Data Mining Techniques

For Marketing, Sales, and Customer Support

Michael J. A. Berry

Gordon Linoff

WILEY COMPUTER PUBLISHING

John Wiley & Sons, Inc.
New York • Chichester • Weinheim
• Brisbane • Singapore • Toronto

Executive Publisher: Katherine Schowalter
Editor: Robert M. Elliott
Managing Editor: Mark Haydon
Text Design & Composition: Publishers' Design and Production Services, Inc.

Designations used by companies to distinguish their products
are often claimed as trademarks. In all instances where John
Wiley & Sons, Inc., is aware of a claim, the product names
appear in initial capital or ALL CAPITAL LETTERS. Readers, however, should contact the appropriate companies for more complete information regarding trademarks and registration.

This text is printed on acid-free paper.

Library of Congress Cataloging-in-Publication Data:

Berry, Michael (Michael J. A.)
    Data mining techniques : for marketing, sales, and customer
support / Michael Berry, Gordon Linoff.
        p.   cm.
    Includes bibliographical references and index.
    ISBN 0-471-17980-9 (pbk. : alk. paper)
    1. Data mining.   2. Marketing—Data processing.   3. Business—Data
processing.   I. Linoff, Gordon.   II. Title.
    HF5415.125.B47   1997
    658.8′02—dc21   97-13601
                                                                    CIP

Printed in the United States of America
10 9 8 7 6 5 4 3 2

To Stephanie, Sasha, and Nathaniel. Without your patience and understanding, this book would not have been possible.

—Michael

To Puccio.
Grazie per essere paziente con me.
Ti amo.

—Gordon

Contents

Acknowledgments

There are many people that have played an important role in supporting us in writing this book, in providing material, and in giving us access to information and future plans. Although any such list is incomplete, we do want to extend thanks to a few people. First and foremost is Sue Osterfelt (now working at NationsBank), who gave us the inspiration to write a book on data mining and the introduction to our esteemed editor Bob Elliott.

Our data mining work has not taken place in a vacuum. Our colleagues at MRJ Technology Solutions have provided the professionalism and dedication through the years that has made this effort worthwhile. Our managers, Rich Cohen and Paul Becker, have been generous in allowing us to spend time on this project. Susan Buchanan, Jim Flynn, and Gregory Lampshire have spent numerous hours helping, discussing data mining, and reading drafts of this book and our seminar materials. And a special thanks to Alan Parker, who truly understands data mining, but has left MRJ to found his own company (http://www.apower.com).

Help with the examples, algorithms, and case studies came from many sources. We particularly want to thank:
Don Peppers, Marketing 1:1
Janet Smith, Case in Point
Ed Horton and Dena d'Ebin, Acxiom
Larry Scroggins, Casablanca Information Services

William Petefish and Syamala Srinivasan, Caterpillar
Marc Goodman, Continuum Software
Wei-Xing Ho, CSC
Bob Flynn, Cogit
Yvonne McCollin, Comcast Cellular
Jerry Modes, HyperParallel
Ric Amari and Marc Reifeis, Victoria's Secret Stores
Dr. Edward F. Ewen, Medical Center of Delaware
Bryan McNeely, NationsBank
Fred Chapman, First Union National Bank

During the course of doing data mining seminars and writing this book, we have had the opportunity to meet with many helpful people working on data mining tools and solutions. We have relished working closely with the following vendors:

Claire Budden, Integral Software
Karen Stewart and Robert Groth, DataMind
Mario Bourgoin and Stephen Smith, Pilot Software
Larry Bookman and Robert Utzschnieder, Torrent Systems
Lars Rohrberg, Tandem
Patsy Campbell, HNC
Jerry Modes, HyperParallel
Diana Lin and Kamran Parsaye, Information Discovery
Gary Drescher, Thinking Machines Corporation
Rakesh Agrawal, IBM
Marge Sherold, Ward Systems Group

Several people reviewed versions of the book at various stages. We hope the final project reflects their valuable comments and directions.

Bob Elliott, John Wiley & Sons
Roland Pesch, Admired Technical Writer
Paul C. Berry, Admired Technical Writer
Jim Flynn, MRJ Technology Solutions

Among many, we want to acknowledge a few individuals who have shared their knowledge and insight, providing guidance in understanding the techniques and where they are applied:

David Isaac, MRJ Technology Solutions
Dr. Michael Jordon, M.I.T.
David Waltz, NEC Research

Finally, without our friends and our immediate families, Stephanie, Sasha, Nathaniel, and Giuseppe, we could never have undertaken and completed this book. Thank you.

Introduction

In May 1995, Sue Osterfelt asked Michael and me whether we would be interested in writing an introduction to data mining. We had been working on data mining algorithms and large databases since the 1980s and, with the help of our colleagues at MRJ, had recently created a seminar on data mining. This seminar received a positive reception wherever we gave it, and it seemed a natural basis for a book.

No one person can be an expert in all areas of data mining—it is simply too vast. Each year, hundreds of doctoral theses extend our knowledge of neural networks, genetic algorithms, decision trees, and parallel databases. Any one chapter in this book is the subject of dozens of monographs. Hundreds of tools support, or claim to support, data mining. And thousands of journal articles published each year push the boundaries of the subject.

Our intention was to write a book that would explain data mining in the context of its most common applications in business—sales, marketing, and customer support. These are not the only areas where advanced data mining techniques are applied, and some examples in the book are taken from other areas as well.

The focus on business is paramount. The first six chapters introduce data mining and discuss it in the business context. Getting value from data is only the beginning. A neural network can predict who will likely respond to a mailing. But this information is only valuable when it is incorporated into business processes. Chapter 2 introduces the

Virtuous Cycle of Data Mining in order to raise awareness of these techniques and their application in business. A good mantra to chant while reading this book is "Analyze, Act, Measure." However, a mantra does not make a good business plan. With that in mind, in this book we introduce our methodology for successful data mining, along with numerous case studies to illustrate success and warn against pitfalls.

Seven techniques are discussed in the book: cluster detection, memory-based reasoning, market basket analysis, genetic algorithms, link analysis, decision trees, and neural networks. Many of the techniques are related to statistical methods and have mathematical explanations beyond the scope of this book. The intention of these chapters is to provide understanding, insight, and background. We illustrate the chapters with examples, and where possible, choose intuitive explanations over abstruse mathematics. Each of these chapters can stand on its own. Taken together they provide a comprehensive overview of how to exploit data in the business environment. This is not the book to learn neural networks in the language of multivariate logistic regression.

The final chapters of the book are devoted to areas related to data mining. On-line analytic processing (OLAP) is one of the fastest growing areas in software, and it also purports to turn data into information. How does data mining fit in with OLAP? Actually quite well. Similarly, data mining and data warehousing are natural allies in the corporate environment—the more data readily available in a warehouse, the more effort can be spent on analyzing data (and not getting it into the tools).

Data mining has the potential to fulfill the promise of turning data into information. Michael and I hope that this book provides insight and inspiration for those embarking on this path.

Why Data Mining?

1

Somerville, Massachusetts, home to one of the authors of this book, is also home to a woman from Cameroon who braids hair. Every few weeks, she arrives at my house with a bag of combs, brushes, and oils, and sets to work transforming my daughter's long, bushy mane into neat cornrows. Some of her clients prefer to come to her, but this particular client finds the four-hour procedure more pleasant if she can set up her chair directly in front of the VCR with her cordless phone, and her Indigo Girls and Ani Difranco tapes, close at hand.

Because she is familiar with the client's likes and dislikes, the hair artist brings no extensions or beads with her to our house. She remembers how each client likes her hair: the diameter of the braids; the distance between braids; the orientation of the cornrows; whether the braids should be formed into fanciful loops or left to hang down straight; whether to weave in ribbons or beads. In short, the customer and the service provider have an established, learning relationship. The longer that relationship lasts—the more the provider learns about the customer—the harder it becomes for the customer to switch to a new provider.

Small retail businesses rely on their knowledge of the customer to inspire loyalty. For nearly 20 years I have done my wine shopping at a small, local store called The Wine Cask. The owner and staff know my tastes and my price range. When I ask them for advice, I know that it will be based on their knowledge of me and my preferences as well as on their knowledge of their stock.

The people at The Wine Cask know a lot about wine. But, while that knowledge does give them an advantage over a big discount liquor store, and even over many specialty wine stores, it is their knowledge of me, the customer, that keeps me coming back. Another shop could open across the street and hire a staff of expert oenophiles, but it would take them many months to get to know me the way those at The Wine Cask do.

LARGE FIRMS NEED LEARNING RELATIONSHIPS TOO

It is widely recognized that firms of all sizes need to learn to emulate what small, service-oriented businesses have always done well—creating one-to-one relationships with their customers. Managers of companies large and small have sent books like *The One to One Future: Building Relationships One Customer at a Time* by Don Peppers and Martha Rogers and *The Loyalty Effect: The Hidden Force behind Growth, Profits, and Lasting Value* by Frederick Reichheld to the top of the business best-seller charts.

In every industry, forward-looking companies are trying to move towards the one-to-one ideal of understanding each customer individually and to use that understanding to make it easier for the customer to do business with them rather than with a competitor. These same firms are learning to look at the lifetime value of each customer so they know which ones are worth investing money and effort to hold on to and which ones to let drop. This change in focus from broad market segments to individual customers requires changes throughout the enterprise, but nowhere more than in marketing, sales, and customer support.

Data Warehousing Provides the Enterprise with a Memory

A small business builds relationships with its customers by *noticing* their needs, *remembering* their preferences, and *learning* from past interactions how to serve them better in the future. How can a large enterprise accomplish something similar when most customers may never interact personally with company employees? Even where there is customer interaction, it is likely to be with a different sales clerk or anonymous call-center employee each time, so how can the enterprise notice, remember, and learn from these interactions? What can replace the creative intuition of the sole proprietor who recognizes customers by name, face, and voice, and remembers their habits and preferences?

In a word, nothing. But through the clever application of information technology, even the largest enterprise can come surprisingly close. In large commercial enterprises, the first step—noticing what the customer does—has already largely been automated. On-line transaction processing (OLTP) systems are everywhere, collecting data on seemingly everything.

These days, we all go through life generating a constant stream of transaction records. When you pick up the phone to order a canoe paddle from L.L. Bean or a satin bra from Victoria's Secret, a transaction record is generated at the local phone company showing the time of your call, the number you dialed, and the long distance company to which you have been connected. At the long distance company, more records are generated recording the duration of your call and the exact routing it takes through the switching system. This data will be combined with other records that store your billing plan, name, and address in order to generate a bill. At the catalog company, your call is logged again along with information about the particular catalog from which you ordered and any special promotions you are responding to. When the customer service representative that answered your call asks for your credit card number and expiration date, the information is immediately relayed to a credit card verification system to approve the transaction. All too soon, the transaction reaches the bank that issued your credit card where it will appear on your next monthly statement. When your order, with its item number, size, and color, goes into the cataloger's order entry system, it will spawn still more records in the billing system and the inventory control system. Within hours, your order is also generating transaction records in a computer system at UPS or FedEx where it may be scanned many times between the warehouse and your home, allowing you to call an 800 number or check the shipper's Web site to track its progress.

The customer-focused enterprise regards every record of an interaction with a client or prospect—each call to customer support, each point-of-sale transaction, each catalog order, each visit to a company Web site—as a learning opportunity. But, learning requires more than simply gathering data. In fact, many companies gather hundreds of gigabytes of data from and about their customers without learning anything! Data is gathered because it is needed for some operational purpose, such as inventory control or billing. And, once it has served that purpose, it languishes on tape or gets discarded.

For learning to take place, data from many sources—billing

records, scanner data, registration forms, applications, call records, coupon redemptions, surveys—must first be gathered together and organized in a consistent and useful way. This is called *data warehousing*. Data warehousing allows the enterprise to remember what it has noticed about its customers. Next, the data must be analyzed, understood, and turned into actionable information. That is where *data mining* comes in.

A Note on Terminology

Data mining brings together ideas and techniques from a variety of fields that have very different vocabularies. Statisticians, artificial intelligence (AI) researchers, database administrators, and marketing people use different words to mean the same thing and the same words to mean different things.

For statisticians, economists, and other quantitative researchers, "data mining" is a pejorative term. It refers to the practice of selectively trying to find data that will support a particular hypothesis. Just as one can find support for any opinion by searching long enough in the Bible, it is usually possible to find data to support any theory.

To a lawyer, to say that something is "actionable" means that it is grounds for a law suit. Yet this is a word that business people use frequently to describe information in response to which some positive action can be taken.

For this book, we have adopted the terminology of the marketing profession, and of database marketing in particular. Where a statistician sees dependent and independent variables, and an AI researcher sees features and attributes, we see records and fields. And when we say that we use data mining to find actionable market information, we certainly don't mean that we are cooking the books and expect to be sued!

Data Mining Provides the Enterprise with Intelligence

The data warehouse provides the enterprise with a memory. But, memory is of little use without intelligence. Intelligence allows us to comb through our memories noticing patterns, devising rules, coming up with new ideas to try, and making predictions about the future. This book describes the tools and techniques that add intelligence to the data warehouse. Using these techniques, you will be able to exploit the vast mountains of data generated by interactions with your customers and prospects in order to get to know them better.

Who is likely to remain a loyal customer and who is likely to jump ship? What products should be marketed to which prospects? What determines whether a person will respond to a certain offer? Which telemarketing script is best for this call? Where should the next branch be located? What is the next product or service this customer will want? Answers to questions like these lie buried in your corporate data, but it takes powerful data mining tools to get at them.

In this book you will learn how these tools work, and the strengths and weaknesses of each. We describe data mining techniques in sufficient detail that even if you have no previous experience with analytical modeling or data mining, you will understand what you can and cannot expect to accomplish with each approach, and how to pick the right tool or tools for a given data mining task. You will also learn a general methodology for data mining, how to select and prepare data sources so as to get the best out of the data mining techniques, and how to evaluate the results you obtain through data mining.

WHAT IS DATA MINING?

Data mining, as we use the term, is the exploration and analysis, by automatic or semiautomatic means, of large quantities of data in order to discover meaningful patterns and rules. For the purposes of this book, we assume that the *goal* of data mining is to allow a corporation to improve its marketing, sales, and customer support operations through better understanding of its customers. Keep in mind, however, that the data mining techniques and tools described here are equally applicable in fields ranging from law enforcement to radio astronomy, medicine, and industrial process control.

In fact, hardly any of the data mining algorithms we describe were first invented with commercial applications in mind. The commercial data miner employs a grab bag of techniques borrowed from statistics, computer science, and artificial intelligence research. The choice of a particular combination of techniques to apply in a particular situation depends on both the nature of the data mining task to be accomplished and the nature of the available data.

Later in the book, we define the tasks well-suited for data mining: *classification, estimation, prediction, affinity grouping, clustering,* and *description.* Some of these tasks are best approached in a top-down manner called *hypothesis testing.* In hypothesis testing, a database recording past behavior is used to verify or disprove preconceived notions, ideas, and hunches concerning relationships in the data.

Other tasks are best approached in a bottom-up manner called *knowledge discovery*. In knowledge discovery, no prior assumptions are made; the data is allowed to speak for itself. Knowledge discovery comes in two flavors—directed and undirected. Directed knowledge discovery attempts to explain or categorize some particular data field such as income or response. Undirected knowledge discovery attempts to find patterns or similarities among groups of records without the use of a particular target field or collection of predefined classes. All of these activities fall under our definition of data mining.

WHY NOW?

Although most of the data mining techniques described in this book have existed, at least as academic algorithms, for years or decades, it is only in the last several years that commercial data mining has caught on in a big way. This is due to the convergence in the 1990s of a number of factors:

- The data is being produced.
- The data is being warehoused.
- The computing power is affordable.
- The competitive pressure is strong.
- Commercial data mining software products have become available.

Let's look at each factor in turn.

Data Is Being Produced

Data mining only makes sense when there are large volumes of data. In fact, most data mining algorithms *require* large amounts of data in order to build and train the models that will then be used to perform classification, prediction, estimation, or other data mining tasks.

A few industries, including telecommunications and credit cards, have long had an automated, interactive relationship with customers that generated many transaction records, but it is only relatively recently that the automation of everyday life has become so pervasive. Today, the rise of supermarket point-of-sale scanners, automatic teller machines, credit and debit cards, pay-per-view television, home shopping, electronic funds transfer, automated order processing, electronic ticketing, and the like means that data is being produced and collected at unprecedented rates.

Data Is Being Warehoused

Not only is a large amount of data being produced, but also, more and more often, it is being extracted from the operational billing, reservations, claims processing, and order entry systems where it is generated and being fed into a data warehouse to become part of the corporate memory.

Data warehousing brings together data from many different sources in a common format with consistent definitions for keys and fields. It is generally not possible (and certainly not advisable) to perform computer- and input/output (i/o)-intensive data mining operations on an operational system that the business depends on just to function. In any case, operational systems store data in a format designed to optimize performance of the operational task. This format is generally not well-suited to decision-support activities like data mining. The data warehouse, on the other hand, is designed exclusively for decision support. This simplifies the job of the data miner.

Computing Power Is Affordable

Data mining algorithms typically require multiple passes over huge quantities of data. Many are computationally intensive as well. The continuing dramatic decrease in prices for disk, memory, processing power, and i/o bandwidth has brought once-costly techniques that were used only in a few government-funded laboratories into the reach of ordinary businesses.

The successful introduction of parallel relational database management software by major suppliers such as Oracle, Informix, Red Brick, Sybase, Tandem, and IBM, has brought the power of parallel processing into many corporate data centers for the first time. These parallel database server platforms provide an excellent environment for large-scale data mining.

Competitive Pressure Is Strong

Some of the most information-rich industries such as telecommunications, insurance, and financial services are experiencing greatly increased competition. Companies in these information-rich sectors of the economy have long had the data and resources to perform data mining. Now, for the first time, they have a strong business incentive to do so. Industries that have not traditionally been information-rich are striving to become so. Several trends are increasing the competitive importance of information:

- An increasingly service-based economy
- The advent of mass customization
- The increasing importance of information as a product in its own right

Every Business Is a Service Business

For companies in the service sector, information confers competitive advantage. That is why hotel chains record your preference for a non-smoking room and car rental companies record your preferred type of car. In addition, companies that have not traditionally thought of themselves as service providers are beginning to think differently. Does an automobile dealer sell cars or transportation? If the latter, it makes sense for the dealership to offer you a loaner car whenever your own is in the shop, as many are now doing.

Even commodity products can be enhanced with service. A home heating oil company that monitors your usage and delivers oil when you need more, sells a better product than a company that expects you to remember to call to arrange a delivery before your tank runs dry and the pipes freeze! Credit card companies, long distance providers, airlines, and even computer retailers often compete as much on service as they do on price.

Mass Customization

Mass customization means producing individually tailored products by combining selections from a large set of standard components. In the process, mass customizers necessarily gather data on sizes or preferences of each customer. In addition to allowing the vendor to understand more about individual customers, this data can be mined for insights on the market as a whole.

Levi-Strauss offers a line of custom-fit jeans. The company has equipped some of its stores with laser devices that record a customer's measurements. This data, along with the customer's stated preferences on fit (tight, baggy, etc.) is sent to the factory where the correct set of standard components will be assembled to order. The Custom

Foot does the same thing with shoes. Andersen Windows uses a mass customization system to allow customers to design their own windows.

Individual, Inc. goes farther by offering a mass customized product that gets smarter over time. Individual has an electronic clipping service. Customers provide a profile of their interests, then rate the articles they are sent as "very relevant," "somewhat relevant," or "not relevant." These ratings are used to automatically adjust the parameters of the information retrieval engine so that after a few weeks, the customer is receiving a customized newsletter containing only relevant articles.

Information as Product

Custom Clothing Technology Corporation, the company that designed the measuring technology used to fit custom Levis is currently working to develop a similar system for fitting brassieres. Eventually, it hopes to supply custom measurements for any type of clothing. When that day comes, the size database itself will be a valuable product.

Many catalog shoppers would be happy to register their individual measurements with an information broker in return for a personal size code. Then, when calling up Lands End or J. Crew they could simply supply their size code once and order everything from hats to shoes. Your grandchildren could put their size codes on their gift wish lists and you could carry your spouse's code in your wallet. Of course, for the system to work, the retailers would have to subscribe to a service provided by the information broker in order to check for the most up-to-date measurements associated with those codes. The information broker could charge a small fee for each inquiry in addition to the subscription charge.

It hasn't happened in body sizes yet, but information brokers are already doing a healthy business in many areas. IMS collects data on prescriptions from pharmacies and sells it back to drug companies who use it to track who is prescribing what to whom and to determine commissions for their sales forces. AC Nielsen does the same with television viewing habits. Market research firms like the NPD Group collect data on purchasing habits and resell it as reports.

Any company that collects valuable data is in a position to become an information broker. The *Cedar Rapids Gazette* takes advantage of its dominant position in a 22-county area of Eastern Iowa to offer direct marketing services to local businesses. The paper uses its own obituary pages and wedding announcements to keep its marketing database current.

Commercial Data Mining Software Products Have Become Available

There is always a lag between the time when new algorithms first appear in academic journals and excite discussion at conferences, and the time when commercial software incorporating those algorithms becomes available. There is another lag between the initial availability of the first products and the time that they achieve wide acceptance. For data mining, the period of widespread availability and acceptance is only just beginning.

Many of the techniques we discuss in this book started out in the artificial intelligence field. After a few years in universities and government labs, a new technique will start to be used by a few early adopters in the commercial sector. At this point in the evolution of a new technique, the software is typically available in source code to the intrepid user willing to retrieve it via FTP, compile it, and figure out how to use it by reading the author's Ph.D. thesis. Only after a few pioneers become successful with a new technique, does it start to appear in real products that come with user's manuals and help lines.

All of the techniques discussed in this book are available in commercial software products, but the techniques are at different points along the road from laboratory to data center. Neural networks and market basket analysis are almost old-hat by now. Decision tree methods and automatic cluster detection are close behind. Genetic algorithms and memory-based reasoning are only just beginning to make the transition.

HOW DATA MINING IS BEING USED TODAY

This whirlwind tour of a few interesting applications of data mining is intended to demonstrate the wide applicability of the data mining techniques discussed in this book. We hope that these vignettes will convey something of the excitement of the field and possibly suggest ways that data mining could be profitably employed in your own work.

> ## Naming Names: Companies Have Privacy Concerns Too
>
> We realize that it is tiresome to read case studies about "a major retailer" or a "regional Bell operating company." Unfortunately, much of the authors' experience in data mining has been inside companies that prefer not to publicize their data mining activities. Many of our clients believe that they gain significant competitive advantage through their data mining activities and would just as soon keep that knowledge to themselves.
>
> Out of respect for these concerns we generally do not name any of the companies with which we have worked and some of the details of case studies drawn from our own experience, or from unpublished conversations with other practitioners, have been changed in ways that do not alter the moral of the story, but do protect the identity of the companies involved.
>
> Wherever the actual names of companies appear in this book, the source of the information is published material from the companies themselves or from the press.

The Feds Use Data Mining to Track Down Criminals

The federal government of the United States was an early adopter of data mining technology. As part of the investigation of the Oklahoma City bombing case, the Unabomber case, and many lower-profile crimes, the FBI used automatic link analysis to sift through thousands of reports submitted by agents in the field looking for connections and possible leads.

The Treasury Department uses data mining to hunt for suspicious patterns in international funds transfer records; patterns that may indicate money laundering or fraud. Data mining tool vendors report that the Internal Revenue Service has expressed a lot of interest as well—so, watch out!

A Supermarket Becomes an Information Broker

Supermarkets are in a position to notice a lot about their customers these days, but most of them do not yet have the technical capability to link the purchase data captured by the check-out scanners with individual purchasers and households. One that does is the Safeway Corporation.

Safeway, like several other large chains, has turned itself into an information broker. The supermarket purchases address and demographic data directly from its customers by offering them discounts in return for using a Safeway Savings Club card when they make their purchases. In order to obtain the card, shoppers voluntarily divulge personal information of the sort that makes good input for predictive computer models.

From then on, each time the shopper presents the discount card, his or her transaction history is updated in a data warehouse somewhere. With every trip to the store, the shoppers teach the retailer a little more about themselves. The supermarket itself is probably more interested in aggregate patterns (what sells well together, what should be shelved together) than in the behavior of individual customers, but the information gathered on individuals is of great interest to the *manufacturers* of the products that line the store's aisles.

Of course, the store assures the customers that the information thus collected will be kept private and it is. Rather than selling Coca-Cola a list of frequent Pepsi buyers and vice-versa, the chain sells *access* to customers who, based on their known buying habits and the data they have supplied, are likely prospects for a particular supplier's product. Safeway charges 5.5 cents per name to suppliers who want their coupon or special promotional offer to reach just the right people. Since the coupon redemption also becomes an entry in the shopper's transaction history file, the precise response rate of the targeted group is a matter of record. Furthermore, a particular customer's response or lack thereof to the offer becomes input data for future predictive models.

American Express and other charge card suppliers do much the same thing, selling advertising space in and on their billing envelopes. The price they can charge for space in the envelope is directly tied to their ability to correctly identify people likely to respond to the ad. That is where data mining comes in.

A Business Based on Community Knowledge

One of the reasons for learning to understand the behavior of individual customers is to be able to generalize so as to make predictions about the behavior of other, similar people. This is what Peppers and Rogers call "developing community knowledge." In their book, *Enterprise One to One: Tools for Competing in the Information Age*, they cite Firefly (http://www.ffly.com) as an example of a business based on community knowledge.

It is also an example of a business entirely dependent on data mining. Firefly asks its members to rate music and movies. Based on the likes and dislikes revealed by these ratings, subscribers are automatically clustered into groups of like-minded people. Once a new subscriber has been assigned to a cluster, the system can make recommendations of movies and music he or she will probably enjoy because other members of the cluster have rated them highly.

The beauty of the system is that the more you use it, the better it understands which other subscribers tastes are similar to your own and the better its advice becomes.

Cross Selling

USAA is an insurance company that markets to active duty and retired military personnel and their families. The company credits information-based marketing, including data mining, with a doubling of the number of products held by the average customer to 4.5. USAA keeps detailed records on its customers and uses data mining to predict where they are in their life cycles and what products they are likely to need.

Another company that has used data mining to improve its cross-selling ability is Fidelity Investments. Fidelity maintains a data warehouse filled with information on all of its retail customers. This information is used to build computer models that predict what other Fidelity products are likely to interest each customer. When an existing customer calls Fidelity, the phone representative's screen shows exactly where to lead the conversation.

In addition to improving the company's ability to cross sell, Fidelity's retail marketing data warehouse has allowed the financial services powerhouse to build models of what makes a loyal customer and thereby increase customer retention. These models caused Fidelity to retain a marginally profitable bill-paying service that would otherwise have been cut. It turned out that people who used the service were far less likely than the average customer to take their business to a competitor. Cutting the service would have encouraged a profitable group of loyal customers to shop around.

A central tenet of the one-to-one marketing philosophy is that it is more profitable to focus on "wallet share" or "customer share," the amount of business you can do with each customer, than on market share. From financial services to heavy manufacturing, innovative companies are using data mining to increase the value of each customer.

Warranty Claims Routing

A diesel engine manufacturer receives a constant stream of warranty claims from independent dealers who have performed maintenance on engines covered by the manufacturer's warranty. Each of the claims must be examined by an expert to determine if the labor and parts used seem reasonable and appropriate. There has long been a set of rules used to exempt certain claims that are considered so routine that they can be paid without any detailed examination.

The company is now investigating the use of data mining to expand the number of claims paid automatically by discovering an expanded set of rules to describe classes of claims always approved by the professional adjusters. This automated claims routing has the potential to save the company millions of dollars.

Holding on to Good Customers

Data mining is being used to promote customer retention in any industry where customers are free to change suppliers at little cost and competitors are eager to lure them away. Banks call it attrition. Cellular phone companies call it churn. By any name, it is a big problem. By gaining an understanding of *who* is likely to leave and *why*, a retention plan can be developed that addresses the right issues and targets the right customers.

Southern California Gas is just one example of a former regulated monopoly that now has to compete for customers. Before deregulation, the company didn't even have a marketing department. Now it has a database marketing program that integrates customer usage and billing data with credit information and U.S. Census data. By applying data mining techniques to this data the utility was able to figure out who would benefit most from a level payment plan. Direct mail based on the model yielded response rates between 7 and 11 percent, a phenomenal result for direct mail. The utility has also learned that some groups of customers are much more price-sensitive than others, with small, commercial heating customers being the quickest to put on a sweater and turn off the gas.

It costs more to bring in a new customer than it does to hold on to an existing one, but often the incentive offered to retain a customer is quite expensive. Data mining is the key to figuring out which customers should get the incentive, which customers will stay without the incentive, and which customers should be allowed to walk.

Weeding Out Bad Customers

In many industries, some customers cost more than they are worth. These might be people who consume a lot of customer support resources without buying much. Or, they might be those annoying folks who carry a credit card they rarely use, are sure to pay off the full balance when they do, but must still be mailed a statement every month. Even worse, they might be people who owe you a lot of money when they declare bankruptcy.

The same data mining techniques that are used to spot the most valuable customers can also be used to pick out those that should be turned down for a loan; those who should be allowed to wait on hold the longest time; and those who should always be assigned a middle seat near the engine (or is that just our paranoia showing?).

Revolutionizing an Industry

In 1988, the idea that a credit card issuer's most valuable asset is the information it has about its customers was pretty revolutionary. It was an idea that Richard Fairbank and Nigel Morris shopped around to 25 banks before Signet Banking Corporation decided to give it a try.

Signet acquired behavioral data from many sources and used it to build predictive models. Using these models it launched the highly successful balance transfer card product that changed the way the credit card industry works. In 1994, Signet spun off the card operation as Capital One which is now one of the top 10 credit card issuers with over $11 billion in loans outstanding. The same aggressive use of data mining technology that fueled such rapid growth is also responsible for keeping Capital One's loan loss rates among the lowest in the industry.

Data mining is at the heart of the marketing strategy of all the so-called monoline credit card banks, First USA, MBNA, Advanta, and Capital One. At least one of these, First USA, having been aquired by Bank One, is now positioned to offer a full range of banking services. Data mining will allow the combined company to mine its extensive credit card portfolio for cross-selling opportunities for car loans, mortgages, and other general banking services.

Capital One is making plans to diversify into other information businesses, both financial and nonfinancial. Meanwhile, Signet, Capital's former parent company, is putting information-based marketing and information-based decision-making at the center of its approach to all its banking services.

Credit card divisions may have led the charge of banks into data mining, but other divisions are not far behind. At First Union, a large North Carolina-based bank, data mining techniques are used to predict which customers are likely to be moving soon. For most people, moving to a new home in another town means closing the old bank account and opening a new one, often with a different company. First Union set out to improve retention by identifying customers who are about to move and making it easy for them to transfer their business to another First Union branch in the new location. Not only has retention improved markedly, but also a profitable relocation business has developed. In addition to setting up a bank account, First Union now arranges for gas, electricity, and other services at the new location.

And Just About Anything Else

These applications should give you a feel for what is possible using data mining, but they do not come close to covering the full range of applications. The data mining techniques described in this book have been used to find quasars, design army uniforms, detect second-press olive oil masquerading as "extra virgin," teach machines to read aloud, and recognize handwritten letters. They will, no doubt, be used to do many of the things your business will require to grow and prosper in the coming century.

The Virtuous Cycle
of Data Mining

2

In the first part of the nineteenth century, textile mills were the industrial success stories. These mills, which populated the growing towns and cities along rivers in England and New England, harnessed the power of these rivers. Water, running over water wheels, drove their spinning, knitting, and weaving machines. For a century, the image of the industrial revolution was the image of water driving these machines.

The business world has changed. Old mill towns are now quaint historical curiosities. The long mill buildings on the sides of rivers are warehouses and shopping malls, artist studios and computer companies. Even manufacturing companies are often providing more value in services than in goods. We were struck by a recent ad campaign by a leading international cement manufacturer, Cemex, that presented concrete as a service. Instead of focusing on the quality of cement, its price, or availability, the ad pictured a bridge over a river and sold the idea that "cement" is a service that connects people by building bridges between them. Concrete as a service? A symbol of the modern economy.

Access to electrical or mechanical power is no longer the criterion for success. For mass-market products, data about customer interactions is the modern equivalent to water power; knowledge drives the turbines of the service economy and, since the line between service and manufacturing is getting blurry, much of the manufacturing economy as well. Information from data focuses marketing efforts by segmenting customers, improves product designs by meeting real customer needs, and improves allocation of resources by understanding and predicting customer preferences.

Data is at the heart of most companies' core business processes. It is generated by transactions that form the foundation of many industries, such as retail, telecommunications, manufacturing, utilities, transportation, insurance, credit cards, and banking. As if the deluge of internal data were not enough, external sources further augment internal data, providing demographic, lifestyle, and credit information on retail customers, and credit, financial, and marketing information on business customers. The promise of data mining is to find the interesting patterns lurking in all these billions and trillions of bytes of data. But merely finding the patterns is not enough. *You must be able to respond to the patterns, to act on them, ultimately turning the data into information, the information into action, and the action into value. This is the virtuous cycle of data mining in a nutshell.*

To really achieve its promise, data mining needs to become an essential business process, incorporated into other processes including marketing, sales, customer support, product design, and inventory control. The virtuous cycle incorporates data mining into the larger context of other business processes. It focuses on action based on discovery and not on the discovery mechanism itself. Throughout this chapter and this book, we will be talking about *actionable* results from data mining. We have adopted the term "actionable" as a descriptive adjective for information that can be acted upon (and this usage should not be confused with its definition in the legal domain).

Marketing literature makes data mining seem so easy. Let us just apply the results created by the best minds in academia, such as neural networks, decision trees, genetic algorithms, and so on, and we are on our way to untold successes. Techniques devised since the 1960s to make sense of a few kilobytes of data are now ready for our terabyte data warehouses. In fact, we now have the computing power and the data to realize the benefits of even the most complex algorithms.

Although the algorithms are important, the data mining solution is more than just a set of powerful techniques and data structures. The techniques have to be applied in the right areas, on the right data. Data mining is not an island. The virtuous cycle of data mining recognizes that data mining is one step in a process that applies knowledge gained from increased understanding of customers, markets, products, and competitors to internal processes. This is a continuous process that builds on results over time. Success in using data will transform an organization from reactive to proactive. This is the virtuous cycle of data mining, used by the authors for extracting maximum benefit from the techniques described later in the book.

A BUSINESS OPPORTUNITY

The marketing group at a large bank needs to increase its overall profitability (sound familiar?). The bank is losing more customers than it is attracting, and the new customers are less profitable than the previous ones. Attrition is causing the bank to lose its *better* customers. In an effort to sustain market share, the bank must recruit new customers but, because of attrition, it is spending too much money trying to attract new customers. What can be done? Before showing how data mining can help in this case, let us examine some cases of what banks have actually done without the benefit of using their data.

One case is to make the bank more competitive over all: Raise interest rates on deposits, lower minimum balances, and reduce interest rates on loans. Such an approach looks appealing; more customers will come, fewer customers will leave. The bank increases its market share. But this is not a panacea. These programs cost money to implement. Existing customers are presumably happy with the current services and many do not need any incentives to remain loyal. Even worse, this method brings in the worst possible customers—the unloyal. A competitor can grab many of them just by offering slightly better interest rates and slightly more attractive terms. The program is attracting the wrong customers and the attrition problem is not solved.

The bank could also decide to stop offering services that are losing money. This seems like a good idea, but it focuses on the profit centers inside the bank instead of on the customers. One financial institution put its bill-paying service on the chopping block because it consistently lost money. Some last-minute analysis, though, showed that their most loyal and most profitable customers used the service. Cutting the service would risk losing these customers. At the eleventh hour, the bill-paying service was saved, preventing a very costly mistake. Cutting such value-added services may further exacerbate the profitability problem by causing the best customers to look elsewhere for service.

Perhaps the customers are dissatisfied with the bank's services. The bank might purchase more automated teller machines (ATMs) placing them in more locations, put more tellers in busy branches, and have more call-center personnel to reduce waiting times. It may introduce new services and bundle products together offering them to all customers in order to increase profitability. Better customer service is a good idea, but trying to improve everything all at once for all customers is often too unfocused. The bank will spend too much money making offers to all its customers and improving service to all customers when it only needs to target a small percentage of them to reduce attrition.

Even data mining may not help. An analyst may pore through the data and learn that a particular transaction—such as a customer walking into a branch bank and asking for the balances of all her accounts—may signal attrition. An analyst may discover this but, not knowing what to do about it, may discard the information. After all, what can an analyst in the corporate headquarters do about a customer walking into a retail branch hundreds or thousands of miles away?

Attrition is a common problem whose solution needs to be targeted. The bank has already made considerable headway by understanding that its profitability problem is related to attrition. Now the bank needs to understand its customers and apply this understanding in the larger context of its business.

SOLVING ATTRITION WITH THE VIRTUOUS CYCLE

Instead of guessing at the solution to its attrition problem, the bank has a wealth of data about its customers that it can put to good use—if it can turn the data into information and the information into action. Let us take one example of how the bank can discover and implement a solution that helps to keep customers. Part of the solution is based on data mining, but much is also based on the bank's experience and knowledge about the business.

First, the bank must *identify the opportunity*. In this example, it has identified that attrition of profitable customers is affecting the bottom line, so reducing attrition is a profitable opportunity. How can the bank determine who is likely to attrite? One very promising approach is by looking at former customers and trying to determine some of the reasons for their leaving.

Faced with this situation, organizations often attempt to survey former customers and try to extract why they left. These surveys may be conducted through a customer service group inside the company or anonymously through an outside vendor. Either way, surveys are not likely to generate good results because:

- People who respond to the survey may not be representative of the population of former customers.
- Former customers have no reason to help you or be honest since they no longer bank with you.
- Former customers may have left for an accumulation of reasons: a branch closed so they had to bank further from home, the bank bounced a check, and they had to wait too long at ATMs. You may only hear about the proximate cause, where the first is probably more significant.

We would argue that a better approach is to look at all the data that the bank has about its current and former customers. How do they differ? Data does not lie and is more available than the former customers.

Next, the bank needs to *analyze data to find a targeted approach for exploiting the opportunity identified in the first phase*. This is where data mining fits in. For illustrative purposes, let's say that the data available for analysis is call-center detail. The bank analyzes the data and finds some interesting clusters, one of which consists of many people who are no longer customers (Chapters 10 and 13 present clustering techniques in more detail). In this cluster, people are considerably older than the average customer and less likely to have a mortgage or credit card. Further analysis suggests that these are customers who have passed away—not a promising cluster for reducing attrition! Knowing about this cluster does not help the bank reduce attrition.

Another cluster has customers with the following characteristics: More of them have attrited than would be expected, they have several accounts, they tend to call after hours and have to wait when they call. Further analysis shows that these customers almost never visit a branch and often use foreign ATMs, making them relatively cheap customers to service. This looks like a promising cluster.

At this point, data mining has done its job by identifying a promising cluster. Merely identifying the cluster is not enough, though. The next step is for the bank to *turn the results of the data mining analysis into action*. Armed with information about the business opportunity and about the cluster, the bank determines several possible courses of action.

- Do nothing. Perhaps the customers that have been identified are not valuable customers and the data analysis should continue until better results come along.

- Hire more call center personnel to reduce after hours wait times. This reduces the wait time, but expanding the call center is expensive.
- Provide customers in this cluster with another telephone number for customer service that is prioritized service.
- Upgrade the call center to identify the telephone number of incoming calls. Using the telephone number, customer information can be looked up and the call prioritized.

In this example, the bank takes the third alternative. It gives customers in the cluster a priority telephone number that provides improved service. This is fairly easy to implement in the call center and less expensive than the other two possible courses of action. Implementing this alternative is a little tricky because the bank needs to be sure that entire households receive the new priority service number and not just one member of the household (the householding problem). Once implemented, customers in this cluster find the bank more responsive to their needs. There are fewer complaints about the new service than about the previous service. But does this reduce attrition?

The final step in the virtuous cycle is to *measure the results*. After several months of using the priority customer service number, have the customers in this cluster actually reduced their attrition? Is profitability improving by keeping these customers? The answer in this case is yes, but you always need to measure the results to be sure.

Are we done yet? Not quite. Now we have more data to analyze. What other customers are likely to attrite? What other customers should be given the prioritized service number? In general, finding a solution to one business opportunity introduces new opportunities for further analysis. This is the virtuous cycle. Finding one solution leads to more information, leading to even better results.

WHAT IS THE VIRTUOUS CYCLE

The four stages of the virtuous cycle of data mining, detailed in the previous section, are shown in Figure 2.1:

1. Identify the business problem.
2. Use data mining techniques to transform the data into actionable information.
3. Act on the information.
4. Measure the results.

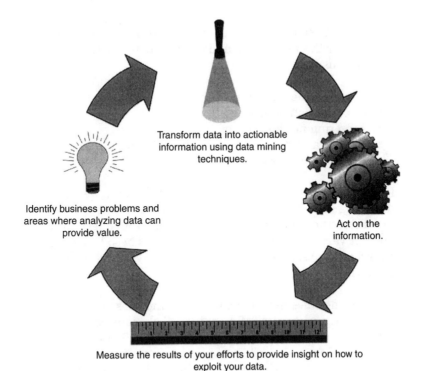

Figure 2.1   These four stages focus on using the *results* of data mining as well as exploiting advanced techniques.

As these steps suggest, the key to success is incorporating data mining into business processes. These stages are highly interdependent: The results from one stage are the inputs into the next phase, much like the steps in a multi-step manufacturing process. The whole approach is driven by results. Each stage depends on the results from the previous stage.

Identify the Business Opportunity

Identifying the business opportunity is the stage that occurs throughout the organization wherever increased information could enable people to better perform their jobs. Its purpose is to identify the areas where data can provide value; these, in turn, are the input in the Data Mining stage. There are several different approaches to this stage. None is the "right" approach. The goal is to identify areas where patterns in data have the potential of providing value.

Some business processes already rely on some amount of data analysis for their operation and can be treated as the Identify stage for the virtuous cycle:

- Planning the marketing effort for a new product
- Pricing existing products and services
- Targeting marketing
- Understanding customer attrition/churn
- Other similar processes

In these cases, the business opportunity is very well understood and the data mining should be an integral part of these processes.

Often the leads for data mining come from questions and observations at various levels in the corporation. These leads are often based on informal observations made by executives and manages questions such as:

- Why do sales in California lag behind those in the Southeast?
- Do long waits at ATM machines likely cause customers to attrite?
- What are the seasonal patterns in long distance usage?
- Should we be spending more money or less on customer support?
- What products should we be promoting with Clorox bleach?

Without access to data, many of these observations are never made. Without a responsive data mining group, many of these questions never get answered. As the group becomes more technically sophisticated, it should encourage following informative leads.

Another approach is formally identifying value areas by interviewing key players throughout the organization. Such an approach is most valuable in the early stages of exploiting data mining because of the chicken and egg problem. Because personnel involved in the business processes have never taken advantage of information, they may not understand how to act upon information when it is available. By explaining the value of data mining to an organization, such interviews provide the forum for two-way communication.

We participated in a series of interviews at a telecommunications company to discuss the value of analyzing call detail records (records of completed calls made by each customer). During one of the interviews, the participants were slow in understanding the value present in this data. A colleague of ours pointed out that lurking inside their data was which customers used fax machines at home. (The details of this are discussed in Chapter 11 on Link Analysis.)

Click! By knowing who had a fax machine at home, they would have a very good idea of who was working at home. And with that information, they had a specific package of products for the work-at-home crowd. Without our prodding, the group marketing to the work-at-home market would never have considered searching through patterns in data.

None of these approaches to identifying the business opportunity is necessarily better than the others. Each environment requires tools specific to that environment. However, identifying actionable business areas is the input into the Data Mining stage. The domain experts who identify the business opportunity should have some idea of how to act on and measure the results from the Data Mining stage. This information is critical to exploiting the virtuous cycle to its fullest advantage.

Data Mining

Data mining is the focus of this book. It takes data and business opportunities and produces actionable results for the Take Action stage. As such, we need to understand what results it must produce to make the virtuous cycle successful. Numerous pitfalls can interfere with the ability to use the results of data mining:

- Bad data formats, such as using five-digit zip codes when nine-digit zip codes are needed by a direct mail application
- Confusing data fields, such as a delivery date that means "planned delivery date" in one system and "actual delivery date" in another system
- Lack of functionality, such as a call-center application that does not allow annotations on a per-customer basis
- Legal ramifications, such as having to provide a legal reason when rejecting a loan (and "my neural network told me so" is not acceptable)
- Organizational factors, since some operational groups are reluctant to change their operations, particularly if they are not provided incentives to change
- Timeliness, since results that come a month late may no longer be actionable

Figure 2.2 illustrates how data comes in many forms, in many formats, and from multiple systems. Identifying the right source of data is crucial to the results of the analysis, as well as bringing the right

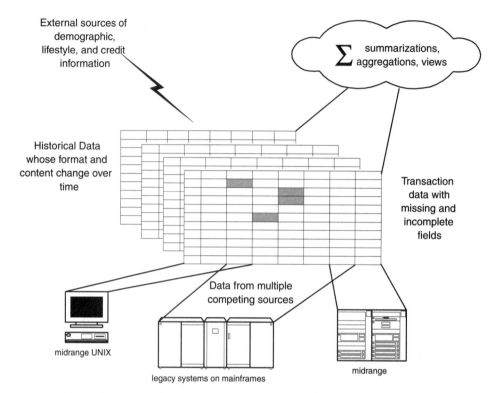

Figure 2.2 Data is never clean. It comes in many forms, from many sources both internal and external.

data together on the computing system used for analysis. In more and more environments, data warehouses are starting to solve this problem. (Chapter 15 talks about developing a data warehouse for effective data mining.)

Is the data you need even being gathered? In the early 1990s, a large health care chain carefully transcribed all doctors' notes from visits into a computer system. What a great idea! Such data, through text analysis algorithms, could yield important information about the spread of diseases, the effects of treatments, and which providers provided the best care. This chain, though, was collecting the data for insurance purposes and every three months the data was thrown out by reusing the tapes for the next set of notes. A wealth of information that cost tens of thousands of dollars was literally thrown away after three months. Other examples abound of surveys and call centers not including customer ids, of survey results sitting on inaccessible desktops, of outsourced operations not providing detailed data of incompatible customer ids, of incompatible computer systems, and of groups that do not communicate well. Gathering and protecting the right data is crucial.

Take Action

This is where the results from data mining are acted upon and results are fed into the Measurement stage. The question here is how to incorporate information into the business processes, so the actions are an integral part of the virtuous cycle.

Different groups responsible for the business processes have to become sensitive to the need for information:

- Don't just launch a product. When launching a new product, you can gather information about a small initial customer base and apply the results to focus future marketing efforts. As the customer base grows, you should continue to track the effects of marketing efforts to provide feedback for future efforts.
- Don't just respond to customer service calls. When responding to customer service calls, be sure that the information gleaned directly from customers can be matched back to profiles. One cellular telephone company learned that profitable, high-volume customers are by far the most likely to use their call center, and it used this information to keep their profitable customers happy.
- Don't just change incentives for the sales force. When implementing new strategies and incentive policies, be sure to collect the data needed to understand the effects of the new policies on customers, as well as on the sales force. A common example is that sales policies that encourage new customers can result in a large amount of *churn*—low-value new customers who stay only long enough for the sales force to collect commissions.

Of course, requiring that all business processes in an organization provide feedback before implementing any data mining solutions has the danger of creating unnecessary delays. To avoid delays, make planning for measuring the results a part of planning the initiative.

You need to change the mindset of operational groups. Increasingly, businesses are taking a strong, proactive stance in favor of customer value. This tends to cause different parts of an organization to focus on common goals. However, the authors still encounter examples of groups that would not consider using the results of data mining, of marketing groups and IS groups that for all practical purposes do not communicate to each other. For successful data mining, the business processes must provide the data feedback needed for the virtuous cycle.

Fortunately, this is not as hard as it sounds. Success breeds success. The virtuous cycle can be implemented to take advantage of one opportunity—for instance, in launching a new product. Successful results (which you measure and communicate) will encourage other groups to start incorporating data-driven information into their processes.

Measure the Results

Measurement provides the feedback for continuously improving results. Measurement here refers specifically to measures of business value that go beyond response rates and costs, beyond averages and standard deviations. These measurements make the virtuous cycle of data mining *virtuous*. Even though the value of measurement and continuous improvement is widely acknowledged, it is usually given less attention than it deserves. How often have you worked on a business case and never returned to the case to measure its success? On an individual level, we improve our efforts by comparing and learning. If this works for individuals, why not for organizations?

Much measurement does happen in an organization, generally as standard reports in one form or another that arrive months after interventions have occurred. The problem is what information is in the reports, when the information is available, and, most importantly, who gets the information. How quickly is information from an effort disseminated to the people who recognized the opportunity or analyzed the data so they can improve their work habits? In most organizations, the answer is months, if at all, and often only after the information has been passed laboriously up through one division, then down another. The introduction of on-line analytic processing tools, discussed in Chapter 16, can greatly improve the dissemination of this information.

It is a good idea to think of every data mining effort as a small business case. By comparing our expectations to the actual results, we can often recognize promising opportunities to exploit on the next round of the virtuous cycle. We are often too busy tackling the next problem to devote energy to measuring the success of our current efforts. This is a mistake. Every data mining effort, whether successful or not, has lessons to apply to future efforts. The question is what to measure and how to approach the measurement so it provides the best input for future use.

The specific measurements needed depend on a number of factors: the business opportunity, the sophistication of the organization, past history of measurements (for trend analysis), and the availability of data. Each group will have different responses to its particular set of factors.

As an example, let's start with what we would want to measure for a targeted marketing campaign. The canonical measurement is the response rate measurement: How many people targeted by the campaign actually responded. This leaves a lot of information lying on the table. For a marketing campaign, some examples of questions that have future value are:

- Did this campaign reach and bring in profitable customers? An organization that has a model for customer profitability can answer this question better than one that does not. However, even in the latter case, questions such as value after one month, six months, and one year can still be measured empirically.
- Are the customers more loyal than average? The success of a campaign should be measured by its long-term benefits—customers that spend more, broaden their relationship, or remain longer are generally more valuable to the business.
- What are the demographics of the most loyal customers reached by this campaign? Demographic profiles of known customers can be applied to future prospective customers. In some circumstances, you want to limit demographics to those characteristics of prospects that can be provided by an external source so the results from the data mining analysis can be applied to prospective customers.
- Do these customers purchase additional products? Can the different systems in an organization detect if one customer purchases multiple products?
- For a multipart campaign (such as direct mail versus telemarketing, or coupons versus discounts), how does the value of customers brought in by different techniques compare?

All of these measurements are really asking how the results from this effort could be used in the future. If a telemarketing campaign brought in good customers, perhaps on the next cycle you might want to compare the results from using different telemarketing scripts—perhaps a lighter approach versus a more direct sales pitch. You might want to know if customers reached by this campaign are profitable in the long term—or do they just grab incentives and shift their loyalties based on the next offer. You might want to measure the effectiveness of advertising agencies or third-party sales organizations—are the customers they bring in valuable, repeat customers or are they the grab-and-shift variety. The answers to questions such as these are hidden inside the data resulting from a given campaign.

Another example is a campaign designed to increase customer retention:

- Were profitable customers more likely to remain customers than unprofitable customers?
- Did the campaign raise the lifetime customer value of the targeted population?
- Did retained customers remain loyal after incentives expired?
- For how long are the predictors of turnover valid?

These questions are driving toward finding measurements of business value and towards focusing the measurements on actionable atomic units—products, customers, markets—instead of on summary measures like expense, revenue, and profitability.

One particularly valuable tool to use in these measurements is a calculation for *lifetime customer value* and associated profitability. As its name implies, this is an estimate of the value of a customer during the entire course of his or her relationship with you. In some industries, quite complicated models have been developed by statisticians to estimate lifetime customer value. Even without sophisticated models, shorter term estimates, such as value after one month, six months, and one year, can prove to be quite useful.

We can see that the Measurement stage depends critically on information provided in the previous stages. We need to ask the right questions early on in order to collect the right information for measurement.

APPLYING THE VIRTUOUS CYCLE

The virtuous cycle is a framework for integrating data mining into other business processes. We already presented an example on how the virtuous cycle helps us to apply data mining to reducing customer attrition. There are numerous other opportunities for data mining and the virtuous cycle.

Inventory control is a problem for a nationwide chain of retailers. The chain buys large quantities of products from manufacturers and must then determine how to allocate these products among its stores. Buying patterns at different locations differ, resulting in a poor distribution of inventory and in increased expenses when inventory has to be moved from one location to another. Red blouses may be the rage in Arizona, but they are not moving in Chicago. Data mining can offer several solutions to this problem. One way is by dividing stores into similarity groups. All the stores in the same group get the same proportions of products. Another way is to analyze historical patterns to predict future needs on a store-by-store basis. Yet another is to test market the product in some key locations and determine the inventory distribution from sales in the test market. There is not a single right answer to this problem, but data mining can be used as a tool for more efficiently allocating inventory.

If a credit card or catalog company knew the next product that a customer wanted to purchase, it could take steps to ensure that the customer uses its credit card or catalog for the purchase. This is a big opportunity. Having identified an opportunity, data mining techniques can help make the prediction. The original company can send direct mail with special offers on the product. Without the targeted approach, the company would waste money sending offers to customers who do not want the product.

Many businesses know that the more business they have with a customer, the more loyal the customer will be—and hence the more profitable. So banks and insurers want to increase the number of accounts, department stores the number of products sold to a household, credit card companies the number of transactions on the card, telephone companies the number of add-on services, and so on. The opportunity here is determining which products to bundle together to broaden customer relationships. Once data mining determines good products to bundle, we need to be sure that these products are marketed and sold vigorously.

DATA MINING IN THE CONTEXT OF THE VIRTUOUS CYCLE

A typical large regional telephone company in the United States has millions of customers. It owns hundreds or thousands of switches located in central offices throughout its region, which typically spans several states in multiple time zones. Each one of these switches can handle thousands of calls simultaneously—including advanced features like call waiting, call-forwarding, voice mail, and digital services. Switches, among the most complex computing devices yet developed, are available principally from three major manufacturers. Our typical telephone company will have multiple versions of several switches from each of the vendors. Each of these switches provides volumes of data in its own format on every call and attempted call—volumes measured in hundreds of megabytes or gigabytes each day. In addition, each state has its own regulations affecting the telecommunications industry, not to mention federal laws and regulations that are subject to rather frequent changes. And, to add to the confusion, our company offers thousands of different billing plans to its customers, which range from occasional users of residential phones to multibillion dollar corporations.

How does this company—or any similar large corporation—manage its billing process, the bread and butter of its business, responsible for the majority of its revenue? The answer is simple: Very carefully! As with all businesses, telecommunications companies have developed detailed processes for handling standard operations; they have policies and procedures. These processes are robust. Bills go out to customers, even when top levels of management change, even when database administrators are on vacation, even when computers are temporarily down, even as laws and regulations change, and switches are upgraded. If an organization can manage a process as complicated as getting accurate bills out every month to millions of residential, business, and government customers, surely incorporating data mining into decision processes should be fairly easy. Is this the case?

Large corporations have decades of experience developing and implementing mission-critical applications for running their business. Data mining is different from the typical operational system, as shown in Figure 2.3. The skills needed for running a successful operational system do not necessarily lead to a successful decision-support system. As we just saw, we need to consider the data mining system in a larger context—in the context of the virtuous cycle.

First, the problem being solved by data mining differs from operational systems—*a data mining system does not seek to replicate previous results exactly*. In fact, replication of efforts can lead to disastrous results. For example, the most profitable market segment for your most recent marketing campaign may have been rental households with under $50,000 in income and no kids. Since you just hit them, you probably do not want to hit them again with the same offer (at least not unintentionally). You do not want to learn from analyzing the data

Typical Operational System	*Data Mining System*
Operations and reports on recent, but past data	Analysis on current and historical data to determine future actions
Predictable and periodic flow of work, typically tied to calendar	Unpredictable flow of work depending on business and marketing needs
Limited use of data from throughout the enterprise	The more data, the better the results (generally)
Focus on line of business (like account, region, product code, minutes of use, etc.), not on customer	Focus on actionable entity, such as product, customer, sales region
Response times often measured in seconds/milliseconds (for interactive systems) or weeks/months (for reports)	Response times often measured in minutes or hours
System of record for data	Copy of data
Descriptive	Creative

Figure 2.3 Data mining differs from typical operational business processes.

that a large cluster of customers fits this profile—which is trivially true if these are the only customers contacted. Your data mining processes need to take this into account. This is an important distinction. For typical operational systems, you want to reproduce the same results over and over—whether it is completing a telephone call, sending a bill, authorizing a credit purchase, tracking inventory, or other countless daily operations.

Data mining is a creative process. Data contains many obvious correlations that are either useless or simply represent current business policies. For example, analysis of data from one large retailer revealed that people who buy household appliances are very likely to buy maintenance contracts. Unless they were analyzing the effectiveness of sales of maintenance contracts with appliances, such information is worse than useless—the maintenance contracts in question are only sold with large appliances. Spending millions of dollars on hardware, software, and analysts to find such results is a waste of resources that can better be applied elsewhere in the business or even distributed to shareholders as dividends. Analysts need to understand what is of value to the business and how to arrange the data to bring out the nuggets.

Data mining results change over time. Models expire and become less useful as time goes on. One cause is that data ages quickly. The moviegoers database that we will use for several examples throughout the book was only valid for a month or two before new movies made the data obsolete. Markets and customers change quickly as well. The introduction of the Pentium processor left large numbers of computers in retailers' inventories—even though these same models had sold very briskly just a month or two earlier. This is an example where previous sales may not be indicative of future sales.

Data mining provides feedback into other processes that may need to change to incorporate the results from data mining. Decisions made in the business world often affect current processes and interactions with customers. For instance, one large bank was studying attrition and learned that customers who come into a branch office for account reconciliations are very likely to close their accounts. This should lead to interventions at the branch level when customers asked for account reconciliations.

THE VIRTUOUS CYCLE IN SUMMARY

We started this chapter by remembering the drivers of the industrial revolution and the creation of large mills in England and New England. These mills are now abandoned, torn down, or converted to other uses. Water is no longer the driving force of business. It has been replaced by electricity and being near a river is no longer needed for manufacturing purposes.

Data is the new force driving business. The virtuous cycle of data mining is about harnessing the power of data and transforming it into actionable business results. Just as water once turned wheels that drove machines throughout a mill, data needs to be gathered and disseminated throughout an organization to provide value. If data is water in this analogy, then data mining is the wheel and the virtuous cycle spreads the power of the data to all the business processes.

The virtuous cycle of data mining places data mining into a context for creating business value. It takes a purposeful approach to data mining, to understanding the reasons for applying particular algorithms, for looking at particular data, and for trying to solve particular problems.

In the business world, data mining provides a fundamentally new capability, the ability to optimize decision-making using automated methods to learn from past actions. In recent years, technology has converged to enable this capability, and in the next few years, more advanced tools, hardware and software, will continue this trend. Parallel processing machines will become more common and less expensive. Software is increasingly available to take advantage of parallel and distributed resources for identifying useful patterns in data. In the past year, many companies have announced or released products in this area.

Different organizations adapt data mining to their own environment, in their own way. In successful environments, the stages of the virtuous cycle will be in place, suitably transformed to fit into the particular environment. The next chapter presents three case studies in detail that show the virtuous cycle in practice.

The Virtuous Cycle
in Practice

3

In this chapter, we take a closer look at several cases where data mining has been employed effectively to support marketing activities. In each case, a marketing challenge is addressed by using data mining techniques to build predictive models. These models are translated into marketing actions whose results are measured and fed back into the data mining process.

We have selected cases from three companies in different industries —wireless communications, automobile manufacturing, and banking.

A WIRELESS COMMUNICATIONS COMPANY MAKES THE RIGHT CONNECTIONS

The wireless communications industry is fiercely competitive. Cellular phone companies are constantly dreaming up new ways to steal customers from their competitors and to keep their own customers loyal. Cellular customers are coming to view the basic service offering as a commodity. As a result, margins are thin and there is little basis for product differentiation.

The wireless companies are responding by coming up with all sorts of novel value-added products which, they hope, will not only be more profitable, but will also promote customer loyalty and reduce churn. The value-added services include:

- Voice mail consolidation
- Routing calls through a user-defined hierarchy of phones and pagers
- Phones that work like a cordless while at home and switch to cellular mode when out of range of the base station

Our first case study concerns the way one cellular phone service provider used data mining to greatly improve its ability to recognize customers who would be attracted to a new service offering.[1]

The Challenge

The cellular phone company wanted to test market a new product. (At the client's request, we can't say exactly what.) For technical reasons, this product could initially only be offered to a few hundred subscribers—a tiny fraction of the customer base in the chosen market. Under the circumstances, it didn't make sense to send out a mass mailing to all customers.

The initial problem, therefore, was to figure out in advance who was likely to want to buy the new product. This is a classic application of data mining. The goal is to find the lowest cost way to reach the desired number of responders. Since the fixed costs of a direct marketing campaign are constant by definition, and the cost per phone call or piece of mail is also fairly constant, the only practical way to reduce the total cost of the campaign is to send fewer pieces of mail and make fewer phone calls.

But remember, the cellular company needed a certain number of people to sign up for the new service in order for the trial to be valid. The company's past experience with new-product introduction campaigns was that about 2 to 3 percent of existing customers would respond favorably and purchase the new product. So, to reach 500 responders, they would expect to have to contact between 16,000 and 25,000 randomly selected prospects.

As long as the prospects for the new product are chosen at random from among all customers, the number of solicitations cannot be reduced without also reducing the number of responders. Of course, the company did not intend to pick prospects at random! Instead, they wanted to pick the prospects most likely to respond. In other words, they intended to run a targeted campaign rather than a mass-marketing campaign.

---

1. We are indebted to our colleague, Alan Parker, for supplying the details of this case study.

But, how should the targets be selected? It would be handy to have a response model that gives each customer a score from, say, 0 to 100, where 0 means "will certainly not purchase the product" and 100 means "will definitely purchase the product." We could then sort the prospects in descending order according to their score and start working down the list until we reach the desired number of responders. As the graph in Figure 3.1 illustrates, by contacting the people most likely to respond first, we can achieve our quota of responders with fewer calls and letters.

Graphs like this one are explained in detail in Chapter 6. For now, it is enough to notice that to obtain the curved line, we have arrayed the customer population along the X-axis with those judged most likely to

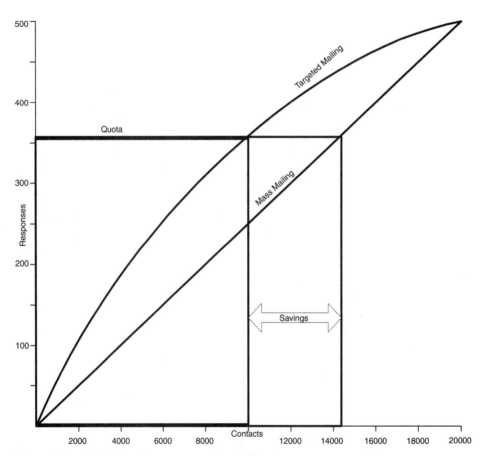

Figure 3.1 Effect of ranking prospects according to a response model.

respond on the left and those judged least likely to respond on the right. The diagonal straight line represents what would happen if prospects were selected at random from an unsorted list of all customers.

The upper line shows what happens if we use the results of a response model to select the prospects. The two lines come together at the left end, since if you contact no one, no one will respond, no matter what model you use, and at the right end, since if you contact everyone, you are bound to find all the responders. In between, you reap the benefits of having a prospect pool that is richer in responders than the population as a whole.

The graph shows that a good response model will lower the cost of a direct marketing campaign by allowing fewer prospects to be contacted. How did the cellular company get such a model? By data mining, of course!

How Data Mining Was Applied

Most data mining methods learn by example. The neural network or decision tree generator or what have you is fed thousands and thousands of training examples. Each of the training examples is clearly marked as being either a responder or a non-responder. After seeing enough of these examples, the data mining tool comes up with a response model. The response model is in the form of a computer program which reads in unclassified records and updates each with a response score or classification.

In this case, however, the offer in question was a new product introduction, so there was no training set of people who had already responded to the offer. One possibility would be to build a model based on people who had ever responded to *any* offer in the past. Such a model would be good for discriminating between people who refuse all telemarketing calls and throw out all junk mail, and those that occasionally respond to some offers. We call models of that kind *non-response models*. Non-response models are very valuable to mass mailers who really do want their message to reach a large, broad market. The American Association of Retired Persons (AARP), for instance, saved millions of dollars in mailing costs when it began using a neural network non-response model. Instead of mailing to every household with a member over 50 years of age, as they once did, they now discard the bottom 10 percent.

But, since the wireless company only wanted to reach a few hundred responders, a model that identified the top 90 percent would not have served the purpose. Instead, they formed a training set of records from a similar new product introduction in another market.

Defining the Inputs

The data mining techniques described in this book automate the central core of the model building process. Given a collection of input data fields, and a target field (in this case, purchase of the new product) they can find patterns and rules that explain the target in terms of the inputs. For data mining to succeed, there must be some relationship between the input variables and the target.

What this means in practice is that it often takes much more time and effort to identify, locate, and prepare input data to build the models than it does to create and run the models once the data has been collected. It is impossible to do a good job of selecting the input variables without knowledge of the business problem being addressed. This is true even when using data mining tools that claim the ability to accept *all* the data and figure out for themselves which fields are important. The problem is that very often the inputs which knowledgeable people in the industry expect from experience to be important are not represented in the raw input data in a way the data mining tools can recognize. We will have more to say about this in Chapter 5.

The cellular company understood the importance of selecting the right input data. Experts from several different functional areas including marketing, sales, and customer support met together with outside data mining consultants to brainstorm about the best way to make use of the available data.

There were three data sources available:

A *Call Detail* database

A *Marketing* database

A *Demographic* database

The call detail database was the largest of the three by far. It contained a record for each call made or received by every customer in the target market. The marketing database contained summarized customer data on usage, tenure, product history, price plans, and payment history. The third database contained purchased demographic and lifestyle data about the customers in the target market.

Derived Inputs

As a result of the brainstorming meetings and preliminary analysis, several summary and descriptive fields were added to the call detail data to be used as input to the predictive model:

Minutes of use

Number of incoming calls

Frequency of calls

Sphere of influence

Voice mail user flag

Roamer flag

Some of these categories require a bit of explanation. Minutes of use (MOU) is the cellular industry's standard measure of how good a customer is. The more minutes of use, the better the customer. Historically, the company had focused on MOU almost to the exclusion of all other variables. But, MOU masks many interesting differences: 2 long calls or 100 short ones? All outgoing calls or half incoming? All calls to the same number or calls to many numbers? The next listed items are intended to shed more light on these questions.

Sphere of influence (SOI) is a particularly interesting measure because it was developed as a result of an earlier data mining effort. A customer's SOI is simply the number of people with whom she or he had cellular conversations during a given time period. It turned out that high SOI customers behaved differently, as a group, than low SOI customers in several ways including frequency of calls to customer service and loyalty.

Roaming is the industry term for leaving the service area of your primary cellular phone service provider. Customers who do this frequently are called *roamers*. A roamer flag was added to the input dataset at the suggestion of people in the sales department who had noticed that roamers tend to have different needs than other customers.

The Results

Data from all three databases was brought together and used to create a computer model. The model was used to identify likely candidates for the new product. Two direct mailings were made: one to a list based on the results of the data mining model and one to a randomly selected control group. As shown in Figure 3.2, 15 percent of the people in the target group purchased the new product, compared to only 3 percent of the control group.

Completing the Cycle

With the help of data mining, the original problem, determining to whom a new product should be offered, was solved. But, that is not the

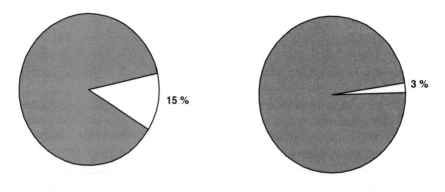

Percent of Target Market Responding   Percent of Control Group Responding

Figure 3.2   A very successful application of data mining.

end of the story. Recall that the group to be mailed was selected on the basis of response data from a different product offering in a different market. Once the results of the new campaign were in, it was possible to apply data mining techniques to get a better picture of the actual responders.

Armed with a buyer profile of the buyers in the initial test market, and a usage profile of the first several months of the new service, the company was able to do an even better job of targeting prospects in the next five markets where the product was rolled out.

NEURAL NETWORKS AND DECISION TREES DRIVE 4 × 4 SALES

In 1992, before any of the commercial data mining tools available today were on the market, one of the big three U.S. auto makers asked a group of researchers at the Pontikes Center for Management at Southern Illinois University in Carbondale to develop an "expert system" to identify likely buyers of a particular sport-utility vehicle.[2]

---

2. We are grateful to Wei-Xiong Ho, one of the researchers who took part in this study, for sharing with us an unpublished paper, *Hybrid Expert Systems: A Marketing Application,* that he co-authored with Joseph Harder of the College of Business and Administration at Southern Illinois in 1992, and for providing additional information in telephone conversations.

Traditional expert systems consist of a large database of hundreds or thousands of rules collected by observing and interviewing human experts who are skilled at a particular classification task. Expert systems have enjoyed some success in certain domains such as medical diagnosis and answering tax questions, but the difficulty of collecting the rules has limited their use. In any case, there are many tasks for which it is hard to find any experts to interview.

The team at Southern Illinois decided to solve these problems by generating the rules directly from historical data provided by the auto maker. In other words, they would replace expert interviews with data mining.

The Initial Challenge

The initial challenge that Detroit brought to Carbondale was to improve response to a direct mail campaign for a particular model. The campaign involved sending an invitation to the prospect to come test-drive the new model. Anyone accepting the invitation would find a free pair of sunglasses waiting for him or her at the dealership. The problem was that very few people were returning the response card or calling the 800 number for more information, and few of those that did ended up buying the vehicle. The company knew it could save itself a lot of money by not sending the offer to people unlikely to respond, but it didn't know who those were.

How Data Mining Was Applied

As is often the case when the data to be mined is from several different sources, the first challenge was to integrate data so that it could tell a consistent story.

The Data

The first file, the "mail file," was a mailing list containing names and addresses of about a million people who had been sent the promotional mailing. This file contained very little information likely to be useful for selection.

The mail file was augmented with data based on zip codes from the commercially available PRIZM database. This database contains demographic and "psychographic" characterizations of the neighborhoods associated with the zip codes.

Zip Codes and Area Codes

For those unfamiliar with the U.S. postal system, the zip code is the first level of a two-tiered postal code. The zip code is a five-digit number that divides the country into postal regions at the level of individual post offices. A single zip code is likely to include a small town and its rural hinterlands, a medium-sized suburb, or a city neighborhood of several thousand people. The ordinary five-digit zip code is used on all mail sent to U.S. addresses.

A second level of encoding, called *zip+4*, appends an additional 4 digits to the zip code, thus dividing each zip code into very fine slices, often consisting of a single building. Bulk mailers get a discount by using zip+4 addresses and presenting the mail to the post office already sorted at the individual mail carrier route level.

Because they are so readily available, demographics and other data are often summarized by zip code. Unfortunately, the five-digit zip codes cover too large an area and the zip+4 codes too small an area to be really well-suited to this purpose. Even the country's most famous zip code, 90210 (Beverly Hills, California) which has given its name to a popular television show about fabulously wealthy teenagers, is probably more diverse than one might suppose from watching the program.

For more information on zip codes, see (http://www.usps.gov/ncsc/). For more information on PRIZM, see (http://www.claritas.com/prizm.htm).

The phone system provides another readily available way to summarize data geographically. The United States, Canada, Bermuda, and a dozen or so Caribbean countries share a common phone numbering system. Within this region, a fully qualified phone number has 10 digits. The first three digits are referred to as the *area code*. Area codes provide an even coarser division than five-digit zip codes. The next three digits are called the *exchange*. Traditionally, and still to a large extent, these three digits identify a local switching office and are strongly associated with a particular neighborhood. So, area code plus exchange together provide a useful level of aggregation intermediate to the short and long forms of the postal zip code.

There are exceptions to the geographical interpretation of the area code. An 800 or 888 in the area code field indicates that a telephone number, wherever located, is toll-free to the caller. A 900 in the area code field indicates that the caller will be assessed an additional fee on his or her bill, and so on.

Two additional files contained information on people who had sent back the response card or called the 800 number for more information. It was simple to tie the response cards back to the original mailing file because the mail file contained a nine-character key for each address. This key was printed on the response cards. Telephone responders presented more of a problem since their reported name and address might not exactly match their address in the database, and there is no guaranty that the call even came from someone on the mailing list since the recipient of the offer may have passed it on to someone else.

Of 1,000,003 people who received the mailing, 32,904 responded by sending back a card and 16,453 responded by calling the toll-free number for a total initial response rate of 5 percent. The auto maker's primary interest, of course, was in the much smaller number of people who both responded to the mailing and bought the advertised model of car. These were to be found in a sales file, obtained from the manufacturer, that contained the names, addresses, and model purchased for all car buyers in the three-month period following the mailing.

An automated name-matching program with loosely set matching standards discovered around 22,000 apparent matches between people who bought cars and people who had received the mailing. Hand editing reduced the intersection to 4,764 people who had received the mailing and bought a car. About half of those had purchased the advertised model. See Figure 3.3 for a comparison of data sources.

Down the Mine Shaft

The experimental design called for the population to be divided into exactly two classes—success and failure. This is certainly a questionable design since it obscures interesting differences. Surely, people who come into the dealership to test-drive one model, but end up buying another should be in a different class than people who simply don't respond, or people who respond, but buy nothing. For that matter, people who weren't considered good enough prospects to be sent a mailing, but who nevertheless bought the car are an even more interesting group.

Be that as it may, success was defined as "received a mailing and bought the car" and failure was defined as "received the mailing, but did not buy the car." A series of trials was run using the decision tree tool, ID3 (a precursor of the currently popular C4.5 described in detail in Chapter 12), and a neural network tool. The tools were tested on various kinds of training sets. Some of the training sets reflected the true proportion of successes in the database, while others were enriched to have up to 10 percent successes.

The results were that the neural network did better on the sparse training sets, while the decision tree tool appeared to do much better

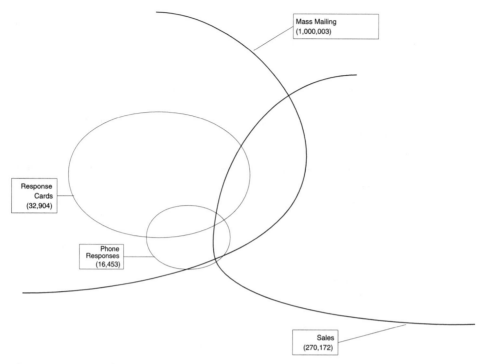

Figure 3.3 How the data sources were merged.

on the enriched sets. Unfortunately, when the decision tree developed using the enriched training set was applied to unseen data containing only the usual number of successes, the apparent advantage was not maintained. These observations led to a two-stage process. First, a neural network determined who was likely to buy a car, any car, from the company. Then, the decision tree tool was used to predict which of the likely car buyers would choose the advertised model. This two-step process proved quite successful. The hybrid model combining decision trees and neural networks missed very few buyers of the targeted model while at the same time screening out many more non-buyers than either the neural net or the decision tree was able to do.

The Resulting Actions

Armed with a model that could effectively reach responders the company decided to take the money saved by mailing fewer pieces and put it into improving the lure offered to get likely buyers into the showroom. Instead of sunglasses for the masses, they offered a nice pair of leather boots to the far smaller group of likely buyers. The new approach proved much more effective than the first.

Completing the Cycle

The university-based data mining project showed that even with only a limited number of broad-brush variables to work with and fairly primitive data mining tools, data mining could improve the effectiveness of a direct marketing campaign for a big-ticket item like a sport-utility vehicle. The next step is to gather more data, build better models, and try again!

INVESTMENT IN DATA MINING IMPROVES YIELDS AT BANK OF AMERICA

Our next case study concerns a bank in the early stages of incorporating data mining into its marketing process. Bank of America was anxious to expand its portfolio of home equity loans, but several direct mail campaigns had yielded disappointing results. The National Consumer Assets Group (NCAG) at B of A decided to use data mining to attack the problem.[3]

The Challenge

Bank of America wanted to gain a better understanding of its current home equity loan customers in order to be able to do a better job of marketing the loans to others. Before applying data mining to this task, the bank had developed two common sense models of likely prospects for the home equity loan product:

- People with college-age children wanting to borrow against their home equity in order to pay tuition bills
- People with high but variable incomes wanting a way to tap into their home equity to smooth out the peaks and valleys

---

3. We would like to thank Larry Scroggins of Casablanca Information Services (B of A public relations) for allowing us to use material from a Bank of America Case Study he wrote. We also benefited from conversations with Bob Flynn of Cogit Corporation and Jerry Modes of HyperParallel.

Marketing literature for the home equity line product reflected this view of the likely customer, as did the lists drawn up for telemarketing. As it turns out, data mining led the bank to a new understanding of its home equity line customers.

How Data Mining Was Applied

NCAG worked with data mining consultants to bring a range of data mining techniques to bear on the problem. There was no shortage of data with which to work. Since the mid-1980s, Bank of America had been storing data on its nine million retail customers in a relational database on a large parallel computer from NCR. The corporate data warehouse is fed by 42 separate *systems of record*. Data from these feeder systems is cleaned, transformed, and aligned into consistent time frames, geographic codes, and customer codes. Because of the corporate data warehouse, B of A is able to see at once all of the relationships each customer maintains with the bank.

This is a historical database truly worthy of the name—some of the records go back to 1914! More recent records contain about 250 fields per customer. In addition to fields collected directly by the bank, the database also contains demographic fields such as income, number of children, type of home, and so forth.

These customer attributes were combined with transaction histories and analyzed using the //Discover suite of parallel data mining software tools from HyperParallel. Three different tools proved to be useful.

First, a decision tree tool was used to derive rules that could be used to classify customers as likely or unlikely to respond to a home equity loan offer. The decision tree software trained on thousands of examples of customers who had obtained the product and thousands who had not. Eventually, it learned to tell the difference. Once the rules were discovered, the resulting computer model was used to add yet another attribute to the record of each potential prospect. The new attribute was the "good prospect" flag generated by the data mining model.

Next, a sequential pattern-finding tool was used to determine *when* a customer was most likely to want a loan of this type. The goal of this analysis was to discover a sequence of events that had frequently preceded successful solicitations in the past.

Finally, a clustering tool was used to automatically segment the customers into groups with many similar attributes. The clustering tool came up with 14 different clusters of customers. As often happens, many of the clusters did not seem particularly interesting. One of them, however, was very interesting indeed. This cluster had two intriguing properties:

1. 39 percent of the people in the cluster had both business and personal accounts with the bank.
2. This cluster accounted for 27 percent of the 11 percent of the customers who had been classified by the decision tree as likely responders to a home equity loan offer.

This data immediately suggested that people might be using home equity loans to start up businesses. Upon further investigation, this hunch proved to be correct.

The Resulting Actions

Upon obtaining this new understanding of the market, NCAG teamed with the Retail Banking Division and several district sales organizations to develop a campaign strategy. The teaming allowed field experience to be combined with the insights gained through data mining to produce new marketing materials. As a result of the new campaign, Bank of America saw the acceptance rate for home equity offers more than double.

Completing the Cycle

According to Dave McDonald, V.P. of the NCAG group, the strategic implications of data mining are nothing short of the transformation of the retail side of Bank of America from a mass-marketing institution to a targeted-marketing, learning institution. "We want to get to the point where we are *constantly* executing marketing programs—not just quarterly mailings, but *programs* on a consistent basis." He goes on to describe his vision of a closed-loop marketing process where data capture feeds a rapid analysis process that leads to program creation for execution and testing which, in turn, generates additional data to rejuvenate the process. In short, the virtuous cycle of data mining.

Bank of America is a pioneer in the application of data mining, but it is by no means alone. Like Bank of America, many banks are now trying to understand the product mix best for each customer. Market basket analysis tools are tailor-made for this purpose.

Finding the right "basket" of products addresses both profitability and retention. As long as each division thinks of the customer only in terms of its product, it is actually training the customers to shop around for each service independently. All too frequently, different divisions work at cross purposes such as when the credit card division spends $500 to acquire a new high balance customer only to have another division pitch the same customer a home equity line as a vehicle for bill consolidation.

By taking a relationship view, banks, like other businesses, are now able to calculate the profitability of a whole basket of products. The lifetime value of the customer may be increased by leaving some products in the basket that are not profitable when measured on a standalone basis. Clustering and affinity grouping are techniques that can be used both to define new customer segments that have similar needs and desires and to find new groupings of products to be bundled.

What Can Data Mining Do?

From the hyperbole surrounding this topic, one might easily conclude that data mining will cure arthritis and let you loose 30 pounds in 30 days without having to diet or exercise. In fact, practical data mining can accomplish a limited set of tasks and only under limited circumstances. The good news is that many problems of intellectual, economic, and business interest can be phrased in terms of the following six tasks:

Classification

Estimation

Prediction

Affinity Grouping

Clustering

Description

No single data mining tool or technique is equally applicable to all the tasks. In this chapter, we define each of the six tasks and, using a small survey of moviegoers, provide examples of each. In later chapters, we introduce a data mining methodology that covers all six tasks and describes the tools that can be applied to them.

CLASSIFICATION

Classification, the most common data mining task, seems to be a human imperative. In order to understand and communicate about the world, we are constantly classifying, categorizing, and grading. We divide living things into phyla, species, and genera; matter into elements; dogs into breeds; people into races; steaks and maple syrup into USDA grades.

Classification consists of examining the features of a newly presented object and assigning it to one of a predefined set of classes. For our purposes, the objects to be classified are generally represented by records in a database and the act of classification consists of updating each record by filling in a field with a class code of some kind.

The classification task is characterized by a well-defined definition of the classes, and a training set consisting of preclassified examples. The task is to build a model of some kind that can be applied to unclassified data in order to classify it.

Examples of classification tasks that have been addressed using the techniques described in this book include:

- Assigning keywords to articles as they come in off the news wire
- Classifying credit applicants as low, medium, or high risk
- Determining which phone numbers correspond to facsimile machines
- Spotting fraudulent insurance claims
- Assigning industry codes and job designations on the basis of free-text job descriptions

In all of these examples, there are a limited number of classes and we expect to be able to assign any record into one or another of them. Decision trees (discussed in Chapter 12) and memory-based reasoning (discussed in Chapter 9) are techniques well-suited to classification. Link analysis (discussed in Chapter 11) is also useful for classification in certain circumstances.

ESTIMATION

Classification deals with discrete outcomes: yes or no; measles, rubella, or chicken pox. Estimation deals with continuously valued outcomes. Given some input data, we use estimation to come up with a value for some unknown continuous variable such as income, height, or credit card balance.

In practice, estimation is often used to perform a classification task. A credit card company wishing to sell advertising space in its billing envelopes to a ski boot manufacturer might build a classification model that put all of its cardholders into one of two classes, skier or nonskier. Another approach is to build a model that assigns each cardholder a "propensity to ski score." This might be a value from 0 to 1 indicating the estimated probability that the card holder is a skier. The classification task now comes down to establishing a threshold score. Anyone with a score greater than or equal to the threshold is classed as a skier and anyone with a lower score is considered not to be a skier.

The estimation approach has the great advantage that the individual records may now be rank ordered. To see the importance of this, imagine that the ski boot company has budgeted for a mailing of 500,000 pieces. If the classification approach is used and 1.5 million skiers are identified, then it might simply place the ad in the bills of 500,000 people selected at random from that pool. If, on the other hand, each cardholder has a propensity to ski score, it can send the ad to the 500,000 most likely candidates.

Examples of estimation tasks include

estimating the number of children in a family,

estimating a family's total household income,

estimating the lifetime value of a customer, and

estimating the probability that someone will respond to a balance transfer solicitation.

Neural networks (discussed in Chapter 13) are well-suited to estimation tasks.

PREDICTION

Prediction is the same as classification or estimation except that the records are classified according to some predicted future behavior or estimated future value. In a prediction task, the only way to check the accuracy of the classification is to wait and see.

Any of the techniques used for classification and estimation can be adapted for use in prediction by using training examples where the value of the variable to be predicted is already known, along with historical data for those examples. The historical data is used to build a model that explains the current observed behavior. When this model is applied to current inputs, the result is a prediction of future behavior.

The market basket analysis technique, used to discover which items are likely to be purchased together in a grocery store, can also be adapted to model what *future* purchases or actions tend to be implied by current data.

Examples of prediction tasks addressed by the data mining techniques discussed in this book include:

- Predicting the size of the balance that will be transferred if a credit card prospect accepts a balance transfer offer
- Predicting which customers will leave within the next six months
- Predicting which telephone subscribers will order a value-added service such as three-way calling or voice mail

Market basket analysis (discussed in Chapter 8), memory-based reasoning (discussed in Chapter 9), decision trees (discussed in Chapter 12), and artificial neural networks (discussed in Chapter 13) are all suitable for use in prediction. The choice of technique depends on the nature of the input data, the type of value to be predicted, and the importance attached to explicability of the prediction.

AFFINITY GROUPING OR MARKET BASKET ANALYSIS

The task of affinity grouping is to determine which things go together. The prototypical example is determining what things go together in a shopping cart at the supermarket, hence the term *market basket analysis*. Retail chains can use affinity grouping to plan arrangement of items on store shelves or in a catalog so that items often purchased together will be seen together.

Affinity grouping can also be used to identify cross-selling opportunities and to design attractive packages or groupings of product and services.

Affinity grouping is one simple approach to generating rules from data. If two items, say cat food and kitty litter, occur together frequently enough, we can generate two *association rules*:

People who buy cat food also buy kitty litter with probability P_1.

People who buy kitty litter also buy cat food with probability P_2.

Association rules are discussed in detail in Chapter 8.

CLUSTERING

Clustering is the task of segmenting a heterogeneous population into a number of more homogeneous subgroups or *clusters*. What distinguishes clustering from classification is that clustering does not rely on predefined classes. In classification, the population is subdivided by assigning each element or record to a predefined class on the basis of a model developed through training on preclassified examples.

In clustering, there are no predefined classes and no examples. The records are grouped together on the basis of self-similarity. It is up to you to determine what meaning, if any, to attach to the resulting clusters. Clusters of symptoms might indicate different diseases. Clusters of leaf and kernel attributes might indicate different strains of corn.

Clustering is often done as a prelude to some other form of data mining or modeling. For example, clustering might be the first step in a market segmentation effort: Instead of trying to come up with a one-size-fits-all rule for "what kind of promotion do customers respond to best," we can first divide the customer base into clusters or people with similar buying habits, and then ask what kind of promotion works best for each cluster. Cluster detection is discussed in detail in Chapter 10.

DESCRIPTION

Sometimes the purpose of data mining is simply to describe what is going on in a complicated database in a way that increases our understanding of the people, products, or processes that produced the data in the first place. A good enough *description* of a behavior will often suggest an *explanation* for it as well. At the very least, a good description suggests where to start looking for an explanation. The famous gender gap in American politics is an example of how a simple description, "women support Democrats in greater numbers than do men," can provoke large amounts of interest and further study on the part of journalists, sociologists, economists, and political scientists, not to mention candidates for public office.

Some of the tools discussed in this book, the market basket analysis tools, for example, are purely descriptive. Others, like neural networks, provide next to nothing in the way of description.

ALL SIX TASKS IN ONE SMALL DATABASE

In real commercial applications, data mining is usually employed on very large databases. The reasons for this are two-fold:

1. In small databases, it is possible to find interesting patterns and relationships by simple inspection of results from familiar tools such as spreadsheets and multidimensional database query tools.
2. Most data mining techniques require large amounts of training data containing many examples in order to generate good classification rules, association rules, clusters, or predictions. Small datasets lead to unreliable conclusions based on chance patterns.

For expository purposes, however, we have created a small database that we use to explore the six basic data mining tasks and the various ways of approaching them.

The Moviegoers Database

The moviegoers database contains the responses to an informal survey conducted during August and September of 1996. The idea was prompted by the frequent use, by movie reviewers, of terms like "date film," "guy movie," and "chick flick." We wondered how much you can tell about a person by what movies they watch and how much you can tell about a movie by who goes to see it.

The Survey Questions

The survey asked for age, sex, and last movie seen in a movie theater. The restriction to movies seen in a movie theater was intended to restrict the choice of titles to a few dozen so that there would be some chance of patterns emerging from a small sample. To be eligible for inclusion in the database, respondents had to have gone to the cinema at least once in the past several months. Respondents who had made more than one trip to the movies recently were asked to list as many films as they could remember seeing.

The Sample Populations

The survey was distributed to four different populations in hopes that interesting intergroup differences might be revealed. Survey forms were made available

- by e-mail to members of the Oberlin College alumni mailing list,
- by e-mail to employees of the Enterprise Systems division of MRJ Technology Solutions,
- next to the coffee machine in an office building in Cambridge, Massachusetts, and
- at a gathering of English Country Dance and New England Contra Dance afficionados at Pinewoods Camp in Plymouth, Massachusetts.

The Database

The data was entered into a relational database so that it could be easily queried and made accessible to a wide range of data mining tools. The database design is illustrated by the Microsoft Access screen in Figure 4.1.

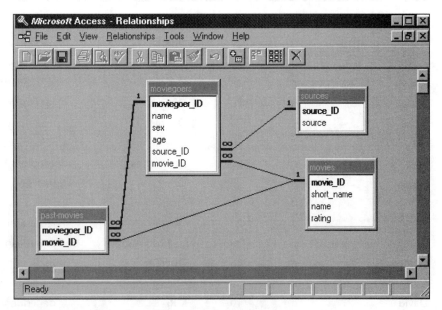

Figure 4.1 The layout of the moviegoers database.

Notice that a given moviegoer may have zero or many entries in the history table. For reasons that will be made clear in Chapter 5, the integer identifiers for categorical variables like movie and survey source will be used for data mining rather than the corresponding strings. The strings are retained for reporting purposes.

The following structured query language (SQL) query produces a table of moviegoers, along with their sex, age, location, and most recent movie, the first few rows of which are shown in Table 4.1.

```
SELECT moviegoers.name, moviegoers.sex, moviegoers.age,
   sources.source, movies.name
FROM moviegoers, sources, movies
WHERE movies.movie_ID = moviegoers.movie_ID AND
   sources.source_ID = moviegoers.source_ID
ORDER BY moviegoers.name;
```

Table 4.1 Moviegoer Survey

moviegoers.name	sex	age	source	movies.name
Amy	f	27	Oberlin	Independence Day
Andrew	m	25	Oberlin	12 Monkeys
Andy	m	34	Oberlin	The Birdcage
Anne	f	30	Oberlin	Trainspotting
Ansje	f	25	Oberlin	I Shot Andy Warhol
Beth	f	30	Oberlin	Chain Reaction
Bob	m	51	Pinewoods	Schindler's List
Brian	m	23	Oberlin	Super Cop
Candy	f	29	Oberlin	Eddie
Cara	f	25	Oberlin	Phenomenon
Cathy	f	39	124 Mt. Auburn	The Birdcage
Charles	m	25	Oberlin	Kingpin
Curt	m	30	MRJ	T2 Judgment Day
David	m	40	MRJ	Independence Day
Erica	f	23	124 Mt. Auburn	Trainspotting

Moviegoer Classification

Classification tasks that might be attempted using this data include:

- Determining sex based on age, source, and movies seen
- Determining source based on sex, age, and movies seen
- Determining most recent movie based on past movies, age, sex, and source

In Chapter 12, we do, in fact, use the moviegoer database to build decision trees for the first of these tasks.

Moviegoer Estimation

As age is the only continuous variable in the database, it is the obvious target for estimation. Using the fields collected directly in the survey, we could estimate age as a function of source, sex, and movies seen. As is often the case, we would probably want to augment the collected data with additional fields that can be derived directly or indirectly from the data provided. For example, we might add a field for total number of movies seen recently. This can be obtained via the SQL statement

```
SELECT moviegoer_ID, COUNT(movie_ID)
FROM past_movies
GROUP BY moviegoer_ID;
```

and a field for movie ratings which can be obtained externally.

With the right data, we could also estimate audience size, profitability, and length of run.

Moviegoer Prediction

The most likely real-world reason for collecting information on who has seen what movies in the past is not, of course, to guess the sex or age of the respondents (we could just ask them), but to predict which of them are likely to see a particular new release.

More broadly, we would like to use the data we have collected to form clusters of both movies and people. For each cluster of people, we would like to find rules that explain the members' taste in movies. For each cluster of movies, we would like to find rules that describe the best target audience. When a new film is released, it is assigned to one of the clusters based on the rules that define the cluster. It is then marketed to the population segments that have responded well to movies in that cluster in the past.

Moviegoer Affinity Grouping

There are several useful ways we can use affinity grouping with the moviegoers data. The most obvious is the standard market basket question: Which movies go together? To perform this analysis, we would group the data into market baskets comprising all the movies seen by each viewer. Based on these baskets, we would calculate the probability that any given movie will be found in a basket containing a known combination of other movies.

We can also use affinity grouping to address the sex classification task by generating association rules. The screen image in Figure 4.2 is taken from the PC version of DataMind, a data mining software package that generates association rules.

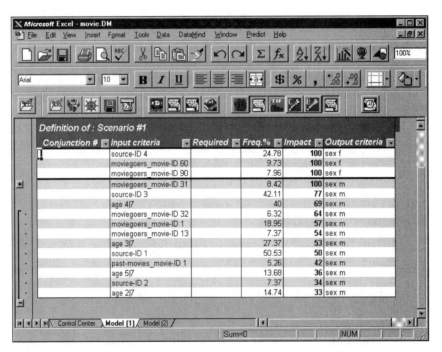

Figure 4.2 A DataMind screen image showing that certain movies are strongly identified with one sex or the other.

The chart tells us that in our sample population, to no one's surprise, only men reported film 31, *Super Cop*, as their most recently seen movie. Somewhat less stereotypically, only women reported films 60 and 90, *Trainspotting* and *The Nutty Professor*, as their most recently seen movie. Astonishingly, nearly 10 percent of women in the sample population had an Eddie Murphy reprise of an old Jerry Lewis role as their most recent cinematic experience.

In the following section, *cluster detection*, we suggest a possible explanation: Parental movie viewing habits are strongly influenced by the tastes of children.

As often happens, the preliminary data mining results suggest other areas for future investigation: 100 percent of the respondents from the office building coffee room are women. Now, as it happens, there are plenty of men in that building and many of them drink coffee. Why did none of them fill out the questionnaire?

Perhaps what is really being revealed is a gender-linked difference in reaction to an empty coffee pot. According to this hypothesis, nobody going up to the coffee machine for a cup of coffee is likely to hang around to fill out a survey form, *unless* the coffee pot is empty and they have to wait several minutes anyway for a new batch to drip through. If, upon finding the coffee pot empty, women tend to make a new pot when it is needed, while men tend to decide they didn't want coffee that much after all, it might explain the skewed response.

Moviegoer Clustering

How might clustering be applied to the moviegoers database? Depending on our goals, we might want to find groups of movies that go together because they are seen by the same people or groups of people that go together because they see the same movies.

One advantage that the algorithms used for clustering have over the other techniques mentioned here is that there is no need to select a single field in the data as the target field or independent variable. As a result, clustering can sometimes reveal information about a variable that is not in the data, but is correlated with variables that are. For example, people with young children form a clearly recognizable cluster in the moviegoers database, even though it contains no explicit information about parental status. People who *are* children would form a different, but also clearly recognizable cluster if there were enough of them in the sample.

As with the other tasks, clustering would be more useful with more data. Before attempting to use clustering to redefine Hollywood's *genre* boundaries, we would want to enhance the data with additional fields such as actors, director, language, country of origin, production budget, and so forth. This is a theme that distinguishes data mining from other forms of analysis: more is better! More records, larger samples, more fields, more variables.

Moviegoer Description

A common goal of data mining, especially data mining in support of marketing, sales, and customer support, is to arrive at a description of the customer population. In the case of the moviegoers, the first level description would be in terms of standard summary statistics—average age, percent female, and so on. The next level of description is provided by affinity grouping—"people who see X also see Y."

Rules, too, can be seen as descriptions. "Males aged 12 to 17 are likely to see X" can be viewed as both a predictive model and a description of the audience for movie X.

Data Mining Methodology

In Chapter 2, we discussed the virtuous cycle of data mining as a business process. In that discussion, we divided the data mining process into four stages:

1. Identifying the problem
2. Analyzing the data
3. Taking action
4. Measuring the outcome

The first and third of these stages raise mainly *business* issues. For data mining to be successful, these business issues must, of course, be properly addressed. The enterprise must identify areas where extracting better information from the available data can lead to better knowledge of what actions to take. Once these improved courses of action have been identified, they must be implemented.

For the most part, however, these topics belong in a book on management and how to improve corporate responsiveness through decision-support technology. In this book we make the bold assumption that management goals are already well-defined and that as management discovers more about the company's market, products, and customers, they will know how to translate that knowledge into actions that further those goals.

In this chapter we concentrate on Stage 2 of the virtuous cycle. This is the stage where the actual mining of data takes place and where the resulting information is smelted to produce knowledge.

Chapter 6 addresses Stage 4, the stage that determines whether all the excavation was worth the effort.

HYPOTHESIS TESTING AND KNOWLEDGE DISCOVERY

There are two basic styles of data mining. The first, *hypothesis testing*, is a top-down approach that attempts to substantiate or disprove preconceived ideas. The second, *knowledge discovery*, is a bottom-up approach that starts with the data and tries to get it to tell us something we didn't already know.

This methodology tackles data mining problems from both directions at once, bouncing back and forth between the two approaches. Wearing our top-down hat, we think up possible explanations for the observed behavior and let those hypotheses dictate the data to be analyzed. Then, putting on our bottom-up hat, we let the data suggest new hypotheses to test (see Figure 5.1).

Figure 5.1 A data mining consultant wearing his "top-down hat" and his "bottom-up hat."

HYPOTHESIS TESTING

Hypothesis testing is what scientists and statisticians spend their lives doing. An hypothesis is a proposed explanation whose validity can be tested. Testing the validity of an hypothesis is done by analyzing data that may simply be collected by observation or generated through an experiment, such as a test mailing.

Whole books are written on the proper design of surveys and experiments. This is not one of them. Our goal in this chapter is to lay out some step-by-step procedures for successful data mining. Following this methodology will increase your chances of using data mining successfully by forcing you to think about each step of the process. Be warned, however, that some of the steps, such as "determining what data would allow these ideas to be tested" can be quite tricky in practice.

The Process of Hypothesis Testing

The hypothesis testing method has several steps:

1. Generate good ideas (hypotheses).
2. Determine what data would allow these hypotheses to be tested.
3. Locate the data.
4. Prepare the data for analysis.
5. Build computer models based on the data.
6. Evaluate computer models to confirm or reject hypotheses.

We examine each of these steps in turn.

Generating Good Ideas—a.k.a. Hypotheses

The key to this step is getting input from a broad spectrum within the organization and, where appropriate, outside it as well. Often, all that is needed to start the ideas flowing is a clear statement of the problem itself—especially if it is something that has not previously been recognized as a problem.

It happens more often than you might suppose that problems go unrecognized because they are not captured by the metrics being used to evaluate the organization's performance. If a company has always measured its sales force on the number of new sales made each month, the sales people may never have given much thought to the question of how long new customers remain active or how much they spend over the course of their relationship with the firm. When asked the right questions, however, the sales force may have insights into customer behavior that the marketing department, with its greater distance from the customer, has missed.

We suggest getting representatives from the various constituencies within the enterprise together in one place, rather than interviewing them separately. That way, people with different areas of knowledge and expertise have a chance to react to each other's ideas.

WARNING

It is important not to allow the brainstorming sessions used to generate hypotheses to degenerate into "pass the blame" sessions. Participants should be made to feel free to toss their ideas into the ring without fear of attack. The discussion leader should be a skilled facilitator who is not too closely tied to any one constituency.

Defining Data Needed to Test Ideas

Once the hypotheses have been gathered, they must be evaluated for amenability to testing. Some hypotheses can be tested by means of simple queries on existing decision-support databases. Others will require information to be culled from operational systems, gathered through surveys, or purchased from an outside vendor.

For each hypothesis, generate a list of data requirements. With these lists in hand, we are ready for the next step.

TIP

When, as often happens, the people who ought to be part of the hypothesis generation meetings are widely scattered geographically, an email discussion list or internal electronic news groups can serve quite well.

Locating the Data

Data mining requires data. In the best of all possible worlds, the required data is already resident in a corporate data warehouse. In fact, it is more often scattered in a variety of operational systems in incompatible formats on computers running different operating systems, accessed through incompatible desktop tools.

The data sources that are useful and available will, of course, vary greatly from problem to problem and industry to industry. Our clients have found uses for all of the following:

- Warranty claims data (including both fixed-format and free-text fields)
- Point-of-sale data (including ring codes, coupons proffered, discounts applied)
- Credit card charge records
- Medical insurance claims data
- Direct mail response records
- Call-center records
- Bridge toll and parking garage records
- Motor vehicle registration records
- Noise level in decibels from microphones placed in communities near an airport
- Telephone call detail records
- Demographic and lifestyle data
- Economic data
- Hourly weather readings (wind direction, wind strength, precipitation)
- Census returns

TIP

As soon as you get your hands on a data file from a new source, it is a good idea to profile it in order to become familiar with it. Profiling includes getting counts and summary statistics for each field, counts of the number of different values taken on by categorical variables, and where appropriate, cross-tabulations such as sales by product by region.

In addition to providing insight into the data, the profiling exercise is likely to raise warning flags about inconsistencies or definitional problems that could destroy the usefulness of later analysis. In one data mining engagement, we encountered 200 different values in a state field. It turned out that the city field had been allowed to overrun the state field in about 5 percent of the records!

Preparing Data for Analysis

It is very uncommon for the data available for data mining to have been collected and stored with that purpose in mind. As a result, it must often be massaged into a form that will allow the data mining tools to be used to best advantage. The precise transformations required vary depending on the technique and the software package. Some tools need to have all continuous variables cut up into ranges.

Others require all values to be normalized to a range from 0 to 1. Some can handle textual data; most cannot.

The specific data transformations required by particular data mining techniques are discussed in the chapters where those techniques are described in detail. In this section, we examine several issues that are likely to arise no matter what tool is used:

- Summarization
- Incompatible computer architectures
- Inconsistent data encoding
- Textual data
- Missing values

Summarization   What is the right level of detail? The answer depends on the analysis to be performed. As a general rule of thumb, you want to obtain the data in completely unsummarized form so as to be free to summarize it several different ways as the need arises. This is not to say that the unsummarized data is necessarily best for analytical purposes. There are several reasons to summarize the data somewhat before beginning analysis:

- The data may reflect details that are simply not of interest for your purposes. In a data mining engagement with a telephone company, we were faced with data collected from the switches that actually route the call from the originating phone to the call's destination. That level of detail might be interesting for an analysis of network congestion problems, but our focus was on customer calling patterns. For our purposes, we were interested in things that are under the customer's control, and which might be influenced by marketing actions. So, we were interested in the caller's telephone number, the telephone number called, the time the call was placed, the length of the call, and the billing plan applied to the call, but *not* which wires the electrons traversed to complete the circuit.
- There may be too few examples at the finest level of detail. Often, in data mining, we are looking for characteristics of groups. If we divide the observations too finely, we may not end up with a sufficient quantity of records in any one bin. In cases like these, zip code may be better than zip+four, and area code plus first 3 digits may be better than phone number, as the expression to use in an SQL GROUP BY clause to aggregate the data.

- Unsummarized data may be too big to handle. This problem is especially vexing in market basket analysis where we may be dealing with tens of thousands of stack-keeping units (SKUs) and a combinatorial explosion of relationships between them. In this situation, we may have no choice but to lump *one-liter bottles of Polar Ginger Ale* into *Soft Drinks* for one analysis and into *Regional Brands* for another.

Incompatible Computer Architectures   Computers do not all speak the same language. Very often the operational system that houses the data we want to analyze speaks COBOL or RPG, stores text in the EBCDIC encoding, and numbers in packed decimal format, while the system used for housing the decision-support database and data mining applications speaks C or C++, stores text in the ASCII encoding, and numbers as integers or single or double precision floating point. Fortunately, there are now data transport tools that take most, though not all, of the pain out of these translations. These tools take a high level description of the desired transformations and produce the code needed to perform them.

Inconsistent Data Encoding   When information on the same topic is collected from multiple sources, the various sources often represent the same data different ways. If these differences are not caught, they add spurious distinctions that can lead to erroneous conclusions. In the call-detail analysis project described in Chapter 3, we discovered that each of the markets studied had a different way of indicating a call to check one's own voice mail. In one city, a call to voice mail from the phone line associated with that mail box was recorded as having the same origin and destination numbers. In another city, the same situation was represented by the presence of a specific nonexistent number as the call destination. In yet another city, the actual number dialed to reach voice mail was recorded. Before we could understand any apparent differences in voice mail habits between the cities, we had to put the data in a common form.

The same data contained multiple abbreviations for some states and some cases a particular city was counted separately from the rest of the state. If issues like this are not resolved, you may find yourself building a model of calling patterns to California based on data that does not include calls to Los Angeles, or analyzing patterns of consumption of carbonated beverages using data that does not include Coca Cola.

Textual Data   Textual data presents many headaches. Unless we hope to actually extract information from what is written in a text field (as in the classification of new stories described in Chapter 9), we generally prefer not to use text fields at all.

In many cases, text fields contain information that is not useful for analytical purposes (name, street address, mother's maiden name, etc.). When the information provided *is* relevant (referral source, country, color, model, etc.), we generally encode it as some other data type that is easier to work with.

If a text field is *very* well constrained, so that the data it contains follows a rigid format that can never vary, it is probably safe to leave it alone. Postal codes, vehicle identification numbers, and product codes are examples of fields that *may* meet these criteria. But, remember: Depending on the software that you use for data mining, `' no'` may not equal `'no '` and `'V0R2J0, "V0R" 2J0,'` and `'V0R-2J0'` will almost certainly appear to be three different postal codes.

The simplest encoding method is to create a table of all the legal strings. Then, in the data to be analyzed, we can replace the string by its index into the table.

If the data source is a relational database, this encoding will already have been done. For every `product_name` field there is a corresponding `product_code` field that is probably the unique key for the product table. If, as is often the case, however, the data source is a flat file created directly from credit application forms, prescription forms, telephone call records, order entry records, or any other operational source, or if you plan to mine fields that were considered merely descriptive by the database designers, text strings should be re-coded before beginning the analysis.

Unfortunately, this is not a task that can safely be left to automatic tools. An automatic tool will not be able to determine that "U.K.," "Scotland," "England," "Wales," "Northern Ireland," and "United Kingdom" should all be mapped to country code 44 in your database, nor even that "F," "W," and "female" should all be mapped to gender code 1.

Missing Values   In the real world, data records are often missing fields or, in relational parlance, contain "nulls." Some data mining tools deal gracefully with missing data; most do not. Even where a tool claims to be able to handle missing data, you may want to give some thought to the issue, because there is no one right way of dealing with it.

When using software that does not accept null values, we have several choices. In some cases, we may be able to afford to simply throw away incomplete records. But that means throwing away useful information from the fields that are filled in and also risks biasing the sample since records that are missing a field may have other things in common as well.

In many cases, we want to fill in the missing value with a likely guess. Clearly, we would not want to fill in all missing salaries as $0.0 nor as $9,999,999.99, but something like that is likely to happen if we rely on defaults. In this example, it might make sense to use the mean or the median of the known salaries. For a missing categorical value, it might make sense to choose the most common value.

In other cases, the fact that data is missing in a field is extremely diagnostic. A missing work telephone number might indicate that an applicant is not really employed or doesn't want anyone to call to verify a salary claim. We would not want to simply fill in an "average" or "most common" telephone number in this case! In fact, we may want to use data mining techniques to address the problem—we might build a neural network to fill in the blanks.

Building Computer Models

In the hypothesis testing style of data mining, a mental model is what you start with. But, there is still a step that must be taken before this *mental* model can be put to the test. Somehow, a mental model such as "frequent roamers are less sensitive than others to the price per minute of cellular phone call time" or "families with high-school age children are most likely to respond to a home equity line offer" must be transformed into a *computer* model that can be tested on real data.

This is where the skills of a good analyst who understands the available data and is well versed in the design of decision-support database queries, statistical packages such as SAS, S-PLUS, and SPSS, and the data mining tools discussed in this book can be invaluable.

Evaluating Computer Models

Finally, we must apply the computer models to real data to see which, if any, of our hypotheses are borne out. Depending on the hypotheses, and the nature of the model, this may mean interpreting a single value returned from a single simple query, or plowing through a collection of association rules generated by market basket analysis, or determining the significance of correlation found by a regression model.

Even when we ask a question that seems to have a simple yes-or-no answer, "Are women more likely than men to respond to a given offer?" the results need to be evaluated and interpreted: How much more likely? Is the difference statistically significant? Even if it is, is it worth designing two different offers? Are men an important part of the market for this product?

Proper evaluation of data mining results requires both analytical and business knowledge. Where these are not present in the same person, it will take cross-functional cooperation to make good use of the new information.

KNOWLEDGE DISCOVERY

Knowledge discovery is the style of data mining that excites the most interest in the media. Reading articles in the popular press, it is easy to imagine that we can now simply turn a smart program loose on our data and have it come back to us with information we can apply at once to make money, win customers, and influence legislation. That sort of undirected learning has long been a goal of artificial intelligence researchers in the academic discipline called *machine learning*. In the real world, discovering valuable patterns is worthwhile, but it is still hard work.

Directed or Undirected?

Knowledge discovery can be either *directed* or *undirected*. In directed knowledge discovery, the task is to explain the value of some particular field (income, response, age, credit worthiness, etc.) in terms of all the others. We select the target field and direct the computer to tell us how to estimate, classify, or predict it. In undirected knowledge discovery, there is no target field. We simply ask the computer to identify patterns in the data that may be significant. Undirected knowledge discovery supplements—but does not seek to replace—the expertise of business analysts.

One way of thinking about it is that we use undirected knowledge discovery to *recognize* relationships in the data and directed knowledge discovery to *explain* those relationships once they have been found.

Undirected learning can be very useful, especially clustering and affinity grouping, but the great majority of knowledge discovery work is much more directed. Instead of "tell me something interesting," we ask "who will go bankrupt?" or "what mix of sweater colors should be stocked at this store?" Knowledge discovery programs have to be *trained* to recognize what we are looking for—and it is much easier to train a neural network or decision tree to recognize a "balance transfer" than to train it to recognize "something interesting."

DIRECTED KNOWLEDGE DISCOVERY

Directed knowledge discovery is goal-oriented. There is a specific field whose value we want to predict, a fixed set of classes to be assigned to each record, or a specific relationship we want to explore. Directed data mining tries to answer questions like these:

- What products show increased sales when cream cheese is discounted?
- Who is likely to purchase credit insurance?
- What is the predicted profitability of this new customer?
- Which options should be bundled with the performance package and which with the luxury package?
- Which advertisement should come up in the web browser window when mjab@data-miners.com performs a keyword search?

The Process of Directed Knowledge Discovery

Knowledge discovery is the process of finding meaningful patterns in data that explain past events in such a way that we can use the patterns to help predict future events. What items sell well together? What pattern of credit card purchases suggests a susceptibility to leather diary offers? What patterns of referrals are suggestive of healthcare providers defrauding an insurance company? Which of several potential sites for a new retail outlet will be the most profitable? What changes in health insurance claim patterns first suggested the emergence of a new virus?

Here are the steps in the process of directed knowledge discovery:

1. Identify sources of preclassified data.
2. Prepare data for analysis.
3. Build and train a computer model.
4. Evaluate the computer model.

Identifying Available Data Sources

Knowledge discovery is based on the premise that the answers to these questions, and others like them, can be found by sifting through data about what has happened in the past. So, the first requirement for successful knowledge discovery is good data.

The ideal source for data is an existing corporate data warehouse. Data in the warehouse has already been cleaned and verified. Data from multiple sources has been integrated. A single data model ensures that similarly named fields have the same meaning throughout the database. The corporate data warehouse is an historical repository; new data is appended, but the historical data is never changed. Since it was designed for decision support, the data warehouse provides the right information at the right level of aggregation to support data mining. Chapter 15 examines the relationship of data mining to data warehousing.

The only problem is that, in most organization, such a data warehouse does not actually exist. That being the case, we must seek out the needed data from various departmental databases and from within the bowels of operational systems.

These operational systems are designed to perform a certain task such as claims processing, call switching, order entry, or billing. They are designed with the primary goal of processing transactions quickly and accurately. The data is in whatever format best suits that goal and the historical record, if any, is likely to be in a tape archive. It may require significant political and programming effort to get the data in a form useful for knowledge discovery.

In some cases, operational procedures have to be changed in order to supply the required data. We know of one major catalog retailer that wanted to analyze the buying habits of its customers and to market differentially to new customers and long-standing customers. Unfortunately, anyone who hadn't ordered anything in the past six months was routinely purged from the records. The substantial population of people who loyally used the catalog for Christmas shopping, but not during the rest of the year, went unrecognized and indeed were *unrecognizable*, until the company began keeping an historical file of customer records.

The Need for Preclassified Data   In directed knowledge discovery, we use the past to build a model of the future. If we want to be able to distinguish people who are likely to default on a loan from people who are not, we look at thousands of examples of people from each class to build a model that distinguishes one from the other. When a new applicant comes along, his or her application is compared with those of past customers, either directly, as in memory-based reasoning, or indirectly through rules or neural networks derived from the historical data. If the new application "looks like" those of people who defaulted in the past, it will be rejected.

Implicit in this model is the idea that we can tell what has happened in the past. If we are going to learn from our mistakes, we first have to recognize that we have made them. This is not always possible. One company had to give up on an attempt to use directed knowledge discovery to build a warranty claims fraud model because, although they suspected that some claims might be fraudulent, they had no idea which ones. Without a training set containing warranty claims clearly marked as fraudulent or legitimate, it was impossible to apply these techniques.

Preparing the Data for Analysis

The same general comments on data preparation made in the earlier section on hypothesis testing apply equally well to knowledge discovery. We still have to deal with data coming from incompatible computer architectures, multiple ways of representing the same thing, free-form textual data, and incomplete data or null values.

In addition, because knowledge discovery relies on tools to find patterns automatically, we often need to augment the data with additional fields derived from the existing ones in ways that might be obvious to the person implementing a hypothesis testing model, but are unlikely to be considered by mere software. This is especially true if we want to look at relationships across multiple fields or at patterns that occur over time.

Examples of the kinds of fields one might want to add are:

```
obesity_index = height2 / weight
delta_balance = current_balance - previous_balance
density = population / area
rpm = passengers * miles
```

By adding fields that represent relationships in the data that we know from experience are likely to be important, we can increase the chance that the knowledge discovery process will yield useful results.

Learning to Recognize the Normal

Fraud detection is a particularly challenging application of data mining, not only because it is hard to build a training set of known fraudulent cases, but also because fraud may take many forms. In fact, as soon as one scam becomes generally known and recognizable, the criminals must come up with a new one in order to avoid detection.

One solution is to build a model of what is normal, then flag records that vary from the norm by more than some threshold. This might be done by applying in clustering algorithms and then examining records that do not fall into any cluster, or by building rules that describe the expected range of values for each field, or by flagging unusual associations.

Credit card companies routinely build neural network models into their charge authorization process. For each card, a neural network learns to recognize an expected usage pattern. If you normally use your card only for airplane tickets, rental cars, and restaurants, but one day you use it to buy stereo equipment or jewelry, don't be surprised if the transaction gets held up until you can speak with a representative of the card issuing company to verify your identity.

Dividing the Data into Training, Test, and Evaluation Sets   Once the pre-classified data has been obtained, our methodology calls for it to be divided into three parts. The first part, the *training set*, is used to build the initial model. The second part, the *test set*, is used to adjust the initial model to make it more general and less tied to the idiosyncrasies of the training set. The third part, the *evaluation set*, is used to gauge the likely effectiveness of the model when applied to unseen data. Three sets are necessary because once data has been used for one step in the process, it can no longer be used for the next step because the information it contains has already become part of the model; therefore, it cannot be used to correct or judge.

People often find it hard to understand why the training set and test set are "tainted" once they have been used to build a model. An analogy may help: Imagine yourself back in the 5th grade. The class is taking a spelling test. Suppose that, at the end of the test period, the teacher asks you to estimate your own grade on the quiz by marking the words you got wrong. You will give yourself a very good grade, but your spelling will not improve. If, at the beginning of the period, you thought there should be an 'e' at the end of "tomato," nothing will have happened to change your mind when you grade your paper. No new data has entered the system. You need a test set!

Now, imagine that at the end of the test the teacher allows you to look at the papers of several neighbors before grading your own. If they all agree that "tomato" has no final 'e,' you may decide to mark your own answer wrong. If the teacher gives the same quiz tomorrow, you will do better. But how much better? If you use the papers of the very same neighbors to evaluate your performance tomorrow, you may still be fooling yourself. If they all agree that "potatoes" has no more need of an 'e' than "tomato," and you have changed your own guess to agree with theirs, then you will overestimate your actual grade on the second quiz as well. That is why the evaluation set should be different from the test set.

How Much Data?   Unfortunately, there is no simple answer to this question. The answer depends on the particular algorithms employed, the complexity of the data, and the relative frequency of possible outcomes. Statisticians have spent years developing tests for determining the smallest training set that can be used to produce a model. Machine learning researchers have spent much time and energy devising ways to let parts of the training set be reused for test and evaluation. All of this work ignores an important point: In the commercial world, statisticians are scarce, but data is not.

In any case, we have argued that where data *is* scarce, data mining is not only less effective, it is also unlikely to be useful. Data mining is most useful when the sheer volume of data obscures patterns that might be detectable by other means in a smaller database. Therefore, our advice is to use so much data that the questions about what constitutes an adequate sample size simply do not arise. We generally start with at least 10,000 preclassified records so that the training, test, and evaluation sets each contain several thousand records. In data mining, more is better.

Adding More Needles to the Haystack

In standard statistical analysis, it is common practice to throw out *outliers*—observations which are far outside the normal range. In data mining, however, these outliers may be just what we are look ing for. Perhaps they represent fraud, some sort of error in our business procedures, or some fabulously profitable niche market. In these cases, we don't want to throw out the outlier, we want to dig for more of them!

The problem is that knowledge discovery algorithms learn by example. If there are not enough examples of a particular class or pattern of behavior, the data mining tools will not be able to come up with a model for predicting it. In this situation, we may be able to improve our chances by artificially enriching the training data with examples of the rare event.

For example, a bank might want to build a model of who is a likely prospect for a private banking program. These programs appeal only to the very wealthiest clients, few of whom will be represented in even a fairly large sample of, say, checking accounts. To build a model capable of spotting these fortunate individuals, we might create a training set of checking transaction histories of a population that includes 10 percent private banking clients even though they represent under 1 percent of all checking accounts.

How Many Variables? If you are accustomed to using standard statistical techniques, you have to become used to a whole new mindset when you start using data mining tools. Instead of carefully choosing the few independent variables that you expect to be important, the data mining approach calls for throwing them all into the hopper and letting the data mining tool itself determine what is important.

Often, variables that had previously been ignored turn out to have predictive value when used in combination with other variables. For example, one credit card issuer, that had never included data on cash advances in its customer profitability models, discovered through data mining that people who do not use cash advances most of the time, but do so in November and December are highly profitable. Presumably, these are people who are prudent enough to avoid borrowing money at 18 percent interest most of the time (a prudence that makes them less likely to default than habitual users of cash advances) but who need some extra cash for the holidays and are willing to pay exorbitant interest to get it.

Building and Training the Model

The details of this step vary from technique to technique and are described in the chapters devoted to each data mining method. In general terms, this is the step where most of the work of creating a model occurs. The training set is used to generate an explanation of the independent (target) variable in terms of the independent (input) variables. This explanation may take the form of a neural network, a decision tree, a linkage graph, or some other representation of the relationship between the field we are trying to estimate, classify, or predict and the other fields in the database.

The Problem of Overfitting   All of the knowledge discovery methods suffer from a tendency to read too much into the training dataset. Working with the training set alone, the algorithms have no way to distinguish relationships that reflect some fundamental truth that will hold across many samples from relationships that just happen to occur in the training set, but have no predictive value. If everyone named Mary in the training set was a profitable customer, the knowledge discovery tools will conclude that anyone else named Mary will be equally profitable. This tendency to assume that the whole world looks just like the training data is called *overfitting*.

The cure for overfitting is to confront the newly generated model with the test dataset. The model, which may do a perfect job of describing the training data, will, at first, perform miserably on the test data. The next step in the process is, therefore, to tune and tweak the model to produce a second model that does about as well on the test set as it does on the training set. Again, this is a process whose details vary from technique to technique—tuning the weights in a neural network, pruning branches from a decision tree, and so forth. The resulting model will not do as well with the training data as the first one did, but it will be more general. Figure 5.2 shows the point we are trying to get to—where the model's error rate on the test set is minimized.

Evaluating the Model

Now we have used the test dataset to optimize the model, but we still don't know how well we can expect it to work on unseen data. By using the test set, we have eliminated rules or relationships that depended entirely on idiosyncrasies of the training set, but it is possible that in optimizing the model's performance on the test data, we have made use of some of its own little quirks.

In order to be confident in our estimate of the model's performance, we need to apply it to the final collection of reserved preclassified records, the evaluation set. The error rate on the evaluation set is a good predictor of the error rate on unseen data.

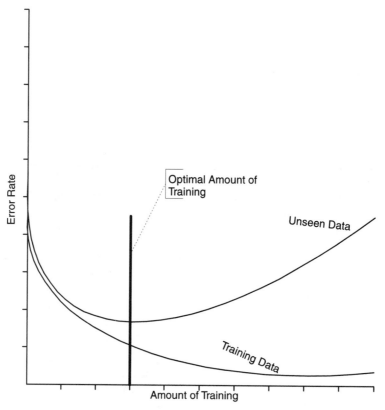

Figure 5.2 A properly trained model minimizes the error rate on unseen data.

UNDIRECTED KNOWLEDGE DISCOVERY

The process previously described is called *directed knowledge discovery*. This is far and away the most common type of knowledge discovery. Directed knowledge discovery is characterized by the presence of a single target field whose value is to be predicted in terms of the other fields in the database.

Undirected knowledge discovery is different—there is no target field. The data mining tool is simply let loose on the data in the hope that it will discover meaningful structure. One common use for undirected knowledge discovery is market basket analysis that asks "what items sell together" rather than "what items sell with tofu." Another application is clustering, where groups of records are assigned to the same cluster if they have something in common.

One very good example of undirected knowledge discovery comes from a market segmentation study of long distance telephone customers. Taken as a whole, the data showed fairly uniform usage patterns with predictable variation between weekdays and weekends, and spikes at certain holidays. But, once the data had been broken into segments, using an undirected clustering technique, it became clear that the aggregate behavior of the customer population was concealing some very interesting patterns in the behavior of various subgroups.

One group, in particular, had an odd profile of both usage and profitability. The long distance usage of this group stayed high and constant for most of the year, but then dropped off precipitously for several months. Furthermore, although the group as a whole scored low on various models of credit worthiness and profitability, they were, in fact, both profitable and reliable. Upon closer examination, the group turned out to be composed of college students. It is obvious, once you think about it: College students have no steady income and no credit history, but they tend to call home a lot. And, if they get in over their heads, their parents are likely to cover their bill.

The Process of Undirected Knowledge Discovery

Here are the steps in the process of undirected knowledge discovery:

1. Identify sources of data.
2. Prepare data for analysis.
3. Build and train a computer model.
4. Evaluate the computer model.
5. Apply the computer model to new data.
6. Identify potential targets for directed knowledge discovery.
7. Generate new hypotheses to test.

You will notice that steps 1 through 5 are the same as for directed knowledge discovery. The two additional steps reflect the fact that undirected knowledge discovery is usually a prelude to further investigation via more directed techniques.

Identifying Potential Targets for Directed Knowledge Discovery

Undirected knowledge discovery is a great way to generate ideas that can then be verified using more directed methods. A market basket report is bound to lead to questions about *why* the products that sell together go together, *who* is buying particular combinations of products, and *when* the purchases tend to be made. These questions move us back into the realm of directed knowledge discovery. The newly discovered clusters or product groupings become target variables in need of explanation.

Generating Hypotheses to Test

Once a clustering program has done its work, we need to study the resulting clusters to see what they have in common and how that information might be put to good use. For example, in the moviegoers data, there is a cluster of adults who have seen many children's movies. This leads us to suspect that parents are an important segment of the moviegoing population. To test that hypothesis we would need to gather more data.

CASE STUDY: KNOWLEDGE DISCOVERY AND HYPOTHESIS TESTING WORKING TOGETHER AT A BANK

In Chapter 3, we describe how a bank used data mining to improve its marketing of a loan product. The methodology employed by the bank illustrates the way that the two styles of data mining—knowledge discovery and hypothesis testing—work together.

The bank first used directed knowledge discovery to learn to recognize likely prospects. Using a training set of current home equity line holders, the bank developed a model for propensity to use a home equity line. Using the model, each customer was given a score.

The scores allowed a customer to be rank-ordered according to their propensity to use a home equity line so that only the 11 percent most likely to respond received solicitations. This was a useful result, but the breakthrough in understanding came only when the results obtained through directed knowledge discovery were combined with results from undirected knowledge discovery in order to generate a new hypothesis about the market. The customer database was segmented using an undirected clustering technique. Of the dozen or so clusters produced, one proved to be very interesting. In this cluster, 39 percent of the customers had both business and personal accounts with the bank. Furthermore, this cluster accounted for 27 percent of the 11 percent of customers who received high scores for propensity to respond to a home equity offer.

The high correlation between business accounts and home equity loans led the bank to the hypothesis that many people tap into their home equity in order to start a new business. After testing this hypothesis and finding it valid, the bank designed a whole new marketing program.

PRACTICAL ISSUES

If you are integrating data mining into your business process for the first time, there are a few issues that need to be considered. By taking them into account, you will be able to produce a more realistic data mining plan.

Applying a Model to New Data

The training set, the test set, and the evaluation set used to build and evaluate the model all consist of records with the target field filled in. But, the whole point of building the model is to be able to fill in the target field in records where its value is unknown. This process is often called *scoring* because one of the most common uses of predictive models is to assign a score that reflects the likelihood that a record falls into a certain category.

It is not uncommon for scoring to take place in a very different environment than model development. Data mining is typically done on a system set aside for decision-support processing. Although the training data may be extracted from an operational system, computing cycles on the operational system are likely to be zealously guarded. In many cases the operational data is not even under the direct control of the company doing the data mining because it resides at a list processor, credit bureau, or service bureau.

This separation often poses a problem because the model generated by the data mining tool in one environment cannot necessarily be run directly in the production environment where the data must be scored. The ease with which a data mining solution can be integrated with a company's production environment is one of the most important, and most often overlooked, criteria for choosing a data mining tool.

What Is the Shelf-life of a Predictive Model?

The ability of a model to classify, cluster, estimate, or predict erodes over time. Maintaining a model is therefore not a one-time effort, but a continuous process. In some cases, a model will remain valid for many years. In other situations, the model will require continual retraining as the environment changes around it. The moviegoers model introduced in the last chapter is a good example: Whatever predictive power it once had has now disappeared because the movies it learned about in the fall of 1996 are no longer in the theaters. An environment where data is constantly changing requires a model that is constantly learning and adapting.

A model based on recent films will degrade at a predictable rate as older movies go to video and get replaced in the theaters by new releases at a fairly constant rate. Sometimes, however, a model works well for years, then is invalidated by sudden changes in the regulatory or competitive environment. A data mining plan should include provisions for frequent assessment of the continuing validity of the generated models.

What Is the Shelf-life of a Prediction?

How often we need to re-score old records depends not only on the volatility of the model, but also on the nature of the thing to be predicted. Once we have made an accurate classification of a particular person as male or female, there is no point in re-scoring this just because new movies have appeared. After all, a change of gender is quite unusual! A person's credit-worthiness, on the other hand, may change more rapidly than the models used to predict it. It makes sense to re-score our customer population on a regular basis even though the model has not changed.

Getting Tools to Work Together

We often recommend that a wide variety of techniques be brought to bear on a data mining task: relational and on-line analytic processing (OLAP) queries, decision trees, neural networks, market basket analysis, link analysis, clustering, visualization, and so on. We must acknowledge, however, that it requires extra effort to set up a data mining environment capable of supporting such a wide range of tools.

Although many data mining tools prefer to store data in a proprietary flat-file format, most can also deal with data stored in any of the popular relational database systems. Storing data in a relational database rather than in a flat file is a good first step, but depending on the particular tools you would like to be able to work with, further integration effort is likely to be needed. This is especially true when the models created through data mining will be used to update or score a production database on a regular basis.

Interpreting the Results

A final source of unexpected difficulty is that the results obtained through data mining must be understood and interpreted by someone who can tell what is and is not relevant and useful. This may mean wading through thousands of trivial or obvious associations looking for one that is both strong and surprising. It may mean being able to calculate whether a 2 percent improvement in classification rate is worth millions of dollars or lost in the noise. Chapter 6 examines these issues in detail.

A SAMPLE DATA MINING PLAN

Not long ago, we were approached by a bank that wanted help putting together a data mining plan to address a customer retention problem. What follows is adapted from the actual plan of action we presented to the client. You will not be surprised to see that this plan is derived fairly directly from the steps laid out in the sections on the hypothesis testing and knowledge discovery processes.

The Problem

The bank was concerned about the rate of attrition for its demand deposit accounts (what the rest of us call checking accounts).

This bank was no stranger to modeling and data mining. Before talking to us, it had already built models for predicting attrition. The problem was that these models did not provide sufficient warning of impending attrition to allow time for corrective action.

The bank knew, for instance, that when customers came into a branch office and asked for an account reconciliation, they were as good as lost. Unfortunately, by that time, the customers have already made up their minds to leave. What was needed was a model that could spot trouble looming before it was too late.

Historically, the bank had based its attrition models on monthly account activity summaries, because that is all that was available. Using these summaries, it was possible to spot broad trends such as several months of declining balances, but once again, a prediction of attrition based on declining balances comes too late; the money has already been shifted somewhere else.

What gave the bank hope, and inspired the new push into data mining, was a new corporate data warehouse on a powerful new parallel database server that made it possible, for the first time, to analyze transaction-level, detailed data instead of summaries. The bank hoped that analysis of the transaction details would reveal a "signature" for impending attrition before the problem showed itself in declining balances and requests for reconciliation.

Hypothesis Testing Plan

Because we suspected that the transaction data alone would not yield good long-range predictors of attrition, we suggested that the bank approach this problem by first trying to come up with good ideas about the many disparate reasons that people might leave a bank, then identifying the additional data sources needed in order to gain insight into those ideas.

The next step is to combine the additional data with the transaction history data before beginning to build models. The various hypotheses can then be tested through analysis of the supplemented transaction data, using a combination of SQL queries and special-purpose analytical software.

Generating Good Ideas

To come up with a set of hypotheses about attrition, we recommended that people from various groups with insight into the problem be interviewed. These groups include call-center personnel, branch managers, present and former customers, and, of course, the marketing analysts themselves. The interviews should be performed by the analysts who will be building the attrition models. Throughout the interview process, they should be alert for ideas that can be tested using the transaction history data, perhaps in combination with other data sources.

Defining Data Requirements

We expect that some of the ideas generated will be verifiable through the transaction history, while others will require the bank to obtain additional data from both internal and external sources. To get them started, we provided some sample hypotheses along with suggestions on how they might be tested.

Table 5.1 lists several reasons a customer might stop using her account along with ways that these reasons might be reflected in the transaction history data:

Table 5.1   Possible Account Termination Explanations

Cause	*Symptom*
She died.	Transactions cease.
She moved to a place where there is no convenient branch of this bank.	Increased use of ATM machines and change in location of most frequently used ATM machines.
She got married to someone who was loyal to another bank and now they have a joint account.	Reduction in balance and number of transactions; request for a change of last name on the account.
She got a new job and no longer gets direct deposit.	Regular bi-weekly direct deposit ceases.
She got a new job and there is a branch of another bank in the lobby of her new office building.	Most ATM transactions now occur at a single location belonging to another bank.

We suggested that the bank pay careful attention to data generated by decisions internal to the bank. Here are a few reasons a customer might be angry at her bank that will not be reflected in her transaction data, but may be available form other sources:

- The bank started charging for debit card transactions that were formerly free.
- The bank started charging for using ATMs belonging to other banks.
- The bank messed up her statement . . . again!
- The bank turned her down for a loan or credit card limit increase.
- She got a loan at another bank with a lower interest rate than her current bank is offering.
- She has had to stand in line for a teller too often.

Locating the Data Needed to Test the Hypotheses

Once the hypotheses have been gathered, the next task is to identify available data that will allow them to be tested. At this point, many promising hypotheses may have to be thrown out for lack of data available for testing them. The authors have heard it claimed that while dog owners are more loyal customers, cat owners are less prone to default. A fascinating hypothesis, but difficult to test if you do not happen to have a `pet_species` field in your customer database.

In addition to the customer information and transaction history databases, a large bank such as this one might be able to examine records from its PC banking system, its credit card division, and its consumer lending group.

Preparing the Data for Analysis

Once hypotheses to be tested have been chosen and the data sources have been identified, the data needs to be gathered together, cleaned and preprocessed as previously described. When data is coming from multiple sources where there is no common key, such as customer number, this can be a fairly painful process. This is a problem facing all banks and many other service establishments.

Building Computer Models

When the data has been prepared, each hypothesis can be tested using tools dictated by the form of the hypothesis itself. Depending on the complexity of the hypothesis, the computer model needed to test it may be as simple as an OLAP query or as complex as a neural network. Typically, many hypotheses will be in the form of expected correlation between some set of observable events and the behavior (attrition, in this case) of interest. Examples of hypotheses of this type are:

- People who have many ATM transactions at machines owned by another bank are at high risk for attrition.
- People who have direct deposit of their paychecks are at low risk for attrition.
- Customers who have recently paid off a loan to the bank or canceled a bank credit card are at high risk for attrition.

These kinds of questions can be addressed through structured queries on the historical data.

Other hypotheses lend themselves to testing through sorting, counting, and other simple queries in a relational or multidimensional on-line analytic processing (OLAP) environment. Do loyal customers average more in-branch transactions than attriters? Count them and see!

Evaluating the Computer Models

In some cases, it will be immediately obvious whether the hypotheses are borne out by the data. In other cases further analysis will be required in order to determine whether observed relationships are statistically significant. Chapter 6 contains more information on how to evaluate the results of data mining.

Knowledge Discovery Plan

We turn now to the question that the bank originally presented to us: How can we employ advanced data mining tools in an attempt to discover patterns in the transaction history that are signatures of attrition? The first step in our knowledge discovery methodology is to identify sources of preclassified data. In this case, the client had already done that. In fact, one of the bank's goals was to justify the inclusion of transaction history data in the warehouse by demonstrating its usefulness for prediction.

Our advice to the bank was that rather than look for an attrition signature, they should instead look for the signatures of many different classes of customers. Different classes of customers have such widely differing transaction history profiles that the differences between classes would tend to overshadow any overall differences between loyal, satisfied customers and those about to close their accounts.

A Tale of Two Checking Accounts

Figure 5.3 shows one month of transaction history for two very different customers. One customer is paid by direct deposit twice a month. Most of the first deposit goes to her mortgage payment. The second deposit goes to paying other bills. Occasionally, the customer makes a withdrawal from a cash machine and on one occasion she transferred money from savings in preparation for the automatic deduction of a car loan payment.

The second customer owns vacation rental property in a foreign country. He rarely visits the bank, but mails in deposits from time to time. Occasionally, he transfers money to an account in the other country so as to be able to pay local currency expenses.

These customers have very different transaction patterns, but they are both happy customers. We should not expect them to look any more similar as *un*happy customers.

If we are able to identify several types of customers based on their habitual transaction patterns, then we will be able to have an alarm go off when a customer of a certain type starts acting in a way inconsistent with our expectations. A customer changing from one type to another one may not be a bad sign; in fact, it may represent a new cross-selling opportunity. The point is that we want to change the

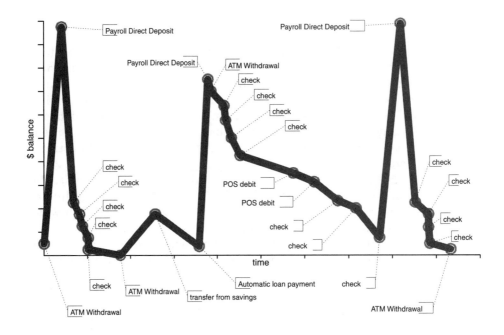

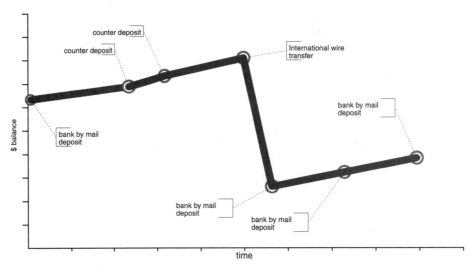

Figure 5.3 Two very different styles of checking.

focus from looking for some specific *bad* pattern of transactions, to looking at *changes* in a customer's usual behavior. Impending attrition is only one of many possible implications of a sudden change in banking behavior; it may reflect some life change such as a new job, a new marital status, or a new home.

Preparing the Data for Analysis

Because we are interested in patterns that occur in time, we recommend that the transaction history database be augmented with fields to explicitly represent changes over time. We also recommend adding fields that summarize activity into daily, weekly, and monthly time windows. These new summary fields will capture information such as number of ATM withdrawals per week, number of direct deposits per month, and so on. These fields, too, will need corresponding delta fields to represent change from one time window to the next.

Applying Undirected Knowledge Discovery Models to Perform Clustering

When faced with a problem of this nature, our approach is to segment the data in various ways, then look for patterns within the segments. There are several plausible ways to segment the population according to predefined categories:

- Account type (ATM convenience account, N.O.W. account, etc.)
- Branch
- Home zip code
- Demographic profile (These profiles, which can be purchased from list-processing companies, contain data on the favorite hobbies, favorite types of car, and dozens of other "lifestyle variables" for neighborhoods defined by zip+four or area code plus 3-digit phone number prefix.)

In this case, however, we want to let the data do the talking, so we would employ one of the cluster detection algorithms described in Chapter 10 to segment the population of checking account holders into subgroups with similar transaction histories. We would perform this clustering without referring to explicit information about attrition in the data; we are not yet trying to form clusters of attriters and non-attriters.

Applying Directed Knowledge Discovery Models to the Cluster

Once the data has been clustered, each cluster becomes a training set for finding patterns that predict attrition within that cluster. As a first step, we would check to see that each cluster has a reasonable number of canceled accounts. If it turned out that some clusters have an unusually high or low concentration of canceled accounts, we would, of course, want to do further investigation. But, assuming that the clusters each have about the same percentage of canceled accounts as the parent population, we would apply sequential pattern recognition tools and rule induction tools to each cluster separately.

Generating New Hypotheses

Examination of the clusters and of the resulting rules is bound to result in new ideas about the causes of attrition. These will become inputs to the next round of hypothesis testing. This process, whereby the results of one investigation become the inputs to the next is the basis of the virtuous cycle of data mining.

SUMMARY OF THE DATA MINING METHODOLOGY

Here, in step-by-step form, is the data mining methodology we have introduced in this chapter. We present three variations of the methodology—one for each of the three styles of data mining.

Hypothesis Testing

1. Generate hypotheses.
2. Define data needed to test hypotheses.
3. Locate data.
4. Prepare data for analysis.
5. Design computer models and database queries to test hypotheses against the data.
6. Evaluate results of queries and computer models.
7. Take action based on the data mining results.
8. Measure the effect of the actions taken.
9. Restart the data mining process taking advantage of new data generated by the actions taken.

Directed Knowledge Discovery

1. Identify sources of preclassified data.
2. Prepare data for analysis.
3. Select appropriate knowledge discovery techniques based on characteristics of the data and the data mining goal.
4. Divide data into training, test, and evaluation sets.

5. Use the training dataset to build a computer model.
6. Tune the model by applying it to the test dataset.
7. Gage the accuracy of the model by applying it to the evaluation dataset.
8. Take action based on the data mining results.
9. Measure the effect of the actions taken.
10. Restart the data mining process taking advantage of new data generated by the actions taken.

Undirected Knowledge Discovery

1. Identify available data sources.
2. Prepare data for analysis.
3. Select an appropriate undirected knowledge discovery technique based on the characteristics of the data and the data mining goal.
4. Use the selected technique to uncover hidden structure in the data.
5. Identify potential targets for directed knowledge discovery.
6. Generate new hypotheses to test.

6

Measuring the Effectiveness of Data Mining

Data mining is expensive. It requires a major effort in data collection, data preparation, software integration, problem formulation, model building, and analysis. How can we be sure that the results are worth all the time, money, and effort?

To answer that question, we need to be able to answer three others:

What is the *goal* of the data mining exercise?

How well can the goal be achieved?

What it is worth to us to achieve the goal?

In this chapter we examine each of these questions in turn. Data mining can be used in different ways for different purposes. Our selection of data mining tools and methods will largely be determined by what we want to achieve. Each of the data mining methods comes with its own vocabulary and its own way of assessing accuracy and performance. Since analysts will use these measures to evaluate the performance of data mining tools, we introduce them here in the section on measuring models.

As we will see, however, it can be hard to make sense of the error rates, confidence measures, and standard deviations used to measure data mining models—especially when trying to compare models of different types. The section on measuring results introduces the concept of *lift*, a measure of the extent to which a model leads to better outcomes. Lift, when applicable, is our preferred method of comparing the performance of data mining models.

In the commercial world, we can never lose sight of the fact that in the end there is only one true measure of a data mining project. That measure is, of course, dollars. In the section on measuring impact, we look at ways of translating lift into return on investment (ROI).

GOALS

A favorite scene from *Alice in Wonderland* is the passage where Alice asks the Cheshire cat for directions:

> "Would you tell me, please, which way I ought to go from here?"
>
> "That depends a good deal on where you want to get to," said the Cat.
>
> "I don't much care where—" said Alice.
>
> "Then it doesn't matter which way you go," said the Cat.
>
> "—so long as I get *somewhere*," Alice added as an explanation.
>
> "Oh, you're sure to do that," said the Cat, "if you only walk long enough."

The Cheshire cat might have added that if you don't have some way of recognizing your destination, you can never tell whether you have walked long enough! For that reason, we are leery of data mining projects whose goals are stated in broad, general terms, such as:

Gaining insight into customer behavior.

Discovering meaningful patterns in the data.

Learning something interesting.

These are all worthy goals, but even when they have been achieved, they are hard to measure. Projects that are hard to measure are hard to put a value on, and projects of unknown value do not tend to get much funding.

Wherever possible, the broad, general goals should be broken down into narrow, more specific ones to make it easier to monitor progress in achieving them. Gaining insight into customer behavior might turn into things like:

Identify customers who are unlikely to renew their subscription.

Design a calling plan that will reduce churn for home-based business customers.

Rank order all customers based on propensity to ski.

List products whose sales will be adversely affected if we discontinue wine and beer sales.

Description or Prediction?

The goals of data mining may be descriptive or predictive. Consider two sets of rules derived from a large database. The first set comprises four rules, each of which is a conjunction of simple true-or-false tests on individual fields. The second set comprises 50 rules, each of which is a linear combination of dozens of fields. The first set of rules correctly classifies 70 percent of cases; the second set, 72 percent. Which is better?

The answer depends entirely on the goal of the data mining exercise. If our goal is to gain understanding of the data and of the relationships it contains, then a set of four simple rules that does nearly as well as a set of 50 complex ones is clearly preferable. On the other hand, if our goal is to reduce the cost of a mass mailing by identifying households that are extremely unlikely to respond to an offer, a 2 percent improvement in the classification rate may literally be worth millions.

Although we identified six kinds of data mining tasks in chapter four, they can all be thought of as either descriptive or predictive. A descriptive task is one whose goal is understanding, explanation, or knowledge discovery. Most of the published definitions of data mining focus on descriptive tasks—finding interesting patterns.

> ### A Typical Definition of Data Mining
>
> "Data mining is the process of discovering meaningful new correlations, patterns, and trends by sifting through large amounts of data stored in repositories and by using pattern recognition technologies as well as statistical and mathematical techniques." The Gartner Group

In contrast, most of the actual *applications* of data mining are for classification and prediction. That is lucky for us, since it is much easier to design a test for whether a prediction is accurate than for whether a pattern is interesting.

Even when the goal of data mining is predictive, it may be important that the model used is sufficiently descriptive to make it clear why a particular prediction was made. We call this trait *explicability* or *explainability*. It can be very difficult to justify an investment decision to your manager by saying "my neural net predicts that this move will have a great outcome." It is even more difficult to use that line on a federal regulator who wants to see proof that the move in question is not discriminatory.

MEASURING MODELS

Imagine that you are the V.P. of marketing for a retail chain. You have asked your analytical staff to forecast sales of a certain style of sweater by store over the coming months and to suggest ways that sales can be improved. Each analyst has a favorite technique to apply and they all come back with what they are sure is the best model. How can you evaluate their claims?

One comes to you with a regression model and assures you that the forecast is quite accurate. As evidence, she points to the *standard deviation*, which is quite small.

Another says that market basket analysis shows that the sale of these sweaters is largely driven by the sales of leggings, so stocking plans for the sweaters shouldn't be made until plans for the legging promotion are finalized. As evidence, she points out that the association of leggings and sweaters has high *confidence* and strong *support*.

A third has used decision trees to come up with a set of rules for identifying customers likely to buy this sweater. He proudly shows you the low *error rates* his model achieved on a test dataset and suggests mailing a two-for-one offer to customers that meet the profile.

How can you compare these models? For that matter, what do the italicized words even *mean?* In the following sections, we make a start at answering these questions. We do not want to burden this book with the lengthy introduction to statistical theory that a full answer would require. On the other hand, we want you to understand that there are objective ways of answering the following questions:

How accurate is the model?

How well does the model describe the observed data?

How much confidence can we place in the model's predictions?

and even, to some extent,

How comprehensible is the model?

The Whole or the Parts?

Whether we are discussing accuracy or explicability, we need to distinguish between the model as a whole and any particular classification or prediction. In the academic field of machine learning—the source of many of the algorithms used for data mining—researchers have a goal of generating models that can be understood in their entirety. A model that is easy to understand is said to have good "mental fit." In the interest of obtaining the best mental fit, these researchers often prefer models that consist of a few simple rules to models that contain many such rules, even when the latter are more accurate. In a business setting, we are more likely to be concerned with the explicability of each individual prediction or classification than with the ability to comprehend the entire model.

When measuring the accuracy of a predictive model, we are interested in both the accuracy of the model as a whole (the percentage of records classified correctly) and the accuracy of individual predictions. Two models with the same overall accuracy may have quite different levels of variance among the individual predictions. In a decision tree, for instance, each branch and leaf of the tree has an error rate associated with it.

Measuring Descriptive Models

The rule, *If home state is in New England then home heating source is oil*, seems more descriptive than the rule, *If area code=207 OR area code=603 OR area code=802 OR area code=413 OR area code=508 OR area code=617 OR area code=203 OR area code=401 then home heating source is oil*. Even if the two rules turn out to be equivalent, the first one seems more expressive.

You might suppose that rating the expressive power of a rule is purely subjective, but there is, in fact, a theoretical measure that can be used to assess it. The measure is called the *minimum description length* or *MDL*. The minimum description length for a model is the number of bits it takes to encode both the rule and the list of all exceptions to the rule. The fewer bits required, the better the rule. Some data mining tools use MDL to decide which sets of rules to keep and which to weed out.

Measuring Predictive Models

Predictive models are assessed on the accuracy of their predictions for previously unseen data. Different data mining tasks call for different ways of assessing performance of the model as a whole and different ways of judging the likelihood that the model yields accurate results for any particular record.

Measuring Classifiers and Predictors

For classification and prediction tasks, accuracy is measured in terms of the error rate. The error rate is simply the percentage of records classified incorrectly. The classification error rate that a model gets on the preclassified evaluation dataset is used as an estimate of the error rate expected when classifying new records. Of course, this procedure is only valid if the evaluation set is a representative sample of the larger population.

Our recommended method of establishing the error rate for a model is to measure it on an evaluation dataset taken from the same population as the training and test datasets, but disjointed from them. In the interest of conserving preclassified records, which in some environments may be a scarce resource, there is several approaches to estimating the error rate of a model even when the only available records are those in the training set. Some data mining tools make use of these techniques, but we do not go into them here because lack of data is rarely a problem in commercial data mining environments.

Measuring Estimators

For estimation tasks, accuracy is expressed in terms of the difference between the predicted score and the actual measured result. Again, we are interested in both the accuracy of any one estimate and of the model as a whole. Calculating the latter can be quite tricky as the size of the error may be a function of where we are in the data. Figure 6.1 shows a linear model that estimates total revenue based on a product's unit price. This simple model works reasonably well in one price range but goes badly wrong when the price reaches the level where the elasticity of demand for the product (the ratio of the percent change in quantity sold to the percent change in price) becomes greater than one. An elasticity greater than one means that any further price increase results in a decrease in revenue because the increased revenue per unit is more than offset by the drop in the number of units sold.

The standard way of describing the accuracy of an estimation model is by measuring how far off the estimates are *on average*. But, simply subtracting the estimated value from the true value at each

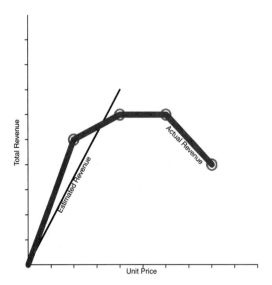

Figure 6.1 The accuracy of an estimator may vary considerably over the range of its inputs.

point and taking the mean results in a meaningless number. To see why, look at Table 6.1.

The average difference between the true values and the estimates is zero; positive differences and negative differences have canceled each other out. The usual way of solving this problem is to sum the squares of the differences rather than the differences themselves. The average of the squared differences is called the *variance*. The estimates in the this table have a variance of 10.

$$(-5^2 + 2^2 + -2^2 + 1^2 + 4^2)/5 = (25 + 4 + 4 + 1 + 16)/5 = 50/5 = 10$$

The smaller the variance, the more accurate the estimate. A drawback to variance as a measure is that it is not expressed in the same

Table 6.1 Estimated versus True Values

True Value	Estimated Value	Difference
127	132	–5
78	76	2
120	122	–2
130	129	1
95	91	4

units as the estimates themselves. If we are estimating prices in dollars, we would like to know how far off we are in dollars, not *square* dollars! For that reason, it is usual to take the square root of the variance which is called the *standard deviation*. The standard deviation of these estimates is the square root of 10 or about 3.16.

For our purposes, all you need to know about the standard deviation is that it is a measure of how widely the estimated values vary from the true values, but if your work brings you in contact with statisticians and analytical model builders, you may want to read the shaded aside which defines some common statistical terminology and explains why the standard deviation is such a useful measure.

Common Statistical Terms

Statistics is the branch of mathematics that deals with the observation and interpretation of data. Statisticians have developed many tools for dealing with situations where there is less than complete information. The word "statistics" is used to refer both to the whole field of study and to individual formulas used in the field. Some statistics, called *descriptive* statistics, are used to characterize data that has actually been collected or measured directly. Others, called *inferential* statistics, are used to generalize from the observed data, providing the ability to describe related data that cannot be measured directly.

To make the definitions of these common statistical terms more concrete, we will refer to the age data from a subset of the moviegoers database, as shown in Table 6.2.

Population The population consists of all members of the group we wish to study, not just those members that we have actually observed. Depending on the application, the population might be "all voters" or "all cans of orange spray paint" or "all fruit flies."

It is important to have a good definition of the population you are studying. Pediatricians' offices often have a chart where you can look up the average height and weight for a child of a given age. At any day care center, you can hear parents discussing what percentile their children are in for each of these measures. They tend to worry if their baby is too far "below normal."

But these charts are not labeled with a definition of the population being described. A Vietnamese mother of our acquaintance looked at the chart with disbelief and said, "These must be *American* babies they're talking about!"

Table 6.2 Moviegoers and Their Ages

name	age	name	age	name	age	name	age
Joel	5	Candy	29	Steve	39	Liz	65
Joan	22	Janie	29	Michael	39		
Michael	22	Karen	30	Cathy	39		
Julie	22	Jeff	30	Jerry	40		
Erica	23	Anne	30	David	40		
Tammy	23	Sean	30	Rich	40		
Brian	23	Patrick	30	Paul	41		
Tracy	24	Karen	30	Ken	41		
Eve	25	Beth	30	Jenny	43		
Cara	25	Curt	30	Joan	44		
Andrew	25	Tom	31	Jim	44		
Shannon	25	Shiela	32	Kathi	45		
Charles	25	Susan	32	Kristin	45		
Ansje	25	Gordon	32	Joanne	46		
Ian	26	Andy	34	Stephanie	46		
Amy	27	Randy	37	Mike	46		
Susan	27	Randy	38	Mary	46		
George	28	Judy	38	Jean	49		
Ravi	28	Esther	39	Bob	51		
John	29	Mark	39	Myrna	59		

Sample   A sample is a subset chosen randomly from the population so as to be representative of it. In general, the larger the sample, the more confidently it can be used to make inferences about the population as a whole. The individual elements of a sample are numbers representing measurements of some aspect of the corresponding member of the sample. These elements are called *observations*.

Bias   A sample chosen by some method that is not completely random is said to be *biased*. By random, we mean that every member of the population has an equal chance of appearing in the sample. When the population under study is made up of human beings, it can be quite difficult to obtain a true random sample. People who bother to fill out registration cards are not representative of the entire population of product owners. People who respond to telephone surveys are not representative of all voters. People whose medical claims appear in an insurance company database are not representative of the entire sick population.

Range The range is the difference between the smallest and largest observation in the sample is the range. In the moviegoers database, the youngest respondent is 5 and the oldest is 65, so we say that the observations range from 5 to 65 or simply that the range is 60.

Arithmetic Mean This is what we call an *average* in every day speech. In statistics, a variety of different ways of defining a central or typical value are all called averages. The arithmetic mean is the one obtained by dividing the sum of the observations by the number of observations. The mean age of the moviegoers is 34.

Median The median value is the one which splits the observations into two equally sized groups, one having observations smaller than the median and another containing observations larger than the median.

The median can be used in some situations where it is impossible to calculate the mean, such as when incomes are reported in ranges of $10,000 dollars with a final category "over $100,000" for which we know the number of observations, but no actual values.

The median is less affected by one or two observations that are out of line with the others. If we added the record "Methuselah, 900" to the moviegoers sample, it would increase the average age from 34 to 48 while the median age would only shift from 31 to 31.5.

Mode The mode of a sample is its most frequently occurring value. The mode of the ages in the moviegoers database is 30.

Distribution Depending on the underlying mechanism that is generating the members of a population, the relative frequencies of different values will vary. The description of how values are distributed in the population is called a *distribution*. A distribution is usually shown graphically by using the X-axis to represent the range of values taken on and the Y-axis to represent the number of observations at each value.

A handful of distributions keep turning up in widely varied settings. These distributions have been exhaustively studied and there are many useful formulas that relate the behavior observed in a sample to characteristics of the parent population that depend on the distribution. Things that can have only two possible values (heads and tails is the usual example) follow one distribution, called the *binomial distribution*. Measurements of natural phenomena often follow another well-known distribution, the *normal distribution*.

Variance   The variance is a measure of the dispersion of a sample or how closely the observations cluster around the mean. The range is not a good measure of dispersion because it takes only two values into account—the extremes. The addition of a single value far from the mean can dramatically increase the range. The variance, on the other hand, takes every value into account. The difference between a given observation and the mean of the sample is called its deviation. The variance is defined as the mean of the squares of the deviations.

Standard Deviation   The standard deviation is the most frequently used measure of dispersion. It is defined as the square root of the variance. The standard deviation is more convenient to use than the variance because it is expressed in the same units as the observations rather than in terms of those units squared. This allows us to use the standard deviation itself as a unit of measurement. Since the mean age of the moviegoers is 34, and the standard deviation is very close to 10, we would say that anyone between 24 and 44 years of age is "within one standard deviation from the mean" while the age of a 54-year-old is "two standard deviations above the mean." An observation's distance from the mean measured in standard deviations is often called its *z-value* or *z-score*.

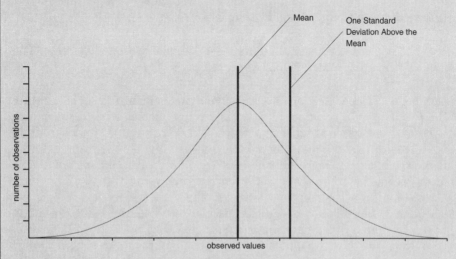

Figure 6.2 The shape of the normal distribution.

The most important reason for the popularity of the standard deviation as a measure is the relationship between the standard deviation and the mean in the normal distribution. The graph of the normal distribution is symmetrical, with its highest point at the mean. Starting from the center, each shape first curves downward, then curves outward. The point where the curve stops curving downward and starts curving outward is called the *point of inflection*. This point is exactly one standard deviation from the mean. When we calculate the area under the bell-shaped curve of the normal distribution, we find that the region between the mean and the points one standard deviation away on either side accounts for 68 percent of the observations. Over 90 percent of observations are within two standard deviations of the mean. These proportions hold for all normal curves, whether tall and skinny (low variance) or short and fat (high variance). That is one reason that z-scores are so useful; they can be used to compare the significance of measurements taken from different experiments.

If one college applicant takes the SAT test and another takes the ACT, their scores cannot be directly compared. But, if we are told that the z-value for the SAT score of the first student is 1 while the z-value for the ACT score of the second is 3, we can assume that the second student will be a shoe-in at even the most selective schools because a score three standard deviations above the mean is quite out of the ordinary. The first student would be well-advised to get good grades and good references and demonstrate a well-rounded personality or ability at sports because, although he scored better than 84 percent of people taking the SAT examination, there will be many applicants that did even better.

Significance   Significance is a measure of how unlikely it is that a difference between two samples happened by chance. The statistical approach is to assume that, in fact, the samples were drawn from the same population, then to calculate the probability of the means of two such samples differing by the observed amount.

As a rule of thumb, if the observed difference is more than 2.5 standard deviations, we call it "statistically significant." At this level, there is only a 5 percent chance of getting two sample means that far apart, so we can say that we believe the parent populations to be different with a confidence level of 95 percent.

There are dozens of other tests for significance. Which one to use depends on the distribution of the population, the size of the sample, and other factors.

Correlation   Correlation is a measure of the extent to which a change in one variable is related to a change in another. Correlation ranges from –1 to 1. A correlation of 0 means that the two variables are not related. A correlation of 1 means that as the first variable changes, the second is guaranteed to change in the same direction, though not necessarily by the same amount. For instance, the circumference and the area of a circle are perfectly correlated, although the latter grows faster than the former. A negative correlation means that the two variables move in opposite directions. Altitude is inversely correlated to air pressure.

Regression   Regression is the process of using the value of one of a pair of correlated variables in order to predict the value of the second. The most common form of regression is *linear regression,* so called because it attempts to fit a straight line through the observed X and Y pairs in a sample. Once the line has been established, it can be used to predict a value for Y given any X and for X given any Y.

Confidence and Support

Market basket analysis may be used purely descriptively, in which case the question of error does not arise. But most often, the reason that we study what sold together in the training data is that we want to be able to predict what will sell together in the future. In fact, market basket analysis can be used for estimation. Based on the correlations in the training data, we might estimate that 60 percent of the people who buy kitty litter next month will also buy cat food.

But, how accurate is that prediction likely to be? And how can we tell which of the many combinations of items found in the training data will be good predictors? To answer these questions, we use two statistics that will be covered in Chapter 8: *confidence* and *support*.

Confidence is a measure of how often the relationship holds true in the training sample. In this case, what percentage of the time did people who bought kitty litter also buy cat food. Support is a measure of how often the combination occurred overall. An association may hold 100 percent of the time and have the highest possible confidence, yet still be of little use because the combination occurs so rarely.

Distance

The concept of distance comes up in several data mining techniques. In clustering, we think of a neighborhood being drawn about a central point with all records within a certain distance of that central point being included in the cluster. In the memory-based reasoning method, we need some way of deciding how near the neighbors are. In regression, the line of best fit minimizes the sum of the distances between the observations and the line.

When all the variables are continuous and numeric, we can often use the familiar geometric formula for distance, the square root of the sum of the squares of the differences along each axis. In other situations, the proper distance function is less obvious.

MEASURING RESULTS

If you take away one thing from the preceding sections of this chapter, it should be that each data mining technique comes with its own set of evaluation criteria; this makes it very hard to compare apple models with orange models.

Fortunately, there is a way to compare models without getting into their inner workings. Predictive models, whether created using neural networks, decision trees, genetic algorithms, or Ouija boards, are all created to accomplish some task. Why not judge them on their ability to classify, estimate, and predict?

Lift

The most common way to compare the performance of classification models is to use a ratio called *lift*. This technique can be adapted to compare models designed for other tasks as well. What lift actually measures is the change in concentration of a particular class when the model is used to select a purposefully biased sample from the general population.

```
lift = P(class_t| sample) / P(class_t | population)
```

Lift is most easily understood in terms of an example. Since the term comes from the direct marketing industry, we will use a marketing response model as our demonstration. Suppose we are building a model to predict who is likely to respond to a direct mail solicitation. As usual, we build the model by using a preclassified training dataset and, if necessary, a preclassified test set as well. Now we are ready to use the evaluation dataset to calculate the model's lift.

The classifier will mark the records as either "predicted to respond" or "not predicted to respond." Of course, it will not be correct every time, but if the model is any good at all, the group of records marked "predicted to respond" will contain a higher proportion of actual responders than the evaluation dataset as a whole. The set of records marked "predicted to respond" becomes our biased sample. If the evaluation set contains 5 percent actual responders and the sample contains 50 percent actual responders, the model provides a lift of 10 (50 divided by 5).

So, is the model that produces the highest lift necessarily the best model? Surely you would always prefer a list of people half of whom will respond to your offer to a list of whom only a quarter will respond, right? Not necessarily—not if the first list has only 10 names on it!

The point is that lift is a function of sample size. If the classifier only picks out 10 likely respondents, and it is right 100 percent of the time, it will achieve a lift of 20—the highest lift possible given that the population contains 5 percent responders. As we relax the confidence level we require in order to classify someone as likely to respond, our mailing list gets longer, but the lift decreases.

Charts like the one in Figure 6.3 will become very familiar as you work with data mining tools. It is created by sorting all the prospects according to their likelihood of responding as predicted by the model. As the size of the mailing list increases, we reach farther and farther down the list. The X-axis shows the percentage of the population getting our mailing. The Y-axis shows the percentage of all responders we reach.

If no model were used, mailing to 10 percent of the population would reach 10 percent of the responders, mailing to 50 percent of the population would reach 50 percent of the responders, and mailing to everyone would reach all the responders. This mass-mailing approach is illustrated by the 45 percent line. The other line shows what happens if the model is used to select recipients for the mailing. Using the model, we can reach 20 percent of the responders by mailing to only 10 percent of the population. If we solicit half the population, we can reach over 70 percent of the responders.

Charts like the one in Figure 6.3 are often referred to as *lift charts*, although what is really being graphed is cumulative response. Figure 6.4 shows the actual lift chart corresponding to the response chart in Figure 6.3. The chart shows clearly that lift decreases as the size of the target list increases.

In this case, the underlying response rate in the population is 5 percent. According to the cumulative response chart, when we send mail to the top 10 percent of the population, we get 20 percent of the responders. To keep the numbers small, let's say that the total population is 100 people of whom 5 will respond if solicited. Figure 6.3 says that if we send mail to the top 10 people, we will get 20 percent of the 5 responders, which is to say one responder. One responder out of 10 prospects means that our mailing list has a 10 percent concentration of responders. That is twice the concentration found in the general population, so for the top decile, our model gets a lift of 2.

By the time we are mailing to 60 percent of the population and getting 80 percent of the responders (four out of five), the lift has decreased to 1.3. As always, when we mail to the entire population, the

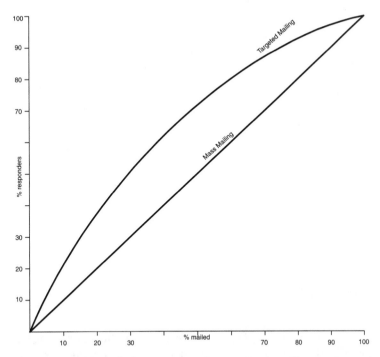

Figure 6.3 Cumulative response for targeted mailing compared with mass mailing.

lift is 1. Lift charts are quite informative, but we recognize that graphs featuring lines that go down and to the right are never as popular as those with lines going up!

Problems with Lift

Lift solves the problem of how to compare the performance of models of different kinds, but it is still not powerful enough to answer the question posed in the opening paragraph of this chapter: Is the model worth the time, effort, and money it cost to build it? The predictive models generated through data mining will not answer that question unless they are tied to the business model as well.

MEASURING IMPACT

The response chart in Figure 6.3 compares the number of responders reached for a given amount of postage, with and without the use of a predictive model. A more useful chart would show how many dollars

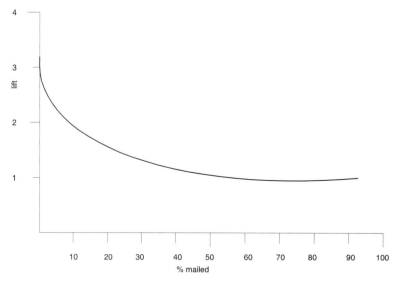

Figure 6.4 A lift chart.

are brought in for a given expenditure on the marketing campaign. After all, if developing the model is very expensive, a mass mailing may be more cost-effective than a targeted one.

- What is the fixed cost of setting up the campaign and the model that supports it?
- What is the cost per recipient of making the offer?
- What is the cost per respondent of fulfilling the offer?
- What is the value of a positive response?

By plugging these numbers into a simple spreadsheet-style model, we can measure the impact that the model will have in dollars. The cumulative response chart can then be turned into a cumulative profit chart which will tell us where the sorted mailing list should be cut off. If, for example, there is a high fixed price of setting up the campaign and also a fairly high price per recipient of making the offer (as when a wireless company buys loyalty by giving away a cellular phone or waiving a renewal fee), we will lose money by going after too few prospects because, even though we are targeting the most responsive segments, there are still not enough respondents to make up for the high fixed cost of the program. On the other hand, if we make the offer to too many people, the high variable cost begins to hurt us as we get into the region where there are few respondents. A good graphical user interface such as the one shown in Figure 6.5 allows the user to flip between cumulative response and cumulative profit at the click of a mouse.

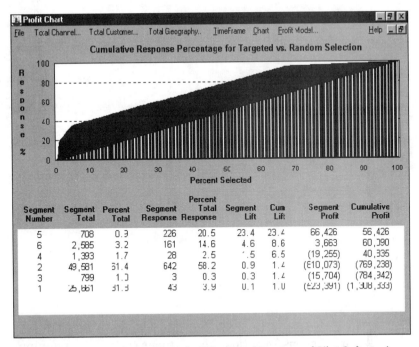

Figure 6.5 A cumulative lift and profit chart (Courtesy of Pilot Software).

Of course, the profit model is only as good as its inputs. While the fixed and variable costs of the campaign are fairly easy to come by, the predicted value of a responder can be very hard to estimate. The process of figuring out what a customer is worth is beyond the scope of this book, but a good estimate helps to measure the true value of a data mining model.

In their 1997 book, *Enterprise One to One*, Don Peppers and Martha Rogers use a measure called *lifetime value* (LTV). This is defined as "the stream of expected future profits, net of costs, on a customer's transactions, discounted at some appropriate rate back to its current, net present value."

Measure Results, not Models

In the end, the only measure that really counts is return on investment. Measuring lift on an evaluation set will help you choose the right model. Profitability models based on lift will help you decide how to apply the results of the model. But, it is very important to measure these things in the field as well. In a database marketing application, this will require always setting aside control groups and carefully tracking customer response to various models.

Overview of Data Mining Techniques

7

The first part of the book has focused on the *hows* of data mining within an organization. The virtuous cycle of data mining incorporates data mining into business processes, resulting in beneficial and actionable information. Lift and related measurements measure the effectiveness of the information and actions returned by the data mining process. The specific tasks descried in Chapter 4—classification, estimation, prediction, affinity grouping, clustering, and description— transform data into information to satisfy needs throughout an organization.

This section of the book moves on to the hows of data mining techniques and introduces seven specific techniques that are discussed in the next seven chapters in considerably more detail. The following seven chapters describe these techniques with attention to

- what you need to know about the technique to take advantage of it in the business environment;
- specific examples of the technique being used to return actionable information;
- advantages and disadvantages; and,
- when the technique is best applied.

No one technique solves all data mining problems. Familiarity with a variety of techniques is necessary to provide the best approach to solving data mining problems. These chapters contain commonly used data mining techniques, with examples of their use. The chapters are guidelines to help people interested in using data mining in their particular environment. In addition, two further chapters delve into data warehousing and on-line analytic processing (OLAP). Although not specifically data mining, they are powerful allies in the goal of extracting information from data.

This chapter provides an overview of the techniques from the perspective of problems and challenges that arise across the spectrum of data mining. For this purpose, we talk about regression and correlation statistics to provide a comparison for other techniques. First, though, to get a common basis for talking about the technical stuff, this chapter talks about some of the history of data analysis and introduces the language of models.

SOME OF THE HISTORY OF DATA ANALYSIS

Since the Renaissance, people have been looking at the world and gathering data to explain natural phenomena. This data has led to theories, observations, and equations that describe the natural world and its laws. Even the ancient Egyptians and Chinese (and later the Greeks) measured the sides of right triangles and induced what is now known as the Pythagorean Theorem. And before them, people observed the movements of the sun, the moon, and the stars and created calendars to describe heavenly events. Without the aid of computers, people have been analyzing data and looking for patterns since before recorded history even began.

What started to change in the past few centuries, though, has been the codification of the mathematics and the creation of machines to facilitate the taking of measurements, their storage, and their analysis. The advent of modern computers owes much to Herman Hollerith's invention of punch cards in 1880 and of a counting machine for the 1890 Census. The company he formed to market the machine later became better known as International Business Machines. Traditional statistics has developed over the past two centuries to help scientists, engineers, and later business analysts to make sense of the data they have collected.

The history of data mining techniques is generally rather different, highlighting the influence of other disciplines. Genetic algorithms and neural networks came from attempts to model biological processes on computers. Memory-based reasoning is a technique coming directly from the field of artificial intelligence (AI), and link analysis arose from graph theory and its application to data structures in computer science. Nevertheless, as these techniques mature, the umbrella of statistics will eventually come to include many of these techniques as well as the more classic ones.

Statistics originated as a way of making sense out of observations made about the world, generally in the name of natural science or political science. Descriptive statistics give general information about observations—what are the average and median values, what are the observed errors, what is the distribution of values. Regression analysis refers to techniques used to interpolate and extrapolate these observations. The most familiar regression technique is undoubtedly linear regression, which attempts to fit a line to observed data (see Figure 7.1).

One major problem with regression is that it works best when the form of the solution is known such as when you expect the solution to look like a line. Correlation analysis is another important technique that describes when different observations occur together. An example of a correlation might be that people with large incomes tend to have large mortgages—although there are much better examples. One problem with correlation analysis is that it often produces trivial results, things that are already known.

Sampling is a very important technique used extensively in statistics (and a bit less so in data mining) to reduce the size of data. A random sample takes every nth record, such as every hundredth record, to reduce the amount of data being worked on. This was mandatory before computers, since all the calculations had to be done by hand. Even in the early days of computing, reducing the size of data was critical, since the cost of memory and storage for data was very expensive. Now, though, statistics packages running on desktops can handle thousands and even millions of data points, so the need for sampling is lessened.

Statistics refers not only to the analytic techniques that process data but also to developing good experiments to collect the data. A great example of meticulously designed experiments was Gregor Mendel's painstaking efforts to describe inheritance. After growing and observing thousands of plants over several generations, he was able to infer the existence of genes. He managed his work lacking any form of automation. Fortunately, as a monk, he had the time to spend collecting and analyzing his data by hand. He devoted his life to the effort.

Today, statistics has some advantages not shared by data mining techniques. There are legions of highly qualified personnel who have studied statistics and its application to virtually all areas. Statistical software is readily available, runs on many platforms, and is increasingly available on high-performance parallel platforms. The techniques

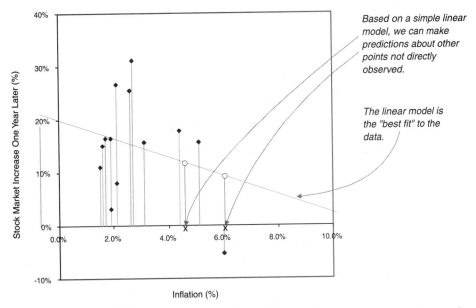

Figure 7.1   Linear regression produces the familiar best fit line that can be used to predict the value of other points.

themselves have been analyzed quite extensively, so statisticians can explain in exceedingly complex mathematics why they do or do not work. And, in some cases, statistics produces results as good as any of the techniques described in the next seven chapters.

Sometimes, but not always. There is definitely room for the data mining techniques. In short, statistics is very useful but does not solve all data mining problems. Sampling to reduce the size of a dataset may miss important subsets of the data, thereby missing important opportunities. Because of its emphasis on continuous functions and already known forms, regressions are not as general-purpose as the data mining techniques. The computational complexity of the statistical approach does not grow well with larger data sizes.

Models

A *model*, as shown in Figure 7.2, produces one or more output values for a given set of inputs. Analyzing data is often the process of building an appropriate model for the data. A linear regression, for instance, builds a model that is a line, having the form

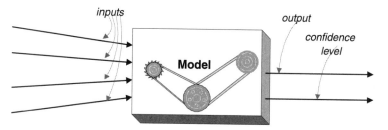

Figure 7.2 A model takes one or more inputs and produces one or more outputs.

```
aX + bY + c = 0
```

where *a, b,* and *c* are parameters of the model and *X* and *Y* are variables. For a given *X* value, we can use the line to estimate a *Y* value, as shown in Figure 7.1. This type of model is one of the simplest models available.

Just because a model exists does not mean that it provides accurate results. For any given set of points, there is some line that best fits the points—even when there is no linear relationship between the values. There are good models and bad models. Measuring the results of a model is a critical step in using and developing them.

The linear model just described is an example of regression—finding the best form of a curve to fit to a bunch of points. A model is broader and can be used for clustering, classification, and time-series analysis. Models provide a common language for talking about data mining.

A *classification model* takes a new record and assigns an existing classification to it. It might also assign a new classification, a probability of correctness, and other information, depending on the nature of the model. A *predictive model* is similar to a classification model, except the output is not limited to a set number of classes. A *clustering model* takes many records and returns, hopefully, a smaller number of clusters. These clusters can then often be applied to new records, by creating a classification model. A *time-series model* is like a classification or predictive model, except the domain includes data taken over time.

When models are created, the input is generally clearly specified. Records in a customer information file are a typical example of a domain that might be useful for a predictive model. In the real world, preparing data from disparate operational systems to match the domain of a model—called data cleansing or data scrubbing—is often more challenging than creating the model itself. The inputs to the model can affect the choice of technique. For physics problems with lots of continuous input variables, statistical regression techniques usually work pretty well. When the inputs have lots of categorical variables, decision trees often work well. When the relationship between the inputs and the output is hard to figure out, neural networks are frequently the technique of choice.

The output of a model is often specified in advance. It is often a category, such as whether a customer will respond to a mailing, or a continuous variable—such as the maximum credit to extend to a customer. In clustering models, the output specifies a cluster, but the cluster may not have any intrinsic meaning. Understanding the cluster requires profiling and analyzing it using other techniques. A model often provides a degree of confidence in its output. This is very useful for determining when to apply the results of the model.

When creating models for data mining, there are some useful things to keep in mind:

- One of the dangers of models is underfitting or overfitting the data.
- Directed and undirected data mining both use models, but in slightly different ways.
- Some models explain what they are doing better than other models.
- Some models are easier to apply than other models.

These are discussed in more detail in the following sections.

Underfitting and Overfitting

Sometimes, models do not work very well. Two common causes are underfitting and overfitting the data. Road maps provide a familiar example to illustrate these problems. Some road maps are very detailed, including every street in a relatively small area, such as a city, with one-way streets laid out, and showing buildings and the names of parks. Other maps are more general, covering the major roads in a larger area, such as a state. Which is the better map to use? If we need to travel a large distance, it may be difficult to figure out the best path from a patchwork of detailed maps. The detailed map *overfits* the information. The route we are looking for is there, but it is difficult to spot among all the detail. On the other hand, we may be looking for a particular street that may not even be present on the larger map. This is an example of *underfitting* the data. The larger map is too general and either does not contain the information we need (the specific road) or does not describe it well.

These concepts apply directly to models as well. Overfitting the data is when the model memorizes the data and predicts results based on idiosyncrasies in the particular data used for training. Such a model produces good results on the training set, but these do not generalize to other data. Overfitting occurs for a variety of reasons. If the dataset is too small, some modeling techniques readily memorize the data. A trivial example of this would be running a linear regression technique on only two input data points. The regression finds the line that connects the two points exactly, but we did not start with enough data to determine if the line is useful.

Overfitting can also occur when the predicted field is redundant. That is, another field or combination of fields contains the same information as the predict field, perhaps in another form. A favorite example of this occurred by accident to one of the authors in the course of analyzing telephone call data. We were investigating differences in calling patterns based on the day of the week to answer questions like: Are weekend calls different from weekday calls? Are calling patterns on Mondays different from calling patterns on other days of the week? To do so, we separated the weekday and weekend calls and used them as a training set for a decision tree algorithm. The results were too good; the resulting model was able to predict with 100 percent accuracy when a call was made. Although we had carefully removed the day-of-the-week field from the data, the date field remained. The decision tree algorithm was able to determine the day of the week with 100 percent accuracy using the date.

Underfitting occurs when the resulting model fails to match patterns of interest in the data. Underfitting is common when applying statistical techniques to data. A common cause is the elimination of variables that have predictive power but are not included in the model. To an analyst, a field may not have much predictive power, so it is never considered as inputs into the model. For instance, on a database used for pet products sold by mail, the type of pet (cat or dog) did not originally seem important for determining the worth of a customer. A closer examination of the data showed that cat owners were slightly more likely to pay their bills on time—quite a useful result for that business.

Another cause is that the technique simply may not work well for the data in question. The following chapters discuss when the various techniques are applicable and when they are not.

Directed versus Undirected

Chapter 5 describes the differences between directed and undirected data mining. From the perspective of applying the data mining techniques, the difference between undirected and directed data mining occurs when creating the data mining model. In a directed data mining, the output of the model is specified prior to creating it. The model trains on examples where the known output provides feedback into refining the model. In an undirected model, the model itself determines its output. It is up to the analyst to determine what is interesting about the results. In both cases, though, the resulting model can be applied to other data.

Explainability

For some purposes, knowing why a particular model produces a particular result is not important. For other purposes, it can be quite insightful and important. Some types of models are easier to understand than others. For instance, decision trees and market basket analysis produce clear sets of rules—that make sense in English. At the other extreme, neural networks and clustering techniques provide little insight into why a particular model does what it does.

Ease of Applying the Model

Similar to explainability is the ease of applying the model to new records. If the data is stored in a relational database, then a model that can be implemented using SQL statements is preferable to one that requires exporting the data into other tools. Increasingly, vendors of data mining products are seeing the value of working with relational databases and other data stores, implementing even very complex models using stored procedures in the database. A stored procedure is written in a computer language inside the database.

TECHNIQUES AND TASKS

This section summarizes the techniques discussed in the following chapters, with specific attention to the tasks they are good for.

Market Basket Analysis

Market basket analysis is a form of clustering used for finding groups of items that tend to occur together in a transaction (or market basket). The models that it builds give the likelihood of different products being purchased together and can be expressed as rules. It is closely tied to analyses in the retail industry, where information on products purchased together may be the only data available for mining customer patterns (other information, such as demographics and history, is not available because the transactions are anonymous). A typical example of results from market basket analysis is that hardware customers purchase 2-by-4s and nails at the same time and customers who purchase paint purchase paint brushes (but not vice versa).

As a clustering technique, market basket analysis is useful on problems where you want to know what items occur together or in a particular sequence. The results are often highly actionable because the results include the specific items. The resulting information can be used for many purposes, such as planning store layouts, limiting specials to one of the products in a set that tend to occur together, bundling the products, offering coupons for the other products when one of them is sold without the others, and so on. When the transactions are not anonymous, market basket analysis can be adapted for use on historical data with a time component.

Memory-Based Reasoning (MBR)

MBR is a directed data mining technique that uses known instances as a model to make predictions about unknown instances. MBR looks for the nearest neighbors in the known instances and combines their values to assign classification or prediction values. For instance, we might maintain a database of claims and whether they were adjusted after investigation. If we want to determine whether a new claim warrants further investigation, we would find similar claims—neighbors—in the database and make the "investigate-further" or "pay-immediately" decision based on the status of the neighbors. The distance to the neighbors gives a measure of correctness of the results.

One of the major advantages of MBR is its ability to run on virtually any source of data, even without data modification. The two key elements in MBR are the distance function used to find the nearest neighbors and the combination function that combines values at the nearest neighbors to make a prediction. For some purposes, these functions can be expressed as SQL statements on a relational database and run directly inside the database for data mining purposes. Although possible, using a relational database tends to be inefficient. In other cases, MBR may be based on more complex data types, such as text and images, when distance functions are available in these domains.

Another major advantage of MBR is its ability to learn about new classifications merely by introducing new instances into the database. Once the right distance function and combination function have been found, they tend to remain pretty stable even as new instances for new categories are incorporated into the known data. This ease of incorporating changes to the domain and range separates MBR from most other data mining techniques, which need to be reapplied to incorporate substantially new information.

Cluster Detection

Cluster detection is the building of models that find data records that are similar to each other. These clumps of self-similarity are called clusters. This is inherently undirected data mining, since the goal is to find previously unknown similarities in the data. There are several techniques for finding clusters, including geometric methods, statistical methods, and neural networks.

Clustering data is a very good way to start any analysis on the data. Self-similar clusters can provide the starting point for knowing what is in the data and for figuring out how to best make use of it.

Link Analysis

Link analysis follows relationships between records to develop models based on patterns in the relationships. This is an application of graph theory constructs to data mining. Relationships between customers are becoming increasingly important, especially as marketing groups focus more on customers, households, and economic marketing units (EMUs) instead of specific accounts. A natural area for the application of link analysis is in telecommunications. Each telephone call links a customer with someone else (potentially another customer). This linkage information can become the basis of highly successful marketing campaigns, such as MCI's original Friends and Family program.

As a data mining tool, link analysis is supported rather inefficiently by relational database technology. The largest area where it is applied is actually in the law enforcement area, where clues about crimes are linked together to help solve them. The few tools available focus on visualizing the links, rather than analyzing the patterns. Too often, the use of link analysis requires writing application-dependent code.

Decision Trees and Rule Induction

Decision trees are a powerful model produced by a class of techniques that include classification and regression trees (CART) and chi-squared automatic induction (CHAID). Decision trees are used for directed data mining, particularly classification. They divide the records in the training set into disjoint subsets, each of which is described by a simple rule on one or more fields.

One of the chief advantages to decision trees is that the model is quite explainable since it takes the form of explicit rules. This allows people to evaluate the results, identifying key attributes in the process. This is also useful where the incoming data is of uncertain quality—spurious results are obvious in the explicit rules. The rules themselves can be expressed easily as logic statements, in a language such as SQL, so they can be applied directly to new records.

Artificial Neural Networks

Neural networks are probably the most common data mining technique, perhaps synonymous with data mining to some readers. They are simple models of neural interconnections in brains, adapted for use on digital computers. In their most common incarnation, they learn from a training set, generalizing patterns inside it for classification and prediction. Neural networks can also be applied to undirected data mining (in the form of self-organizing maps and related structures) and time-series prediction. New applications and new structures for neural networks are being investigated and appear monthly at various conferences and publications devoted to them.

One of the chief advantages of neural networks is their wide applicability. Because of their utility, tools supporting neural networks are available from multiple vendors on a wide variety of platforms. Neural networks are also interesting because they detect patterns in data in a matter analogous to human thinking—an intriguing basis for a data mining tool.

Neural networks have two major drawbacks. The first is the difficulty in understanding the models they produce. Increasingly this objection is being overcome as tools delve into the underlying neural network structure to make them more explainable. The second is their particular sensitivity to the format of incoming data. Different data representations can produce different results; therefore, setting up the data is a significant part of the effort of using them.

Genetic Algorithms

Genetic algorithms (GA) applies the mechanics of genetics and natural selection to a search used for finding the optimal sets of parameters that describe a predictive function. As such, it is used for directed data mining. Genetic algorithms are similar to statistics, in that the form of the model needs to be known in advance. Genetic algorithms uses the selection, crossover, and mutation operators to evolve successive generations of solutions. As the generations evolve, only the most predictive survive, until the functions converge on an optimal solution.

Although other optimization techniques are not discussed in this book, genetic algorithms is appropriate because it is used to solve the same types of problems as other data mining techniques. It has also been used to enhance MBR and neural networks. In the next few years, the authors expect more, rather than fewer, applications of GA in the area of data mining.

On-Line Analytic Processing (OLAP)

Not all that is useful for data analysis is necessarily data mining. OLAP is a way of presenting relational data to users to facilitate understanding the data and important patterns inside it. Like visualization, it is not specifically a tool for data mining, but it is an important tool in the arsenal of weapons used for extracting and presenting information.

The OLAP methods discussed are based on multidimensional databases (MDDs). MDDs are a representation of data that allows users to drill down into the data to understand various important summarizations. In the authors' experiences, most areas where there is interest in data mining can also benefit from OLAP. We include it here because such tools help with the goal of transforming data into information.

Market Basket Analysis

To conjure up an image of market basket analysis, consider the shopping cart in Figure 8.1 filled with various products purchased by someone on a quick trip to the supermarket. This basket contains an assortment of products—orange juice, bananas, soda, window cleaner, and detergent—that tells us what one customer purchased on one trip. One basket tells us about one customer, but all the purchases made by all the customers have much more information. Customers are not all the same. Each customer purchases a different set of products, in different quantities, at different times during the week. Market basket analysis uses the information about *what* customers purchase to give us insight into *who* they are and *why* they make certain purchases. Market basket analysis gives insight into the merchandise by telling us *which* products tend to be purchased together and which are most amenable to promotion. This information is actionable: It can suggest new store layouts; it can determine which products to put on special; it can indicate when to issue coupons, and so on.

Although its roots are in analyzing point-of-sale transactions, market basket analysis can be applied outside the retail industry. Whenever a customer purchases multiple products at the same time or does multiple things in close proximity, there is a potential application:

- Items purchased on a credit card, such as rental cars and hotel rooms, give insight into the next product that customers are likely to purchase.

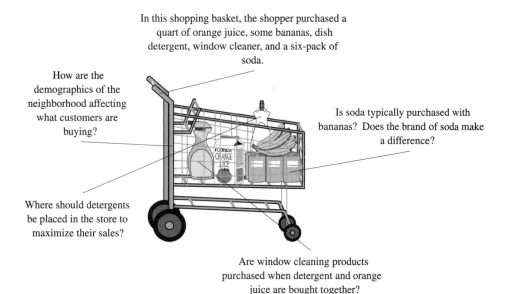

In this shopping basket, the shopper purchased a quart of orange juice, some bananas, dish detergent, window cleaner, and a six-pack of soda.

How are the demographics of the neighborhood affecting what customers are buying?

Is soda typically purchased with bananas? Does the brand of soda make a difference?

Where should detergents be placed in the store to maximize their sales?

Are window cleaning products purchased when detergent and orange juice are bought together?

Figure 8.1 Market basket analysis helps us understand what items are likely to be purchased together.

- Optional services purchased by telecommunications customers (call waiting, call forwarding, ISDN, speed call, etc.) help determine how to bundle these services together to maximize revenue.
- Banking services used by retail customers (money market accounts, CDs, investment services, car loans, etc.) identify customers likely to want other services.
- Unusual combinations of insurance claims can be a sign of fraud and can spark further investigation.
- Medical patient histories can give indications of complications based on certain combinations of treatments.

Often, market basket analysis is used as a starting point when transaction data is available and you do not know what specific patterns to look for. Interesting patterns often suggest some profitable course of action. This is an example of undirected data mining, introduced in Chapter 4. When we have a hunch about where interesting differences lie in the data—such as differences between new stores and established stores—we can still use market basket analysis to investigate these areas. Market basket analysis is suitable for both directed and undirected data mining.

Unfortunately, market basket analysis often fails to live up to expectations. This chapter covers its pitfalls as well as its uses and explores ways to maximize the benefit when using it. The techniques underlying market basket analysis are borrowed from probability and statistics. The ideas are presented with a minimum of explanation of the underlying theory. Readers familiar with statistical packages and even spreadsheets can implement market basket analysis without much effort on small datasets.

WHEN IS MARKET BASKET ANALYSIS USEFUL?

An appeal of market basket analysis comes from the clarity and utility of its results, which are in the form of *association rules*. There is an intuitive appeal to an association rule because it expresses how tangible products and services relate to each other, how they tend to group together. A rule like, *"if a customer purchases three-way calling, then that customer will also purchase call waiting,"* is clear. Even better, it suggests a specific course of action, like bundling three-way calling with call waiting into a single service package.

While association rules are easy to understand, they are not always useful. The following three rules are examples of real rules generated from real data:

- On Thursdays, grocery store consumers often purchase diapers and beer together.
- Customers who purchase maintenance agreements are very likely to purchase large appliances.
- When a new hardware store opens, one of the most commonly sold items is toilet rings.

These three examples illustrate the three common types of rules produced by market basket analysis: the *useful*, the *trivial*, and the *inexplicable*.

The useful rule contains high quality, actionable information. In fact, once the pattern is found, it is often not hard to justify. The rule about diapers and beer on Thursdays suggests that on Thursday evenings, young couples prepare for the weekend by stocking up on diapers for the infants and beer for dad (who, for the sake of argument, we stereotypically assume is watching football on Sunday with a six-pack). Even more important than suggesting causes is that managers can now take action. By locating their own brand of diapers near the aisle containing the beer, they can increase sales of a high-margin product. Because the rule is easily understood, it suggests plausible causes, leading to other interventions: placing other baby products within sight of the beer so customers do not "forget" anything and putting other leisure foods, like potato chips and pretzels, near the baby products.

Trivial results are already known by anyone at all familiar with the business. The second example ("Customers who purchase maintenance agreements are very likely to purchase large appliances") is an example of a trivial rule. In fact, we already know that customers purchase maintenance agreements and large appliances at the same time. Why else would they purchase maintenance agreements? The maintenance agreements are advertised with large appliances and rarely sold separately. This rule, though, was based on analyzing hundreds of thousands of point-of-sale transactions from Sears. Although it is valid and well-supported in the data, it is still useless. Similar results abound: People who buy 2-by-4s also purchase nails; customers who purchase paint buy paint brushes; oil and oil filters are purchased together as are hamburgers and hamburger buns, and charcoal and lighter fluid.

A subtler problem falls into the same category. A seemingly interesting result—like the fact that people who buy the three-way calling option on their local telephone service almost always buy call waiting—may be the result of marketing programs and product bundles. In the case of telephone service options, three-way calling is typically bundled with call waiting, so it is difficult to order it separately. In this case, the analysis is not producing actionable results; it is producing already acted-upon results. Although a danger for any data mining technique, market basket analysis is particularly susceptible to reproducing the success of previous marketing campaigns because of its dependence on unsummarized point-of-sale data—exactly the same data that defines the success of the campaign. *Results from market basket analysis may simply be measuring the success of previous marketing campaigns.*

Inexplicable results seem to have no explanation and do not suggest a course of action. The third pattern ("When a new hardware store opens, one of the most commonly sold items is toilet rings") is intriguing, tempting us with a new fact but providing information that does not give insight into consumer behavior or the merchandise, or suggest further actions. In this case, a large hardware company discovered the pattern for new store openings, but did not figure out how to profit from it. Many items are on sale during the store openings, but the toilet rings stand out. More investigation might give some explanation: Is the discount on toilet rings much larger than for other products? Are they consistently placed in a high-traffic area for store openings but hidden at other times? Is the result an anomaly from a handful of stores? Are they difficult to find at other times? Whatever the cause, it is doubtful that further analysis of just the market basket data can give a credible explanation.

WARNING

When applying market basket analysis, many of the results are often either *trivial* or *inexplicable*. Trivial rules reproduce common knowledge about the business, wasting the effort used to apply sophisticated analysis techniques. Often, trivial results simply measure previous actions, like marketing campaigns, but provide no guidance for future actions. Inexplicable rules are flukes in the data and are not actionable. They may suggest further investigation outside the realm of data mining to understand them better. Determining which rules are valuable can require factoring in knowledge about previous marketing campaigns, bundling of services, and other external and historical factors.

Market Basket Analysis to Compare Stores

Market basket analysis is commonly used to make comparisons between locations within a single chain. The rule about toilet ring sales in hardware stores is an example where sales at new stores are compared to sales at existing stores. Different stores exhibit different selling patterns for many reasons: regional trends, the effectiveness of management, and demographic patterns in the catchment area, for example. Air conditioners and fans are often purchased during heat waves, but heat waves affect only a limited region. Within smaller areas, demographics of the catchment area can have a large impact; we would expect stores in wealthy suburbs to exhibit different sales patterns from those in inner city neighborhoods. These are examples where market basket analysis can help to describe the differences and serve as an example of using market basket analysis for directed data mining.

How do you use market basket analysis to make these comparisons? First, we need to augment the transactions in the data with *virtual items* that specify which group, such as an existing location or a new location, the transaction comes from. Virtual items help describe the transaction, although the virtual item is not a product or service. For instance, a sale at an existing hardware store might include the following products:

A hammer

A box of nails

Extra-fine sandpaper

After we augment the data to specify where it came from, the transaction becomes

a hammer,

a box of nails,

extra fine sandpaper,

"at existing hardware store."

Later in this chapter, we will talk more about virtual items, when they are useful, and some caveats to their use.

To compare sales at store openings versus existing stores, the process is:

1. Gather data for a specific period (such as two weeks) from store openings. Augment each of the transactions in this data with a virtual item saying that the transaction is from a store opening.
2. Gather about the same amount of data from existing stores. Here you might use a sample across all existing stores or you might take all the data from stores in comparable locations. Augment the transactions in this data with a virtual item saying that the transaction is from an existing store.
3. Apply market basket analysis to find association rules in each set.
4. Pay particular attention to association rules containing the virtual items.

The rules generated from market basket analysis act as starting points for further hypothesis testing. Why does one pattern exist at existing stores and another at new stores? The rule about toilet rings and store openings, for instance, suggests looking more closely at toilet ring sales in existing stores at different times during the year.

Using this technique, market basket analysis can be used for many other types of comparisons:

- To compare sales during promotions versus sales at other times
- To compare sales in various geographic areas, by county, standard statistical metropolitan area (SSMA), direct marketing area (DMA), or country
- To compare urban versus suburban sales
- To detect seasonal differences in sales patterns

Adding virtual items to each basket of goods enables the standard market basket analysis techniques to make these comparisons.

HOW DOES MARKET BASKET ANALYSIS WORK

Market basket analysis starts with transactions containing one or more products or service offerings and some rudimentary information about the transaction. For the purpose of analysis, we call the products and service offerings *items*. Table 8.1 illustrates five transactions in a grocery store that carries five products.

These transactions are simplified to include only the items purchased. How to use information like the date and time and whether the customer used cash will be discussed later in this chapter.

Each of these transactions gives us information about which products are purchased with which other products. Using this data, we can create a co-occurrence table that tells the number of times that any pair of products was purchased together (see Table 8.2).

This table tells us the number of times that two products *co-occur* in a transaction. For instance, by looking at the box where the "Soda" row intersects the "OJ" column, we see that two transactions contain both soda and orange juice. This is easily verified against the original transaction data, where customers 1 and 4 purchased both these items. The values along the diagonal (for instance, the value in the

Table 8.1 Grocery Point-of-Sale Transactions

Customer	Items
1	orange juice, soda
2	milk, orange juice, window cleaner
3	orange juice, detergent
4	orange juice, detergent, soda
5	window cleaner, soda

Table 8.2 Co-Occurrence of Products

	OJ	Window Cleaner	Milk	Soda	Detergent
OJ	4	1	1	2	1
Window Cleaner	1	2	1	1	0
Milk	1	1	1	0	0
Soda	2	1	0	3	1
Detergent	1	0	0	1	2

"OJ" column and the "OJ" row) represent the number of transactions containing just that item.

The co-occurrence table contains some simple patterns:

- Orange juice and soda are more likely to be purchased together than any other two items.
- Detergent is never purchased with window cleaner or milk.
- Milk is never purchased with soda or detergent.

These simple observations are examples of associations and may suggest a formal rule like: *"If a customer purchases soda, then the customer also purchases milk."* For now, we defer discussion of how we find this rule automatically. Instead, we ask the question: How good is this rule?

In the data, two of the five transactions include both soda and orange juice. These two transactions *support* the rule. Another way of expressing this is as a percentage. The support for the rule is two out of five or 40 percent.

Since both the transactions that contain soda also contain orange juice, there is a high degree of *confidence* in the rule as well. In fact, every transaction that contains soda also contains orange juice, so the rule *"if soda, then orange juice"* has a confidence of 100 percent. We are less confident about the inverse rule, *"if orange juice then soda,"* because of the four transactions with orange juice, only two also have soda. Its confidence, then, is just 50 percent. More formally, confidence is the ratio of the number of the transactions supporting the rule to the number of transactions where the conditional part of the rule holds. Another way of saying this is that confidence is the ratio of the number of transactions with all the items to the number of transactions with just the "if" items.

The ideas behind the co-occurrence table extend to any combinations with any number of items, not just pairs of items. For combinations of three items, imagine a cube with each side split into five different parts as shown in Figure 8.2. This gets to be a bit difficult to interpret for combinations of three. Even with just five items in the data, there are already 125 different subcubes to fill in. By playing with symmetries in the cube, this can be reduced a bit (by a factor of six), but the number of subcubes to fill in three dimensions is proportional to the third power of the number of different items. In general, the number of combinations with n items is proportional to the number of items raised to the nth power—a number that gets very large, very fast. And generating the co-occurrence table requires doing work for each of these combinations.

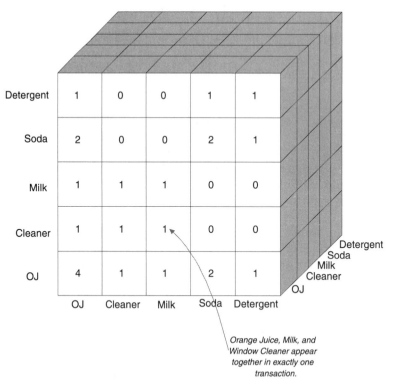

Figure 8.2 A co-occurrence table in three dimensions is a bit cumbersome to visualize.

THE BASIC PROCESS

This basic process for market basket analysis is illustrated in Figure 8.3. There are three important concerns using market basket analysis:

- Choosing the right set of items
- Generating rules by deciphering the counts in the co-occurrence matrix
- Overcoming the practical limits imposed by thousands or tens of thousands of items appearing in combinations large enough to be interesting

These areas are covered in more detail in the next three sections.

Choosing the Right Set of Items

The data used for market basket analysis is typically the detailed transaction data captured at the point of sale. Gathering and using this data is a critical part of applying market basket analysis, depending crucially on the items chosen for analysis. What constitutes a particular item depends on the business need. Within a grocery store where there are tens of thousands of products on the shelves, a frozen pizza might be considered an item for analysis purposes—regardless of its toppings (extra cheese, pepperoni, or mushrooms), its crust (extra thick, whole wheat, or white), or its size. So, the purchase of a large whole wheat vegetarian pizza contains the same "frozen pizza" item as the purchase of a single-serving, pepperoni with extra cheese. A sample of such transactions at this summarized level might look like Table 8.3.

On the other hand, the manager of frozen foods or a chain of pizza restaurants may be very interested in the particular combinations of toppings that are ordered. He or she might decompose a pizza order into constituent parts, as shown in Table 8.4.

At some later point in time, the grocery store may become interested in more detail in its transactions, so the single "frozen pizza" item would no longer be sufficient. Or, the pizza restaurants might broaden their menu choices and become less interested in all the different toppings. *The items of interest may change over time*. This can pose a problem when trying to use historical data if the transaction data has been summarized.

Choosing the right level of detail is a critical consideration for the analysis. If the transaction data in the grocery store keeps track of every type, brand, and size of frozen pizza—which probably account

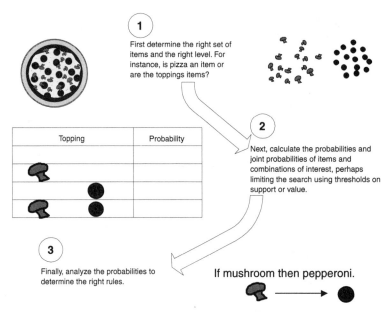

Figure 8.3 The basic steps in market basket analysis.

Table 8.3 Transactions with More Summarized Items

Customer	pizza	milk	sugar	apples	coffee
1	√				
2		√	√		
3	√			√	√
4		√			√
5	√		√	√	√

Table 8.4 Transactions with More Detailed Items

Customer	extra cheese	onions	peppers	mushrooms	olives
1	√	√			√
2			√		
3	√	√		√	
4		√			√
5	√		√	√	√

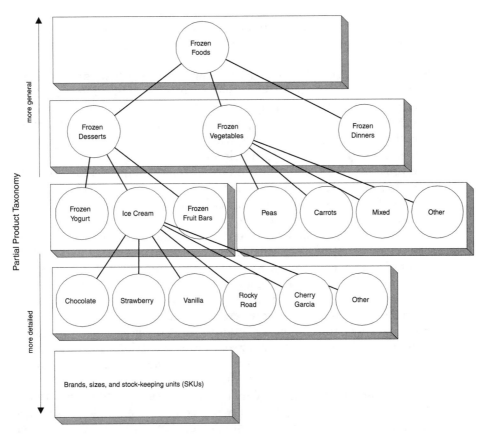

Figure 8.4 Taxonomies start with the most general and move to increasing detail.

for several dozen products—then all these items need to map down to the "frozen pizza" item for analysis.

Taxonomies Help to Generalize Items

In the real world, items have product codes and stock-keeping unit codes (SKUs) that fall into hierarchical categories (see Figure 8.4), called a *taxonomy*. When approaching a problem with market basket analysis, what level of the taxonomy is the right one to use? This brings up issues such as

- Are large fries and small fries the same product?
- Is the brand of ice cream more relevant than its flavor?
- Which is more important: the size, style, pattern, or designer of clothing?

- Is the energy-saving option on a large appliance indicative of customer behavior?

The number of combinations to consider grows very fast as the number of items used in the analysis increases. This suggests using items from higher levels of the taxonomy, "frozen desserts" instead of "ice cream." On the other hand, the more specific the items are, the more likely the results are actionable. Knowing what sells with a particular brand of frozen pizza, for instance, can help in managing the relationship with the producer. One compromise is to use more general items initially, then to repeat the rule generation to hone in on more specific items. As the analysis focuses on more specific items, use only the subset of transactions containing those items.

The complexity of a rule refers to the number of items it contains. The more items in the transactions, the longer it takes to generate rules of a given complexity. So, the desired complexity of the rules also determines how specific or general the items should be. In some circumstances, customers do not make large purchases. For instance, customers purchase relatively few items at any one time at a convenience store or through some catalogs, so looking for rules containing four or more items may apply to very few transactions and be a wasted effort. In other cases, like in a supermarket, the average transaction is larger, so more complex rules are useful.

Moving up the taxonomy hierarchy reduces the number of items. Dozens or hundreds of items may be reduced to a single generalized item, often corresponding to a single department or product line. An item like a pint of Ben & Jerry's Cherry Garcia gets generalized to "ice cream" or "frozen desserts." Instead of investigating "orange juice," investigate "fruit juices." Instead of looking at 2 percent milk, map it to "dairy products." Often, the appropriate level of the hierarchy ends up matching a department with a product-line manager, so using generalized items has the practical effect of finding interdepartmental relationships. Because the structure of the organization is likely to hide relationships between departments, these relationships are more likely to be actionable. Generalized items also help find rules with sufficient support. There will be many times as many transactions supported by higher levels of the taxonomy than lower levels.

Just because some items are generalized does not mean that all items need to move up to the same level. The appropriate level depends on the item, on its importance for producing actionable results, and on its frequency in the data. For instance, in a department store, big-ticket items (like appliances) might stay at a low level in the hierarchy while less expensive items (such as books) might be higher. This hybrid approach is also useful when looking at individual products. Since there are often thousands of products in the data, generalize everything else except for the product or products of interest.

TIP

Market basket analysis produces the best results when the items occur in roughly the same number of transactions in the data. This helps prevent rules from being dominated by the most common items. Taxonomies can help here. Roll up rare items to higher levels in the taxonomy, so they become more frequent. More common items may not have to be rolled up at all.

Virtual Items Go beyond the Taxonomy

The purpose of virtual items is to enable the analysis to take advantage of information that goes beyond the taxonomy. Virtual items do not appear in the product taxonomy of the original items, because they cross product boundaries. Examples of virtual items might be designer labels like Calvin Klein that appear in both apparel departments and perfumes, low-fat and no-fat products in a grocery store, and energy-saving options on appliances.

Virtual items may even include information about the transactions themselves, such as whether the purchase was made with cash, a credit card, or check, and the day of the week or the time of the day the transaction occurred. However, it is not a good idea to crowd the data with too many virtual items. *Only include virtual items when you have some idea of how it could turn into actionable information if found in well-supported, high-confidence association rules.*

For instance, a good use of virtual items is to represent seasonal information. By including a virtual item for the "month" or "season" when a transaction occurred, you can start to detect differences between the seasons and seasonal trends. Market basket analysis can produce rules like:

If "May" and "soil" then "gardening gloves"

There is a danger, though. Virtual items are a prime cause of redundant rules. You have to be careful that the analysis does not just simply reproduce the definitions of the virtual items in terms of other items as shown in Figure 8.5. In this example, a rule like *"if Coke product then Coke"* simply repeats the definition of the virtual item. All the

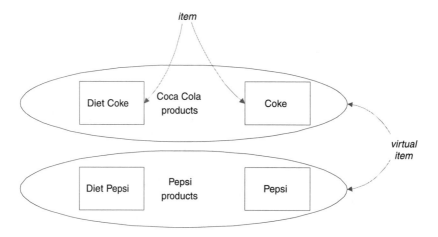

The rules:

> if Coca Cola product, then Coke
> if Pepsi product, then Pepsi

are redundant, useless rules, since they simply repeat the definition
of the virtual items.

Figure 8.5 This is an example of a poor choice of virtual items since the rules
are likely to be redundant.

items that are compatible with the virtual item "Coke products," like
"Diet Coke" and "Coke," are associated only with that virtual item. The
risk of redundant rules arises because each item chosen from the taxonomy is entirely associated with just one virtual item.

Figure 8.6 shows how to avoid this situation. Be sure that the
items from the taxonomy overlap the virtual items. In this case, by replacing "Diet Coke" and "Diet Pepsi" with "diet soda" from the product
taxonomy, the problem goes away. This overlap helps prevent the market basket analysis from generating rules that just repeat the definition of the virtual items.

A more subtle danger of using virtual items occurs when a virtual
item and a generalized item appearing together are a proxy for individual items. For instance, if "diet Coke" is replaced by "diet soda"
from the taxonomy and "Coke product" is included as a virtual item,
then rules containing both "diet soda" and "coke product" may really
be talking about "diet coke." For instance,

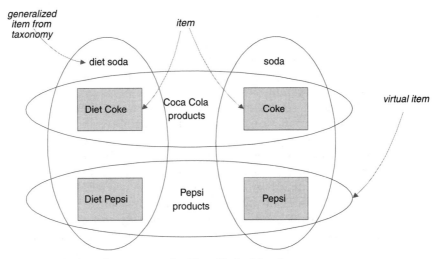

To avoid redundant rules, use generalized items like "soda" and "diet soda" that overlap virtual items.

Figure 8.6   Make sure that the virtual items do not totally encompass the items used for analysis.

If "coke product" and "diet soda" then "pretzels"

probably means,

If "diet coke" then "pretzels"

If most of the rules are of this form, then you need to reconsider how you are breaking up items. Looking for rules with three items instead of two is a bad idea because it increases the computational effort needed to generate the rules.

TIP

When applying market basket analysis, it is useful to have a taxonomy of the items being considered for analysis. You can replace the items in the analysis with generalized items from different levels in the taxonomy. By judiciously choosing the right levels of the taxonomy, these generalized items should occur about the same number of times in the data, improving the results of the analysis. For specific lifestyle features that provide insight into customer behavior, such as sugar-free items and specific brands, augment the data with virtual items.

Data Quality

The data used for market basket analysis is generally not of very high quality. It is gathered directly at the point of customer contact and used mainly for operational purposes like inventory control. Data from operational systems is often dirty and needs extensive cleansing before being a good source for decision support. The data is likely to have multiple formats, corrections, incompatible code types, and so on. Much of the explanation of various code values is likely to reside buried deep in code running in legacy systems and may be difficult to extract. Different stores within a single chain sometimes have slightly different product hierarchies or different ways of handling situations like discounts. Some systems are more up-to-date than other systems. These problems are typical when using any sort of data for data mining. However, they are exacerbated for market basket analysis because this type of analysis depends heavily on the unsummarized point-of-sale transactions.

Anonymous versus Signed

Market basket analysis has proven particularly useful for mass-market retail, such as supermarkets, convenience stores, drug stores, and fast food chains, where many of the purchases have traditionally been made with cash. Cash transactions are anonymous, meaning that the store has no knowledge about specific customers because there is no information identifying the customer in the transaction. For anonymous transactions, the only information known about the purchase is the date and time, the location of the store, the cashier, the items purchased, any coupons redeemed, and the amount of change. With market basket analysis, even this limited data yields interesting and actionable results.

The increasing use of credit cards, debit cards, and purchasing clubs at stores is resulting in fewer and fewer anonymous transactions, providing analysts with more possibilities for information about customers and their behavior over time. Demographic and trending information is available on individuals and households to further augment customer profiles. This additional information can be incorporated into the analysis using virtual items.

In other industries like banking and medical care, anonymous transactions are not an issue. All interactions with a customer include his or her account number, patient id, or the like. This allows the same data to be used for time-series analysis, which we will touch on later in this chapter and in more detail in the next few chapters.

Generating Rules from All This Data

Calculating the number of times that a given combination of items appears in the transaction data is well and good, but a combination of items is not a rule. Sometimes, just the combination is interesting in itself, as in the diaper, beer, and Thursday example. But in other circumstances, it makes more sense to find an underlying rule.

What is a rule? A rule has two parts, a condition and a result, and is usually represented as a statement:

If *condition* then *result*.

Notice that this is just shorthand. If the rule says,

If *3-way calling* then *call-waiting*

we read it as: "if a customer has 3-way calling, then the customer also has call-waiting." In practice, the most actionable rules have just one item as the result. So, a rule like

If *diapers* and *Thursday*, then *beer*

is more useful than

If Thursday, then diapers and beer.

Constructs like the co-occurrence table provide the information about which combination of items occur most commonly in the transactions. For the sake of illustration, let's say the most common combination has three items, A, B, and C. The only rules to consider are those with all three items in the rule and with exactly one item in the result:

- If A and B, then C
- If A and C, then B
- If B and C, then A

Table 8.5 provides an example, showing the probabilities of items and various combinations.

Because these three rules contain the same items, they have the same support in the data, 5 percent. What about their confidence level? Confidence is the ratio of the number of transactions with all the

Table 8.5 Probabilities of Three Items and Their Combinations

Combination	Probability
A	45 %
B	42.5%
C	40 %
A and B	25 %
A and C	20 %
B and C	15 %
A and B and C	5 %

items in the rule to the number of transactions with just the items in the condition. The confidence for the three rules is shown in Table 8.6. What is confidence really saying? Saying that the rule *"if B and C then A"* has a confidence of 0.33 is equivalent to saying that when B and C appear in a transaction, there is a 33 percent chance that A also appears in it. That is, one time in three A occurs with B and C, and the other two times, A does not.

The most confident rule is the best rule, so we are tempted to choose *"if B and C then A."* But there is a problem. This rule is actually worse than if just randomly saying that A appears in the transaction. A occurs in 45 percent of the transactions but the rule only gives 33 percent confidence. The rule does worse than just randomly guessing.

This suggests another measure called *improvement*. Improvement tells how much better a rule is at predicting the result than just assuming the result in the first place. It is given by the following formula:

$$\text{improvement} = \frac{p(\text{condition and result})}{p(\text{condition}) \, p(\text{result})}$$

Table 8.6 Confidence in Rules

Rule	p(condition)	p(condition and result)	confidence
If A and B then C	25%	5%	0.20
If A and C then B	20%	5%	0.25
If B and C then A	15%	5%	0.33

When improvement is greater than 1, then the resulting rule is better at predicting the result than random chance. When it is less than 1, it is worse. The following table (Table 8.7) shows the improvement for the three rules and for the rule with the best improvement.

None of the rules with three items shows any improvement. The best rule in the data actually only has two items. The rule "*if A then B*" is 1.31 times better at predicting when B is in a transaction than randomly guessing. In this case, as in many cases, the best rule actually contains fewer items than other rules being considered.

When improvement is less than 1, *negating* the result produces a better rule. If the rule

If B and C then A

has a confidence of 0.33, then the rule

If B and C then NOT A

has a confidence of 0.67. Since A appears in 45 percent of the transactions, it does NOT occur in 55 percent of them. Applying the same improvement measure shows that the improvement of this new rule is 1.22 (0.67/0.55). The negative rule is useful. The rule "*if A and B then NOT C*" has an improvement of 1.33, better than any of the other rules.

Rules are generated from the basic probabilities available in the co-occurrence table. Useful rules have an improvement that is greater than 1. When the improvement scores are low, you can increase them by negating the rules. However, you may find that negated rules are not as useful as the original association rules when it comes to acting on the results.

Table 8.7 Improvement Measurement for Four Rules

Rule	support	confidence	improvement
If A and B then C	5%	0.2	0.5
If A and C then B	5%	0.25	0.59
If B and C then A	5%	0.33	0.74
If A then B	25%	0.59	1.31

Overcoming Practical Limits

Generating association rules is a multi-step process. The general algorithm is:

1. Generate the co-occurrence matrix for single items.
2. Generate the co-occurrence matrix for two items. Use this to find rules with two items.
3. Generate the co-occurrence matrix for three items. Use this to find rules with three items.
4. And so on.

For instance, in the grocery store that sells orange juice, milk, detergent, soda, and window cleaner, the first step calculates the counts for each of these items. During the second step, the following counts are created:

- OJ and milk, OJ and detergent, OJ and soda, OJ and cleaner
- Milk and detergent, milk and soda, milk and cleaner
- Detergent and soda, detergent and cleaner
- Soda and cleaner

This is a total of 10 counts. The third pass takes all combinations of three items and so on. Of course, each of these stages may require a separate pass through the data or multiple stages can be combined into a single pass by considering different numbers of combinations at the same time.

Although it is not obvious when there are just five items, increasing the number of items in the combinations requires exponentially more computation. This results in exponentially growing run times—and long, long waits when considering combinations with more than three or four items. The solution is *pruning*. Pruning is a technique for reducing the number of items and combinations of items being considered at each step. At each stage, the algorithm throws out a certain number of combinations that do not meet some threshold criterion.

The most common pruning mechanism is called *minimum support pruning*. Recall that support refers to the number of transactions in the database where the rule holds. Minimum support pruning requires that a rule hold on a minimum number of transactions. For instance, if there are 1 million transactions and the minimum support is 1 percent, then only rules supported by 10,000 transactions are of interest. This makes sense, because the purpose of generating these rules is to pursue some sort of action—such as putting own-brand diapers in the same aisle as beer—and the action must affect enough transactions to be worthwhile.

The minimum support constraint has a cascading effect. Say we are considering a rule with four items in it, like

If A, B, and C, then D.

Using minimum support pruning, this rule has to be true on at least 10,000 transactions in the data. It follows that:

A must appear in at least 10,000 transactions; and,
B must appear in at least 10,000 transactions; and,
C must appear in at least 10,000 transactions; and,
D must appear in at least 10,000 transactions.

In other words, minimum support pruning eliminates items that do not appear in enough transactions! There are two ways to do this. The first way is to eliminate the items from consideration. The second way is to use the taxonomy to generalize the items so the resulting generalized items meet the threshold criterion.

The threshold criterion applies to each step in the algorithm. The minimum threshold also implies that:

A and B must appear together in at least 10,000
    transactions; and,
A and C must appear together in at least 10,000
    transactions; and,
A and D must appear together in at least 10,000
    transactions;
And so on.

Each step of the calculation of the co-occurrence table can eliminate combinations of items that do not meet the threshold, reducing its size and the number of combinations to consider during the next pass.

Figure 8.7 is an example of how the calculation takes place. In this example, choosing a minimum support level of 10 percent would eliminate all the combinations with three items—and their associated rules—from consideration. This is an example where pruning does not have an effect on the best rule since the best rule has only two items. In the case of pizza, these toppings are all fairly common, so are not pruned individually. If anchovies were included in the analysis—and

A pizza restaurant has sold 2000 pizzas, of which:
100 are mushrooms, 150 are pepperoni, 200 are extra cheese
400 are mushroom and pepperoni, 300 are mushroom and extra cheese, 200 are pepperoni and extra cheese
100 are mushrom, pepperoni, and extra cheese.
550 have no extra toppings.

We need to calculate the probabilities for all possible combinations of items.

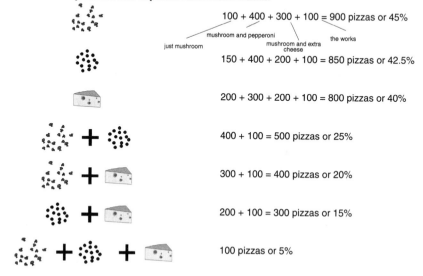

100 + 400 + 300 + 100 = 900 pizzas or 45%

just mushroom   mushroom and pepperoni   mushroom and extra cheese   the works

150 + 400 + 200 + 100 = 850 pizzas or 42.5%

200 + 300 + 200 + 100 = 800 pizzas or 40%

400 + 100 = 500 pizzas or 25%

300 + 100 = 400 pizzas or 20%

200 + 100 = 300 pizzas or 15%

100 pizzas or 5%

There are three rules with all three items

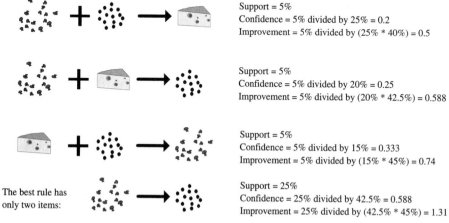

Support = 5%
Confidence = 5% divided by 25% = 0.2
Improvement = 5% divided by (25% * 40%) = 0.5

Support = 5%
Confidence = 5% divided by 20% = 0.25
Improvement = 5% divided by (20% * 42.5%) = 0.588

Support = 5%
Confidence = 5% divided by 15% = 0.333
Improvement = 5% divided by (15% * 45%) = 0.74

The best rule has
only two items:

Support = 25%
Confidence = 25% divided by 42.5% = 0.588
Improvement = 25% divided by (42.5% * 45%) = 1.31

Figure 8.7 Counting up the frequencies on pizza sales for market basket analysis.

there are only 15 pizzas containing them out of the 2,000—then a minimum support of 10 percent, or even 1 percent, would eliminate anchovies during the first pass.

The best choice for minimum support depends on the data and the situation. It is also possible to vary the minimum support as the algorithm progresses. For instance, using different levels at different stages you can find uncommon combinations of common items (by decreasing the support level for successive steps) or relatively common combinations of uncommon items (by increasing the support level). Varying the minimum support helps to find actionable rules, so the rules generated are not all like finding that peanut butter and jelly are often purchased together.

THE PROBLEM OF BIG DATA

A typical fast-food restaurant offers several dozen items on its menu, say there are a 100. To use probabilities to generate association rules, counts have to be calculated for each combination of items. The number of combinations of a given size tends to grow exponentially. A combination with three items might be a small fries, cheeseburger, and medium diet Coke. On a menu with 100 items, how many combinations are there with three menu items? There are 161,700! Table 8.8 shows how fast the number of combinations grows.

(This is based on the binomial formula from mathematics.) On the other hand, a typical supermarket has at least 10,000 different items in stock, and more typically 20,000 or 30,000.

Table 8.8 The Number of Combinations of Items Grows Fast

# in combination	# of combinations
1	100
2	4,950
3	161,700
4	3,921,225
5	75,287,520
6	1,192,052,400
7	16,007,560,800
8	186,087,894,300

Calculating the support, confidence, and improvement quickly gets out of hand as the number of items in the combinations grows. There are almost 50 million possible combinations of two items in the grocery store and over 100 billion combinations of three items. Although computers are getting faster and cheaper, it is still very expensive to calculate the counts for this number of combinations. Calculating the counts for five or more items is prohibitively expensive. The use of taxonomies reduces the number of items to a manageable size.

The number of transactions is also very large. In the course of a year, a decent-size chain of supermarkets will generate tens of millions of transactions. Each of these transactions consists of one or more items, often several dozen at a time. So, determining if a particular combination of items is present in a particular transaction may require a bit of effort—multiplied a million-fold for all the transactions.

DISSOCIATION RULES

A *dissociation rule* is similar to an association rule except that it can have the connector "and not" in the condition in addition to "and." A typical dissociation rule looks like:

If *A* and not *B* then *C*.

Dissociation rules can be generated by a simple adaptation of the basic market basket analysis algorithm. The adaptation is to introduce a new set of items that are the inverses of each of the original items. Then, modify each transaction so it includes an inverse item if, and only if, it does not contain the original item. For example, Table 8.9 shows the transformation of a few transactions. The ¬ before the item denotes the inverse item.

There are three downsides to including these new items. First, the total number of items used in the analysis doubles. Since the amount of computation grows exponentially with the number of items, doubling the number of items seriously degrades performance. Second, the size of a typical transaction grows because it now includes inverted items. The third issue is that the frequency of the inverse items tends to be much larger than the frequency of the original items. So, minimum support constraints tend to produce rules in which all items are inverted, such as:

If *NOT A* and *NOT B* then *NOT C*.

Table 8.9 Transformation of Transactions to Generate Dissociation Rules

Customer	Items		Customer	
1	{A, B, C}	⟶	1	{A, B, C}
2	{A}	⟶	2	{A, ¬B, ¬C}
3	{A, C}	⟶	3	{A, ¬B, C}
4	{A}	⟶	4	{A, ¬B, ¬C}
5	{}	⟶	5	{¬A, ¬B, ¬C}

These rules are less likely to be actionable.

Sometimes it is useful to invert only the most frequent items in the set used for analysis. This is particularly valuable when the frequency of some of the original items is close to 50 percent, so the frequencies of their inverses are also close to 50 percent.

SEQUENTIAL TIME-SERIES ANALYSIS USING MARKET BASKET ANALYSIS

Market basket analysis analyzes things that happen at the same time—what items are purchased at a given time. The next natural question concerns sequences of events and what they mean. Examples of results in this area are:

- New homeowners purchase shower curtains before purchasing furniture.
- When a customer goes into a bank branch and asks for an account reconciliation, there is a good chance that he or she will close all his or her accounts.

Time-series data usually requires some way of identifying the customer. Anonymous transactions cannot reveal that new homeowners buy shower curtains before they buy furniture. This requires tracking each customer, as well as knowing which customers recently purchased a home. Since larger purchases are often made with credit cards or debit cards, this is often not a problem. For problems in other domains, such as investigating the effects of medical treatments or customer behavior inside a bank, all transactions typically include identity information.

> **WARNING**
>
> In order to consider time-series analyses on your customers, there has to be some way of identifying customers over time. Without a way of tracking individual customers, there is no way to analyze their behavior.

For the purposes of this section, a *time series* is an ordered sequence of items. It differs from a transaction only in being ordered. In general, the time series contains identifying information about the customer, since this information is used to tie the different transactions together into a series. Although there are many techniques for analyzing time series, such as neural networks, this section discusses only how to manipulate the time-series data to apply the market basket analysis.

From Transactions to Series

In order to use time series, our transaction data must have two additional features:

- A time stamp or sequencing information to determine when transactions occurred relative to each other
- Identifying information, such as account number, household id, or customer id that identifies different transactions as belonging to the same customer or household (sometimes called an economic marketing unit)

The transactions corresponding to the same customer are gathered together into a time series using this information. Unlike the transactions we have looked at so far, this series shows which items came before, after, or at the same time as other items. Also, these series can contain duplicate items. Figure 8.8 is an example of a time series for banking data, showing simplified transactions (only four types of transactions are allowed) for two customers. One of the customers is a happy customer—she deposits money once, withdraws a few times, and repeats the process. The other is a former customer. The time series indicates customer behavior and should be able to help us understand the ex-customer better.

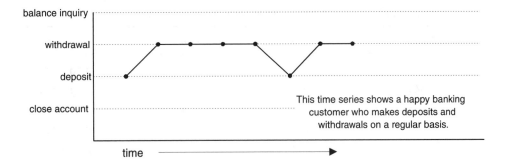

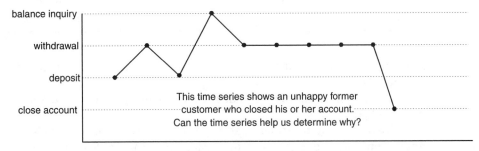

Figure 8.8 Time series provide snapshots of customer behavior through time.

A Simple Case of Cause and Effect

A simple but powerful way to use time series is for analyzing cause and effect. This is a directed method to find the causes of an event that occurs at a particular time. For instance, the problem may be to understand more about attrition of credit card customers. Less often, but also of importance, are the effects of an event, such as how a promotion affects behavior or the treatments given a patient after being diagnosed with a particular disease.

The strategy presented here is to convert the time-series problem into a market basket analysis problem. Each time series is converted into a transaction by including the items before the event of interest (for causes) or after the event of interest (for effects) and removing duplicate items from the transaction. Then there is a set of transactions amenable to market basket analysis. In this case, the interest is just in

Table 8.10 Some Medical Care Records for Time Series Analysis

Patient ID	Provider	Sequence	Item
1356	Jones	1	diagnosis X
5690	Jones	2	diagnosis X
1356	Jones	3	prescription 2
7573	Smith	4	diagnosis X
7573	Smith	5	prescription 2
5690	Jones	6	prescription 1
1356	Jones	7	prescription 1
7573	Smith	8	prescription 2

finding common combination items so there is no need to generate actual rules.

As a simple example, consider the following patient data, shown in Table 8.10.

To analyze the treatments after patients are diagnosed with X, we might generate the following transactions (refer to Table 8.10):

- {Jones, prescription 2, prescription 1}   for patient 1356
- {Jones, prescription 1}   for patient 5690
- {Smith, prescription 2}   for patient 7573

In this case, the transaction includes the provider's name since this may give some insight into the follow-ups to the diagnosis. If the prognosis of all the patients is the same, then perhaps Dr. Jones is over-prescribing prescription 1.

This example created new transactions that span multiple treatments over time, then applied market basket analysis to these transactions to study the effect of an event.

Time Windows

Time windows are another way of interpreting time series for market basket analysis. It is particularly useful when there are few items that occur over a span of time, such as ATM transactions. A *time window* is a snapshot of all items that occur within a certain time period.

An example of a time window is to gather all the transactions made in a single month into a single transaction. So, if the data in Figure 8.8 were all from one month, then the time-window approach would use the following two transactions:

- Happy Customer: {deposit, withdrawal}
- Unhappy Customer: {deposit, withdrawal, balances, close}

Unfortunately, it is not easy to capture the different number of times that each item occurs during the month. However, this approach can help understand trends in behavior.

This is also a case where virtual items can capture other information that might be important. For instance, such items might say,

- the average account balance increased from the last time window;
- this catalogue customer purchased less in this time window than in the last; or
- this cellular customer called customer service more this month than last month.

These trend items can be included with all the items from the time period, creating rules with some trend information available. However, we are reaching into the limits of market basket analysis. Its purpose is to understand how discrete items interrelate with each other. At this point, we need more powerful techniques to help us understand how continuous variables change over time.

STRENGTHS OF MARKET BASKET ANALYSIS

The strengths of market basket analysis are:

- It produces clear and understandable results.
- It supports undirected data mining.
- It works on variable-length data.
- The computations it uses are simple to understand.

Results Are Clearly Understood

The results of market basket analysis are association rules; these are readily expressed as English or as a statement in SQL. The expression of patterns in the data as "if-then" rules makes the results easy to understand and facilitates turning the results into action. In some circumstances, merely the set of related items is of interest and rules do not even need to be produced.

Market Basket Analysis Is Strong for Undirected Data Mining

Undirected data mining is very important when approaching a large set of data and you do not know where to begin. Market basket analysis is an appropriate technique, when it can be applied, to analyze data and to get a start. Most data mining techniques are not primarily used for undirected data mining. Market basket analysis, on the other hand, is used in this case and provides clear results.

Market Basket Analysis Works on Variable-length Data

Market basket analysis can handle variable-length data without the need for summarization. Other techniques tend to require records in a fixed format, which is not a natural way to represent items in a transaction. Market basket analysis can handle transactions without any loss of information.

Computationally Simple

The computations needed to apply market basket analysis are rather simple, although the number of computations grows very quickly with the number of transactions and the number of different items in the analysis. Smaller problems can be set up on the desktop using a spreadsheet. This makes the technique more comfortable to use than complex techniques, like genetic algorithms or neural networks.

WEAKNESSES OF MARKET BASKET ANALYSIS

The weaknesses of market basket analysis are:

- It requires exponentially more computational effort as the problem size grows.
- It has a limited support for attributes on the data.
- It is difficult to determine the right number of items.
- It discounts rare items.

Exponential Growth as Problem Size Increases

The computations required to generate association rules grow exponentially with the number of items and the complexity of the rules being considered. The solution is to reduce the number of items by generalizing them. However, more general items are usually less actionable. Methods to control the number of computations, such as minimum support pruning, may eliminate important rules from consideration.

Limited Support for Data Attributes

Market basket analysis is a technique specialized for items in a transaction. Items are assumed to be identical except for one identifying characteristic, such as the product type. When applicable, market basket analysis is very powerful. However, not all problems fit this description. The use of item taxonomies and virtual items helps make rules more expressive.

Determining the Right Items

Probably the most difficult problem when applying market basket analysis is determining the right set of items to use in the analysis. By generalizing items up their taxonomy, you can ensure that the frequencies of the items used in the analysis are about the same. Although this generalization process loses some information, virtual items can then be reinserted into the analysis to capture information that spans generalized items.

Market Basket Analysis Has Trouble with Rare Items

Market basket analysis works best when all items have approximately the same frequency in the data. Items that rarely occur are in very few transactions and will be pruned. Modifying minimum support threshold to take into account product value is one way to ensure that expensive items remain in consideration, even though they may be rare in the data. The use of item taxonomies can ensure that rare items are rolled up and included in the analysis in some form.

WHEN TO APPLY MARKET BASKET ANALYSIS

Market basket analysis is applied to undirected data mining problems that consist of well-defined items that group together in interesting ways. These problems occur commonly in the retail industry where point-of-sale transactions are the basis for the analysis. Similar problems can be found in other industries.

Market basket analysis can also be applied to some directed data mining problems in these industries. It can be run on a well-defined subset of transactions, such as transactions from new stores or medicines prescribed by physicians in a particular HMO, to find outliers in a subset of interest. The basic algorithm can also be modified to only consider rules that contain a particular item, such as a new product, to understand patterns in its selling patterns.

Time-series problems are another area where these methods can be applied. Many time-series problems can be adapted for market basket analysis by relatively simple transformations on the data in the time series.

9

Memory-Based Reasoning

People are very good at making decisions based on their past experience. When someone picks out a face in a crowd, he or she is comparing that face to all the faces he or she knows. When physicians diagnose diseases, they are applying their experience of similar patients and symptoms to the current case. When analysts find fraudulent insurance claims, they are often relying on similarities to previous cases of fraud and differences from non-fraud cases. Whether identifying faces in a crowd, diagnosing diseases, or flagging fraudulent insurance claims, the process is similar: The first step is *identifying* similar cases from experience, then *applying* the information from these cases to the problem at hand. This is the essence of memory-based reasoning (MBR), a directed data mining technique that similarly exploits experience. By maintaining a database of known records, MBR finds neighbors similar to a new record and uses the *neighbors* for classification and prediction.

One of the broad appeals of MBR is its ability to use data "as is." Unlike other data mining techniques, it does not care about the format of the records. It only cares about the existence of two operations: The *distance function* assigns a distance between any two records and the *combination function* combines the results from the neighbors to arrive at an answer. These functions are readily defined for the standard data types in most records. In addition, they are also available for more complex data types such as geographic locations, images, and full-text that are usually difficult to handle with other analysis techniques. A case study later in the chapter shows MBR's successful application to the classification of news stories—an example where it takes advantage of the full-text in the news story to assign subject codes.

MBR is also suitable to the relational data more commonly found in business environments. The distance and combination functions needed by MBR handle the complexities of records in the business environment and can sometimes even help when values in certain fields are missing. Applications of MBR span many areas:

- Fraud detection. New cases of fraud are likely to be similar to known cases. MBR can find and flag them for further investigation.
- Customer response prediction. The next customers likely to respond to an offer are probably similar to previous customers that have responded. MBR can easily identify the next likely customers.
- Medical treatments. The most effective treatment for a given patient is probably the treatment that resulted in the best outcomes for similar patients. MBR can find the treatment that produces the best outcome.
- Classifying responses. Free-text responses, such as those on the U.S. Census form for occupation and industry, need to be classified into a fixed set of codes. MBR can process the free-text and assign the codes.

The simplicity of MBR belies much of its power and its advantages when compared to other techniques. The vagueness of the definition of similarity is a strength that allows the application of MBR to almost all types of data, including non-atomic types such as geographic coordinates and free-text. For data in a relational database, the technique can be implemented in SQL, although performance is an issue. Another strength is its ability to adapt. By merely incorporating new data into the historical database, MBR learns about new categories and new definitions of old ones. MBR also produces good results without a long period devoted to training or to massaging incoming data into the right format.

All these advantages come at a cost. MBR tends to be a resource hog—since a large amount of historical data must be readily available for finding neighbors. Classifying new records can require processing all the historical records to find the most similar neighbors—a more time-consuming process than applying an already-trained neural network or an already-built decision tree. New techniques point to ways to reduce the size of the historical data. Although finding good distance and combination functions is not very difficult, finding the optimal functions can take some effort.

HOW DOES MBR WORK?

Let's consider how MBR works for a simple classification problem, illustrated by the moviegoers database introduced in Chapter 4: What is the most likely movie last seen by a respondent based on the source of the record and the age of the individual? This example uses only four of the most popular movies. A good way to visualize MBR is to use a scatter plot of the movies, by source and age as shown in Figure 9.1. In the scatter plot, the age and source for each respondent is marked with the movie seen by that individual.

Figure 9.2 is the same scatter graph with three unknown respondents included. Using the graph, it is easy to pick out the nearest

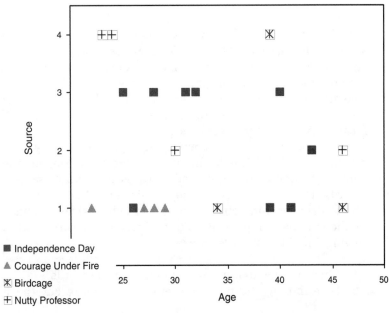

Figure 9.1 The age and source of respondents for the four most popular movies.

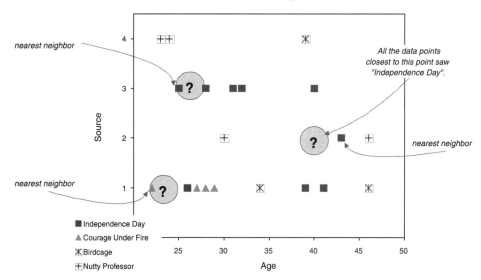

Figure 9.2 To predict the last movie seen by three unknown people, find where they land on the scatter graph and make a prediction based on the nearest neighbor.

neighbor for each of the new respondents. For the sake of prediction, say that the last movie seen by the new respondents is the last movie seen by each one's nearest neighbor. This process works without deriving any rules about the original data and without a long training cycle. The nearest neighbor approach is strictly local. That is, only the records similar to the new record play any part in assigning the value for the most recently seen movie.

This example is quite simple. It does, however, show the main elements of MBR. MBR determines unknown categories for the respondents, by finding the most similar cases in a database of historical records with categories already assigned. MBR has two distinct phases: The learning phase generates the historical database and the prediction phase applies MBR to new cases. The three main issues in solving a problem with MBR are:

1. Choosing the appropriate set of historical records
2. Determining the most efficient way to represent the historical records

3. Determining the distance function, the combination function, and the number of neighbors

MBR works for both classification—the assignment of discrete categories to the data like the movies in the previous example—and prediction—the assignment of continuous values, as we will see later.

Choosing the Historical Records

The historical records, also known as the training set, is a subset of available records. The training set needs to provide good coverage of the records so that the nearest neighbors to an unknown record are useful for predictive purposes. A random sample does not usually provide sufficient coverage. Some categories are much more frequent than others and the more frequent categories will dominate the random sample. For instance, the most popular movies had 38 respondents, whereas 23 movies had only 1 respondent. To avoid movies with too few respondents, the moviegoers example limited the database to only the four most popular movies. This is a common situation: Fraudulent transactions are much rarer than non-fraudulent transactions, heart disease is much more common than liver cancer, news stories about the computer industry more common than about plastics, and so on. To achieve balance, the training set should contain roughly equal numbers of records representing the different categories.

TIP

When selecting the training set for MBR, be sure that each category has roughly the same number of records supporting it. As a general rule of thumb, several dozen records for each category are a minimum to get adequate support and hundreds or thousands of examples are not unusual.

Representing the Historical Records

The performance of MBR in making predictions depends on how the training set is represented in the computer. The scatter graph approach works for people using a few dozen simple data points, but it does not map well to a computer. The simplest method for finding the nearest neighbors requires finding the distance from the unknown case to each of the records in the training set and choosing the historical records with the smallest distances. As the number of records grows, the time needed to find the neighbors for a new record grows just as fast.

This is especially true if the records are stored in a relational database. In this case, the query looks something like:

```
SELECT distance(),rec.category
FROM historical_records rec
ORDER BY 1 ASCENDING;
```

The notation *distance()* fills in for whatever the particular distance function happens to be. In this case, all the historical records need to be sorted in order to get the handful needed for the nearest neighbors. This requires a full-table scan plus a sort—quite an expensive couple of operations. It is possible to eliminate the sort by walking through table and keeping another table of the nearest, inserting and deleting records as appropriate. Unfortunately, this technique is not readily expressible in SQL without using a procedural language.

Some specialized databases, like those supporting geographic information systems, do provide the ability to find records that are close to each other without doing a full-table scan. Text databases also have similar functions. Increasingly, these functions are appearing in relational databases, so more efficient operations may be on the way.

The other way to make MBR more efficient is to reduce the number of records in the historical database. Figure 9.3 shows a scatter graph for categorical data. This graph has a well-defined boundary between the two regions. The points above the line are all diamonds and those below the line are all squares. Although this graph has forty points in it, most of the points are redundant. That is, they are not really necessary for classification purposes. Figure 9.4 shows that only eight points in it are needed to get the same results. Given that the size of the training set has such a large influence on the performance of MBR, being able to reduce the size is a significant performance boost.

How can this reduced set of records be found? The most practical method is to look for clusters containing the records of the different categories. The centers of the clusters can then be used as a reduced set. This works well when the different categories are quite separate. However, when there is some overlap and the categories are not so well-defined, using clusters to reduce the size of the training set can

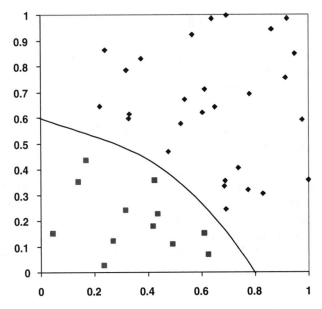

Figure 9.3 An example where the training set divides neatly into two disjoint sets is an example of a data set that can be used for MBR.

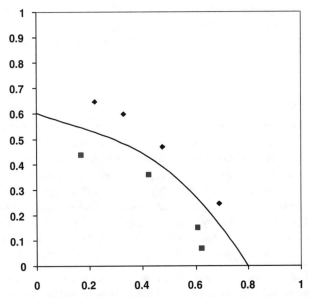

Figure 9.4 These same points return the same results using MBR.

cause MBR to produce poor results. Finding an optimal set of "support records" has been an area of recent research. When such an optimal set can be found, the historical records can sometimes be reduced to the level where they fit inside a spreadsheet, making it quite efficient to apply MBR to new records on less powerful machines.

Determining the Distance Function, Combination Function, and Number of Neighbors

The distance function, combination function, and number of neighbors are the key ingredients in determining how good MBR is at producing results. The same set of historical records can prove very useful or not useful at all for predictive purposes, depending on these criteria. Fortunately, simple distance functions and combination functions usually work quite well. But, before discussing these issues in detail, let's look at a detailed case study.

CASE STUDY: CLASSIFYING NEWS STORIES

This case study uses MBR to assign classification codes to news stories and is based on work conducted by one of the authors. The results from this case study show that MBR can perform as well as people on a problem involving hundreds of categories and data on a difficult-to-use type of data, free-text.[1]

What Are the Codes?

Dow Jones, like many news providers, assigns codes to news stories in order to describe the content of the stories. These codes help users search for stories of interest, help automate the process of routing particular stories to particular customers, and help implement personalized profiles. For instance, an industry analyst who specializes in the automotive industry can simplify searches by looking for documents with the "automotive industry" code. Because knowledgeable experts, also known as editors, set up the codes, the industry analyst has confi-

---

1. This case study is a summarization of research conducted by one of the authors. Complete details are available in the article "Classifying News Stories using Memory Based Reasoning," by David Waltz, Brij Massand, and Gordon Linoff, in *Proceedings*, SIGIR '92, published by ACM Press.

Table 9.1 Six Types of Codes Used to Classify News Stories

Category	# Codes	# Docs	# Occurrences
Government (G/)	28	3,926	4,200
Industry (I/)	112	38,308	57,430
Market Sector (M/)	9	38,562	42,058
Product (P/)	21	2,242	2,523
Region (R/)	121	47,083	116,358
Subject (N/)	70	41,902	52,751

dence in the stories retrieved. In fact, the analyst can also set up a profile so stories assigned the "automotive industry" code are routed automatically to the analyst's desktop computer. Editors or expert systems have traditionally assigned these codes. This case study investigated the use of MBR for this purpose.

The codes used in this study fall into six categories: government agency, industry, market sector, product, region, and subject. The data contained 361 separate codes, distributed as follows in the training set (Table 9.1).

The number and types of codes assigned to stories varied. Almost all the stories had region and subject codes—and, on average, almost three region codes per story. At the other extreme, relatively few stories contained government and product codes, and such stories rarely had more than one such code.

Applying MBR

This section explains how MBR facilitated assigning codes to news stories. The important steps were:

1. Choosing the training set
2. Determining the distance function
3. Choosing the number of nearest neighbors
4. Determining the combination function

Choosing the Training Set

The training set consisted of 49,652 news stories, provided by Dow Jones for this purpose. These stories came from about three months of news and from almost 100 different sources. Each story contained, on average, 2,700 words and had eight codes assigned to it. The training set was not specially created, so the frequency of codes in the training set varied a great deal, mimicking the overall frequency of codes in news stories in general. Although this training set yielded good results, a better constructed training set with more examples of the rarer codes would probably have performed even better.

Choosing the Distance Function

The next step is choosing the distance function. In this case, a distance function already existed, based on a notion called *relevance feedback* that measures the similarity of two documents based on the words they contain. Relevance feedback was originally designed to return documents similar to a given document, as a way of refining searches. The most similar documents are the neighbors used for MBR.

Choosing the Combination Function

The next decision is the combination function. Assigning classification codes to news stories is a bit different from most classification prob-

---

Using Relevance Feedback to Create a Distance Function

Relevance feedback is a powerful technique that allows users to refine searches on text databases by asking the database to return documents similar to one they already have. In the course of doing this, the text database scores all the other documents in the database and returns those that are closest—along with a measure of closeness. This is the relevance feedback score. Calculating it goes as follows:

1. Common, noncontent-bearing words, such as "it," "and," and "of," were removed from the text of all stories in the training set. A total of 368 words in this category were identified and removed.
2. The next most common words, accounting for 20 percent of the words in the database, were removed from the text. Because these words are so common, they provide little information in distinguishing between documents.
3. The remaining words were collected into a dictionary of *searchable terms*. Each was assigned a weight inversely proportional to its frequency in the database. The particular weight was the negative of log in base 2 of the term's frequency in the training set.

lems because more than one code was assigned to each story. The ability to adapt MBR to this problem highlights its flexibility.

The combination function used a weighted summation technique. Each neighbor was assigned a weight proportional to the inverse of the distance between the neighbor and the unknown story—so weights would be big for neighbors at small distances. For example, say the neighbors of a story had the following region codes and weights, shown in Table 9.2.

The total score for a code was then the sum of the weights of the neighbors containing it. Then, codes with scores below a certain threshold value were eliminated. For instance, the score for R/FE (which is the region code for the Far East) is the sum of the weights of neighbors 1, 2, 3, and 4, since all of them contain the R/FE, yielding a score of 2.816. Table 9.3 gives the results for the six region codes contained by the neighbors. For these examples, a threshold of 1.0 leaves only three codes: R/CA, R/FE, and R/JA. The particular choice of threshold was based on experimenting with different values and is not important to understanding MBR.

---

4. Capitalized word pairs, such as "United States" and "New Mexico," were identified (automatically) and included in the dictionary of searchable terms.

5. To calculate the relevance feedback score for two stories, the weights of the searchable terms in both stories are added together. The algorithm used for this case study included a bonus when terms appeared close together.

The relevance feedback score is an example of the adaptation of an already-existing function for use as a distance function. However, the score itself does not quite fit the definition of a distance function. In particular, a score of 0 indicates that two stories have no words in common, instead of implying that the stories are identical. The following transformation converts the relevance feedback score to a distance function:

$$d_{\text{classification}}(A,B) = 1 - \frac{\text{score}(A,B)}{\text{score}(A,A)}$$

This is the function used to find the nearest neighbors.

Table 9.2 Classified Neighbors of an Not-Yet-Classified Story

Neighbor	Distance	Weight	Codes
1	0.076	0.924	R/FE,R/CA,R/CO
2	0.346	0.654	R/FE,R/JA,R/CA
3	0.369	0.631	R/FE,R/JA,R/MI
4	0.393	0.607	R/FE,R/JA,R/CA

Table 9.3 Code Scores for the Not-Yet-Classified Story

Code	1	2	3	4	Score
R/CA	0.924	0	0	0.607	1.531
R/CO	0.924	0	0	0	0.924
R/FE	0.924	0.654	0.631	0.607	2.816
R/JA	0	0.654	0.631	0.607	1.892
R/MI	0	0.654	0	0	0.624

Choosing the Number of Neighbors

The investigation varied the number of nearest neighbors between 1 and 11 inclusive. The best results came from using more neighbors. However, this case study is different from many applications of MBR because it is assigning multiple categories to each story. The more typical problem is to assign only a single category or code and fewer neighbors would be the rule in this case.

The Results

To measure the effectiveness of MBR on coding, the study asked a panel of editors to rate all the codes assigned, whether by editors or by MBR, to 200 stories. Only codes agreed upon by a majority of the panel were considered "correct."

The comparison of the "correct" codes to the codes originally assigned by human editors was interesting. Eighty-eight percent of the codes originally assigned to the stories were correct. However, the human editors made mistakes. A total of 17 percent of the codes originally assigned by human editors were incorrect (see Figure 9.5).

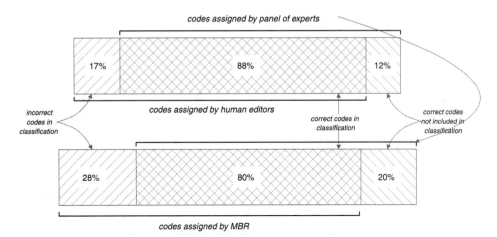

Figure 9.5 A comparison of results by human editors and by MBR on assigning codes to news stories.

MBR did not do quite as well. For MBR, the corresponding percentages were 80 percent and 28 percent. That is, 80 percent of the codes assigned by MBR were correct, but the cost was that 28 percent of the codes assigned were incorrect.

The mix of editors assigning the original codes, though, included novice, intermediate, and experienced editors. The MBR system actually performed as well as intermediate editors and better than novice editors. Also, MBR was using stories classified by the same mix of editors, so the training set was not consistently coded. Given the inconsistency in the training set, it is surprising that MBR did as well as it did. The study was not able to investigate using MBR on a training set verified by the panel of experts because there were not enough verified stories for a viable training set.

This case study illustrates that MBR can be used for solving difficult problems that might not easily be solved by other means. Most data mining techniques cannot handle textual data and assigning multiple categories at the same time is problematic. With some experimentation, this case study shows that MBR can produce results comparable to human experts. This study achieved these results with about two person-months of effort (not counting development of the relevance feedback engine). By comparison, other automated classification techniques, such as those based on expert systems, require many person-years of effort to achieve equivalent results for classifying news stories.

Measuring the Effectiveness of Assigning Codes: Recall and Precision

Recall and *precision* are two measurements that are useful when measuring how well a set of codes gets assigned. They are particularly useful when multiple codes are being assigned. The case study on coding news stories, for instance, is assigning many codes to news stories and shows how these measurements are used.

Recall answers the question: "How many of the correct codes did MBR assign to the story?" It is the ratio of codes assigned by MBR that are correct (as verified by editors) to the total number of correct codes on the story. If MBR assigns all available codes to every story, then recall is 100 percent because the correct codes all get assigned, along with many other irrelevant codes. If MBR assigns no codes to any story, then recall is 0 percent.

Precision answers the question: "How many of the codes assigned by MBR were correct?" It is the percentage of correct codes assigned by MBR to the total number of codes assigned by MBR. Precision is 100 percent when MBR assigns only correct codes to a story. It is close to 0 percent when MBR assigns all codes to every story. Table 9.4 gives some insight into these measurements.

The original codes assigned to the stories by individual editors had a recall of 83 percent and a precision of 88 percent with respect to the validated set of correct codes. For MBR, the recall was 80 percent and the precision 72 percent. However, Table 9.5 is an average across all categories. MBR did significantly better in some of the categories.

The variation in the results by category suggests that the original stories used for the training set may not have been coded consistently. The re-

---

MEASURING DISTANCE

Say your travels take you to a small town and you want to know the weather. There is no information from the usual sources—the Weather Channel, Web pages, the newspaper—because these sources only cover major cities. What you would typically do (if you can't call someone in the town) is find the weather for larger cities near the small town. You might look at the closest city and just take its weather, or do some sort of combination of the forecasts for, say, the three closest cities. This is an example of using MBR to find the weather forecast. The distance function being used is the geographic distance between the two locations.

sults from MBR can only be as good as the examples chosen for the training set. Even so, MBR performed as well as many experienced editors.

Table 9.4 Examples of Recall and Precision

Codes by MBR	Correct Codes	Recall	Precision
A,B,C,D	A,B,C,D	100%	100%
A,B	A,B,C,D	50%	100%
A,B,C,D,E,F,G,H	A,B,C,D	100%	50%
E,F	A,B,C,D	0%	0%
A,B,E,F	A,B,C,D	50%	50%

Table 9.5 Recall and Precision Measurements by Code Category

Category	Recall	Precision
Government	85%	87%
Industry	91%	85%
Market Sector	93%	91%
Product	69%	89%
Region	86%	64%
Subject	72%	53%

What Is a Distance Function?

Distance is the way the MBR measures similarity. Fortunately, distance has a very intuitive meaning. The distance from point A to point B, denoted by d(A,B), has four key properties:

1. **Well-defined.** The distance between two points is always defined and is a non-negative real number, $d(A,B) \geq 0$.
2. **Identity.** The distance from one point to itself is always zero, so $d(A,A) = 0$.
3. **Commutativity.** Direction does not make a distance, so the distance from A to B is the same as the distance from B to A: $d(A,B) = d(B,A)$. This property precludes one-way roads, for instance.

4. Triangle Inequality. Visiting an intermediate point C on the way from A to B never shortens the distance, so d(A,B) ≥ d(A,C) + d(C,B).

For MBR, the points are really records in a database. This formal definition of distance is the basis for measuring similarity, but MBR still works pretty well when some of these constraints are relaxed a bit. For instance, the distance function in the news story classification case study was not *commutative*; that is, the distance from a news story A to another B was not always the same as the distance from B to A. However, the similarity measure was still useful for classification purposes.

What makes these properties useful for MBR? The fact that distance is well-defined implies that every record has a neighbor somewhere in the database—and MBR needs neighbors in order to work. The identity property makes distance conform to the intuitive idea that the most similar record to a given record is the original record itself. Commutativity and the Triangle Inequality make the nearest neighbors local and well-behaved. Adding a new record into the database will not bring an existing record any closer. Similarity is a matter reserved for just two records.

Although distance is used to find nearest neighbors, the set of nearest neighbors can have some peculiar properties. For instance, the nearest neighbor to a record B may be A, but A may have many neighbors closer than B, as shown in Figure 9.6.

Building a Distance Function One Field at a Time

It is easy to understand distance as a geometric concept, but how can we build a distance function for records consisting of many different fields of different types? The answer is, one field at a time. Consider some sample records like those shown in Table 9.6.

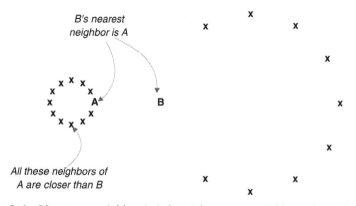

Figure 9.6 B's nearest neighbor is A, but A has many neighbors closer than B.

Table 9.6 Five Customers in a Marketing Database

Recnum	Gender	Age	Salary
1	female	27	$ 19,000
2	male	51	$ 64,000
3	male	52	$105,000
4	female	33	$ 55,000
5	male	45	$ 45,000

Figure 9.7 illustrates a scatter graph in three dimensions. The records are a bit complicated, with two numeric fields and one categorical. This example shows how to define field distance functions for each field, then combine them into a single record distance function that gives a distance between two records.

The three most common distance functions for numeric fields are:

- Absolute value of the difference: $|A-B|$
- Square of the difference: $(A-B)^2$
- Normalized absolute value: $|A-B|/(\text{maximum difference})$

The advantage of the normalized absolute value is that it is always between 0 and 1. Since the ages are much smaller than the salaries in this example, the normalized absolute value is the best choice for both of them—so neither field will dominate the record distance function. For the ages, the distance matrix looks like Table 9.7.

Gender is an example of categorical data. The simplest distance function is the "identical to" function, which is 1 when the genders are the same and 0 otherwise:

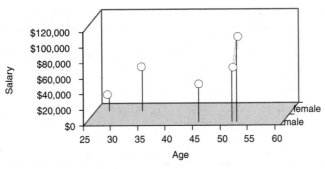

Figure 9.7 This scatter graph is for five records in three dimensions.

Table 9.7 Distance Matrix of Customers from Each Other

	27	*51*	*51*	*33*	*45*
27	0.00	0.96	0.96	0.24	0.72
51	0.96	0.00	0.00	0.72	0.24
52	1.00	0.04	0.04	0.76	0.28
33	0.24	0.72	0.72	0.00	0.48
45	0.72	0.24	0.24	0.48	0.00

d_{gender}(female, female) = 0
d_{gender}(female, male)   = 1
d_{gender}(female, female) = 1
d_{gender}(male, male)   = 0

So far, so simple. There are now three field distance functions that need to merge into a single record distance function. There are three common ways to do this:

- Summation: $d_{sum}(A,B) = d_{gender}(A,B) + d_{age}(A,B) + d_{salary}(A,B)$
- Normalized summation: $d_{norm}(A,B) = d_{sum}(A,B) / max(d_{sum})$
- Euclidean distance: $d_{euclid}(A,B) = sqrt(d_{gender}(A,B)^2 + d_{age}(A,B)^2 + d_{salary}(A,B)^2)$

Table 9.8 shows the nearest neighbors for each of the points using the three functions.

In this case, the sets of nearest neighbors are exactly the same for all three functions. This is a coincidence, caused by the fact that the five records fall into two well-defined clusters. One of the clusters is

Table 9.8 Set of Nearest Neighbors for Three Distance Functions

	d_{sum}	$D_{normalized}$	D_{euclid}
1	1,4,5,2,3	1,4,5,2,3	1,4,5,2,3
2	2,5,3,4,1	2,5,3,4,1	2,5,3,4,1
3	3,2,5,4,1	3,2,5,4,1	3,2,5,4,1
4	4,1,5,2,3	4,1,5,2,3	4,1,5,2,3
5	5,2,3,4,1	5,2,3,4,1	5,2,3,4,1

lower-paid, younger females and the other is better-paid, older males. These clusters imply that if two records are close to each other relative to one field, then they are close on all fields, so the way the distances on each field are combined is not important. This is not a very common situation.

Consider what happens when a new record (Table 9.9) is used for the comparison.

This new record is not in either of the clusters. Table 9.10 shows her respective distances from the training set with the list of her neighbors, from nearest to furthest.

Now the set of neighbors depends very much on how the record distance function combines the field distance functions. In fact, the second nearest neighbor using the summation function is the farthest neighbor using the Euclidean and vice versa. Compared to the summation or normalized metric, the Euclidean metric tends to favor neighbors where all the fields are relatively close. It punishes Record 3 because the genders are different and are maximally far apart (a distance of 1.00). Correspondingly, it favors Record 1 because the genders are the same. Note that the neighbors for d_{sum} and d_{norm} are identical. The definition of the normalized distance preserves the ordering of the summation distance—the distances values are just shifted to the range from 0 to 1.

The summation, Euclidean, and normalized functions can also incorporate weights so each field contributes a different amount to the record distance function. MBR usually produces good results when all the weights are equal to 1. However, sometimes weights can be used to incorporate a priori knowledge, such as a particular field suspected of having a large effect on the classification.

Table 9.9 New Customer

Recnum	Gender	Age	Salary
new	female	45	$100,000

Table 9.10 Set of Nearest Neighbors for New Customer

	1	2	3	4	5	Neighbors
d_{sum}	1.662	1.659	1.338	1.003	1.640	4,3,5,2,1
d_{norm}	0.554	0.553	0.446	0.334	0.547	4,3,5,2,1
d_{euclid}	0.781	1.052	1.251	0.494	1.000	4,1,5,2,3

Distance Functions for Other Data Types

A 5-digit American zip code is usually represented as a simple numeric type. Do any of the default distance functions for numeric fields make any sense? No. The difference between two randomly chosen zip codes has no meaning, so perhaps a zip code is more like a categorical data type. Well, almost, except that a zip code does encode location information. The first three digits represent a postal zone—for instance, all zip codes on Manhattan start with "100." One way of handling zip codes is to just drop the last two digits and treat the remaining digits as a category. For instance, the codes "10014," "10001," and "10016" would all become "100." The distance between any two of these would be 0, but between them and any other zip code (like "101" or "954") would be 1.

Another way of handling this problem would be to define a special distance function. This function might look like:

- $d_{zip}(A,B) = 0$ when the first three digits are the same
- $d_{zip}(A,B) = 1$ when the first three digits differ

What is the advantage to defining a special function? The major advantage is that it allows experimentation. Instead of massaging the original zip code to have just three digits, the special functions allows the zip code to stay the same and just the function to change. For instance, further refining of the function might be useful:

- $d_{zip-refined}(A,B) = 0.0$ if the zip codes are identical
- $d_{zip-refined}(A,B) = 0.1$ if the first three digits are identical (e.g., "20008" and "20015"
- $d_{zip-refined}(A,B) = 0.5$ if the first digits are identical (e.g., "95050" and "98125")
- $d_{zip-refined}(A,B) = 1.0$ if the first digits are not identical (e.g., "02138" and "90024")

This distance function captures more of the information in a zip code. After all, codes that start with a "0" are in New England and codes that start with a "9" are in the West—and this information could be relevant for predictive purposes. This function still preserves the fact that fields with identical zip codes are closer than fields where the zip codes merely start with the same digit.

This is just one example of code values that might have special distance functions. Telephone numbers and product codes are two other examples where a special function might prove useful to capture information about a value hierarchy. Developing distance metrics for these hierarchies can increase the effectiveness of MBR.

When a Distance Metric Already Exists

There are some situations where a distance metric already exists, although it may be difficult to spot. These situations generally arise in one of two forms. Sometimes there are hidden categorical fields that can really be used as the basis for a distance function. In other cases, a function exists that provides a distance measure between two records. The news story case study provides a good example of adapting an existing function, relevance feedback, for use as a distance function.

An example of a hidden categorical field is solicitation history. Two customers who were chosen for a particular solicitation in the past are "close," even though the reasons why they were chosen may no longer be available; two who were not, are close, but not as close; and one that was chosen and one that was not are far apart. The advantage of this metric is that it can incorporate previous decisions, even if the basis for the decisions is no longer available. On the other hand, it does not work well for customers who were not around during the original solicitation; so some sort of neutral weighting must be applied to them.

Considering whether the original customers responded to the solicitation can extend this function further, resulting in a solicitation metric like:

- $d_{solicitation}(A, B) = 0$, when A and B both responded to the solicitation
- $d_{solicitation}(A, B) = 0.1$, when A and B were both chosen but neither responded
- $d_{solicitation}(A, B) = 0.2$, when neither A nor B was chosen, but both were available in the data
- $d_{solicitation}(A, B) = 0.3$, when A and B were both chosen, but only one responded
- $d_{solicitation}(A, B) = 0.3$, when one or both were not considered
- $d_{solicitation}(A, B) = 1.0$, when one was chosen and the other was not

Of course, the particular values are not sacrosanct; they are only meant as a guide for measuring similarity and showing how previous information and response histories can be incorporated into a distance function.

THE COMBINATION FUNCTION: ASKING THE NEIGHBORS FOR THE ANSWER

Let's return to the example of travelling to a small town and trying to determine its weather. The previous section gave us guidelines for establishing a distance function (although in this case, the distance between two geographic sites is easy to figure out from their latitude and longitude). This section presents different ways that the data from the neighbors can be gathered together. The vagaries of weather provide a good example. For instance, depth of snowfall tends to be highly local. A hurricane hitting a few hundred miles away may have no effect on rain or wind in a particular location—or could have disastrous effects depending on the storm's path. A tornado may hit in one location, while the sun shines five miles away. Although hurricanes, blizzards, and tornadoes do not generally exist in the data used for data mining, the shifting patterns of weather are a useful analogy for understanding the patterns that may exist inside a database. The nature of these patterns places limits on making decisions based strictly on local neighborhoods. However, despite occasional exceptions, nearby conditions are, more often than not, the best predictors for weather—and for the patterns found in databases used for data mining. This section illustrates common types of combination functions.

The Basic Approach: Democracy

The basic combination function used for MBR is to have the k nearest neighbors vote on the answer—"democracy" in data mining. This approach starts by determining the number of neighbors to consider. The classification for the instance is simply the majority vote of the classifications of the neighbors. To avoid tie-breaking situations, k should be odd when there are only two categories. In general, a good rule of thumb is to use $c+1$ neighbors when there are c categories.

An example is provided by augmenting the five test cases seen earlier with a flag that signals whether the customer has attrited (Table 9.11).

Table 9.11 Customers with Attrition History

Recnum	Gender	Age	Salary	Attriter
1	female	27	$19,000	no
2	male	51	$64,000	yes
3	male	52	$105,000	yes
4	female	33	$55,000	yes
5	male	45	$45,000	no
new	female	45	$100,000	?

For this example, three of the customers have attrited and two have not; this is typical since we want about the same number of examples for each category in the training set. For illustration purposes, let's try to determine if the new record is or is not an attriter using different values of k for the two distance functions already considered, d_{euclid} and d_{norm} (Table 9.12).

The question marks indicate that there is a tie among the neighbors, so no prediction can be made. In practice you would arbitrarily assign the classification of the nearest neighbor when there is a tie. The first thing to notice is that different values of k do affect the classification. This suggests incorporating a confidence level in the prediction, by using the percentage of neighbors in agreement (Table 9.13).

The confidence level works just as well when there are more than two categories. However, with more categories, there is a greater chance that no single category will have a majority vote. One of the key assumptions about MBR (and data mining in general) is that the training set provides sufficient information for predictive purposes. If the neighborhoods of new cases consistently produce no obvious choice of classification, then the data simply may not contain the necessary information and the choice of training set needs to be reevaluated. By measuring the effectiveness of MBR on the test set, you can determine whether the training set has a sufficient number of examples.

Table 9.12   Using MBR to Determine if the New Customer Will Attrite

	Neighbors	Neighbor Attrition	$k = 1$	$k = 2$	$k = 3$	$k = 4$	$k = 5$
d_{sum}	4,3,5,2,1	Y,Y,N,Y,N	yes	yes	yes	yes	yes
d_{Euclid}	4,1,5,2,3	Y,N,N,Y,Y	yes	?	no	?	yes

Table 9.13   Attrition Prediction with Confidence

	$k = 1$	$k = 2$	$k = 3$	$k = 4$	$k = 5$
d_{sum}	yes, 100%	yes, 100%	yes, 67%	yes, 75%	yes, 60%
d_{Euclid}	yes, 100%	yes, 50%	no, 67%	yes, 50%	yes, 60%

> ### TIP
>
> The effectiveness of MBR is only as good as the training set it uses. To measure whether the training set is effective, measure the results of its predictions on the test set using two, three, and four neighbors. If the results often disagree with each other, are inconclusive, or inaccurate, then the training set is not large enough.

Weighted Voting

Weighted voting is similar to voting except that the neighbors are not all created equal—more like shareholder democracy instead of one-person, one-vote. The size of the vote is inversely proportional to the distance from the new record, so closer neighbors have stronger votes than neighbors farther away do. To prevent problems when the distance might be 0, it is common to add 1 to the distance before taking the inverse. Adding 1 also makes all the votes between 0 and 1.

Let's apply this voting scheme to the previous example. In Table 9.14 the "yes, this is an attriter" vote is the first; the "no, this is a good customer" vote is second.

Now, there are no ambiguities. Weighted voting usually introduces enough variation to prevent ties, although the votes can still be close. The same confidence level can still be introduced, this time as the fraction of winning votes to total votes (Table 9.15).

Table 9.14 Attrition Prediction with Weighted Voting

	k = 1	*k = 2*	*k = 3*	*k = 4*	*k = 5*
d_{sum}	**0.749** to 0	**1.441** to 0	**1.441** to 0.647	**2.085** to 0.647	**2.085** to 1.290
d_{Euclid}	**0.669** to 0	**0.669** to 0.562	0.669 to **1.062**	**1.157** to 1.062	**1.601** to 1.062

Table 9.15 Confidence with Weighted Voting

	1	*2*	*3*	*4*	*5*
d_{sum}	yes, 100%	yes, 100%	yes, 69%	yes, 76%	yes, 62%
d_{Euclid}	yes, 100%	yes, 54%	no, 61%	yes, 52%	yes, 60%

Weighting the votes has had only a small effect on the results and the confidence. The biggest effect is the elimination of ambiguous results for even numbers of nearest neighbors. Weighting the votes has its largest effect when some of the neighbors are considerably further away than closer neighbors. Without weighting, the further neighbors are equal to the nearer neighbors. With weighting, the vote of the distant neighbors is much less significant. The decision to use weighted voting or unweighted voting can be determined by using the test set and checking which performs better on the particular problem.

Combining Statistical Regression Techniques with MBR for Numeric and Ordered Values

The voting and weight voting combination functions do not produce very good results for numeric and continuous values. For a numeric prediction, it is likely that the values on the neighbors will all be different, so there is little use in tallying votes. The simplest way to combine the neighbors is using interpolation, where the neighboring values are simply averaged together. This has some distinct disadvantages since interpolation smoothes out the data. For instance, the value for the new record can never be larger than the largest value in the training set and can never be smaller than the smallest value.

A better approach is to borrow some ideas from statistics. The key idea here is regression, which fits a particular function, usually a line, to some points and uses the function to calculate the unknown value. Figure 9.8 shows an example of using linear regression to make a prediction in the financial markets. This example is overly simple, since it is trying to calculate one variable (change in stock market) from just a single other variable (current inflation rate). Typically, the prediction would be made using several other variables—but that would be hard to illustrate. This graph shows the inflation at a point in time on the horizontal axis for a specific country and the change in the stock market in that country one year later on the vertical axis. Using this information for several countries, can the change in the stock market value be predicted based on the current inflation rate? Figure 9.8 shows the *best fit* line for the data. For any given inflation rate in a country, the estimated change in the stock market one year later can be found along this line.

In this example, regression may not be working as well as it could. The reason is that no single function does a good job of capturing all the local variations in the data. However, combining regression with the nearest neighbor approach of MBR incorporates the best of the two

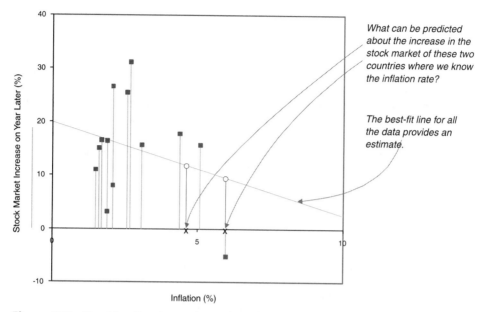

Figure 9.8 Graphing the change in stock market indexes based on inflation for different countries provides an example of how linear regression can be used to make a prediction given only one variable, the inflation rate.

methods. Applying regression just to the nearest neighbors focuses it on local phenomena. Figure 9.9 shows an example of this. The best-fit line for the last three points in the data is quite different from the best-fit line for all the data. It is taking into account local behavior.

GETTING THE BEST RESULTS

MBR is a very powerful data mining technique that can be used to solve a wide variety of directed data mining problems. This section provides some hints and guidance for obtaining the best results from MBR.

Choosing the right training set is perhaps the most important step in MBR. The training set needs to include sufficient numbers of instances for all possible classifications. This may mean enriching it by including a disproportionate number of instances for rare classifications, such as customers who have attrited or examples of fraud, so it includes a balance of roughly the same number of instances for all cat-

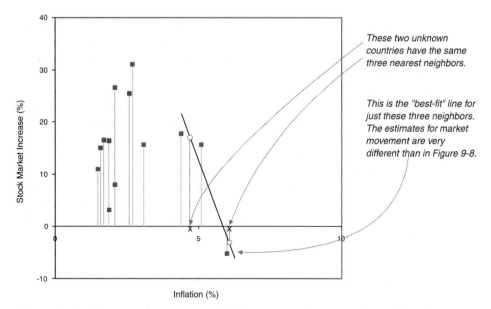

These two unknown
countries have the same
three nearest neighbors.

This is the "best-fit" line for
just these three neighbors.
The estimates for market
movement are very
different than in Figure 9-8.

Figure 9.9   This example uses MBR with linear regression to predict stock market movement for countries based on their measured inflation rate. The regression is applied only to
the nearest neighbors (i.e., those countries with the most similar inflation rates).

egories. A training set that includes only instances of bad customers
will predict that all customers are bad. In general, the size of the training set should measure in the thousands, preferably the hundreds of
thousands, depending on the application, available data, and available
computing power.

The basic distance functions presented in this chapter produce
good results. The field distance functions should return values in the
same range, typically normalized to between 0 and 1. One important
decision is how to combine the field distance functions into a record
distance function, using the summation metric or Euclidean metric.
The Euclidean method wants as many fields as possible to have similar values; the summation is more forgiving—a large difference on one
field can more easily be offset by close values on other fields. The particular data being used may suggest one method over another, by applying both to the test set and seeing which produces better results.
Sometimes, the right choice of neighbors depends on modifying the distance function to favor some fields over others. This is easily accomplished by incorporating weights into the record distance function.

The next question is the number of neighbors to choose. Once again, investigating different numbers of neighbors using the test set can help determine the optimal number. There is no right number of neighbors. The number depends on the distribution of the data and is highly dependent on the problem being solved. When using MBR with statistical regression techniques, the number of neighbors must be at least one more than the number of fields in the records to ensure that there are enough samples for the regression.

The basic combination function, weighted voting, does a good job for categorical data, using weights inversely proportional to distance. For predicting continuous values, the best approach is to incorporate statistical regression techniques into the nearest neighbor approach. Calculate the best-fit line for the set of nearest neighbors, and use the line for predictive purposes.

STRENGTHS OF MEMORY-BASED REASONING

The strengths of MBR are:

- It produces results that are readily understandable.
- It is applicable to arbitrary data types, even non-relational data.
- It works efficiently on almost any number of fields.
- Maintaining the training set requires a minimal amount of effort.

Results Are Readily Understandable

The list of nearest neighbors provides an explanation of how MBR arrives at a specific result. This is not the explicit if-then rules generated by market basket analysis or decision trees that can readily be turned into SQL, though. Instead of rules, the list is saying, "I made this prediction because the new record is a lot like these records." This provides enough information to tell if the distance function and training set are working well or if they need to be updated, but it does not give global insight into the data.

Applicable to Arbitrary Data Types, Even Non-relational Data

MBR is a very general technique that does not depend on the underlying representation of the data. Unlike most of the other data mining techniques, MBR only depends upon the existence of two functions, the distance function and the combination function, and not on the representation of the data.

For common types of data, such as numeric and categorical data, MBR can make use of standard functions that perform well. However, MBR has been applied to a wide variety of other data, including images, text, and audio, that are not as amenable to other data mining techniques.

Works Well on Any Number of Fields

The performance of MBR depends more on the size of the training set than on the number of fields in the records. This makes it practical to use when other techniques, like neural networks, cannot make sense of the data. Being able to work on many fields is an advantage when using MBR on summarized data, such as credit bureau histories purchased from outside vendors or records containing extensive roll-ups of customer behavior.

Minimal Effort to Maintain Training Set

The training set defines how well MBR works and it is remarkably easy to maintain. As new categories are introduced, new records for those categories can be added directly into the training set—and MBR takes advantage of them. This is a stark contrast to neural networks or decision trees that require an extensive period of retraining in order to ingest new information.

WEAKNESSES OF MEMORY-BASED REASONING

Weaknesses of MBR are:

- It is computationally expensive when doing classification and prediction.
- It requires a large amount of storage for the training set.
- Results can be dependent on the choice of distance function, combination function, and number of neighbors.

Computationally Intensive during Prediction Phase

The performance penalty for MBR usually occurs during the prediction phase instead of the training phase. Although it is possible to optimize the storage of the training set to improve the performance of prediction, this phase is always rather expensive because finding the nearest neighbors involves applying the distance function to all the fields in the record and all the records in the training set. By contrast, decision trees and neural networks incorporate the training set into their models, then discard the training set.

Large Amount of Storage for Training Set

The training set used by MBR is the model, and the larger the training set the better the results. Although there are some techniques for reducing the number of records in the training set, the remaining records must still be represented. By contrast, the size of a neural network model depends only on the topology of the network and has no dependency on the size of the training set.

Dependence on Distance Function and Combination Function

The results from MBR do depend on the particular choice of distance function, combination function, and k, the number of neighbors chosen. Different choices can affect the results. Fortunately, common choices work pretty well. It is fairly easy to use a test set to find the best choice of k. Only if the results for all values of k are disappointing should you consider changing the distance and combination functions.

WHEN TO APPLY MEMORY-BASED REASONING

Memory-based reasoning is a directed data mining technique useful for both classification and prediction. In comparison with other techniques, it works well when the patterns in the data are likely to be highly local, so global rules and global functions do not make sense. For example, there may be many reasons why customers stop buying from a particular catalog—new shops open in their neighborhood, they are inundated by other catalogs, they lose their job, get a big promotion, and so forth. This is a good example of where MBR would be very applicable. On the other hand, there are fewer reasons why customers regularly make purchases in December—probably for giving gifts—so MBR is probably less useful to predict which customer needs a holiday catalog.

In short, MBR is a powerful technique that incorporates local information for classification and prediction purposes. The more complicated the data, the more likely it is that local patterns dominate the patterns, making MBR useful in many different circumstances.

10

Automatic Cluster Detection

We are always being told to "look at the big picture." But the fact is, sometimes the big picture is too confusing to be understood. A large database may contain so many variables, so many dimensions, and so much complex structure that even the best-directed data mining techniques are unable to coax meaningful patterns from it. In many cases, the problem is not that there are no patterns to be found, but that there are too many. When mining such a database for the answer to some specific question, we often find nothing but noise. Competing explanations cancel each other out.

When human beings try to make sense of complex questions, our natural tendency is to break the subject into smaller pieces, each of which can be explained more simply. If someone were to ask you to describe the color of trees in the forest, your answer would probably make distinctions between deciduous trees, conifers, and other evergreens, and between winter, spring, summer, and fall. You know enough about woodland flora to predict that, of all the hundreds of variables associated with the forest, season and foliage type, rather than say altitude and soil acidity, are the best discriminators to use for forming clusters of trees that follow similar coloration rules.

In marketing terms, subdividing the population according to variables already known to be good discriminators is called "segmentation." But in many cases, although we may suspect that a very noisy dataset is actually composed of a number of better behaved clusters, we have no idea how to define them. That's where techniques for automatic cluster detection come in—when you can't see the forest without knowing a bit more about the trees.

SEARCHING FOR ISLANDS OF SIMPLICITY

Clustering is one of the few data mining activities that can properly be described as undirected knowledge discovery or unsupervised learning. For most data mining tasks, we start out with a preclassified training set and attempt to develop a model capable of predicting how a new record will be classified. In clustering, there is no preclassified data and no distinction between independent and dependent variables. Instead, we are searching for groups of records—the clusters—that are similar to one another, in the expectation that similar records represent similar customers or suppliers or products that will behave in similar ways.

Automatic cluster detection is rarely used in isolation because finding clusters is not an end in itself. Once clusters have been detected, other methods must be applied in order to figure out what the clusters mean. When clustering is successful, the results can be dramatic: One famous early application of cluster detection led to our current understanding of stellar evolution.

Star Light, Star Bright

Early in this century, astronomers trying to understand the relationship between the luminosity (brightness) of stars and their temperatures, made scatter plots like the one in Figure 10.1. The vertical scale measures luminosity in multiples of the brightness of our own sun. The horizontal scale measures surface temperature in degrees Kelvin (degrees centigrade above absolute 0, the theoretical coldest possible temperature where molecular motion ceases).

As you can see, the stars plotted by astronomers, Hertzsprung and Russell, fall into three clusters. We now understand that these three clusters represent stars in very different phases in the stellar life cycle. The relationship between luminosity and temperature is consistent within each cluster, but the relationship is different in each cluster because a fundamentally different process is generating the heat and light. The 80 percent of stars that fall on the main sequence are generating energy by converting hydrogen to helium through nuclear fusion. This is how all stars spend most of their life. But after 10 bil-

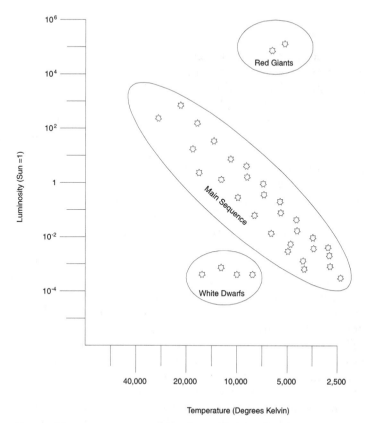

Figure 10.1   The Hertzsprung-Russell diagram clusters stars by temperature and luminosity.

lion years or so, the hydrogen gets used up. Depending on the star's mass, it then begins fusing helium or the fusion stops. In the latter case, the core of the star begins to collapse, generating a great deal of heat in the process. At the same time, the outer layer of gasses expands away from the core. A red giant is formed. Eventually, the outer layer of gasses is stripped away and the remaining core begins to cool. The star is now a white dwarf.

A recent query of the Alta Vista web index using the search terms "HR diagram" and "main sequence" returned many pages of links to current astronomical research based on cluster detection of this kind. This simple, two-variable cluster diagram is being used today to hunt for new kinds of stars like "brown dwarfs" and to understand pre-main sequence stellar evolution.

Fitting the Troops

We chose the Hertzsprung-Russell diagram as our introductory example of clustering because with only two variables, it is easy to spot the clusters visually. Even in three dimensions, it is easy to pick out clusters by eye from a scatter plot cube. If all problems had so few dimensions, there would be no need for automatic cluster detection algorithms. As the number of dimensions (independent variables) increases, our ability to visualize clusters and our intuition about the distance between two points quickly break down.

When we speak of a problem as having many dimensions, we are making a geometric analogy. We consider each of the things that must be measured independently in order to describe something to be a *dimension*. In other words, if there are N variables, we imagine a space in which the value of each variable represents a distance along the corresponding axis in an N-dimensional space. A single record containing a value for each of the N variables, can be thought of as the vector that defines a particular point in that space. Figure 10.2 plots the height and weight of a group of teenagers as points on a graph. Notice the clustering of boys and girls.

The chart in Figure 10.2 begins to give a rough idea of people's shapes. But if we wanted to fit them for clothes, we would need many more measurements! The U.S. army recently commissioned a study on how to redesign the uniforms of female soldiers. The army's goal is to reduce the number of different uniform sizes that have to be kept in inventory while still providing each soldier with well-fitting khakis.

As anyone who has ever shopped for women's clothing is aware, there is already a surfeit of classification systems (odd sizes, even sizes, junior, petite, etc.) for categorizing garments by size, but none of these systems was designed with the needs of the U.S. military in mind. Susan Ashdown and Beatrix Paal, researchers at Cornell University, went back to the basics; they designed a new set of sizes based on the actual shapes of women in the army.

Unlike the traditional clothing size systems, the one Ashdown and Paal came up with is not an ordered set of graduated sizes where all dimensions increase together. Instead, they came up with sizes that fit particular body types. So, one size might be for short-legged, small-waisted, large-busted women with long torsos, average arms, broad shoulders, and skinny necks while other sizes fit other constellations of measurements.

The database they mined contained more than 100 measurements for each of nearly 3,000 women. The clustering technique employed in

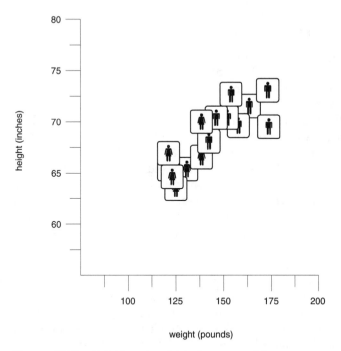

Figure 10.2   Height and weight of a group of teenagers.

this case was the K-means algorithm. In this approach, the first step is to choose the number of clusters (uniform sizes, in this case) that you want to form. That number is the *K* in K-means. Next, K "seeds" are chosen to be the initial guess at the centroids of the clusters. Each seed is just a particular combination of values for each measurement. Each seed might record the actual measurements of one of the women in the sample, but that is not a requirement.

Next, each record in the database is given a preliminary cluster assignment based on the seed to which it is closest. Then the centroids (or *means*) of the new clusters are calculated and the whole process starts over with the new centroids taking on the role of the seeds. Since the new centroids will not be in the same place as the original seeds, some of the records will be moved from the first cluster to which they were assigned to another one. (Actually, it is the cluster boundaries that move, not the points described by the records.) After a few iterations, this motion stops and the centroid of each cluster contains the measurements that define one of the new uniform sizes.

Spotting the Entrepreneurs

A third application of automatic cluster detection is described in Chapter 3. In that example, a bank used an automatic cluster detection technique to find clusters of similar customers in its customer information warehouse.

Although the clothing size example was undirected data mining in the sense that there were no pre-defined size categories to be found, the bank's quest was even less-directed. In the former case, the number of clusters to be found was imposed externally by the army which only wants to deal with a certain small number of uniform sizes. Furthermore, there could be no doubt about the meaning of the clusters once found. Since all the variables are body measurements, they are all in comparable units and each cluster clearly represents a certain body type.

The bank, on the other hand, has variables that measure many different things in many different units. There is no clear right way to compare outstanding balances with customer tenure or home zip code. The clusters found will depend greatly on the way these dissimilar values are scaled and weighted. With the bank's data, there is no obvious way to chose a value for K, the number of clusters to be formed. Worse, there is no readily available interpretation of any clusters that are found.

In fact, the bank found 14 clusters and only came up with a useful interpretation of one of them. But, that one cluster was so useful that nobody minded that they couldn't make sense of the other 13. The useful cluster was very rich in people who had both personal and business accounts with the bank and with people rated likely to respond to a home equity loan offer. This combination of traits led the bank to a new marketing premise—that people take out home equity loans in order to start a small business.

THE K-MEANS METHOD

The K-means method of cluster detection is the most commonly used in practice. It has many variations, but the form described here was first published by J. B. MacQueen in 1967. For ease of drawing, we illustrate the process using two-dimensional diagrams, but bear in mind that in practice we will usually be working in a space of many more dimensions. That means that instead of points described by a two-element vector (x_1, x_2), we work with points described by an n-element vector $(x_1, x_2, \ldots, x_n)$. The procedure itself is unchanged.

In the first step, we select K data points to be the seeds. Mac-Queen's algorithm simply takes the first K records. In cases where the records have some meaningful order, it may be desirable to choose widely spaced records instead. Each of the seeds is an embryonic cluster with only one element. In this example, we use outside information about the data to set the number of clusters to 3.

In the second step, we assign each record to the cluster whose centroid is nearest. In Figure 10.3 we have done the first two steps. Drawing the boundaries between the clusters is easy if you recall from high school geometry that given two points, X and Y, all points that are equidistant from X and Y fall along a line that is half way along the line segment that joins X and Y and perpendicular to it. In Figure 10.3, the initial seeds are joined by dashed lines and the cluster boundaries constructed from them are solid lines. Of course, in three dimensions, these boundaries would be planes and in N dimensions they would be hyperplanes of dimension $N - 1$.

As we continue to work through the K-means algorithm, pay particular attention to the fate of the point with the box drawn around it.

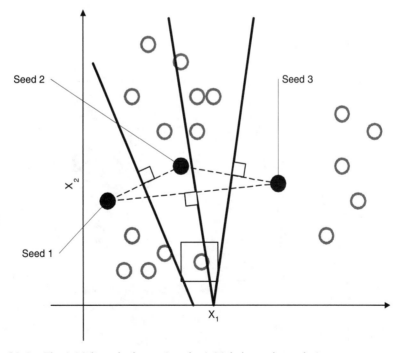

Figure 10.3   The initial seeds determine the initial cluster boundaries.

On the basis of the initial seeds, it is assigned to the cluster controlled by seed number 2 because it is closer to that seed than to either of the others.

At this point, every point has been assigned to one or another of the three clusters centered about the original seeds. The next step is to calculate the centroids of the new clusters. This is simply a matter of averaging the positions of each point in the cluster along each dimension. If there are 200 records assigned to a cluster and we are clustering based on four fields from those records, then geometrically we have 200 points in a 4-dimensional space. The location of each point is described by a vector of the values of the four fields. The vectors have the form (X_1, X_2, X_3, X_4). The value of X_1 for the new centroid is the mean of all 200 X_1s and similarly for X_2, X_3, and X_4.

In Figure 10.4, the new centroids are marked with a cross. The arrows show the motion from the position of the original seeds to the new centroids of the clusters formed from those seeds.

Once the new clusters have been found, each point is once again

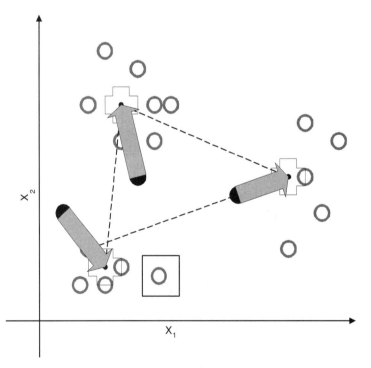

Figure 10.4 Calculating the centroids of the new clusters.

assigned to the cluster with the closest centroid. Figure 10.5 shows the new cluster boundaries—formed, as before, by drawing lines equidistant between each pair of centroids. Notice that the point with the box around it, which was originally assigned to cluster number 2, has now been assigned to cluster number 1. The process of assigning points to cluster and then re-calculating centroids continues until the cluster boundaries stop changing.

Similarity, Association, and Distance

After reading the preceding description of the K-means algorithm, we hope you agree that once the records in a database have been mapped to points in space, automatic cluster detection is really quite simple—a little geometry, some vector means, *et voilà*!

The problem, of course, is that the databases we encounter in marketing, sales, and customer support are not about points in space. They are about purchases, phone calls, airplane trips, car registrations,

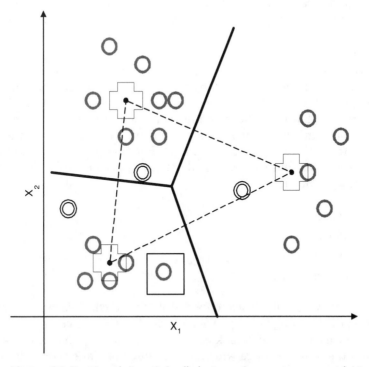

Figure 10.5 At each iteration, all cluster assignments are re-evaluated.

and a thousand other things that have no obvious connection to the dots in a cluster diagram.

When we speak of clustering records of this sort, we have an intuitive notion that members of a cluster have some kind of *natural association*; that they are more *similar* to each other than to records in another cluster. Since it is difficult to convey intuitive notions to a computer, we must translate the vague concept of association into some sort of numeric measure of the degree of similarity. The most common method, but by no means the only one, is to translate all fields into numeric values so that the records may be treated as points in space. Then, if two points are close in the geometric sense, we assume that they represent similar records in the database. There are two main problems with this approach:

1. Many variable types, including all categorical variables and many numeric variables such as rankings, do not have the right behavior to properly be treated as components of a position vector.
2. In geometry, the contributions of each dimension are of equal importance, but in our databases, a small change in one field may be much more important than a large change in another field.

A Variety of Variables

Variables can be categorized in various ways—by mathematical properties (continuous, discrete), by storage type (character, integer, floating point), and by other properties (quantitative, qualitative). For this discussion, however, the most important classification is how much the variable can tell us about its placement along the axis that corresponds to it in our geometric model. For this purpose, we can divide variables into four classes, listed here in increasing order of suitability for the geometric model.

Categories

Ranks

Intervals

True measures

Categorical variables only tell us to which of several unordered categories a thing belongs. We can say that this ice cream is pistachio while that one is mint-cookieo, but we cannot say that one is greater than the other or judge which one is closer to black cherry. In mathematical terms, we can tell that $X \neq Y$, but not whether $X > Y$ or $Y < X$.

Ranks allow us to put things in order, but don't tell us how much bigger one thing is than another. The valedictorian has better grades than the salutatorian, but we don't know by how much. If X, Y, and Z are ranked 1, 2, and 3, we know that X > Y > Z, but not whether (X – Y) > (Y – Z).

Intervals allow us to measure the distance between two observations. If we are told that it is 56° in San Francisco and 78° in San Jose, we know that it is 22 degrees warmer at one end of the bay than the other.

True measures are interval variables that measure from a meaningful zero point. This trait is important because it means that the ratio of two values of the variable is meaningful. The Fahrenheit temperature scale used in the United States and the Celsius scale used in most of the rest of the world do not have this property. In neither system does it make sense to say that a 30° day is twice as warm as a 15° day. Similarly, a size 12 dress is not twice as large as a size 6 and gypsum is not twice as hard as talc though they are 2 and 1 on the hardness scale. It does make perfect sense, however, to say that a 50-year-old is twice as old as a 25-year-old or that a 10-pound bag of sugar is twice as heavy as a 5-pound one. Age, weight, length, and volume are examples of true measures.

Geometric distance metrics are well-defined for interval variables and true measures. In order to use categorical variables and rankings, it is necessary to transform them into interval variables. Unfortunately, these transformations add spurious information. If we number ice cream flavors 1 through 28, it will appear that flavors 5 and 6 are closely related while flavors 1 and 28 are far apart. The inverse problem arises when we transform interval variables and true measures into ranks or categories. As we go from age (true measure) to seniority (position on a list) to broad categories like "veteran" and "new hire," we lose information at each step.

There is further discussion of these conversion issues as they apply to distance metrics in Chapter 9.

Formal Measures of Association

There are dozens if not hundreds of published techniques for measuring the similarity of two records. Some have been developed for specialized applications such as comparing passages of text. Others are designed especially for use with certain types of data such as binary variables or categorical variables. Of the three we present here, the first two are suitable for use with interval variables and true measures while the third is suitable for categorical variables.

The Distance between Two Points

Each field in a record becomes one element in a vector describing a point in space. The distance between two points is used as the measure of association. If two points are close in distance, the corresponding records are considered similar. There are actually a number of metrics that can be used to measure the distance between two points (see aside), but the most common one is the Euclidian distance we all learned in high school. To find the Euclidian distance between X and Y, we first find the differences between the corresponding elements of X and Y (the distance along each axis) and square them. The distance is the square root of the sum of the squared differences.

Distance Metrics

Any function that takes two points and produces a single number describing a relationship between them is a candidate measure of association, but to be a true distance metric, it must meet the following criteria:

- `Distance(X,Y)` $= 0$ if and only if $X = Y$
- `Distance(X,Y)` ≥ 0 for all X and all Y
- `Distance(X,Y)` $=$ `Distance(Y,X)`
- `Distance(X,Y)` $\leq$ `Distance(X,Z)` $+$ `Distance(Z,Y)`

The Angle between Two Vectors

Sometimes we would like to consider two records to be closely associated because of similarities in the way the fields *within* each record are related. We would like to cluster minnows with sardines, cod, and tuna, while clustering kittens with cougars, lions, and tigers even though in a database of body-part lengths, the sardine is closer to the kitten than it is to the tuna.

The solution is to use a different geometric interpretation of the same data. Instead of thinking of X and Y as points in space and measuring the distance between them, we think of them as *vectors* and measure the *angle* between them. In this context, a vector is the line segment connecting the origin of our coordinate system to the point described by the vector values. A vector has both magnitude (the distance from the origin to the point) and direction. For our purposes, it is the direction that matters.

If we take the values for length of whiskers, length of tail, overall body length, length of teeth, and length of claws for a lion and a house cat and plot them as single points, they will be very far apart. But if the ratios of lengths of these body parts to one another are similar in the two species, than the vectors will be nearly parallel.

The angle between vectors provides a measure of association that is not influenced by differences in magnitude between the two things being compared (see Figure 10.6). Actually, the sine of the angle is a better measure since it will range from 0 when the vectors are closest (most nearly parallel) to 1 when they are perpendicular without our having to worry about the actual angles or their signs.

The Number of Features in Common

When the preponderance of fields in the records we wish to compare are categorical variables, we abandon geometric measures and turn instead to measures based on the degree of overlap between records. As with the

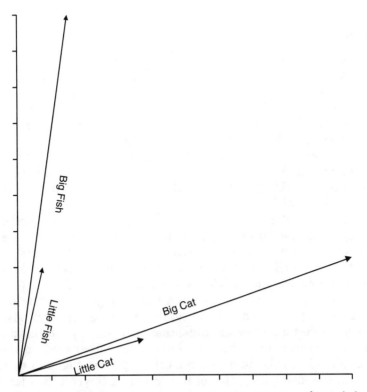

Figure 10.6 The angle between vectors as a measure of association.

geometric measures, there are many variations on this idea. In all variations, we compare two records field by field and count the number of fields that match and the number of fields that don't match. The simplest measure is the ratio of matches to the total number of fields.

In its simplest form, this measure counts two null fields as matching with the result that everything we don't know much about ends up in the same cluster. A simple improvement is to not include matches of this sort in the match count. Other variations are useful under various conditions. If the usual degree of overlap is high, you can give extra weight to unmatched fields by counting them double so that any minor mismatch is punished. If, on the other hand, the usual degree of overlap is low, you can give extra weight to matches to make sure that even a small overlap is rewarded.

The most sophisticated measures weight the matches by the prevalence of each class in the general population. After all, a match on "1956 Chevy Nomad" ought to count for more than a match on "1997 Ford Taurus."

What K Means

Clusters form some subset of the field variables tend to vary together. If all the variables are truly independent, no clusters will form—the entire space will be filled with an even haze of data points. At the opposite extreme, if all the variables are dependent on the same thing (in other words, if they are co-linear), then all the records will form a single cluster. In between these extremes, we don't really know how many clusters to expect. If we go looking for a certain number of clusters, we may find them. But that doesn't mean that there aren't other perfectly good clusters lurking in the data where we could find them by trying a different value of K.

In his excellent 1973 book, *Cluster Analysis for Applications*, Michael Anderberg uses a deck of playing cards to illustrate many aspects of clustering. We have borrowed his idea to illustrate the way that the initial choice of K, the number of cluster seeds, can have a large effect on the kinds of clusters that will be found.

In descriptions of K-means and related algorithms, the selection of K is often glossed over. But since, in many cases, there is no a priori reason to select a particular value, there is really an outermost loop to these algorithms that occurs in the analyst rather than in the computer program. This outer loop consists of performing automatic cluster detection using one value of K, evaluating the results, then trying again with another value of K.

After each trial, the strength of the resulting clusters can be evaluated by comparing the average distance between records in a cluster with the average distance between clusters, and by other procedures described later in this chapter. But the clusters must also be evaluated on a more subjective basis to determine their usefulness for a given application. As shown in Figures 10.7, 10.8, 10.9, 10.10, and 10.11, it is easy to create very good clusters from a deck of playing cards using various values for K and various distance measures. In the case of

A ♠	A ♣	A ♦	A ♥
K ♠	K ♣	K ♦	K ♥
Q ♠	Q ♣	Q ♦	Q ♥
J ♠	J ♣	J ♦	J ♥
10 ♠	10 ♣	10 ♦	10 ♥
9 ♠	9 ♣	9 ♦	9 ♥
8 ♠	8 ♣	8 ♦	8 ♥
7 ♠	7 ♣	7 ♦	7 ♥
6 ♠	6 ♣	6 ♦	6 ♥
5 ♠	5 ♣	5 ♦	5 ♥
4 ♠	4 ♣	4 ♦	4 ♥
3 ♠	3 ♣	3 ♦	3 ♥
2 ♠	2 ♣	2 ♦	2 ♥

Figure 10.7 K = 2 clustered by color.

	A ♠	A ♣	A ♦	A ♥
	K ♠	K ♣	K ♦	K ♥
Q ♠		Q ♣	Q ♦	Q ♥
	J ♠	J ♣	J ♦	J ♥
	10 ♠	10 ♣	10 ♦	10 ♥
	9 ♠	9 ♣	9 ♦	9 ♥
	8 ♠	8 ♣	8 ♦	8 ♥
	7 ♠	7 ♣	7 ♦	7 ♥
	6 ♠	6 ♣	6 ♦	6 ♥
	5 ♠	5 ♣	5 ♦	5 ♥
	4 ♠	4 ♣	4 ♦	4 ♥
	3 ♠	3 ♣	3 ♦	3 ♥
	2 ♠	2 ♣	2 ♦	2 ♥

Figure 10.8 K = 2 clustered by Old Maid rules.

A ♠	A ♣	A ♦	A ♥
K ♠	K ♣	K ♦	K ♥
Q ♠	Q ♣	Q ♦	Q ♥
J ♠	J ♣	J ♦	J ♥
10 ♠	10 ♣	10 ♦	10 ♥
9 ♠	9 ♣	9 ♦	9 ♥
8 ♠	8 ♣	8 ♦	8 ♥
7 ♠	7 ♣	7 ♦	7 ♥
6 ♠	6 ♣	6 ♦	6 ♥
5 ♠	5 ♣	5 ♦	5 ♥
4 ♠	4 ♣	4 ♦	4 ♥
3 ♠	3 ♣	3 ♦	3 ♥
2 ♠	2 ♣	2 ♦	2 ♥

Figure 10.9 K = 2 clustered by rules for War, Beggar My Neighbor, and many other games.

	A ♠	A ♣	A ♦	A ♥
	K ♠	K ♣	K ♦	K ♥
Q ♠		Q ♣	Q ♦	Q ♥
	J ♠	J ♣	J ♦	J ♥
	10 ♠	10 ♣	10 ♦	10 ♥
	9 ♠	9 ♣	9 ♦	9 ♥
	8 ♠	8 ♣	8 ♦	8 ♥
	7 ♠	7 ♣	7 ♦	7 ♥
	6 ♠	6 ♣	6 ♦	6 ♥
	5 ♠	5 ♣	5 ♦	5 ♥
	4 ♠	4 ♣	4 ♦	4 ♥
	3 ♠	3 ♣	3 ♦	3 ♥
	2 ♠	2 ♣	2 ♦	2 ♥

Figure 10.10 K = 3 clustered by rules for Hearts.

A ♠	A ♣	A ♦	A ♥
K ♠	K ♣	K ♦	K ♥
Q ♠	Q ♣	Q ♦	Q ♥
J ♠	J ♣	J ♦	J ♥
10 ♠	10 ♣	10 ♦	10 ♥
9 ♠	9 ♣	9 ♦	9 ♥
8 ♠	8 ♣	8 ♦	8 ♥
7 ♠	7 ♣	7 ♦	7 ♥
6 ♠	6 ♣	6 ♦	6 ♥
5 ♠	5 ♣	5 ♦	5 ♥
4 ♠	4 ♣	4 ♦	4 ♥
3 ♠	3 ♣	3 ♦	3 ♥
2 ♠	2 ♣	2 ♦	2 ♥

Figure 10.11 K = 4 clustered by suit.

playing cards, the distance measures are dictated by the rules of various games. The distance from Ace to King, for example, might be 1 or 12 depending on the game.

K = N?

Even with playing cards, some values of K don't lead to good clusters—at least not with distance measures suggested by the card games known to the authors. There are obvious clustering rules for K = 1, 2, 3, 4, 8, 13, 26, and 52. For these values we can come up with "perfect" clusters where each element of a cluster is equidistant from every other member of the cluster, and equally far away from the members of some other cluster. For other values of K, we have the more familiar situation that some cards do not seem to fit particularly well in any cluster.

The Importance of Weights

It is important to differentiate between the notions of *scaling* and *weighting*. They are not the same, but they are often confused. Scaling deals with the problem that different variables are measured in different units. Weighting deals with the problem that we care about some variables more than others.

In geometry, all dimensions are equally important. Two points that differ by 2 in dimensions X and Y and by 1 in dimension Z are the same distance from one another as two other points that differ by 1 in dimension X and by 2 in dimensions Y and Z. We don't even ask what units X, Y, and Z are measured in; it doesn't matter, so long as they are the same.

But what if X is measured in yards, Y is measured in centimeters, and Z is measured in nautical miles? A difference of 1 in Z is now equivalent to a difference of 185,200 in Y or 2,025 in X. Clearly, they must all be converted to a common scale before distances will make any sense.

Unfortunately, in commercial data mining there is usually no common scale available because the different units being used are measuring quite different things. If we are looking at plot size, household size, car ownership, and family income, we cannot convert all of them to acres or dollars. On the other hand, it seems bothersome that a difference of 20 acres in plot size is indistinguishable from a change of $20 in income. The solution is to map all the variables to a common *range* (often 0 to 1 or –1 to 1). That way, at least the ratios of change become comparable—doubling plot size will have the same effect as doubling income. We refer to this remapping to a common range as *scaling*.

But what if we think that two families with the same income have more in common than two families on the same size plot, and we want that to be taken into consideration during clustering? That is where weighting comes in.

TIP

Here are three common ways of scaling variables to bring them all into comparable ranges:

1. Divide each variable by the mean of all the values it takes on.
2. Divide each variable by the range (the difference between the lowest and highest value it takes on) after subtracting the lowest value.
3. Subtract the mean value from each variable and then divide by the standard deviation. This is often called "converting to z scores."

Use Weights to Encode Outside Information

Scaling takes care of the problem that changes in one variable appear more significant than changes in another simply because of differences in the speed with which the units they are measured in get incremented. Many books recommend scaling all variables to a normal form with a mean of zero and a variance of one. That way, all fields contribute equally when the distance between two records is computed.

We suggest going farther. The whole point of automatic cluster detection is to find clusters that make sense to *you*. If, for your purposes, whether people have children is much more important than the number of credit cards they carry, there is no reason not to bias the outcome of the clustering by multiplying the number of children field by a higher weight than the number of credit cards field. After scaling to get rid of bias that is due to the units, you should use weights to introduce bias based on your knowledge of the business context.

Of course, if you want to evaluate the effects of different weighting strategies, you will have to add yet another outer loop to the clustering process. In fact, choosing weights is one of the optimization problems that can be addressed with genetic algorithms as discussed in Chapter 14.

Variations on the K-Means Method

The basic K-means algorithm has many variations. It is likely that the commercial software tools you find to do automatic clustering will incorporate some of these variations. Among the differences you are likely to encounter are:

- Alternate methods of choosing the initial seeds
- Alternate methods of computing the next centroid
- Using probability density rather than distance to associate records with clusters.

Of these, only the last is important enough to merit further discussion here.

Gaussian Mixture Models

The K-means method as we have described it has some drawbacks.

- It does not do well with overlapping clusters.
- The clusters are easily pulled off center by outliers.
- Each record is either in or out of a cluster; there is no notion of some records being more or less likely than others to really belong to the cluster to which they have been assigned.

Gaussian mixture models are a probabilistic variant of K-means. Their name comes from the Gaussian distribution, a probability distribution often assumed for high-dimensional problems. As before, we start by choosing K seeds. This time, however, we regard the seeds as means of Gaussian distributions. We then iterate over two steps called the estimation step and the maximization step.

In the estimation step, we calculate the *responsibility* that each Gaussian has for each data point (see Figure 10.12). Each Gaussian has strong responsibility for points that are close to it and weak responsibility for points that are distant. The responsibilities will be used as weights in the next step.

In the maximization step, the mean of each Gaussian is moved towards the centroid of the entire data set, *weighted by the responsibilities* as illustrated in Figure 10.13.

These steps are repeated until the Gaussians are no longer moving. The Gaussians themselves can grow as well as move, but since the

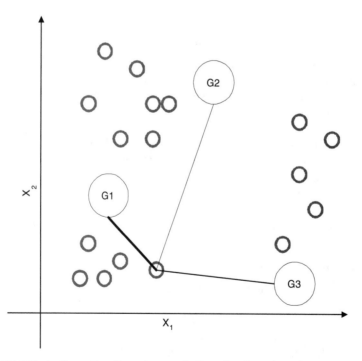

Figure 10.12 In the estimation step, each Gaussian is assigned some responsibility for each point. Thicker lines indicate greater responsibility.

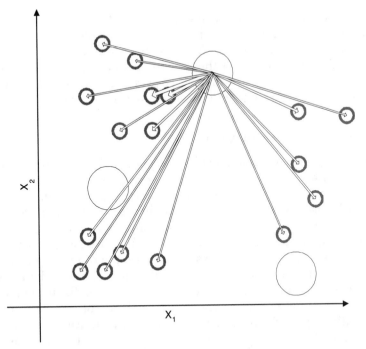

Figure 10.13 Each Gaussian mean is moved to the centroid of all the data points weighted by the responsibilities for each point. Thicker arrows indicate higher weights.

distribution must always integrate to one, a Gaussian gets weaker as it gets bigger. Responsibility is calculated in such a way that a given point may get equal responsibility from a nearby Gaussian with low variance and from a more distant one with higher variance.

The reason this is called a "mixture model" is that the probability at each data point is the sum of a mixture of several distributions. At the end of the process, each point is tied to the various clusters with higher or lower probability. This is sometimes called *soft clustering*.

AGGLOMERATION METHODS

In the K-means approach to clustering, we start out with a fixed number of clusters and gather all records into them. There is another class of methods that work by agglomeration. In these methods, we start out with each data point forming its own cluster and gradually merge clusters until all points have been gathered together in one big cluster. Towards the beginning of the process, the clusters are very small and very pure—the members of each cluster are few, but very closely related. Towards the end of the process, the clusters are large and less well-defined. The entire history is preserved so you can choose the level of clustering that works best for your application.

The Agglomerative Algorithm

The first step is to create a *similarity matrix*. The similarity matrix is a table of all the pair-wise distances or degrees of association between points. As before, we can use any of a large number of measures of association between records, including the Euclidean distance, the angle between vectors, and the ratio of matching to nonmatching categorical fields. The issues raised by the choice of distance measures are exactly the same as previously discussed in relation to the K-means approach.

At first glance you might think that if we have N data points we will need to make N^2 measurements to create the distance table, but if we assume that our association measure is a true distance metric, we actually only need half that because all true distance metrics follow the rule that Distance(X,Y) = Distance(Y,X). In the vocabulary of mathematics, the similarity matrix is lower triangular. At the beginning of the process there are N rows in the table, one for each record.

Next, we find the smallest value in the similarity matrix. This identifies the two clusters that are most similar to one another. We merge these two clusters and update the similarity matrix by replacing the two rows that described the parent cluster with a new row that describes the distance between the merged cluster and the remaining clusters. There are now N–1 clusters and N–1 rows in the similarity matrix.

We repeat the merge step N–1 times, after which all records belong to the same large cluster. At each iteration we make a record of which clusters were merged and how far apart they were. This information will be helpful in deciding which level of clustering to make use of.

Distance between Clusters

We need to say a little more about how to measure distance between clusters. On the first trip through the merge step, the clusters to be merged consist of single records so the distance between clusters is the same as the distance between records, a subject we may already have said too much about. But on the second and subsequent trips around the loop, we need to update the similarity matrix with the distances from the new, multi-record cluster to all the others. How do we measure this distance?

As usual, there is a choice of approaches. Three common ones are:

- Single linkage
- Complete linkage
- Comparison of centroids

In the single linkage method, the distance between two clusters is given by the distance between the *closest* members. This method produces clusters with the property that every member of a cluster is more closely related to at least one member of its cluster than to any point outside it.

In the complete linkage method, the distance between two clusters is given by the distance between their *most distant* members. This method produces clusters with the property that all members lie within some known maximum distance of one another.

In the third method, the distance between two clusters is measured between the centroids of each. The centroid of a cluster is its average element. Figure 10.14 gives a pictorial representation of all three methods.

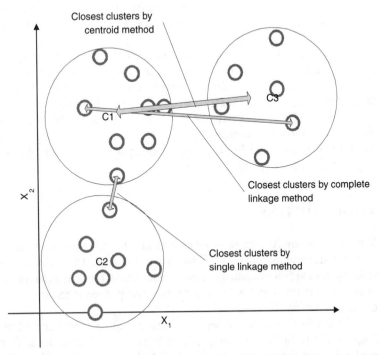

Figure 10.14 Three methods of measuring the distance between clusters.

Clusters and Trees

The agglomeration algorithm creates hierarchical clusters. At each level in the hierarchy, clusters are formed from the union of two clusters at the next level down. Another way of looking at this is as a tree, much like the decision trees discussed in Chapter 12 except that cluster trees are built by starting from the leaves and working towards the root.

Clustering People by Age: An Example of Agglomerative Clustering

To illustrate agglomerative clustering, we have chosen an example of clustering in one dimension using the single linkage measure for distance between clusters. These choices should enable you to follow the algorithm through all its iterations in your head without having to worry about squares and square roots.

The data consists of the ages of people at a family gathering. Our goal is to cluster the participants by age. Our metric for the distance between two people is simply the difference in their ages. Our metric for the distance between two clusters of people is the difference in age between the oldest member of the younger cluster and the youngest member of the older cluster. (The one dimensional version of the single linkage measure.)

Because the distances are so easy to calculate, we dispense with the similarity matrix. Our procedure is to sort the participants by age, then begin clustering by first merging clusters that are 1 year apart, then 2 years, and so on until there is only one big cluster.

Figure 10.15 shows the state of the clusters after six iterations, with three clusters remaining. This is the level of clustering that seems the most useful. The algorithm appears to have clustered the population into three generations.

EVALUATING CLUSTERS

When using the K-means approach to cluster detection, we need a way to determine what value of K finds the best clusters. Similarly, when using a hierarchical approach, we need a test for which level in the hierarchy contains the best clusters. But what does it mean to say that a cluster is good?

In general terms, we want clusters whose members have a high degree of similarity—or in geometric terms, are close to each other—and we want the clusters themselves to be widely spaced.

A standard measure of the within-cluster similarity is the variance—the sum of the squared differences of each element from the mean, so we might simply look for the solutions that produce the clusters with the lowest variance. But for hierarchical clustering, this does not make sense since we always start out with clusters of one which have no variance at all. A good measure to use with hierarchical clusters is the difference between the distance value at which it was formed and the distance value at which it is merged into the next level. Strong clusters, like the one linking 1 to 13-year-olds at distance 3 in Figure 10.15, last a long time.

A general-purpose measure that works with any form of cluster detection is to take whatever similarity measure or distance metric you used to form the clusters and use it to compare the average distance within clusters to the average distance between clusters. This can be done for each cluster individually and for the entire collection of clusters.

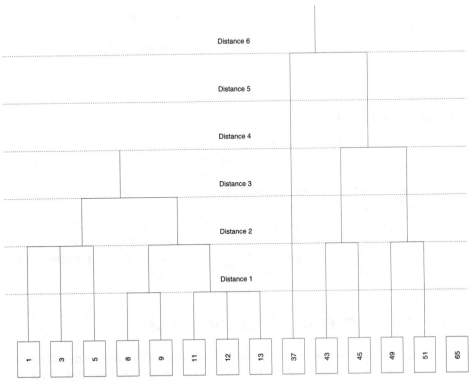

Figure 10.15 Single linkage clustering by age.

If you find that there are one or two good clusters along with a number of weaker ones, you may be able to improve your results by removing all members of the strong clusters. You will want to isolate the strong clusters for further analysis anyway, and removing their strong pull may allow new clusters to be detected in the records left behind.

Inside the Cluster

Once you have found a strong cluster, you will want to analyze what makes it special. What is it about the records in this cluster that causes them to be lumped together? Even more importantly, is it possible to find rules and patterns within this cluster now that the noise from the rest of the database has been eliminated?

The easiest way to approach the first question is to take the mean of each variable within the cluster and compare it to the mean of the same variable in the parent population. Rank order the variables by the magnitude of the difference. Looking at the variables that show the largest difference between the cluster and the rest of the database will go a long way towards explaining what makes the cluster special.

As for the second question, that is what all the other data mining techniques are for!

Outside the Cluster

Clustering can be useful even when only a single cluster is found. When screening for a very rare defect, there may not be enough examples to train a directed data mining model to detect it. One example is testing electric motors at the factory where they are made. Cluster detection methods can be used on a sample containing only good motors to determine the shape and size of the "normal" cluster. When a motor comes along that falls outside the cluster for any reason, it is suspect. This approach has been used in medicine to detect the presence of abnormal cells in tissue samples.

OTHER APPROACHES TO CLUSTER DETECTION

In addition to the two approaches to automatic cluster detection described in this chapter, there are two other approaches that make use of variations of techniques discussed in Chapters 12 and 13—decision trees and neural networks.

Divisive Methods

We have already noted the similarity between the tree formed by the agglomerative clustering techniques and the ones formed by decision tree algorithms such as CART and CHAID. Although the agglomerative methods work from the leaves to the root, while the decision tree algorithms work from the root to the leaves, they both create a similar hierarchical structure. The hierarchical structure reflects another similarity between the methods. Decisions made early on in the process are never revisited, which means that some fairly simple clusters will not be detected if an early split or agglomeration destroys the structure.

Seeing the similarity between the trees produced by the two methods, it is natural to ask whether the algorithms used for decision trees may also be used for clustering. The answer is yes. A decision tree algorithm starts with the entire collection of records and looks for a way to spit it into clusters that are *purer*, in some sense defined by a diversity function. All that is required to turn this into a clustering algorithm is to supply a diversity function chosen to either minimize the average intra-cluster distance or maximize the inter-cluster distances.

Self-Organizing Maps

Self-organizing maps are a variant of neural networks that have been used for many years in applications such as feature detection in two-dimensional images. More recently, they have been applied successfully for more general clustering applications. There is a discussion of self-organizing networks in Chapter 13.

STRENGTHS OF AUTOMATIC CLUSTER DETECTION

The strengths of automatic cluster detection are:

- Automatic cluster detection is an undirected knowledge discovery technique.
- Automatic cluster detection works well with categorical, numeric, and textual data.
- Easy to apply.

Automatic Cluster Detection Is Undirected

The chief strength of automatic cluster detection is that it is undirected. This means that it can be applied even when you have no prior knowledge of the internal structure of a database. Automatic cluster detection can be used to uncover hidden structure that can be used to improve the performance of more directed techniques.

Clustering Can Be Performed on Diverse Data Types

By choosing different distance measures, automatic clustering can be applied to almost any kind of data. It is as easy to find clusters in collections of news stories or insurance claims as in astronomical or financial data.

Automatic Cluster Detection Is Easy to Apply

Most cluster detection techniques require very little massaging of the input data and there is no need to identify particular fields as inputs and others as outputs.

WEAKNESSES OF AUTOMATIC CLUSTER DETECTION

Weaknesses of this technique are:

- It can be difficult to choose the right distance measures and weights.
- Sensitivity to initial parameters.
- It can be hard to interpret the resulting clusters.

Difficulty with Weights and Measures

The performance automatic cluster detection algorithms is highly dependent on the choice of a distance metric or other similarity measure. It is sometimes quite difficult to devise distance metrics for data that contains a mixture of variable types. It can also be difficult to determine a proper weighting scheme for disparate variable types.

Sensitivity to Initial Parameters

In the K-means method, the original choice of a value for K determines the number of clusters that will be found. If this number does not match the natural structure of the data, the technique will not obtain good results.

Difficulty Interpreting Results

A strength of automatic cluster detection is that it is an undirected knowledge discovery technique. The flip side is that when you don't know what you are looking for, you may not recognize it when you find it! The clusters you discover are not guaranteed to have any practical value.

WHEN TO USE CLUSTERING

Clustering is a great tool to use when you are faced with a large, complex data set with many variables and a lot of internal structure. At the start of a new data mining project, clustering is often the best first technique to turn to. It is rarely the only tool, however. Once automatic cluster detection has discovered regions of the data space that contain similar records, other data mining tools have a better chance of discovering rules and patterns within them.

Link Analysis

The world of business is a world of relationships, connecting people, places, and things together (see Figure 11.1). Airlines, truckers, and other transportation companies link cities together. Telecommunications customers link to each other when they talk over landline

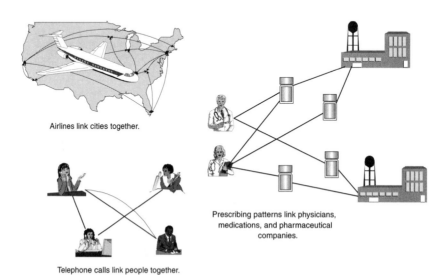

Airlines link cities together.

Telephone calls link people together.

Prescribing patterns link physicians, medications, and pharmaceutical companies.

Figure 11.1   Links represent relationships.

phones and mobile phones. Physicians recommend some medicines over others, creating prescribing patterns that link physicians to certain pharmaceutical companies. Credit card customers prefer particular restaurants or retailers. Web users browse particular sites and respond to particular ads. Relationships are everywhere and these relationships contain a wealth of information that most data mining techniques are not able to take direct advantage of. Link analysis (LA) is the technique that exploits these relationships.

Link analysis is based on a branch of mathematics called *graph theory*. This chapter reviews the key notions of graphs, then shows how link analysis can be applied to solve real problems. Link analysis is not applicable to all types of data or to solve all types of problems. However, when it can be used, it often yields very insightful and actionable results. Some areas where it has yielded promising results are:

- Analyzing telephone call patterns. Each telephone call is a relationship between two end points and contains valuable information. Calling patterns are naturally represented as graphs.
- Understanding physician referral patterns. A referral is a relationship between two physicians, once again, naturally susceptible to LA.
- Combining leads. A system in place at the FBI helps the bureau to combine information from disparate sources to help in solving crimes.

There are just a few tools that explicitly support link analysis and, for the most part, they have specialized in the law enforcement area. These tools often focus on the visualization of links, so they assist people with knowledge discovery rather than finding patterns themselves. However, even SQL queries on relational databases can be the basis for link analysis. The only downside is performance; link analysis queries are generally quite expensive to run, since links are equivalent to joins in the relational model. For smaller amounts of data, object-oriented technology often encapsulates the links into the database, providing an efficient way of traversing them.

Another problem addressed in this chapter is the recognition of when links exist between items. In the case of telephone calls, the links are obvious—one person calls another person and the call itself is the link. In other cases, the links need to be generated automatically. The lead analysis system in place at the FBI determines the relationships between items using techniques similar to MBR.

SOME BASIC GRAPH THEORY

The language of graphs is the language of links and relationships. The purpose of this section is to describe some fundamentals of graph theory to provide a vocabulary for talking about link analysis. The basic ideas are quite simple and this section should give a feel for how graphs are formed and what they can do.

What Is a Graph?

Graphs are an abstraction developed specifically to represent relationships. They have proven very useful both in mathematics and in computer science for developing algorithms that exploit these relationships. Fortunately, graphs are quite intuitive and there is a wealth of examples that illustrate how to take advantage of them.

A *graph* consists of two distinct parts:

- *Nodes* (sometimes called *vertices*) are the things in the graph that have relationships. These have names and often have additional useful properties.
- *Edges* are pairs of nodes connected by a relationship. An edge is represented by the two nodes that it connects, so *(A, B)* or *AB* represents the edge that connects A and B.

Figure 11.2 illustrates two graphs. The graph on the left has four nodes connected by six edges and has the property that there is an edge between every pair of nodes. We say that the graph is *fully-connected*. It could be representing daily flights between Miami, New York, Nashville, and Dallas on an airline where these four cities serve as regional hubs. It could also be representing four people, all of whom know each other, or four related leads for a criminal investigation. The graph on the right has one node in the center connected to four other nodes. This could represent daily flights connecting Atlanta to Birmingham, Greenville, Charlotte, and Savannah on an airline that serves the Southeast and has a hub in Atlanta, or a restaurant frequented by four credit card customers. The graph itself captures the information about what is connected to what. Without any labels, it can describe many different situations. This is the power of abstraction.

A few points of terminology about graphs. Because graphs are so useful for visualizing relationships, it is nice when the nodes and edges can be drawn so no edges intersect each other. The graphs in Figure 11.2 have this property. They are *planar* graphs since they can be drawn on a sheet of paper (what mathematicians call a *plane*) with-

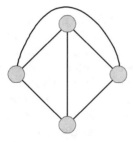 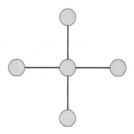

A fully-connected graph with four nodes and six edges. In a fully-connected graph, there is an edge between every pair of nodes

A graph with five nodes and four edges.

Figure 11.2 Two examples of graphs.

out having any edges intersect. Figure 11.3 shows two graphs that cannot be drawn without having at least two edges cross. There is, in fact, a result in graph theory that says that if a graph is non-planar, then lurking inside it is one of these two graphs.

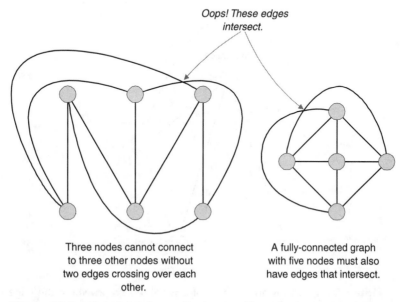

Oops! These edges intersect.

Three nodes cannot connect to three other nodes without two edges crossing over each other.

A fully-connected graph with five nodes must also have edges that intersect.

Figure 11.3 Not all graphs can be drawn without having some edges cross over each other.

When a path exists between any two nodes in a graph, we say that the graph is *connected*. For the rest of this chapter, we assume that all graphs are connected, unless otherwise specified. A *path*, as its name implies, is an ordered sequence of nodes connected by edges. Consider a graph where each node represents a city and the edges are flights between them. On such a graph, a node is a city and an edge is a flight segment—two cities that are connected by a non-stop flight. A path is an itinerary of flight segments that go from one city to another, such as from Greenville, South Carolina to Atlanta, from Atlanta to Chicago, and from Chicago to Peoria.

Figure 11.4 is an example of a *weighted graph* in which the edges have a weight associated with them. In this case, the nodes represent products purchased by customers. The weights on the edges represent the number of purchases containing both products. Such a graph provides an approach for solving problems in market basket analysis, as discussed in Chapter 8. It is also a useful means of visualizing market basket data.

One very common problem in link analysis is to find the shortest path between two nodes. Shortest, though, depends on the weights as-

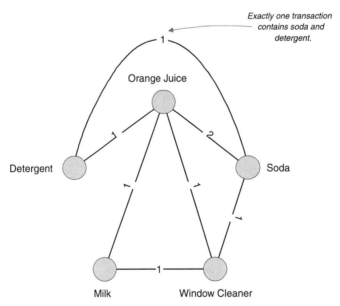

Figure 11.4 This is an example of a weighted graph where the edge weights are the number of transactions containing the items represented by the nodes at either end.

signed to each edge. Consider the graph of flights between cities. Does shortest refer to distance? To the fewest number of flight segments? Or the least expensive? All these questions are answered the same way using graphs—the only difference is the weights on the edges.

The following two sections describe two classic problems in graph theory that illustrate the power of graphs to represent and solve problems. Few data mining problems are exactly like these two problems, but the problems give a flavor of how the simple construction of graphs leads to some interesting solutions. They are presented to familiarize the reader with graphs by providing examples of key concepts in graph theory and to provide a stronger basis for discussing link analysis.

Seven Bridges of Königsberg

One of the earliest problems in graph theory originated with a simple challenge posed in the eighteenth century by the Swiss mathematician Leonhard Euler. As shown in the simple map in Figure 11.5, Königsberg had two islands in the Pregel River connected to each other and to the rest of the city by a total of seven bridges. On either side of the river or on the islands, it is possible to get to any of the bridges. Figure 11.5 shows one path through the town that crosses over five bridges exactly once. Euler posed the question: Is it possible to walk over all

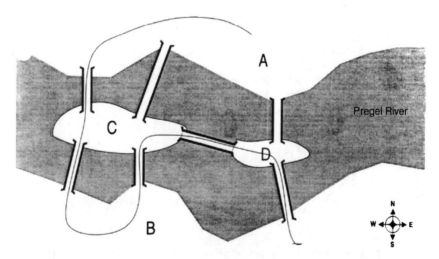

Figure 11.5 The Pregel River in Königsberg has two islands connected by a total of seven bridges.

seven bridges exactly once, starting from anywhere in the city, without getting wet? As an historical note, the problem has survived longer than the name of the city. In the eighteenth century, Königsberg was a prominent Prussian city on the Baltic Sea nestled between Lithuania and Poland. Now, it is known as Kaliningrad, the westernmost Russian enclave, separated from the rest of Russia by Lithuania.

In order to solve this problem, Euler invented the notation of graphs. He represented the map of Königsberg as the simple graph with four vertices and seven edges in Figure 11.6. Some pairs of nodes are connected by more than one edge, indicating that there is more than one bridge between them. Finding a route that traverses all the bridges in Königsberg exactly one time is equivalent to finding a path in the graph that visits every edge exactly once. Such a path is called an *Eulerian Path* in honor of the mathematician who posed and solved this problem.

Euler devised a solution based on the number of edges going into or out of each node in the graph. The number of such edges is called the *degree* of a node. For instance, in the graph representing the seven bridges of Königsberg, the nodes representing each shore both have a

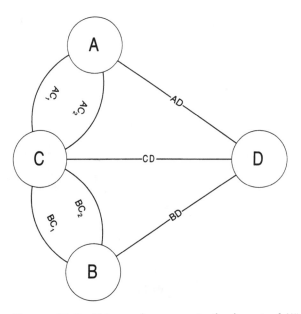

Figure 11.6 This graph represents the layout of Königsberg. The edges are bridges and the nodes are the riverbanks and islands.

degree of three—corresponding to the fact that there are three bridges connecting each shore to the islands. The other two nodes, representing the islands, have degrees of 5 and 3. Euler showed that an Eulerian Path exists only when the degrees of all the nodes in a graph are even, except at most two (see technical aside). So, there is no way to walk over the seven bridges of Königsberg, since there are four nodes whose degrees are odd.

Why Do the Degrees Have to Be Even?

Showing that an Eulerian path exists only when the degrees on all nodes are even (except at most two) rests on a simple observation. This observation is about paths in the graph. Consider one path through the bridges:

$$A \rightarrow C \rightarrow B \rightarrow C \rightarrow D$$

The edges being used are:

$$\underline{AC}_1 \rightarrow \underline{BC}_1 \rightarrow \underline{BC}_2 \rightarrow \underline{CD}$$

The edges connecting the intermediate nodes in the path come in pairs. That is, there is an outgoing edge for every incoming edge. For instance, node C has four edges visiting it and node B has two. Since the edges come in pairs, each intermediate node has an even number of edges in the path. Since an Eulerian path contains all edges in the graph and visits all the nodes, such a path exists only when all the nodes in the graph (minus the two end nodes) can serve as intermediate nodes for the path. This is another way of saying that the degree of those nodes is even.

Euler also showed that the opposite is true. When all the nodes in a graph (save at most two) have an even degree, then an Eulerian path exists. This proof is a bit more complicated, but the idea is rather simple. To construct an Eulerian path, start at any node or at one of the nodes with an odd degree and move to any other node connected to it with an even degree. Remove the edge from the graph and make it the first edge in the Eulerian path. Now, the problem is to find an Eulerian path starting at the second node in the graph. By keeping track of the degrees of the nodes, it is possible to construct such a path when there are at most two nodes whose degree is odd.

Travelling Salesman Problem

A more modern problem in graph theory is the "Travelling Salesman Problem." In this problem, a salesman needs to visit customers in a set of cities. He plans on flying to one of the cities, renting a car, visiting the customer there, then driving to each of other cities to visit each of the rest of his customers. He leaves off the car in the last city and flies home. There are many possible routes that the salesman can take, but he would like to minimize the total distance he travels. What route minimizes the total distance while still allowing him to visit each city one time?

The Travelling Salesman Problem is easily reformulated using graphs, since graphs are a natural representation of cities connected by roads. In the graph representing this problem, each edge has a weight corresponding to the distance between the two cities. The Travelling Salesman Problem therefore is asking: "What is the shortest path that visits all the nodes in a graph exactly one time?" Notice that this problem is different from Seven Bridges of Königsberg. We are not interested in simply finding a path that visits all nodes exactly once, but of all possible paths we want the shortest one. Notice that all Eulerian paths have exactly the same length since they contain exactly the same edges. Asking for the shortest Eulerian path does not make sense.

Solving the Travelling Salesman Problem for three or four cities is not difficult. The most complicated graph with four nodes is a completely connected graph where every node in the graph is connected to every other node. In this graph, 24 different paths visit each node exactly once. To count the number of paths, start at any of nodes (there are four possibilities), then go to any of the other three remaining ones, then to any of the other two, and finally to the last node ($4 \times 3 \times 2 \times 1 = 24 = 4!$). A completely connected graph with n nodes has $n!$ (*n factorial*) distinct paths that contain all nodes. Each path has a slightly different collection of edges, so their lengths are usually different. From the 24 possibilities, we can choose the shortest path.

The problem of finding the shortest path connecting nodes was first investigated by the Irish mathematician Sir William Rowan Hamilton. His study of minimizing energy in physical systems led him to investigate minimizing energy in certain discrete systems that he represented as graphs. In honor of him, a path that visits all nodes in a graph exactly once is called a *Hamiltonian path*.

The Travelling Salesman Problem is difficult to solve. In the lingo of graph theory, this means that any solution must consider all of the possible paths through the graph in order to determine which one is the shortest. The number of paths in a completely connected graph grows very fast—as a factorial. What is true for completely connected graphs is true for graphs in general: The number of possible paths visiting all the nodes grows like an exponential function of the number of nodes (although there are a few graphs where this is not true). So, as the number of cities increases, the effort required finding the shortest path grows exponentially. Adding just one more city (with associated roads) can result in a solution that takes twice as long—or more—to find.

This lack of scalability is so important that mathematicians have given it a name: NP—where NP means that all known algorithms used to solve the problem scale exponentially—not like a polynomial. These problems are considered difficult.

All of this graph theory aside, there are pretty good heuristic algorithms for computers that provide reasonable solutions to the Travelling Salesman Problem. The resulting paths are relatively short paths, although they are not guaranteed to be the shortest possible one. This is a useful fact if you have a similar problem. One common algorithm is the greedy algorithm: start the path with the shortest edge in the graph, then lengthen the path with the shortest edge available at either end that visits a new node. The resulting path is generally pretty short, although not necessarily the shortest (see Figure 11.7).

There is a lesson here for data mining: Often it is better to use an algorithm that yields good, but not perfect results, instead of trying to analyze the difficulty of arriving at the ideal solution. The imperfect result is actionable; the analysis is just, well, analysis.

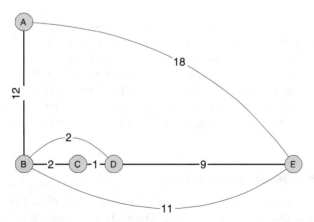

Figure 11.7 In this graph, the shortest path (ABCDE) has a length of 24 but the greedy algorithm can find a much longer path (CDBEA).

> ## Biological Computers
>
> The difficulty of finding the shortest Hamiltonian path is a well-studied problem and is still the topic of much current research. One of the most interesting recent results in this area has been the application of biological mechanisms to solve the problem. Sequences of DNA are much, much smaller than the components used in standard computers. Jostling them around in a test tube allows them to grow into longer and longer sequences. This only results in fast computation when the sequences of DNA are carefully chosen to represent a particular problem. Finding the shortest Hamiltonian path is one problem where biological mechanisms have been successfully applied.
>
> A researcher at the University of Southern California, Dr. Adleman, devised a way to represent the problem of finding the shortest Hamiltonian Path using sequences of DNA in a test tube. By analyzing the DNA, he was able to find a Hamiltonian Path for a small graph, estimating that this molecular computer was millions of times faster than the fastest supercomputer. Since he published his paper in *Science* in 1994, an entire field of computational biology has been developing around this idea.

CASE STUDY: WHO IS USING FAX MACHINES FROM HOME?

Mobile, local, and long distance telephone service providers have records of every telephone call that their customers make and receive. This data contains a wealth of information about the behavior of their customers: when they place calls, who calls them, whether they benefit from their calling plan. As this case study shows, link analysis can be used to analyze the records of local telephone calls to identify which residential customers have a high probability of having fax machines in their home.

Why Finding Fax Machines Is Useful

What is the use of knowing who owns a fax machine? How can a local telephone provider act on this information? In this case, the provider had developed a package of services for residential work-at-home customers. Targeting such customers for marketing purposes was a revolutionary concept at the company. In the tightly regulated local phone market not so long ago, local service providers lost revenue from work-at-home customers. They could have been charging these customers higher business rates instead of the lower residential rates. Far from targeting such customers for marketing campaigns, the local telephone providers would deny such customers residential rates—punishing them for behaving like a small businesses. For this company, developing and selling work-at-home packages to improve service to work-at-home customers represented a new foray into customer service. But which customers should be targeted for the new package?

There are many approaches to defining a set of customers to target. The company could effectively use neighborhood demographics, household surveys, estimates of computer ownership by zip code, and similar data. Although this data improves the definition of a market segment, it is still far from identifying a *market of one* that customizes services to meet the needs of individual customers. A team, including one of the authors, suggested that the ability to find residential fax machine usage would improve this marketing effort, since fax machines are often (but not always) used for business purposes. Knowing who uses a fax machine would help target the work-at-home package to a very well-defined market segment and this segment should have a better response rate than a segment defined by less precise segmentation techniques based on statistical properties. The actual case study does demonstrate the ability to find fax machines. Unfortunately, we were unable to carry out the marketing effort and measure the improvement on this particular segment.

The customers with fax machines offer other opportunities as well. Customers that are sending and receiving faxes should have at least two lines—if they only have one, there is an opportunity to sell them a second line. To provide better customer service, the customers who use faxes on a line with call waiting should know how to turn off call waiting to avoid annoying interruptions on fax transmissions. There are other possibilities as well: perhaps owners of fax machines would prefer receiving their monthly bills by fax instead of by mail, saving both postage and printing costs. In short, being able to identify who is sending or receiving faxes from home is valuable information that provides opportunities for increasing revenues, reducing costs, and increasing customer satisfaction.

The Data as a Graph

The raw data used for this analysis is the call detail data fed into the billing system to generate monthly bills. Each record contains 80 bytes of data, with information like

- the 10-digit telephone number that originated the call, three digits for the area code, three digits for the exchange, and four digits for the line;
- the 10-digit telephone number of the line where the call terminated;
- the 10-digit telephone number of the line being billed for the call;
- the date and time of the call;
- the duration of the call;
- miscellaneous flags, such as the day of the week and whether the call was placed at a pay phone.

This analysis reduced the data to just three fields: a duration, an originating number, and a terminating number. The telephone numbers are the nodes of the graph and the calls themselves are the edges, weighted by the duration of the calls (see Figure 11.8). A sample of telephone calls is shown in Table 11.1.

This graph is a bit different from the graphs previously described. First, notice that the graph is not connected. It consists of two entirely separate *components*. The second difference is more important. The edges have arrows on them, indicating that they are *directed*. The edge goes *from* the number originating the call *to* the number receiving it. We will return to the discussion of directed graphs or *digraphs* (as they are sometimes called) after the case study.

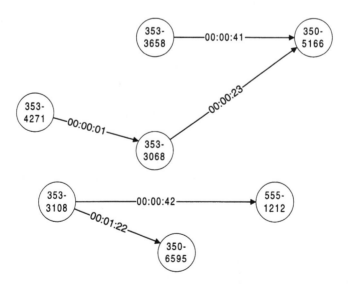

Figure 11.8 Five calls link together seven telephone numbers.

Table 11.1 Five Telephone Calls

ID	Originating Number	Terminating Number	Duration
1	353-3658	350-5166	00:00:41
2	353-3068	350-5166	00:00:23
3	353-4271	353-3068	00:00:01
4	353-3108	555-1212	00:00:42
5	353-3108	350-6595	00:01:22

The Approach

Finding fax machines is based on a simple observation: Fax machines tend to call other fax machines. A set of known numbers with fax machines can be expanded based on the calls made or received at the known numbers, and so on. This simple characterization is good for guidance, but is an oversimplification. There are actually several types of fax machine usage expected at a residential customer:

- Dedicated fax. Some fax machines are on dedicated lines and the line is used only for fax communication.
- Shared. Some fax machines share their line with voice calls.
- Data. Some fax machines are on lines dedicated to data use, either via fax or via computer modem.

TIP

Characterizing expected behavior is a good way to start any directed data mining problem. The better the problem is understood, the better the results are likely to be. Incorporating domain knowledge such as the behavior of fax machines, is particularly valuable for link analysis, since it takes advantage of relationships.

The presumption that fax machines call other fax machines is generally true for machines on dedicated lines, although wrong numbers provide exceptions to this rule. To distinguish shared lines from dedicated or data lines, we assumed that any number that calls information—411 or 555-1212—is used for voice communications, and therefore a voice line or a shared fax line. For instance, call #4 in the example data contains a call to 555-1212, signifying that this is likely to be a shared line or just a voice line. When a shared line calls another number, there is no way to know if the call is voice or data. We cannot identify fax machines based on calls to and from such a node in the call graph. On the other hand, these shared lines do represent a marketing opportunity to sell additional lines.

The process used to find fax machines consisted of the following steps:

1. Start with a set of known fax machines (gathered from the Yellow Pages).
2. Determine all the numbers that make or receive calls to any number in this set where the call's duration was longer than 10 seconds. These numbers are candidates.

   - If the candidate number has called 411, 555-1212, or a number identified as a shared fax number, then it is included in the set of shared voice/fax numbers.
   - Otherwise, then it is included in the set of known fax machines.

3. Repeat steps 1 and 2 until no more numbers are identified.

One of the challenges was identifying wrong numbers. In particular, incoming calls to a fax machine may sometimes represent a wrong number and give no information about the originating number (actually, if it is a wrong number then it is probably a voice line). We made the assumption that such incoming wrong numbers would last a very short time, such as Call #3. In a larger-scale analysis of fax machines, it would be useful to eliminate other anomalies, such as outgoing wrong numbers and modem/fax usage.

The process needs to start with an initial set of fax numbers. Since this was a demonstration project, several fax numbers were gathered manually from the Yellow Pages based on the annotation "fax" by the number. For a larger-scale project, all fax numbers could be retrieved from the database used to generate the Yellow Pages. These numbers are only the beginning, the seeds, of new numbers. Although it is common for retail businesses to advertise their fax numbers, it is not so common for fax machines at home.

Some Results

The sample of telephone records used consisted of 3,011,819 telephone calls made over one month by 19,674 households. In the world of telephony, this is a very small sample of data, but it was sufficient to show the power of link analysis. The analysis was performed using special-purpose C++ code that stored the call detail and allowed us to expand a list of fax machines efficiently.

Finding the fax machines is an example of a *graph coloring algorithm*. This type of algorithm walks through the graph and label nodes with different "colors." In this case, the colors are "fax," "shared," "voice," and "unknown" instead of red, green, yellow, and blue. Initially, all the nodes are "unknown" except for the handful labeled "fax" from the starting set. As the algorithm proceeds, more and more nodes with the "unknown" label get a more informative label.

Figure 11.9 shows a call graph with 15 numbers and 19 calls. The weights on the edges are the duration of each call in seconds. Nothing is really known about the specific numbers.

Figure 11.10 shows how the algorithm proceeds. First, the numbers that are known to be fax machines are labeled "F" and the number of information is labeled "I." Any edge for a call that lasted less than 10 seconds has been dropped. The algorithm colors the graph by assigning labels to each node using an iterative procedure:

- Any "voice" node connected to a "fax" node gets the label "shared."
- Any "unknown" node connected mostly to "fax" nodes gets the label "fax."

This procedure continues until all nodes connected to "fax" nodes have a "fax" or "shared" label.

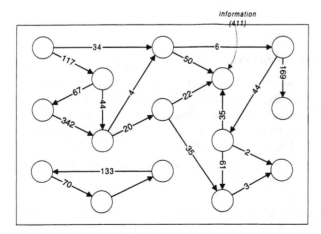

Figure 11.9 A call graph for 15 numbers and 19 calls.

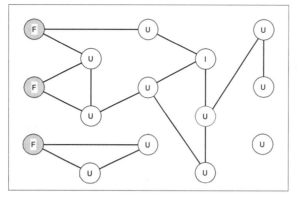

This is the initial call graph with short calls removed and with nodes labeled as "fax," "unknown," and "information."

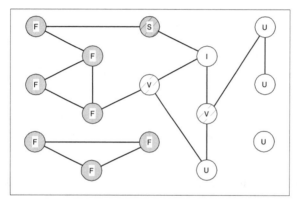

Nodes connected to the initial fax machines are assigned the "fax" label.

Those connected to "information" are assigned the "voice" label.

Those connected to both, are "shared."

The rest are "unknown."

Figure 11.10 Applying the graph coloring algorithm to the call graph shows which numbers are fax numbers and which are shared.

Using a Relational Database

Although the case study implemented the graph coloring using special-purpose C++ code, these operations are suitable for data stored in a relational database. Assume there are three tables: `call_detail`, `dedicated_fax`, and `shared_fax`. The query for finding the numbers that call a known fax number is

```
SELECT originating_number
FROM call_detail
WHERE terminating_number IN (SELECT number FROM dedicated_fax)
  AND duration > 9
GROUP BY originating_number;
```

A similar query can be used to get the calls made by a known fax number. However, this does not yet distinguish between dedicated fax lines and shared fax lines. To do this, we have to know if any calls were made to information. For efficiency reasons, it is best to keep this list in a separate table, `voice_numbers`:

```
SELECT originating_number
FROM call_detail
WHERE terminating_number = '5551212'
  OR terminating_number = ' 411'
GROUP BY originating_number;
```

So the query to find dedicated fax lines is

```
SELECT originating_number
FROM call_detail
WHERE terminating_number IN (SELECT number FROM dedicated_fax)
  AND duration > 9
  AND originating_number NOT IN (SELECT number FROM
voice_numbers)
GROUP BY originating_number;
```

and for shared lines is

```
SELECT originating_number
FROM call_detail
WHERE terminating_number IN (SELECT number FROM dedicated_fax)
  AND duration > 2
  AND originating_number IN (SELECT number FROM voice_numbers)
GROUP BY originating_number;
```

These SQL queries are intended to show that finding fax machines is possible on a relational database. They are probably not the most efficient SQL statements for this purpose, depending on the layout of the data, the database engine, and the hardware it is running on. Also, if there is a significant number of calls in the database, any SQL queries for link analysis will require joins on very large tables.

DIRECTED GRAPHS

The previous case study introduced directed graphs. In undirected graphs, the edges are like expressways between nodes: They go in both directions. In a directed graph the edges are like one-way roads. An edge going from A to B is distinct from an edge going from B to A. A directed edge from A to B is an *outgoing edge* of A and an *incoming edge* of B.

Directed graphs are a powerful way of representing data:

- Flight segments that connect a set of cities
- Referral patterns of doctors
- Telephone calling patterns
- State transition diagrams
- Decision trees

Two types of nodes are of particular interest in directed graphs. All the edges connected to a *source node* are outgoing edges. Since there are no incoming edges, no path exists from any other node in the graph to any of the source nodes. When all the edges on a node are incoming edges, the node is called a *sink node*. The existence of source nodes and sink nodes is an important difference between directed graphs and their undirected cousins.

An important property of directed graphs is whether the graph contains any paths that start and end at the same vertex. Such a path is called a *cycle*, implying that the path could repeat itself endlessly: ABCABCABC and so on. If a directed graph contains at least one cycle, it is called *cyclic*. Cycles in a graph of flight segments, for instance, might be the path of a single airplane. In a call graph, members of a cycle call each other—these are good candidates for a "friends and family-style" promotion where the whole group gets a discount or for marketing conference call services. In a graph representing referral patterns for physicians, cycles might indicate potentially fraudulent referrals.

Detecting Cycles in a Graph

A simple cycle detection algorithm detects whether a directed graph has any cycles. This algorithm starts with the observation that if a directed graph has no sink vertices, and it has at least one edge, then any path can be extended arbitrarily. Without any sink vertices, the terminating node of a path is always connected to another node, so the path can be extended by appending that node. Similarly, if the graph has no source nodes, then we can always prepend a node to the beginning of the path. Once the path contains more nodes than there are nodes in the graph, we know that the path must visit at least one node twice. Call this node X. The portion of the path between the first X and the second X in the path is a cycle, so the graph is cyclic.

Now consider the case when a graph has one or more source nodes and one or more sink nodes. It is pretty obvious that source nodes and sink nodes cannot be part of a cycle. Removing the source and sink nodes from the graph, along with all their edges, does not affect whether the graph is cyclic. If the resulting graph has no sink nodes or no source nodes, then it contains a cycle, as just shown. The process of removing sink nodes, source nodes, and their edges is repeated until one of the following occurs:

- No more edges or no more nodes are left. In this case, the graph has no cycles.
- Some edges remain but there are no source or sink nodes. In this case, the graph is cyclic.

If no cycles exist, then the graph is called an *acyclic graph*. These graphs are useful for describing dependencies or one-way relationships between things. For instance, different products often belong to nested hierarchies that can be represented by acyclic graphs. In Chapter 8, we saw such a hierarchy describing taxonomies (Figure 8.4). Decision trees are another example of acyclic graphs, explained in Chapter 12.

In an acyclic graph, any two nodes have a well-defined precedence relationship with each other. If node A precedes node B in any path that contains both A and B, then A will precede B in all paths containing both A and B (otherwise there would be a cycle). In this case, we say that A is a *predecessor* of B and that B is a *successor* of A. If no paths contain both A and B, then A and B are *disjoint*. This strict ordering can be an important property of the nodes and sometimes useful for data mining purposes.

CASE STUDY: SEGMENTING CELLULAR TELEPHONE CUSTOMERS

This case study applies link analysis to cellular telephone calls for the purpose of segmenting existing customers for selling new services. Analyses similar to those presented here were used with a leading cellular provider. The results from the analysis were used for a direct mailing for a new product offering. On such mailings, the cellular company typically measured a response rate of 2 percent to 3 percent. With some of the ideas presented here, it increased its response rate to over 15 percent, a very significant improvement. Because the company views these new techniques as a competitive advantage, it is not willing to be identified or to use its specific data here.[1]

The Data

Cellular telephone data is similar to the call detail data seen in the previous case study for finding fax machines. There is a record for each call that includes fields like

- the originating and terminating numbers;
- the location where the call was placed;
- the account number of the person who originated the call;
- the duration of the call;
- the time and date; and
- various flags, not of interest here.

Although the analysis did not use the account number, it plays an important role in this data because the data did not otherwise distinguish between business and residential accounts. Accounts for larger businesses have thousands of phones, while most residential accounts have only a single phone.

Analyses without Graph Theory

Prior to using link analysis, the marketing department used a single indicator for segmentation: minutes of use (MOU) which is the number of minutes each month that a customer uses on the cellular phone. MOU is a useful measure, since there is a direct correlation between MOU and the amount billed to the customer each month. This correlation is not exact, since it does not take into account discount periods and calling plans that offer free nights and weekends, but it is a good guide nonetheless.

The marketing group did use external data, like demographics, for prospective customers. They could also distinguish between individual customers and business accounts. In addition to MOU, though, their only understanding of customer behavior was the total amount billed and whether customers paid the bills in a timely matter. They were leaving a lot of information on the table.

---

1. The authors would like to thank their colleagues Alan Parker, William Crowder, and Ravi Basawi for their contributions to this section.

A Comparison of Two Customers

Figure 11.11 illustrates two customers and their calling patterns during a typical month. These two customers have similar MOU, but the patterns are strikingly different. John's calls generate a small, tight graph, while Jane's explodes with many different calls. If Jane is happy with her cellular service, her use will likely grow and she might even influence many of her friends and colleagues to switch to the cellular provider. For instance, offering her a third minute free on each call might induce her to lengthen her many short calls. On the other hand, offering John a third minute free would probably just reduce his bill.

In fact, looking at these two customers more closely reveals important differences. Although John racks up 150 to 200 MOU every month on his car phone, his use of the cellular telephone consists almost exclusively of two types of calls:

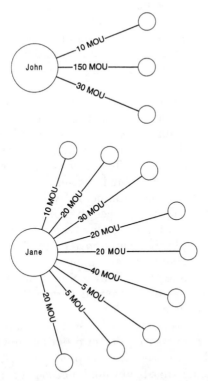

Figure 11.11 John and Jane have about the same minutes of use each month, but their behavior is quite different.

- On his way home from work, he calls his wife to let her know what time to expect him. Sometimes they chat for three or four minutes.
- Every Wednesday morning, he has a 45-minute conference call that he takes in the car on his morning commute.

The only person who has John's car phone number is his wife and she rarely calls him when he is driving. In fact, John has another cellular phone that he carries with him for business purposes, but he does not like to use the portable one in the car—his car phone service provider does not know this, though.

Jane also racks up about the same usage every month on her car phone. She only uses her car phone one or two days a week. She has four salespeople reporting to her that call her throughout the day, often leaving messages on her cellular phone voice mail when they do not reach her in the car. Her calls include calls to management, potential customers, and other colleagues. Her calls, though, are always quite short—almost always a minute or two. Working in a small business, she is sensitive to the cost of the calls and prefers to use landlines for longer discussions. She also has a minimal commute to work, so rarely makes calls early in the morning or late in the afternoon.

Now, what happens if Jane and John both get an offer from a competitor? Who is more likely to accept the competing offer (or *churn* in the vocabulary of cellular telecommunications companies)? At first glance, we might suspect that Jane is the more price-sensitive and therefore the more susceptible to another offer. However, a second look reveals that changing carriers would be a big inconvenience because it would require her to change telephone numbers. By looking at the number of different people who call her, we see that Jane is quite dependent on her cellular telephone number; she even uses the voice mail feature. The number of people she would have to notify is inertia to keep her from changing providers on her car phone. John has no such inertia and might have no allegiance to his cellular provider—as long as the provider can provide uninterrupted service for his 45-minute call on Wednesday mornings.

Jane also has a lot of *influence*. Since she talks to so many different people, they will all know if she is satisfied or dissatisfied with her service. She is a customer that the cellular company wants to keep happy. But, she is not a customer that traditional methods of segmentation would have located.

The Power of Link Analysis

Link analysis is playing two roles in analyzing the cellular phone data. The first is the power of visualization. The ability to see some of the graphs representing call patterns makes patterns for things like inertia or influence much more obvious. Visualizing the data allows us to see patterns that lead to further questions. For this example, we chose two profitable customers considered similar by previous segmentation techniques. Link analysis showed their specific calling patterns and suggested how the customers differ. On the other hand, looking at the call patterns for all customers at the same time would require drawing a graph with hundreds of thousands or millions of nodes and hundreds of millions of edges. This is not feasible.

Second, link analysis can apply the concepts generated by visualization to larger sets of customers. For instance, a churn reduction program might avoid targeting customers who have a large inertia or be sure to target customers with a large influence. This requires traversing the call graph to calculate the inertia or influence for all customers. Such derived characteristics can play an important role in marketing efforts.

Different marketing programs might suggest looking for other features in the call graph. For instance, perhaps the ability to place a conference call would be desirable, but who would be the best prospects? One idea would be to look for groups of customers that all call each other. Stated as a graph problem, this group is a fully-connected subgraph. When these subgraphs are larger than two nodes, perhaps we have a set of customers who would be interested in the ability to place conference calls.

UNEQUAL NODES: GRAPHS AND NETWORKS

So far, graphs have been defined so that the nodes in them represent the same thing: cities on an airline network, telephone customers, products in a market basket, and so on. A more general definition is useful in many situations where there are different things interacting with each other. For this purpose, we expand the notion of nodes to include different types of things and the resulting structure is called a *network*. A common example of a network is a computer network where the nodes connected to the network can be workstations, midrange systems, mainframes, network gateways, servers, and so forth.

Edges in a network represent relationships as they do in a graph. However, in a network, the connections between different types of nodes may represent different types of relationships. Figure 11.1 showed an example of a network—physicians prescribing drugs made by particular pharmaceutical companies. This network has three types of nodes: physicians, drugs, and pharmaceutical companies, and two types of edges:

- Edges between doctors and prescriptions represent the number of prescriptions the physician makes of the drug.
- Edges between prescriptions and pharmaceutical companies represent which pharmaceutical companies make which drug.

This network can be used to answer specific questions like: What is the value of physician D to pharmaceutical company P? This is answered by finding all paths from D to P. Each path has a value, calculated as the number of units of that medicine prescribed by D times its value to the pharmaceutical P. The sum of this value for all paths from D to P is the value of the physician to the company.

STRENGTHS OF LINK ANALYSIS

Link analysis has several strengths:

- It capitalizes on relationships.
- It is useful for visualization.
- It creates derived characteristics.

Most Appropriate for Linked Data

Some data and data mining problems naturally involve links. As the two case studies about telephone data show, link analysis is very useful for telecommunications—a telephone call is a link between two people. Links appear in other areas like transportation, where a graph often corresponds to an actual map. In these cases, link analysis is readily applied. Link analysis is also appropriate in other areas where the connections do not have such a clear manifestation, such as physician referral patterns.

Useful for Visualization

Links are a very natural way to visualize some types of data. Direct visualization of the links can be a big aid in knowledge discovery. Even when automated patterns are found, visualization of the links helps to better understand what is happening. Link analysis offers an alternative way of looking at data, different from the formats of relational databases and OLAP tools. Links may suggest important patterns in the data, but the significance of the patterns requires a person for interpretation.

Creates Derived Attributes

Links containing items contain information. Often, this information is used to create a new attribute on the data. Sphere of influence is an example of a new attribute generated from link analysis. This attribute is more useful as a predictor than minutes of use (MOU) that had previously been used.

WEAKNESSES OF LINK ANALYSIS

Link Analysis has weaknesses:

- It is not applicable to many types of data.
- Few tools support it.
- Implementations in relational databases are inefficient.

Not Applicable to Many Types of Data

Although link analysis is very powerful when applicable, it is not appropriate for many types of problems. It is not a prediction tool or classification tool like a neural network that takes data in and produces an answer. Many types of data are simply not appropriate for link analysis. Its strongest use is probably in finding specific patterns, such as the types of outgoing calls, which can then be applied to data. These patterns can be turned into new features of the data, for use in conjunction with other directed data mining techniques.

Few Tools

Tools that support link analysis are primarily specialized in visualizing relationships in the law enforcement area. These tools provide visualization of a few hundred or few thousand data elements. Special-purpose code is required to analyze data like call detail data or prescribing patterns of physicians.

Inefficient in SQL

Traversing links is a very expensive operation for data stored in relational tables. Typically, links are at a very detailed level in the data, so using the links for analysis requires joins (an expensive operation) on large tables (considerably worse). This can make it difficult to apply link analysis to large data sets.

WHEN TO APPLY LINK ANALYSIS

Link analysis is a knowledge discovery tool that is applicable to some specific types of problems. When it is applicable, it can find patterns in data that cannot be found with other techniques. With this power comes some limitations. It is not applicable on most types of data. It is for discovery, not for prediction or classification. However, once patterns are found in the data, they often have value as attributes for other data mining techniques, like neural networks and decision trees.

Decision Trees

Decision trees are powerful and popular tools for classification and prediction. The attractiveness of tree-based methods is due in large part to the fact that, in contrast to neural networks, decision trees represent *rules*. Rules can readily be expressed in English so that we humans can understand them or in a database access language like SQL so that records falling into a particular category may be retrieved.

In some applications, the accuracy of a classification or prediction is the only thing that matters; if a direct mail firm obtains a model that can accurately predict which members of a prospect pool are most likely to respond to a certain solicitation, they may not care how or why the model works. The automotive industry case study in Chapter 3 is a case in point. The company wanted to improve the targeting of a test-drive promotion, but was not interested in the details of what makes some people more likely than others to respond to an offer of free sunglasses or boots. The model developed by the University of Southern Illinois made use of both neural networks and decision trees. In other situations, the ability to explain the reason for a decision is crucial. In health insurance underwriting, for example, there are legal prohibitions against discrimination based on certain variables. An insurance company could find itself in the position of having to demonstrate to the satisfaction of a court of law that it has not used illegal discriminatory practices in granting or denying coverage. Similarly, it is more acceptable to both the loan officer and the credit applicant to hear that an application for credit has been denied on the basis of a computer-generated rule such as `income < $20,000 and number of existing revolving accounts > 3` than to hear that the decision has been made by a neural network which provides no explanation for its action.

There are a variety of algorithms for building decision trees which share the desirable trait of explicability. Two of the most popular go by the acronyms CART and CHAID which stand, respectively, for classification and regression trees and chi-squared automatic interaction detection. A newer algorithm, C4.5, is gaining popularity and is now available in several software packages.

In this chapter, we first examine the way decision trees work and how they can be applied to classification and prediction problems. We then go on to provide a detailed examination of the CART, C4.5, and CHAID algorithms for building decision trees. Case studies drawn from the authors' experience are used to illustrate practical considerations to take into account when using decision-tree methods.

HOW A DECISION TREE WORKS

Anyone who has played the game of Twenty Questions will have no difficulty understanding the way a decision tree classifies records. In the game, one player thinks of a particular place, person, or thing that would be known or recognized by all the participants, but the player gives no clue to its identity. The other players try to discover what it is by asking a series of yes-or-no questions. A good player rarely needs the full allotment of 20 questions to move all the way from "Is it bigger than a bread box?" to "Michael Johnson's gold running shoes."

A decision tree represents such a series of questions. As in the game, the answer to the first question determines what follow-up question is asked next. If the questions are well chosen, a surprisingly short series is enough to accurately classify an incoming record.

Decision trees are traditionally drawn with the root at the top and the leaves at the bottom, perhaps indicating that mathematicians ought to get out more. The binary decision tree in Figure 12.1 uses the Twenty Questions approach to classify musical instruments.

A record enters the tree at the root node. At the root, a test is applied to determine which *child node* the record will encounter next. There are different algorithms for choosing the initial test, but the goal is always the same: To choose the test that best discriminates among the target classes. This process is repeated until the record arrives at a *leaf node*. All the records that end up at a given leaf of the tree are classified the same way. There is a unique path from the root to each leaf. That path is an expression of the *rule* used to classify the records.

Many different leaves may make the same classification, but each leaf makes that classification for a different reason. For example, in a tree that classifies fruits and vegetables by color, the leaves for apple, tomato, and cherry might all predict "red," albeit with varying degrees of confidence since there are likely to be examples of green apples, yellow tomatoes, and black cherries as well.

Trees Grow in Many Forms

The tree in Figure 12.1 is a binary tree of non-uniform depth; that is, each node has two children and the distance of a leaf to the root varies. In this case, each node represents a yes-or-no question, the answer to which determines by which of two paths a record proceeds to the next level of the tree. Decision trees need not be binary. Figure 12.2 illustrates a tree that has a mixture of binary and ternary nodes.

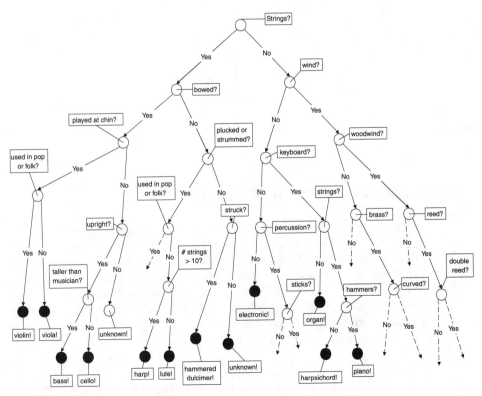

Figure 12.1 A partial binary tree for the classification of musical instruments.

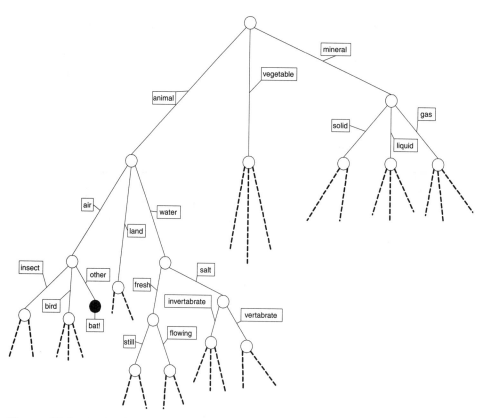

Figure 12.2 A mixed binary and ternary tree.

SOME RULES ARE BETTER THAN OTHERS

We measure the effectiveness of a decision tree, taken as a whole, by applying it to a collection of previously unseen records and observing the percentage classified correctly. We must also pay attention to the quality of the individual branches of the tree. Each path through the tree represents a rule and some rules are better than others. Sometimes, the predictive power of the whole tree can be improved by pruning back some of its weaker branches.

At each node in the tree, we can measure:

- the number of records entering the node
- the way those records would be classified if this were a leaf node
- the percentage of records classified correctly at this node

Decision-tree-building algorithms begin by trying to find the test which does the best job of splitting the data among the desired categories. At each succeeding level of the tree, the subsets created by the preceding split are themselves split according to whatever rule works best for them. The tree continues to grow until it is no longer possible to find better ways to split up incoming records .

Figure 12.3 shows the result of applying C4.5, a popular decision-tree program, to the moviegoers database introduced in Chapter 4. As you will recall, respondents were asked to report their age, sex, most recently seen movie, and other movies seen recently. We then used a decision-tree program to create rules for determining the sex of a

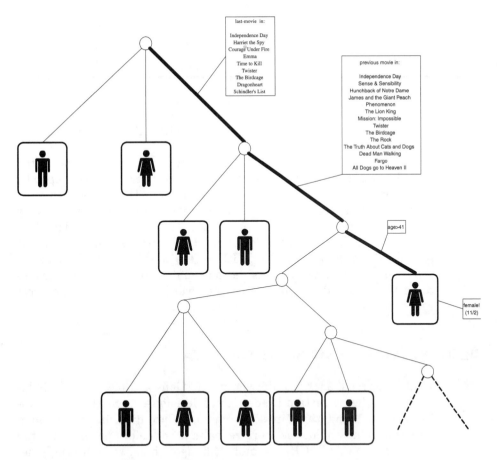

Figure 12.3 Decision tree generated from the moviegoers database.

Table 12.1 An Extract from the Moviegoers' Database of Records Meeting the Criteria Shown in Figure 12.3

age	source_ID	moviegoers.movie_ID	past_movies.movie_ID	sex	predicted
59	4	23	1	f	f
43	2	1	12	f	f
43	2	1	30	f	f
45	1	25	63	m	f
45	1	25	2	f	f
45	1	25	26	f	f
46	1	26	2	f	f
45	2	32	111	f	f
39	3	1	63	m	f
45	1	25	63	f	f
45	2	32	17	f	f

moviegoer based on his or her responses to the other questions on the questionnaire.

As we can see from Table 12.1, this node misclassifies some of the records. Closer examination shows that some of the rules developed by this particular tree work better than others. The rules also vary greatly in their *coverage* of the data. Some leaves of the tree have very few records associated with them, while others have many. The data box next to the highlighted leaf node in Figure 12.3 shows that 11 records (the ones listed in Table 12.1) were classified by this node. Of those, nine were correctly classified as female while two were males incorrectly classified as female. In other words, this rule has an error rate of 0.182.

DECISION TREES CREATE BOXES FOR DATA

While the tree diagram and Twenty Questions analogy are very helpful in visualizing certain properties of decision-tree methods, the authors have found that, in some cases, a box diagram based on a different game analogy is more revealing. So, before getting into the details of the CART, CHAID, and C4.5 algorithms, we will briefly describe the box diagrams we use to represent classification rules produced by all three.

This time, the game in question is the carnival game where the rubes are invited to throw a ball at an array of boxes, plates, or baskets. Each box is labeled with a different score or outcome. Depending on which box the ball ends up in, the player may go home with a giant teddy-bear or with only a small trinket worth less than the game ticket. We may view the array of boxes as a classification device; it classifies players as either winners or losers depending on where their toss lands.

A decision tree creates a set of boxes or bins into which we can toss our records. The leaf nodes from any of the tree diagrams above already form a one-dimensional version of the box diagram. The test associated with the root node of the decision tree divides the line into two or more sections. Each section is further subdivided by tests deeper in the tree. In Figure 12.4, the gap in the center of the row of bins corresponds to the root node of the tree. All stringed instruments fall to the left of the gap.

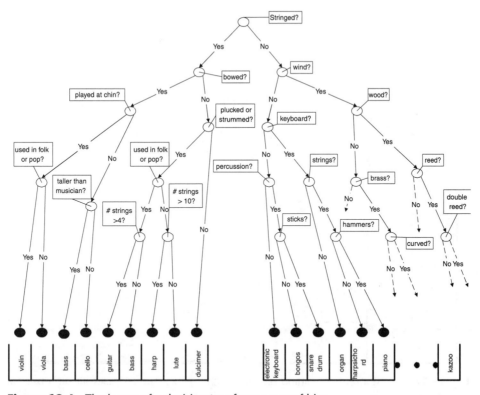

Figure 12.4 The leaves of a decision tree form a row of bins.

There are several ways we might expand on this mapping from tree leaves to record bins:

- The width of the bins can be varied to indicate the relative likelihood of a record landing in a particular bin.
- The diagram can be turned into a histogram with the height of each bar indicating the number of records that landed in the corresponding bin. Such a diagram could use the color or shading of the bars is an indication of the error rate for the corresponding rule (see Figure 12.5).
- Individual records can be represented as balls or dots that are colored according to the values taken on by the target variable. This gives an immediate feel for how well the classifier is performing.

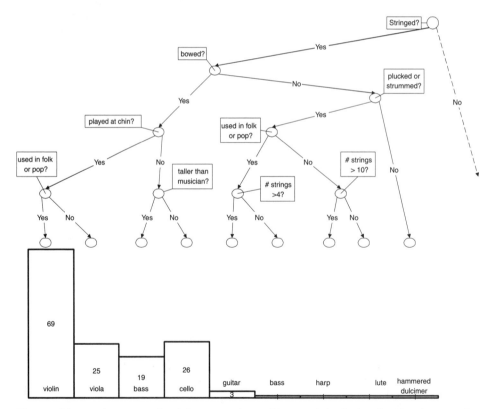

Figure 12.5 Histogram of training records reaching each leaf of a classification tree for stringed instruments.

Representing Many Dimensions

Most of us are familiar with two-dimensional graphs that plot one variable against another. In the final form of our box diagram, we take advantage of that skill by representing a decision tree, and the records it has classified, as a sort of nested collection of two-dimensional scatter plots.

At the root node of a decision tree, a split is performed based on some particular field in the data. In the outermost box of the box diagram, the horizontal axis represents that field. We divide the outermost box into sections, one for each node at the next level of the tree. If the split field represents a categorical variable such as "animal, vegetable, or mineral," we generally choose the positions of the splits so that the size of each section is proportional to the number of records that fall into it. If the field contains a continuous variable, we have the additional option of considering our horizontal line to be the X-axis of a graph and placing the vertical lines according to the values used in the splitting function. In either case, we now use the vertical axis of each box to represent the field which is used as the splitter for that node. In general, this will be a different field for each box.

We now have a new set of boxes, each of which represents a node at the third level of the tree. We continue dividing boxes until we get to the leaves of the tree. Since decision trees often have non-uniform depth, some boxes may be subdivided more often than others. Box diagrams like the one below allow us to represent classification rules that depend on any number of variables on a two-dimensional chart.

The resulting diagram is very expressive. As we toss records onto the grid, they fall into a particular box and are classified accordingly. A box chart allows us to look at the data at several levels of detail. In Figure 12.6, we can see at a glance that the bottom left contains a high concentration of males.

Taking a closer look, we find some boxes that seem to do a particularly good job at classification or collect a large number of records. Viewed this way, it is natural to think of decision trees as a way of drawing boxes around groups of similar points. All of the points within a particular box are classified the same way because they all meet the rule which defines that box. This is in contrast to classical statistical classification methods such as linear, logistic, and quadratic discriminants which attempt to partition data into classes by drawing a line or elliptical curve through the data space. This is a fundamental distinction: Statistical approaches that use a single line to find the boundary between classes are weak when there are several very different ways for a record to become part of the target class.

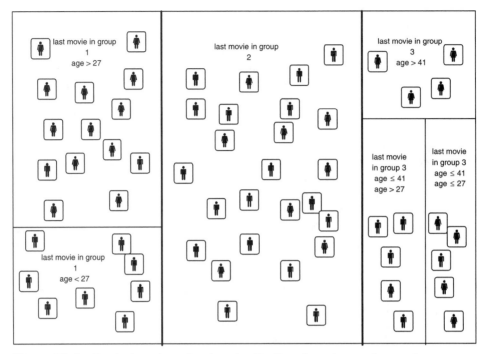

Figure 12.6 Gender box chart showing classification of moviegoers by gender.

In the credit card industry, for example, there are several ways that a customer can be profitable. Some profitable customers have low transaction rates, but keep high revolving balances without defaulting. Others pay off their balance in full each month, but are profitable due to the high transaction volume they generate. Two very dissimilar customers may be equally profitable. We use the illustration in Figure 12.7 to convey the advantage of decision trees over purely statistical methods for classification problems of this kind.

CART

The CART algorithm described here is one of the most popular methods of building a decision tree. Since its publication by L. Briemen and associates in 1984, it has been a staple of machine-learning experiments. Many of the commercially available rule induction tools use

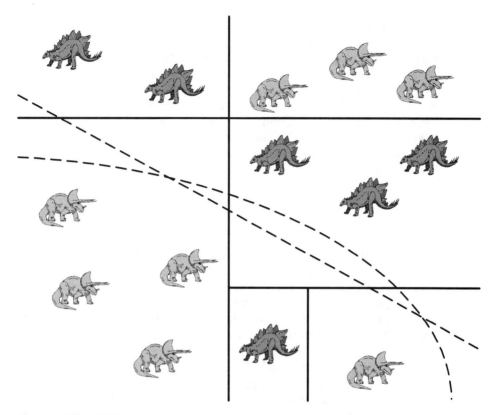

Figure 12.7 Often a line or simple curve cannot separate the regions.

some variant of this algorithm to generate their rules, although the vendors are sometimes a bit coy about describing their algorithms in detail and tend to invent new fancy names for what are, in fact, minor variations.

Finding the Initial Split

At the start of the process, we have a *training set* consisting of preclassified records. By preclassified, we mean that the target field, or *dependent variable*, has a known class. The goal is to build a tree that will allow us to assign a class to the target field of a new record based on the values of the other fields or *independent variables*.

CART builds a binary tree by splitting the records at each node according to a function of a single input field. The first task, therefore, is to decide which of the independent fields makes the best splitter. The best split is defined as one that does the best job of separating the records into groups where a single class predominates.

The measure used to evaluate a potential splitter is *diversity*. There are several ways of calculating the *index of diversity* for a set of records. With all of them, a high index of diversity indicates that the set contains an even distribution of classes, while a low index means that members of a single class predominate. The best splitter is the one that decreases the diversity of the record sets by the greatest amount. In other words, we want to maximize

```
diversity(before split) - ( diversity(left child) +
   diversity(right child) )
```

The CART algorithm as originally described by Briemen and associates, adapted a diversity measure from economics. An Italian economist named Gini devised a standard measure for the level of income inequality in a country. Consider a plot with percent of total income on the Y-axis and percent of population, ordered from poorest to richest, on the X-axis. If income was distributed equally, this would be a straight 45° line; the first 10 percent of the population would account for 10 percent of income, and the first 90 percent of population would account for 90 percent of income. In the real world, the curve sags below the line of perfect equality since the poorest 10 percent of the population receives well under 10 percent of the income while the richest 10 percent receive considerably more than their share. The Gini ratio compares area between the true curve and the 45° line to the total area under the line. Australia has a low score because income is fairly well distributed, whereas Venezuela gets a high score.

The commercial CART package most familiar to the authors is the StarTree module of *Darwin* from Thinking Machines Corporation. This program allows the user a choice of three diversity measures:

```
min( P(c1), P(c2) )
2P(c1)P(c2)
[P(c1)logP(c1)] + [P(c2)logP(c2)]
```

All of these functions have a maximum where the probabilities of the classes are equal and evaluate to zero when the set contains only a single class. Between the extremes of full diversity and complete uniformity, these functions have slightly different shapes. As a result, they produce slightly different rankings of the proposed splits, but these differences need not concern us here. There is a slightly fuller explanation of the last of these measures, called *entropy* or *information*, in the section on C4.5, which uses the concept of *information gain* to make splitting decisions.

To choose the best splitter at a node, we consider each independent field in turn. Assuming the field takes on multiple values, we sort it and then, using decrease in diversity as the measure of goodness, perform a binary search for the best split. We compare the decrease in diversity provided by the best splitter from each field. The winner is chosen as the splitter for the root node.

Growing the Full Tree

The initial split produces two nodes, each of which we now attempt to split in the same manner as the root node. Once again, we examine all the input fields to find candidate splitters. If the field only takes on one value, we eliminate it from consideration since there is no way it can be used to create a split. A categorical field which has been used as a splitter higher up in the tree is likely to become single-valued fairly quickly. The best split for each of the remaining fields is determined. When no split can be found that significantly decreases the diversity of a given node, we label it a leaf node.

Eventually, only leaf nodes remain and we have grown the full decision tree. As we will see, however, the full tree is generally not the tree that does the best job of classifying a new set of records.

Measuring Error Rate at Each Node

At the end of the tree-growing process, every record of the training set has been assigned to some leaf of the full decision tree. Each leaf can now be assigned a class and an error rate. Look again at Figure 12.3 which highlights the path from the root to one of the leaves that assigns records to the class "female." The fact that this is a leaf node means that no splitter was found that would significantly decrease its diversity. That does not mean, however, that all records reaching this leaf actually have the same class. In this case, since the majority of the training records that reached this leaf have the value "female" in the target field, we assign the class "female" to this leaf.

Using the definition of simple probability, we see that 9 of 11 are correctly classified. This tells us that, based on the training data, respondents whose records reach this node have a 0.818 probability of being female. Equivalently, this leaf has an error rate of 1–0.818 or 0.182.

Calculating the Error Rate of an Entire Tree

The error rate of an entire decision tree is a weighted sum of the error rates of all the leaves. Each leaf's contribution to the total is the error rate at that leaf multiplied by the probability that a record will end up in there.

Pruning the Tree

As previously described, the decision tree keeps growing as long as new splits can be found that improve the ability of the tree to separate the records of the training set into classes. If the training data were used for evaluation, any pruning of the tree would only increase the error rate. Does this imply that the full tree will also do the best job of classifying new datasets? Certainly not!

The CART algorithm makes its best split first, at the root node where there is a large population of records. Each following split has a smaller and less representative population with which to work. Towards the end, idiosyncrasies of the particular training records at a node come to dominate the process.

If we are trying to predict height and we come to a node containing one tall Martin and several shorter people with other names, we can decrease diversity at the node by a new rule saying that "people named Martin are tall." This rule helps classify the training data, but if, in the wider universe, Martin turns out to be a fairly rare name and, in any case, not particularly well-correlated with stature, the rule will be worse than useless.

Figure 12.8 shows graphically what has happened. The boxes have become so small and drawn so precisely around the training records that new records are unlikely to fit. Clearly, we need to prune the tree in order to get more accurate predictions in the general case. The problem is to determine how far back to prune and to determine which of the many possible subtrees will perform best.

Identifying Candidate Subtrees

To determine how far back to prune the tree, we first identify candidate subtrees through a process of repeated pruning. The goal is to prune first those branches which provide the least additional predic-

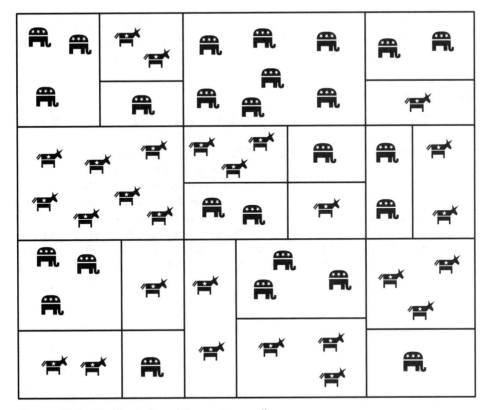

Figure 12.8 The boxes have become too small.

tive power per leaf. In order to identify these least useful branches, we introduce the concept of the *adjusted error rate* of a tree. This is a measure that imposes a per-leaf penalty that identifies weak branches (those that do not decrease the error rate of the tree enough to overcome the penalty) and marks them for pruning.

The formula for the adjusted error rate is

```
AE(T) = E(T) + αleaf_count(T)
```

When α is zero, the adjusted error rate equals the error rate. To find the first subtree, the adjusted error rates for all possible subtrees containing the root node are evaluated as α is gradually increased. When the adjusted error rate of some subtree becomes less than or equal to the adjusted error rate for the complete tree, we have found the first candidate subtree, α_1. All branches that are not part of α_1 are pruned and the process starts again. The α_1 tree is pruned to create an α_2 tree. The process ends when the tree has been pruned all the way down to the root node.

Evaluating Subtrees

The final task is to select from the pool of candidate subtrees, the tree that will best classify new data. For this purpose, we use a second pre-classified dataset, the *test set*. The test set is drawn from the same population as the training set, but contains different records.

Each of the candidate subtrees is used to classify the records in the test set. The tree that performs this task with the lowest overall error rate is declared the winner. The winning subtree has been pruned enough to remove the effects of overtraining, but not so much as to lose valuable information. The graph in Figure 12.9 illustrates the effect of pruning on classification accuracy.

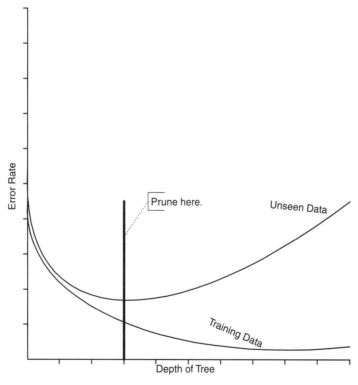

Figure 12.9 Effect of pruning on error rate.

Evaluating the Best Subtree

The winning subtree was selected on the basis of its overall error rate when applied to the task of classifying the records in the test set. But, while we can expect that the selected subtree will continue to be the best performing subtree when applied to other datasets, the error rate that caused it to be selected may slightly overstate its effectiveness. There are likely to be a large number of subtrees that all perform about as well as the one selected. To a certain extent, the one of these that delivered the lowest error rate on the test set may simply have "gotten lucky" with that particular collection of records. For that reason, we apply the selected subtree to a third preclassified dataset that is disjoint with both the test set and the training set. This third dataset is called the *evaluation set*. We use the error rate obtained on the evaluation set to predict expected performance of the classification rules represented by the selected tree when applied to unclassified data.

Taking Cost into Account

In our discussion so far, we have used the error rate as the sole measure for evaluating the fitness of rules and subtrees. In many applications, however, the costs of misclassification vary from class to class. Certainly, in a medical diagnosis, a false negative can be more harmful than a false positive; a scary Pap smear result which, on further investigation, proves to have been a false positive, is much preferable to an undetected cancer. We can take these issues into account by replacing the error rate with a cost function that multiplies the probability of misclassification by a weight indicating the cost of that misclassification.

C4.5

C4.5 is the most recent available snapshot of the decision-tree algorithm that Australian researcher, J. Ross Quinlan has been evolving and refining for many years. An earlier version, ID3, published in 1986, has been very influential in the field of machine learning and is still being used in several commercial products. (The name ID3 stands for "Iterative Dichotomiser 3." We have not heard an explanation for the name C4.5, but we can guess that Professor Quinlan's background is mathematics rather than marketing.)

The version of C4.5 described here is available in source code form Professor Quinlan. It is also used in *Clementine*, a commercial data mining package from Integral Solutions, Ltd. Clementine, under a different name, is also sold by NCR for use on their parallel database servers. The decision tree for classifying people by gender based on movie viewing habits, Figure 12.3 was generated using C4.5.

Differences from CART

C4.5 is so similar to CART, that we will describe it primarily in terms of how the former differs from the latter. For that reason, it is a good idea to read the previous section on CART, even if your primary interest is in C4.5.

Growing the Decision Tree

The first difference we notice between C4.5 and CART is that while CART performs a binary split at each node and so always produces a binary tree, C4.5 produces trees with varying numbers of branches per node. This is because, although C4.5 treats continuous variables in pretty much the same way that CART does, it treats categorical variables quite differently. When C4.5 assesses a categorical field's value as a splitter, its default behavior is to assume that there will be one branch for each value taken on by that variable. So, if `color` is chosen as the best field on which to split the root node, and the training set includes records that take on the values red, orange, yellow, green, blue, purple and white, then there will be seven nodes in the next level of the tree.

Trees versus Bushes

Is the extra bushiness of a C4.5-generated tree a good thing? The answer depends on the domain. Many things, besides Caesar's Gaul, are divided into three parts. An insistence on binary splits, on an attribute that is inherently more various, only leads to unnecessary complication in the generated tree. On the other hand, high branching factors quickly reduce the population of training records available at each node in lower levels of the tree, making further splits less reliable.

Of course, the field being split was chosen for that role because it outperformed all other fields in a competition to find the split that made the most progress towards fully classifying the training records. The choice of metric for the "goodness" of the result of a split has a strong impact on the likelihood of selecting splits with high branching factors.

Gain and Gain Ratio

ID3, the precursor to C4.5, uses a criterion called *information gain* to compare potential splits. A comprehensive introduction to information theory is far beyond the scope of this book. For our purposes, the important notion is that the number of bits required to describe a particular situation or outcome depends on the size of the set of possible outcomes. If there are eight equally probable classes, it takes $\log_2(8)$, or three bits, to identify a particular one. If, on the other hand, there are only four such classes represented, it takes only $\log_2(4)$, or two bits, to identify any one of them. So, a split that takes a node that has examples of eight classes and splits it into nodes which average 4 classes each is said to have an information gain of one bit.

As a split evaluation criterion, information gain is highly biased towards very bushy decision trees. If we used this criterion to build a decision tree from the moviegoers database, we would pick name as a very good field on which to split, no matter what other field we were attempting to predict: Since relatively few people have the same name, a split on that field leads to many nodes that contain a single record. Each of these records necessarily belongs to only a single class. In this situation, the average information is close to zero, so the information gain is maximized. (For a business problem, we would rename fields such as name and address prior to using any data mining techniques.)

A decision tree based on first names might actually do a pretty good job at classifying people by gender *if* we had a training set so large that a high proportion of names of previously unseen moviegoers are represented in the training set. It would be unlikely to do a very good job at predicting age or group membership, however.

In reaction to this problem, C4.5 now uses the ratio of the total information gain due to a proposed split to the information gain attributable solely to the number of subsets created as the criterion for evaluating proposed splits. This test leads to fairly conservative branching, but even so, C4.5 ran into trouble on the moviegoers data when applied with its default options. It chose moviegoers.movie_ID as the root node splitter, leading to a 61-way initial split. Most of the 61 nodes at the second level of the tree had too few records to form reasonable further splits with the result that potentially useful fields, such as the past movies, were ignored. C4.5 did better when an optional grouping flag was used to restrain the bushiness of the initial tree. With this option turned on, the program attempts to form groups of values for each categorical variable by finding combinations of values which have greater discriminatory power than any of the values taken alone. This procedure produced the binary and ternary splits illustrated in Figure 12.3.

Pruning the Tree

Another area in which C4.5 differs substantively from CART is in its approach to pruning. CART, you will recall, uses a measure of the complexity of the tree to label various subtrees, then tests those subtrees on previously unseen preclassified data (the test set). In contrast, C4.5 attempts to prune the tree it has grown without reference to any data beyond the training set.

As an aside, C4.5's choice of pruning strategy clearly reflects its academic origins. Judging from the technical literature, universities seem to have a hard time getting their hands on substantial quantities of real data to use for training sets. Consequently, they spend much time and effort trying to coax the last few drops of information from their impoverished datasets.

In our experience, having a small volume of data is never a problem in commercial applications of data mining. The data may be in the wrong place or in the wrong format, but there is plenty of it. Businesses already know how to deal with small amounts of data using tools like spreadsheets and on-line analytic processing (OLAP). It is only when the data gets really large that the data miners are called in.

Be that as it may, C4.5 uses the same data it used to grow the tree to decide how the tree should be pruned.

Pessimistic Pruning

C4.5 prunes the tree by examining the error rate at each leaf and assuming that the true error rate will be substantially worse. If N records arrive at a leaf, and E of them are classified incorrectly, then the error rate at that leaf is E/N. Now the whole point of the tree-growing algorithm is to minimize this error rate, so we assume that E/N is the best we can do.

C4.5 uses an analogy with statistical sampling to come up with an estimate of the worst error rate likely to be seen at a leaf. The analogy works by thinking of the data at the leaf as representing the results of a series of trials each of which can have one of two possible results. (Heads or tails, to use the usual example.) As it happens, statisticians have been studying this particular situation since at least 1713, the year that Jacques Bernoulli's famous binomial formula was posthumously published. So there are well-known formulas for determining what it means to have observed E occurrences of some event in N trials.

In particular, there is a formula which, for a given confidence level, gives the confidence interval, the range of expected values of E. C4.5 assumes that the observed error rate on the training data is the low end of this range and substitutes the high end to get a leaf's predicted error rate on unseen data. Out towards the leaves, where there are few records, substituting this pessimistic error rate for the observed one often causes the error rate of a whole subtree to be higher than that of one of the nodes above it, in which case, it gets pruned. Unlike CART, which always prunes an entire subtree, C4.5 sometimes replaces a subtree with one of its branches.

From Trees to Rules

C4.5 comes with a companion program for turning the decision trees it generates into sets of rules. We have already seen that the path from the root node to any one leaf can trivially be expressed as a rule, but if there are many leaves, the resulting set of rules can be very confusing. If one of the purposes of the data mining exercise is to gain understanding of the problem domain, it can be useful to reduce this huge tangle of rules to a smaller, more comprehensible collection.

We can take the first step in that direction without changing the classification behavior of the tree by combining paths that lead to leaves that make the same classification. The partial decision tree in Figure 12.10 yields the following rules:

> *Watch the game* and *home team wins* and *out with friends* then **beer**.
>
> *Watch the game* and *home team wins* and *sitting at home* then **diet soda**.
>
> *Watch the game* and *home team loses* and *out with friends* then **beer**.
>
> *Watch the game* and *home team loses* and *sitting at home* then **milk**.

The two rules that predict beer can be combined by eliminating the test for whether the home team wins or loses. That test is important for discriminating between milk and diet soda, but has no bearing on beer consumption. The new, simpler rule is:

> *watch the game* and *out with friends* then **beer**.

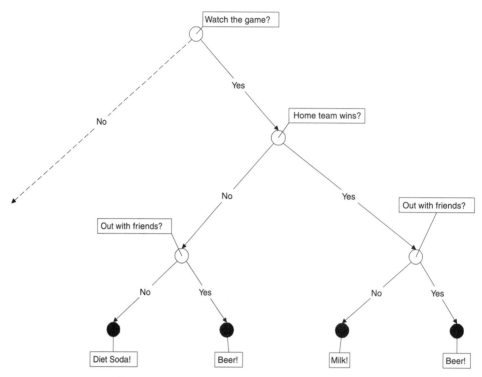

Figure 12.10   A beverage prediction tree.

Up to this point, we have not done anything controversial, but C4.5's rule generator goes farther. It attempts to generalize each rule by removing clauses, then comparing the predicted error rate of the new, briefer rule with that of the original using the same pessimistic error rate assumption used to prune the tree in the first place. Often, the rules for several different leaves generalize to the same rule, so this process results in fewer rules than the decision tree had leaves.

In the decision tree, every record ends up at some one leaf, so we know how to classify any record that comes along. After the rule-generalization process, however, we may end up with rules that are not mutually exclusive and with records that are not covered by any rule. The first problem can be solved by simply picking one rule when more than one is applicable. The second problem requires the introduction of a *default class* assigned to any record not covered by any of the rules. We might choose the most frequently occurring class to be the default.

Once it has created a set of generalized rules, Quinlan's algorithm groups the rules for each class together and eliminates those that do not seem to contribute much to the accuracy of the set of rules as a whole. The end result is a small number of easy to understand rules. Quinlan's claim is that this reduced rule set is generally about as accurate as the entire pruned decision tree, but we are suspicious of this claim, at least for complex problem domains. After all, a complex decision tree may reflect a complex situation.

The reduced set of generalized rules may produce very useful insights, but our preference is to stick with the complete decision tree for classification.

CHAID

CHAID, an algorithm first published by J. A. Hartigan in 1975, is the oldest of the algorithms discussed in this chapter. It is also the most widely used since it is distributed as part of popular statistics packages like SPSS and SAS. CHAID is descended from an earlier automatic interaction detection system, AID, which was described by J. A. Morgan and J. N. Sonquist in 1963.

As the phrase "automatic interaction detection" implies, the original motivation for CHAID was for detecting statistical relationships between variables. It does this by building a decision tree, so the method has come to be used as a classification tool as well and it is in that context that we discuss it here.

Differences from CART and C4.5

The largest difference between CHAID and the two decision-tree generation algorithms that we have already discussed is that rather than first overfitting the data, then pruning, CHAID attempts to stop growing the tree before overfitting occurs. Another difference is that CHAID is restricted to categorical variables. Continuous variables must be broken into ranges or replaced with classes such as *high, low, medium*.

Growing the Tree

As in the other two methods, the algorithm searches for a way to use the input variables to split the training data into two or more child nodes. The child nodes are chosen in such a way that the probability of the target field taking on a particular value differs from node to node.

Choosing a Splitter

Each of the input, or *predictor*, fields is considered as a potential splitter. The first step in this investigation is to merge any categories that correspond to the same value of the target variable. This step is best explained by an example. We start with the correspondences shown in Table 12.2.

After this first step, we have:

Truite Amandine, Tunafish Salad, Sashimi	fish
Foie Gras d'Oie, Buffalo Wings, Chopped Liver	fowl
Chateaubriand, Big Mac, Spam, Lamb Chop	good red meat

Of course, in practice, any given value of the predictor field may occur many times. Not every instance of a particular value of the predictor will correspond to the same classification of the target variable, so predictors are grouped together if the proportion of classes in the corresponding target fields are not *significantly* different. In statistics, the word "significant" has a well-defined meaning and there are a variety of tests for significance. One of these tests, the X^2 (chi-squared), is responsible for the first two letters of the acronym CHAID.

The X^2 Test

The X^2 test is a test of statistical significance developed by the English statistician, Karl Pearson, in 1900. X^2 is defined as the sum of the

Table 12.2 Correspondences

Truite Amandine	fish
Foie Gras d'Oie	fowl
Chateaubriand	good red meat
Buffalo Wings	fowl
Tunafish Salad	fish
Big Mac	good red meat
Chopped Liver	fowl
Spam	good red meat
Sashimi	fish
Lamb Chop	good red meat

squares of the standardized differences between the expected and observed frequencies of some occurrence in each sample. The test is a measure of the probability that an apparent *association* is due to chance or, inversely, that the probability that an observed *difference* between samples is due to chance.

Deciding whether two predictors ought to be merged is only the first of several uses of this test in the CHAID algorithm.

Re-Splitting the Categories

During the first step, all the predictor fields that do not produce statistically significant differences in the target field values are merged. In the second step, each group of three or more predictors is re-split by all possible binary divisions. If any of these splits yields a statistically significant difference in outcomes, it is retained.

Evaluating the Candidate Splitters

Once each predictor field has been grouped to produce the maximum possible diversity of classes in the target field, the X^2 test is applied to the resulting groupings. The predictor that generates the groupings that differ the most according to this test is chosen as the splitter for the current node.

Limiting the Growth of the Tree

In CHAID, the tree keeps growing until no more splits are available that lead to statistically significant differences in classification. The precise level of significance used as the cut-off value affects the size of the tree and its value as a classifier or predictor. This is the main tuning parameter available to the CHAID user.

In the research community, the current fashion is away from methods that continue splitting only as long as it seems likely to be useful and towards methods that involve pruning. Some researchers, however, still prefer the CHAID approach and believe that the pruning camp has a bias towards simpler trees that does not reflect the trees' performance on real-world data.

PRACTICAL CONSIDERATIONS IN USING DECISION-TREE METHODS

In the course of their work with MBJ Technology Solution, a specialty systems integration and consulting company, the authors are sometimes called upon to use the data mining techniques described in this book to produce one or two interesting results very quickly to demonstrate the value of data mining to prospective clients. When it works, this is a very effective sales tool; when we can show prospects that their data can tell them things they need to know to run their businesses more profitably, they tend to become customers.

This is the story of an occasion when the "quick hit" approach failed to yield good results. Success stories are fun to talk about, but in this case, a failure story is more appropriate. This little vignette illustrates many of the practical issues in data preparation and representation that need to be taken into account when using decision trees.

Case Study: Credit Card Division of a Bank

One of our company's regional managers was working on a proposal to build a decision-support system for the credit card division of a medium-size bank based in his area. A week before the proposal was due, the bank agreed to supply us with a sample of some of the data that would be going into the proposed database. We hoped to be able to spice up our proposal with an example of the kind of exciting results the bank would be able to obtain once it created the right decision-support environment. Thinking Machines Corporation, a data mining software vendor provided us with access to a pre-release version of their CART tool, knowing that our success could bring them a sale as well.

Unfamiliarity with the Data

The first problem we encountered was that no one that we were in contact with at the bank was familiar with the data at the detail level. The data was collected and maintained by an outside service provider that handled most of the operational side of the bank's credit card business. The bank received the data in the form of paper reports. We did not feel that we could expect much help from the outside vendor since part of our proposal was to eliminate the need for its service.

Data Translation Issues

The tool we were using included a data import facility capable of dealing with many of the data translation issues we faced such as translating EBCDIC to ASCII and packed decimal to `int` or `double`. Despite this, data translation proved difficult. To import the data, the CART tool needed a description of every field, including a field name, record position, input type, output type, and whether it was to be treated as continuous or categorical.

The only description we had of the data came in the form of COBOL record descriptions. Our COBOL being a bit rusty, we made a trip to the Cambridge bookstore where we generally go for technical books. There, in alphabetical order after the shelves and shelves of titles on C and C++, was a lone COBOL reference. With the aid of that book we were able to create EMACS editor macros to translate the COBOL record descriptors into the form required by the CART tool. All this took longer to accomplish than it does to describe, and by the time the data was imported and ready to be fed to the CART tool, there was only one day left for analysis.

Difficulties with the Time Component of the Data

One issue we faced in translating the COBOL record descriptors was how to deal with the OCCURS statement used in COBOL to describe repeated subfields. The credit card data records consisted of number of fixed fields containing general account information such as account number, name, address, and date of issue. The rest of the record contained 16 monthly snapshots of account information such as balance for purchases, balance for cash advances, payments, and so forth. In the COBOL record descriptor, each of the fields in this repeating section had a single name such as purbal or cabal. In order to import the data we had to give each occurrence of a field a unique name. This we accomplished by simply appending a month number between 0 and 15 to the end of each field name.

This approach, while straightforward, does not make any information about the sequential nature of the data available to the CART tool. It has no way of knowing that purbal3 precedes purbal2 which in turn precedes purbal1. Likewise, it has no way of knowing that purbal3 and cabal3 are related by being in the same month. This poor choice of how to represent the sequential data made it difficult for CART to find patterns such as "three months of declining balance" or even "three consecutive months with no activity."

A better approach is to normalize the historical data for each closed account so that month when the account was closed becomes month 0 and the month before the account was closed becomes month 1 and so on. Of course, this would destroy any pattern that was truly seasonal such as "people close their accounts after Christmas," but in fact, no such seasonal pattern was found. In our judgment, the month on month patterns that would be revealed by looking at time in terms of the number of months before attrition are more important.

When using CART with time-series data, it also makes sense to enrich the dataset with derived fields that represent period-to-period changes explicitly. In this case, fields such as delta_balance, delta_interest_rate, and delta_credit_limit would probably have helped a great deal.

CART's Disregard of Relationships between Fields

In the CART algorithm, as in CHAID and C4.5, the records at a node are split according to some function of the one field whose splitter yields the greatest decrease in diversity. As a consequence, CART can never generate a rule that combines information from multiple fields. This means that relationships that seem intuitively likely to be important, such as "available balance is less than minimum payment" or even "current month is account renewal month" may not be captured unless the data is enriched with derived fields.

Defining the Target Classes

The early version of the Darwin decision-tree tool that we used for this exercise required that the target field, that is, the field to be predicted, be a categorical variable that only takes on two values. In this case, we needed the values "attriter" or "non-attriter." The relevant field in the data actually took on half a dozen values indicating the account's reason for closure. One of these values clearly represented a voluntary closure at the request of the customer. We re-coded the field so that one value represented an attriter while all the others were lumped together in a single category that included customers who had not (yet) closed their account, people who had had their accounts closed by the bank for various reasons, and unknowns. It might have been more informative to attempt to predict the reason for closure.

A larger problem with the definition of the target class is that it ignores "silent attrition." Back when most credit cards carried a yearly renewal fee, customers who had stopped using a credit card had an incentive to take some positive action to close the account. This is the sort of action captured in the closure field of a database. In recent years, however, banks and other card issuers have had to drop renewal fees in order to stay competitive. This has led to a rise in silent attrition. Customers no longer bother to report that they have stopped using their credit card, they simply pay off the balance and stop using it. This sort of attrition is even more costly that the nonsilent variety since it costs money to keep an inactive customer on the books. Careful definition of the target classes is a prerequisite for success with any classification technique.

Data Representation Issues

The bank had grown through a series of recent acquisitions. Presumably, customers acquired from different institutions have different products, different histories, different demographic profiles, and different loyalties from each other and from those who initially opened their accounts with the bank. Unfortunately, this account origin information was not included in the database.

We hoped that since the acquired banks were locally focused institutions, various geographic variables, such as state, might serve as proxies for the account source. As it turned out, the account holder's state was represented by the two-letter post office abbreviation. The tool handled all array variables, including strings, by treating each element independently. CART did come up with a few rules of the form "`if state[0] = N and state[1] = Y ...`" which served mainly to convince us that we should have assigned numeric codes to the states before attempting to analyze the data.

Noisy Data

Although the data contained fields for 16 months of history, it quickly became apparent that most of the accounts did not actually contain 16 months of historical data. There was no formal null value defined so fields without a real value contained whatever meaningless bits had been deposited there after many translation steps.

Clearly, the data needed to be masked so that only meaningful values would be considered, but this sort of masking requires time and thought. For each field, we needed to choose a null value appropriate to the type of data (date, dollar amount, zip code, etc.) that would serve as an identity element for the field and be clearly recognizable in any rules based on it.

Fields That Cheat

Decision-tree algorithms classify a target field, the dependent variable, based on rules expressed in terms of the independent variables. If we are trying to predict a future event such as attrition, the dependent variable is something we don't yet know, while the independent variables are things we can expect to know in advance.

The problem is that with unfamiliar data, it can be hard to know which fields truly are independent. If the training set contains fields that encode future information, decision trees will use them to produce rules that work very well on the test and evaluation datasets (which also contain that future information) but will be useless on real unclassified data.

The good news is that since decision trees are very good at taking advantage of future information, the fields that contain it will reveal themselves by their presence near the root of decision trees with suspiciously low error rates. The authors have seen many examples of rules such as "prospects with an account number not equal to zero respond to the offer." Well, yes, of course: Prospects do not get assigned an account number until they respond! This rule will yield perfect predictions if the training and test data, taken from a past campaign, includes an account number field, but has no predictive value for real prospects, none of whom have non-zero account numbers.

The credit card data that we were working with in this case contained many fields for which we had no clear definition. We started by flagging them all as independent fields and quickly discovered several that were actually markers for closed accounts. It took several iterations to get down to a set of input fields that were truly free of future information.

Over-Summarization

As is often the case with data that was not originally intended for data mining, the credit card data was highly summarized. For each period, we had total charges, total cash advances, and total payments, but all transaction-level detail had been summarized away. That was a pity because the transaction detail contains a wealth of information that might be predictive.

Of course, overly detailed data is also problematic. With transaction-level data we could potentially recognize when a card holder who used to travel a lot begins to stay at home and when a card that once used only at gas stations starts being used in grocery stores. These changes may be very predictive for the relevant subpopulations, but they imply some fairly sophisticated advance segmentation. In general, however, it is better to have detailed data that can be summarized in various ways as required than to have summarized data from which information has been lost irretrievably.

Lessons Learned

It is a tribute to the power of decision-tree methods that, despite all the problems previously described, we did come up with a few rules that were interesting enough to provoke discussion and further exploration. We would undoubtedly have done much better if we had kept in mind the following rules:

- Take the time to get to know the data: Understand the definition of each field and how it is used. If a good data dictionary does not exist, this information must be obtained through interviews.
- Get access to domain expertise. If you are not a practitioner in the field from which the data comes, you will not be able to appreciate

which rules are important and which relationships within or between fields should be made explicit.

- Make data transformations that will increase the effectiveness of the method: Transform continuously valued target fields into a few broad ranges; encode names and other character strings as numeric indexes into a name table.
- Add derived fields to capture important data relationships.
- Choose values for missing data that will make sense when incorporated into rules.
- Screen out input fields that are dependent on the target field.

APPLYING DECISION-TREE METHODS TO SEQUENTIAL EVENTS

Predicting the future is one of the most important applications of data mining. The task of analyzing trends in historical data in order to predict future behavior recurs in every domain we have examined.

One of our clients, a major bank, is looking at the detailed transaction data from its customers in order to spot earlier warning signs for attrition in its demand deposit (checking) accounts. ATM withdrawals, payroll-direct deposits, balance inquiries, visits to the teller, and hundreds of other transaction types and customer attributes are being tracked over time. The database records over 1 billion transactions per year. The bank believes that this data contains "signatures" or patterns that will allow it to recognize that a customer's loyalty is beginning to weaken while there is still time to take corrective action.

Another client, a manufacturer of diesel engines, has been highly successful using *Clementine*, a commercial implementation of the C4.5 algorithm, to forecast diesel engine sales based on historical truck registration data collected by R. L. Polk. The engine manufacturer even expects to be able to identify individual owner-operators who are likely to be ready to trade in the engines of their big rigs.

Sales, profits, failure modes, fashion trends, commodity prices, operating temperatures, interest rates, call volumes, response rates, and return rates: People are trying to predict them all. In some fields, notably economics, the analysis of time-series data is a central preoccupation of statistical analysts, so you might expect there to be a large collection of ready-made techniques available to be applied to predictive data mining on time-ordered data. Unfortunately, this is not the case.

For one thing, much of the time-series analysis work in other fields focuses on analyzing patterns in a single variable such as the dollar-yen exchange rate or unemployment *in isolation*. Our corporate data warehouses may well contain data that exhibits cyclical patterns. Certainly, we would expect average daily balances in checking accounts to reflect that rents are typically due on the first of the month and that many people are paid on Fridays, but, for the most part, these sorts of patterns are not what interest us because they are neither unexpected nor actionable.

In commercial data mining, our focus is on how a large number of independent variables combine to predict some future outcome. We have already seen in Chapter 8 how time can be integrated into association rules in order to find sequential patterns. Decision-tree methods have also been applied very successfully in this domain, but it is generally necessary to enrich the data with derived fields such as differences and derivatives that explicitly represent change over time. The following section describes an application that automatically generates these derived fields and uses them to build a tree-based simulator that can be used to project an entire database into the future.

Simulating the Future

PV Future View, from Continuum Software, provides a good example of the use of decision trees to extrapolate sequential patterns. *PV Future View* is the commercial name for an approach to simulation described by Marc Goodman in his 1995 doctoral dissertation. Goodman calls this approach "projective visualization" or PV. It uses a database of snapshots of historical data to develop a simulator. The simulation can be run to project the values of all variables into the future. The result is an extended database whose new records have exactly the same fields as the original, but with values supplied by the simulator rather than by observation.

Cases, Attributes, Features, and Interpretations

Using Goodman's terminology, which comes from the machine learning field, each snapshot of a moment in time is called a *case*. A case is made up of *attributes*, which are the fields in the case record. Attributes may be of any data type and may be continuous or categorical. The attributes are used to form *features*. Features are Boolean (yes/no) variables that are combined in various ways to form the internal nodes of a decision tree. For example, if the database contains a salary field of type integer, that is a continuous attribute that might lead to creation of a feature such as `salary<38,500`.

For a continuous variable like salary, a feature of the form `attribute≤value` is generated for every value observed in the training set. This means that there are potentially as many features derived from an attribute as there are cases in the training set. Features based on equality or set membership are generated for symbolic attributes and literal attributes such as names of people or places.

The attributes are also used to generate *interpretations*; these are new attributes derived from the given ones. Interpretations generally reflect knowledge of the domain and what sorts of relationships are likely to be important. In the current problem, finding patterns that occur over time, we know that the amount, direction, and rate of change in the value of an attribute from one time period to the next is likely to be important. Therefore, for each numeric attribute, PV Future View automatically generates interpretations for the difference and the discrete first and second derivatives of the attribute.

In general, however, interpretations are supplied by the user. For example, in a credit risk model, it is likely that the ratio of debt to income is more predictive than the magnitude of either. With this knowledge we might add an interpretation that was the ratio of those two attributes. Often, user-supplied interpretations combine attributes in ways that the program would not come up with automatically. Examples include calculating a great-circle distance from changes in latitude and longitude or taking the product of three linear measurements to get a volume.

From One Case to the Next

The central idea behind projective visualization is to use the historical cases to generate a set of rules for generating case n+1 from case n. When this model is applied to the final observed case, it generates a new projected case. To project more than one time step into the future, we continue to apply the model to the most recently created case. Naturally, confidence in the projected values decreases as we run the simulation for more and more time steps.

Figure 12.11 illustrates the way a single attribute is projected using a decision tree based on the features generated from all the other attributes and interpretations in the previous case. During the training process, a separate decision tree is grown for each attribute. This entire forest is evaluated in order to move from one simulation step to the next.

Case Study: Process Control in a Coffee Roasting Plant

The Nestlé company uses a number of continuous-feed coffee roasters to produce a variety of coffee products including Nescafé Granules, Gold Blend, Gold Blend Decaf, and Blend 37. Each of these products has a "recipe" that specifies target values for a plethora of roaster variables such as the temperature of the air at various exhaust points, the

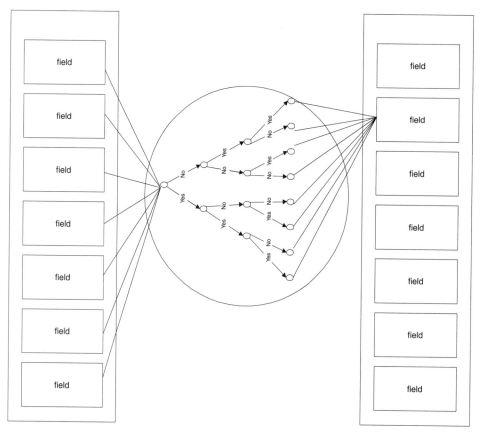

Figure 12.11 Moving from snapshot to snapshot.

speed of various fans, the rate that gas is burned, the amount of water introduced to quench the beans, and the positions of various flaps and valves. There are a lot of ways for things to go wrong ranging from a roast coming out too light in color to a costly and damaging roaster fire.

To help operators keep the roaster running properly, data is collected from around 60 sensors. Every 30 seconds, this data, along with control information, is written to a log and made available to operators in the form of graphs. In 1994, a project began at a Nestlé research laboratory in York, England to use projective visualization to build a coffee roaster simulation based on the sensor logs.

Goals for the Simulator Nestlé saw several ways that a coffee roaster simulator could improve its processes.

- By using the simulator to try out new recipes, a large number of new recipes could be evaluated without interrupting production. Furthermore, recipes that might lead to roaster fires or other damage could be eliminated in advance.
- The simulator could be used to train new operators and expose them to routine problems and their solutions. Using the simulator, operators could try out different approaches to resolving a problem.
- The simulator could track the operation of the actual roaster and project it several minutes into the future. When the simulation ran into a problem, an alert could be generated while the operators still had time to do something to avert it.

Evaluation of the Roaster Simulation   The simulation was built using a training set of 34,000 cases. The simulation was then evaluated using a test set of around 40,000 additional cases that had not been part of the training set. For each case in the test set, the simulator generated projected snapshots 60 steps into the future. At each step the projected values of all variables were compared against the actual values. As expected, the size of the error increases with time. For example, the error rate for product temperature turned out to be 2/3°C per minute of projection, but even 30 minutes into the future the simulator is doing considerably better than random guessing.

The roaster simulator turned out to be more accurate than all but the most experienced operators at projecting trends, and even the most experienced operators were able to do a better job with the aid of the simulator. Operators report that they enjoy using the simulator and that it has given them new insight into corrective actions. Although Nestlé has not yet incorporated the simulator into the roaster control system, they are considering adapting the simulator for use in training new operators. The technique worked well enough in the roaster domain that the company is now investigating its applicability to other processes such as spray drying and aroma extraction.

OTHER DECISION-TREE VARIATIONS

The three decision-tree methods previously described, CART, CHAID, and C4.5, are the most widely used in commercial data mining software packages. A number of other interesting variations are worth discussing as they are finding their way from research labs into actual products.

Using More Than One Field at a Time

All three of the algorithms so far discussed make use of a test on a single variable to perform each split. This approach can be problematic for several reasons, not least of which is that it can lead to trees with many more nodes than necessary. Extra nodes are cause for concern because only the training records that arrive at a given node are available for inducing the subtree below it. The fewer examples there are per node, the less reliable will be the resulting classification.

Suppose we are interested in a condition for which both age and gender are important indicators. If the root node split is on the median age, than each child node contains only half the women. If the initial split is on gender, then each child node contains only half the old folks.

Several algorithms have been developed to allow multiple attributes to be used in combination to form the splitter. One technique, employed by the PV Future View program previously discussed, forms Boolean conjunctions of features (which, you will recall, are always binary) in order to reduce the complexity of the tree. After finding the feature that forms the best split, the algorithm looks for the feature which, when combined with the feature chosen first, does the best job of improving the split. Features continue to be added as long as there continues to be a statistically significant improvement in the resulting split.

This procedure can lead to a much more efficient representation of classification rules. As an example, consider the task of classifying the results of a vote according to whether the motion was passed unanimously. For simplicity, we will consider the case where there are only three votes cast. (The degree of simplification to be made only increases with the number of voters.)

Table 12.3 contains all the possible combinations of three votes and an added column which indicates the unanimity of the result.

Table 12.3 All Possible Combinations of Voting

First Voter	Second Voter	Third Voter	Unanimous?
Nay	Nay	Nay	**TRUE**
Nay	Nay	Aye	**FALSE**
Nay	Aye	Nay	**FALSE**
Nay	Aye	Aye	**FALSE**
Aye	Nay	Nay	**FALSE**
Aye	Nay	Aye	**FALSE**
Aye	Aye	Nay	**FALSE**
Aye	Aye	Aye	**TRUE**

Given this table as training data, CART, or any other algorithm that builds binary trees whose splits are based on the values of a single attribute, will build the decision tree shown in Figure 12.12. This tree perfectly classifies the training data, but it requires five internal splitting nodes to do it.

By allowing features to be combined using the logical and function to form conjunctions, we achieve the much simpler tree in Figure 12.13. The second tree illustrates another potential advantage that can arise from using combinations of fields. The tree now comes much closer to expressing the notion of unanimity that inspired the classes: "When all voters agree, the decision is unanimous."

A tree that can be understood all at once in this way is said, by machine learning researchers, to have good "mental fit." Some researchers in the machine learning field attach great importance to this notion, but that seems to be an artifact of the tiny, well-structured problems around which they build their studies. In the real world, if a classification task is so simple that you can get your mind around the entire decision tree that represents it, you probably don't need to waste your time with powerful data mining tools to discover it. We believe that the ability to understand the rule that leads to any particu-

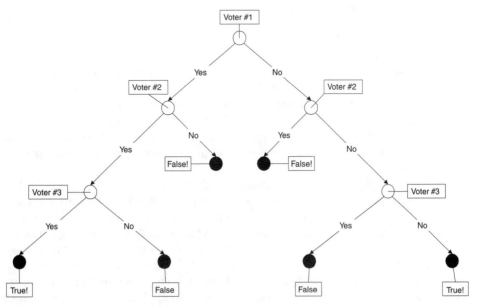

Figure 12.12 The best binary tree for the unanimity function when splitting on single fields.

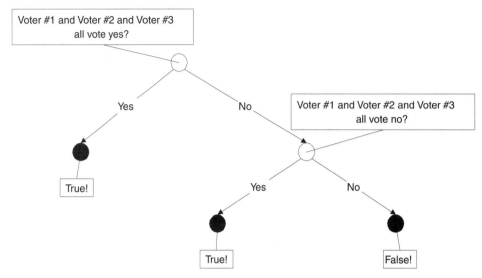

Figure 12.13 Simplifying the unanimity tree by combining features.

lar leaf is very important, but the ability to interpret an entire decision tree at a glance is neither important nor likely to be possible outside of the laboratory.

Tilting the Hyperplane

Classification problems are sometimes presented in geometric terms. This way of thinking is especially natural for datasets having continuous variables for all fields. In this interpretation, each record is a point in a multidimensional space. Each field represents the position of the record along one axis of the space. Decision trees are a way of carving the space into regions, each of which is labeled with a class. Any new record that falls into one of the regions is classified accordingly.

Traditional decision trees, which test the value of a singe field at each node, can only form *rectangular* regions. In a two-dimensional space, a test of the form Y≤N, forms a region bounded by a line perpendicular to the Y-axis and parallel to the X-axis. By choosing different values for N, we can move the line up and down, but we cannot change its slope. Similarly, in a space of higher dimensionality, a test on a single field defines a hyperplane that is orthogonal to the axis represented by the field used in the test and parallel to all the other axes. In a two-dimensional space, with only horizontal and vertical lines to work with, we can only hope to form rectangular regions. In three-dimensional space, we can create rectangular solids and, in general, we can divide any multidimensional space into hyper-rectangles.

The problem is that some things don't fit neatly into rectangular boxes. Figure 12.14 illustrates the problem: The two regions are really divided by a diagonal line; it takes a deep tree to generate enough rectangles to approximate it adequately.

In this case, the true solution can be found easily by allowing linear combinations of the attributes to be considered. Several software packages now attempt to tilt the hyperplanes by basing their splits on a weighted sum of the values of the fields. There are a variety of hill-climbing approaches to selecting the weights.

Of course, it is easy to come up with regions that will not be captured easily even when diagonal lines are allowed. Regions may have

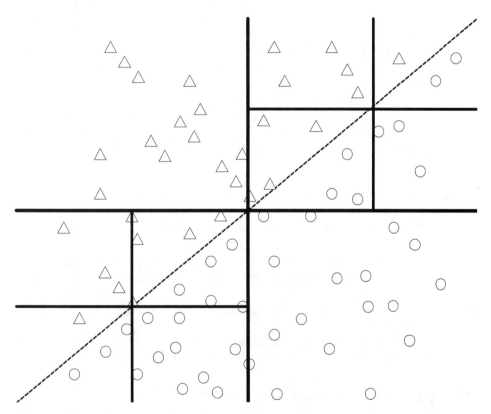

Figure 12.14 The upper left and lower right quadrants are easily classified while the other two quadrants must be carved up into many small boxes to approximate the boundary between the regions.

curved boundaries and fields may have to be combined in more complex ways (such as multiplying length by width to get area). There is no substitute for the careful selection of fields to be inputs to the tree-building process and, where necessary, the creation of derived fields that capture relationships known or suspected by the domain experts. These derived fields may be functions of several other fields or they may be the logarithm, square root, cube, absolute value, or other function of a single field.

Neural Trees

One way of combining input from many fields at every node is to have each node consist of a small neural network. This approach is used by one of the tools that makes up the data mining suite from Torrent Systems. For domains where rectangular regions do a poor job describing the true shapes of the classes, neural trees can produce more accurate classifications while remaining quicker to train and to execute than pure neural networks.

From the point of view of the user, this hybrid technique has more in common with other neural-network variants than it does with other decision-tree variants because, in common with other neural-network techniques, it is not capable of explaining its decisions. Even a rule of the form $(w_1x_1 + w_2x_2 + w_3x_3 + . . .) \leq N$, such as might be generated by a tree method that forms linear combinations of field values at each node, is easier to puzzle out than a neural network.

STRENGTHS OF DECISION-TREE METHODS

The strengths of decision tree methods are:

- Decision trees are able to generate understandable rules.
- Decision trees perform classification without requiring much computation.
- Decision trees are able to handle both continuous and categorical variables.
- Decision trees provide a clear indication of which fields are most important for prediction or classification.

Ability to Generate Understandable Rules

The ability of decision trees to generate rules that can be translated into comprehensible English or SQL is the greatest strength of this technique. Even when a complex domain or a domain that does decompose easily into rectangular regions causes the decision tree to be large and complex, it is generally fairly easy to follow any one path through the tree. So the explanation for any particular classification or prediction is relatively straightforward.

Ability to Perform in Rule-Oriented Domains

It may sound obvious, but rule induction in general, and decision trees in particular, are an excellent choice in domains where there really are rules to be found. The authors had this fact driven home to them by an experience at Caterpillar. Caterpillar called upon MRJ to help design and oversee some experiments in data mining. One of the areas where we felt that data mining might prove useful was in the automatic approval of warranty repair claims.

If an automated system could reliably recognize that the claim for a given repair was reasonable and that the failure was expected given the history of the part in question, then the company could save a considerable amount of money by paying the claim without first waiting for a human analyst to approve it.

Caterpillar already had a policy by which certain claims were paid automatically. The proposed data mining techniques were unfamiliar to most people at Caterpillar, so as a confidence-building first step we decided to use neural networks and decision trees to build models that would predict which claims would be paid using the existing rules. Naturally, we did not ask what the current rules were, but we did obtain a training set consisting of warranty claims and a field indicating whether the claim had been approved automatically.

Because Caterpillar is an industrial partner in the National Center for Supercomputer Applications at the University of Illinois, the actual experiments were performed by NCSA staff using Darwin running on a CM5 parallel supercomputer from Thinking Machines corporation. The results were startling: Darwin's StarTree CART tool generated a model that was 100 percent accurate on unseen test data. In other words, it had discovered the exact rules used by Caterpillar to classify the claims. On this problem, Darwin's neural network tool, StarNet, was less successful.

Many domains, ranging from genetics to industrial processes really do have underlying rules, though these may be quite complex and obscured by noisy data. Decision trees are a natural choice when you suspect the existence of underlying rules.

Ease of Calculation at Classification Time

Although, as we have seen, a decision tree can take many forms, in practice, the algorithms used to produce decision trees generally yield trees with a low branching factor and simple tests at each node. Typical tests include numeric comparisons, set membership, and simple conjunctions. When implemented on a computer, these tests translate into simple Boolean and integer operations that are fast and inexpensive. This is an important point because in a commercial environment, a predictive model is likely to be used to classify many millions or even billions of records.

Ability to Handle Both Continuous and Categorical Variables

Decision-tree methods are equally adept at handling continuous and categorical variables. Categorical variables, which pose problems for neural networks and statistical techniques, come ready-made with their own splitting criteria: one branch for each category. Continuous variables are equally easy to split by picking a number somewhere in their range of values.

Ability to Clearly Indicate Best Fields

Decision-tree building algorithms put the field which does the best job of splitting the training records at the root node of the tree. It is not uncommon for SAS users to run the SAS CHAID module for no other purpose than deciding which independent variables to use when building a regression module.

WEAKNESSES OF DECISION-TREE METHODS

Decision trees are less appropriate for estimation tasks where the goal is to predict the value of a continuous variable such as income, blood pressure, or interest rate. Decision trees are also problematic for time-series data unless a lot of effort is put into presenting the data in such a way that trends and sequential patterns are made visible.

Error-Prone with Too Many Classes

Some decision-tree algorithms can only deal with binary-valued target classes (yes/no, accept/reject). Others are able to assign records to an arbitrary number of classes, but are error-prone when the number of training examples per class gets small. This can happen rather quickly in a tree with many levels and/or many branches per node.

Computationally Expensive to Train

The process of growing a decision tree is computationally expensive. At each node, each candidate splitting field must be sorted before its best split can be found. In some algorithms, combinations of fields are used and a search must be made for optimal combining weights. Pruning algorithms can also be expensive since many candidate subtrees must be formed and compared.

Trouble with Non-Rectangular Regions

Most decision-tree algorithms only examine a single field at a time. This leads to rectangular classification boxes that may not correspond well with the actual distribution of records in the decision space.

APPLICATION OF DECISION-TREE METHODS

Decision-tree methods are a good choice when the data mining task is classification of records or prediction of outcomes. Use decision trees when your goal is to assign each record to one of a few broad categories. Decision trees are also a natural choice when your goal is to generate rules that can be easily understood, explained, and translated into SQL or a natural language.

13

Artificial Neural Networks

Artificial neural networks are popular because they have a proven track record in many data mining and decision-support applications. Neural networks—the "artificial" is usually dropped—are a class of very powerful, general-purpose tools readily applied to prediction, classification, and clustering. They have been applied across a broad range of industries, from predicting financial series to diagnosing medical conditions, from identifying clusters of valuable customers to identifying fraudulent credit card transactions, from recognizing numbers written on checks to predicting the failure rates of engines.

Whereas people are good at generalizing from experience, computers usually excel at following explicit instructions over and over. The appeal of neural networks is that they bridge this gap by modeling, on a digital computer, the neural connections in human brains. When used in well-defined domains, their ability to generalize and learn from data mimics our own ability to learn from experience. This ability is useful for data mining and it also makes neural networks an exciting area for research, promising new and better results in the future.

There is a drawback, though. The results of training a neural network are internal weights distributed throughout the network. These weights provide no more insight into *why* the solution is valid than asking many human experts why a particular decision is the right decision. They just know that it is. The weights are not readily understandable although, increasingly, sophisticated techniques for probing into neural networks help provide some explanation. Neural networks are best approached as black boxes with mysterious internal workings, as mysterious as the origins of our own consciousness. Like the Oracle at Delphi worshipped by the Greeks, the answers produced by neural networks are often correct. They have business value, in many cases a more important feature than explainability.

A BIT OF HISTORY

Neural networks have an interesting history in the annals of computer science. The original work on how neurons work took place in the 1940s—before digital computers really even existed. In 1943, Warren McCulloch, a neurophysiologist, and Walter Pits, a logician, postulated a simple model to explain how biological neurons work. While their focus was on understanding the anatomy of the brain, it turned out that this model provided a new approach to solving certain problems outside the realm of neurobiology.

In the 1950s, when digital computers first became available, computer scientists implemented models called perceptrons based on the work of McCulloch and Pits. An example of a problem solved by these early networks was how to balance a broom standing upright on a moving cart by controlling the motions of the cart back and forth. As the broom starts falling to the left, the cart learns to move to the left to keep it upright. Although there were some limited successes with perceptrons in the laboratory, the results were disappointing for general problem-solving.

One reason for the limited usefulness of early neural networks is that most powerful computers of that era were less powerful than inexpensive desktop computers today. Another reason was that these simple networks had theoretical deficiencies, as shown by Seymour Papert and Marvin Minsky in 1968—two researchers at the Massachusetts Institute of Technology. Because of these deficiencies, the study of neural network implementations on computers slowed down drastically during the 1970s. Then, in 1982, John Hopfield invented backpropagation, a way of training neural networks that sidestepped the theoretical pitfalls of earlier approaches. This development sparked a renaissance in neural network research. Through the 1980s, research moved from the labs into the commercial world, where it has since been applied in virtually every industry to solve both operational problems—like detecting fraudulent credit card transactions as they occur and recognizing numeric amounts written on checks—and data mining applications.

At the same time that artificial neural networks were being developed as a model of biological activity, statisticians were taking advantage of computers to extend the capabilities of statistical models. A technique called logistic regression proved particularly valuable for understanding complex functions of many variables. Like linear regression, logistic regression tries to fit a curve to observed data. Instead of a line, though, it uses a function called the logistic or sigmoid function, which we will be visiting again later. Logistic regression, and even its more familiar cousin linear regression, can be represented as special cases of neural networks. In fact, the entire theory of neural networks can be explained using statistical methods, like probability distributions, likelihoods, and so on. For expository purposes, though, this chapter leans more heavily toward the biological model than on the theoretical mathematics.

Neural networks became popular in the 1980s because of a convergence of several factors. First, computing power was readily available, especially in the business community where data was available. Second, analysts became more comfortable with neural networks by realizing that they are closely related to known statistical methods. Third, there was relevant data since operational systems in most companies had already been automated. Fourth, useful applications became more important than the holy grails of artificial intelligence. Building tools to help people superseded building artificial people. Because of their proven utility, neural networks are and will continue to be popular tools for data mining, as well as encouraging further research that will make them even more powerful in the future.

REAL ESTATE APPRAISAL

Neural networks have the ability to learn from examples in much the same way that human experts gain from experience. The following example applies neural networks to solve a problem familiar to most readers, real estate appraisal.

Why do we want to automate appraisals? Clearly, automated appraisals help real estate agents better match prospective buyers to prospective homes, improving the productivity of even inexperienced agents. Another use would be to set up kiosks or Web pages where prospective buyers could describe the home that they want—and get immediate feedback on how much their dream home costs. Good, consistent appraisals are critical to assessing the risk of individual loans and loan portfolios. For this purpose, Freddie Mac, the Federal Home Loan Mortgage Corporation, has developed a product called Loan Prospector that does these appraisals automatically for homes throughout the United States. Loan Prospector is based on neural network technology provided by HNC, Inc.

The neural network is going to replace the appraiser who estimates the market value of a home based on features of the property (see Figure 13.1). She knows that houses in one part of town are worth more than those in other areas. Additional bedrooms, a larger garage, the style of the house, and the size of the lot are other factors that figure into her mental calculation. She is not applying some set formula, but balancing her experience and knowledge of the sales prices of similar homes. And, her knowledge about housing prices is not static. She is aware of recent sale prices for homes throughout the region and can recognize trends in prices over time—fine-tuning her calculation to fit the latest data.

The appraiser or real estate agent is a good example of a human expert in a well-defined domain. Houses are described by a fixed set of standard features taken into account by the expert and turned into an appraised value. In 1992, researchers at IBM recognized this as a good

Figure 13.1   Real estate agents and appraisers combine the features of a house to come up with a valuation.

problem for neural networks. Figure 13.2 illustrates why. A neural network takes specific inputs—in this case the information from the housing sheet—and turns them into a specific output, an appraised value for the house. The list of inputs is well-defined and even standardized because of the extensive use of the multiple listing service (MLS) to share information about the housing market among different real estate agents and the standardization of housing descriptions for mortgages sold on the secondary market. The desired output is well-defined as well, a specific dollar amount. In addition, there is a wealth of experience in the form of previous sales for teaching the network how to value a house.

TIP

Neural networks are good for prediction problems. A good problem has the following three characteristics:

- *The inputs are well understood.* You have a good idea of which features of the data are important, but not necessarily how to combine them.
- *The output is well understood.* You know what you are trying to predict.
- *Experience is available.* You have plenty of examples where both the inputs and the output are known. This experience will be used to train the network.

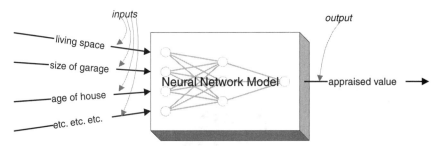

A neural network model calculates the appraised value (the output) from the inputs. The calculation is a complex process that we do not need to understand to use the appraised values.

Figure 13.2 Think of a neural network as an opaque box that processes inputs to create an output.

Table 13.1   Common Features Describing a House

Feature	Description	Values
Num_Apartments	Number of dwelling units	1–3
Year_Built	Year built	1850–1986
Plumbing_Fixtures	Number of plumbing fixtures	5–17
Heating_Type	Heating system type	coded as A or B
Basement_Garage	Basement garage (number of cars)	0–2
Attached_Garage	Attached frame garage area (in square feet)	0–228
Living_Area	Total living area (square feet)	714–4185
Deck_Area	Deck / open porch area (square feet)	0–738
Porch_Area	Enclosed porch area (square feet)	0–452
Recroom_Area	Recreation room area (square feet)	0–672
Basement_Area	Finished basement area (square feet)	0–810

In order to appraise values for a single area, we need to capture the features of a house that affect its sales price. Some possible common features are shown in Table 13.1. These features work for homes in a single geographical area. To extend the appraisal example to handle homes in many neighborhoods, the input data would include ZIP code information, neighborhood demographics, and other neighborhood quality-of-life indicators, such as ratings of schools and proximity to transportation. These additional features are not included here to simplify the example.

During the first phase of using a neural network for prediction, we need to train the network using examples of previous sales. The training examples need two more additional features: the sales price of the home and when it sold. An example from the training is shown in Table 13.2.

Now we arrive at a technical detail. Neural networks work best when all the input and output values are between 0 and 1. This requires massaging all the values, both continuous and categorical, to get new values between 0 and 1. Continuous values, such as sales price or the size of the basement, range between two known values. Categorical values take one value from a list of values. The only example in this data is the *Heating_Type* that takes on the value of A or B. In other data, marital status, gender, account status, product code, vendor id, and so on are categorical values.

Table 13.2 Training Set Example

Feature	Value
Sales_Price	$171,000
Months_Ago	4
Num_Apartments	1
Year_Built	1923
Plumbing_Fixtures	9
Heating_Type	A
Basement_Garage	0
Attached_Garage	120
Living_Area	1,614
Deck_Area	0
Porch_Area	210
Recroom_Area	0
Basement_Area	175

To massage continuous values, we subtract the lower bound of the range from the value and divide the result by the size of the range. For instance, to get a massaged value for *Year_Built* (1923), we recenter the value by subtracting 1850 (the year the oldest house was built) and get 73. This is then normalized by dividing by the number of years in the range (1986 − 1850 + 1 = 137) to get 0.5328. This basic procedure can be applied to any continuous feature to get a value between 0 and 1. If we do not know the size of the range a priori, we can make a guess. If some values slightly exceed the range from 0 to 1, this will not significantly change how well the network performs.

For categorical features, we assign fractions between 0 and 1 to each of the categories. For *Heating_Type*, we arbitrarily assign B to have the massaged value of 1 and A, the massaged value of 0. If we had three values, we would assign one to 0, another to 0.5, and the third to 1.0.

With these simple techniques, we can massage all the fields in the sample house shown earlier (see Table 13.3).

The network is ready to be trained when the training examples have all been massaged. During the training phase, we repeatedly feed the examples in the training set through the neural network. The net-

Table 13.3 Massaged Values for Training Set Example

Feature	Range of Values	Original Value	Massaged Value
Sales_Price	$103,000–$250,000	$171,000	0.4626
Months_Ago	0–23	4	0.1739
Num_Apartments	1-3	1	0.0000
Year_Built	1850–1986	1923	0.5328
Plumbing_Fixtures	5–17	9	0.3333
Heating_Type	coded as A or B	B	1.0000
Basement_Garage	0–2	0	0.0000
Attached_Garage	0–228	120	0.5263
Living_Area	714–4185	1,614	0.2593
Deck_Area	0–738	0	0.0000
Porch_Area	0–452	210	0.4646
Recroom_Area	0–672	0	0.0000
Basement_Area	0–810	175	0.2160

work compares its predicted output value to the actual sales price and adjusts all its internal weights to improve the prediction. By going through all the training examples (sometimes many times), the network calculates a good set of weights. By arriving at a good set of weights, it has really figured out how to calculate the right sales price. Training is complete when the weights no longer change very much or until the network has gone through the training set a maximum number of times.

In practice, we would next run the network on a test set that it had never seen before to guarantee that the network learned to recognize the best patterns in the training set. When the performance on the test set is satisfactory, then we have a neural network model. This model has learned from the training examples and figured out how to calculate the sales price from all the inputs. The model is ready for use. It takes descriptive information about a house, suitably massaged, and produces an output. There is one caveat here. The output is a number between 0 and 1, so we need to unmassage the value to turn it back into a sales price. If we get a value like 0.75, then we multiply it by the size of the range ($147,000) and then add the base number in the range ($103,000) to get an appraisal value of $213,250.

NEURAL NETWORKS FOR DIRECTED DATA MINING

The previous example illustrates the most common use of neural networks: building a model for classification or prediction. The steps in this process are:

1. Identify the input and output features.
2. Massage the inputs and outputs so their range is between 0 and 1.
3. Set up a network with an appropriate topology.
4. Train the network on a representative set of training examples.
5. Test the network on a test set strictly independent from the training examples. If necessary, repeat the training, adjusting the training set, network topology, and parameters. Evaluate the network using the evaluation set to see how well it performs.
6. Apply the model generated by the network to predict outcomes for unknown inputs.

Although an intimate knowledge of their internal workings is not necessary, there are some keys to using networks successfully. The first is choosing the right training set. The second is representing the data in such a way as to maximize the ability of the network to recognize patterns in it. The third is interpreting the results from the network. Finally, understanding some specific details about the internals of the network, such as the network topology and parameters controlling training, can help you get better results.

One of the dangers with any model for prediction or classification is that the model becomes stale as it gets older—and neural networks are no exception to this rule. For the appraisal example, the neural network has learned about historical patterns that allow it to predict the appraised value from descriptions of houses based on the contents of the training set. There is no guarantee that current market conditions match those of last week, last month, or six months ago—when the training set might have been made. New homes are bought and sold every day, creating and responding to market forces that are not present in the training set. A rise or drop in interest rates, or an increase in inflation, may rapidly change appraisal values. The problem of keeping a neural network model up-to-date is made more difficult by two factors. First, the model does not readily express itself in the form of rules, so it may not be obvious when it has grown stale. Second, neural networks are particularly robust. When they degrade, they tend to degrade gracefully making the reduction in performance less obvious. In short, the model gradually expires and it is not always clear exactly when to update it.

The solution is to incorporate more recent data into the neural network. One way is to take the same neural network back to training mode and start feeding it new values. This is a good approach if the network only needs to tweak results such as when the network is pretty close to being accurate, but you think you can improve its accuracy even more by giving it more recent examples. Another approach is to start over again by adding new examples into the training set (perhaps removing older examples) and training an entirely new network, perhaps even with a different topology (we'll talk more about network topologies later). This is appropriate when market conditions may have changed drastically and the patterns found in the original training set are no longer applicable.

The virtuous cycle of data mining described in Chapter 2 put a premium on measuring the results from data mining activities. These measurements help you understand how susceptible a given model is to aging and when a neural network model should be retrained.

WARNING

A neural network is only as good as the training set used to generate it. The model is static and must be explicitly updated by adding more recent examples into the training set and retraining the network (or training a new network) in order to keep it up-to-date and useful.

WHAT IS A NEURAL NET?

Even without delving into the internals of neural networks, the real estate appraisal example shows how to use them to solve a problem not readily amenable to other analysis techniques. As this example suggests, a neural network creates a model of the training set. Its results can be no better than the data used to train it. It is also important to realize that the network may age and atrophy as the real world marches beyond the information covered in the training set. There are many tools, both freeware and commercial off-the-shelf products, that are available for experimenting with networks. The more sophisticated tools let you train networks and use them with no more knowledge than needed for the real estate appraisal example. Others, though, give users much more power over the networks, allowing them to experiment with different options. Such experimentation can lead to better results or all the options can just cause confusion and waste time in solving a problem.

Neural networks consist of basic units modeled on biological neurons. Each unit has many inputs that it combines into a single output value. These units are connected together, as shown in Figure 13.3, so the outputs from some units are used as inputs into other units. All the examples in Figure 13.3 are examples of feed-forward neural networks, meaning there is a one-way flow through the network from the inputs to the outputs and there are no cycles in the network.

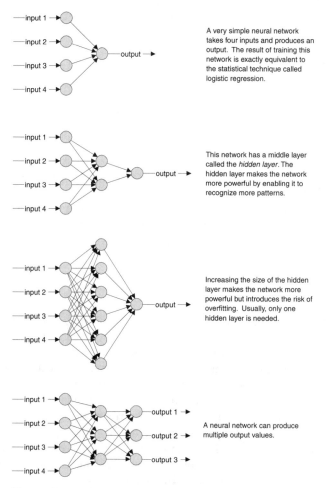

A very simple neural network takes four inputs and produces an output. The result of training this network is exactly equivalent to the statistical technique called logistic regression.

This network has a middle layer called the *hidden layer*. The hidden layer makes the network more powerful by enabling it to recognize more patterns.

Increasing the size of the hidden layer makes the network more powerful but introduces the risk of overfitting. Usually, only one hidden layer is needed.

A neural network can produce multiple output values.

Figure 13.3 Four examples of feed-forward neural networks.

Feed-forward networks are the simplest and most useful type of network. There are three basic questions to ask about them:

- What are units and how do they behave? That is, what is the activation function?
- How are the units connected together? That is, what is the topology of a network?
- How does the network learn to recognize patterns? That is, what is backpropagation?

The answers to these questions provide the background for understanding basic neural networks, an understanding that provides guidance for getting the best results from this powerful data mining technique.

What Is the Unit of a Neural Network?

As previously mentioned, artificial neural networks are composed of basic units designed to model the behavior of biological neurons (see Figure 13.4). The unit combines its inputs into a single output value. This combination is called the unit's *activation function*. The most common activation functions are based on the biological model. The output remains very low until the combined inputs reach a threshold value. When the combined inputs reach the threshold, the unit is *activated* and the output is high.

Like its biological counterpart, the unit in a neural network has the property that small changes in the inputs (when the combined inputs are near the threshold value) can have large effects on the output. Conversely, large changes in the inputs of the unit may have little effect on the output (when the combined inputs are far from the threshold). This property, where sometimes small changes matter and sometimes they do not, is called *non-linear behavior*.

An activation function has two parts. The first part is the *combination function* that merges all the inputs into a single value. As shown in Figure 13.4, each input into the unit has its own weight. The most common combination function is the weighted sum, where each input is multiplied by its weight and these products are added together. Other combination functions are sometimes useful and include the maximum of the weighted inputs, the minimum, or the logical AND or OR of the values. Although there is a lot of flexibility in the choice of combination functions, the standard weighted sum works well in most situations. The element of choice is a common trait of neural networks. The basic structure is quite flexible, but the defaults

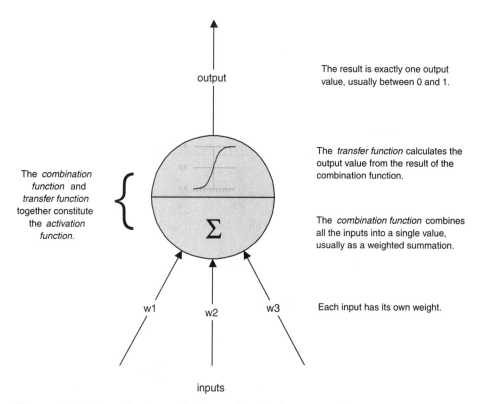

The result is exactly one output value, usually between 0 and 1.

output

The *transfer function* calculates the output value from the result of the combination function.

The *combination function* and *transfer function* together constitute the *activation function.*

The *combination function* combines all the inputs into a single value, usually as a weighted summation.

Σ

Each input has its own weight.

w1   w2   w3

inputs

Figure 13.4 The unit of an artificial neural network is modeled on the biological neuron. The output of the unit is a non-linear combination of its inputs.

that correspond to the original biological models, such as the weighted sum for the combination function, work well in practice.

The second part of the activation function is the *transfer function*, which gets its name from the fact that it transfers the value of the combination function to the output of the unit. Figure 13.5 compares three typical transfer functions: the sigmoid, linear, and hyperbolic tangent functions. The specific values that the transfer function takes on are not as important as the general form of the function. The linear transfer function has limited practical value. A feed-forward neural network consisting only of units with linear transfer functions is really just doing a linear regression—what statisticians call fitting the best line to a bunch of data points. The sigmoid and hyperbolic tangents are non-linear functions and result in non-linear behavior. The major difference between them is the range of their outputs, between 0 and 1 for the sigmoid and between –1 and 1 for the hyperbolic tangent.

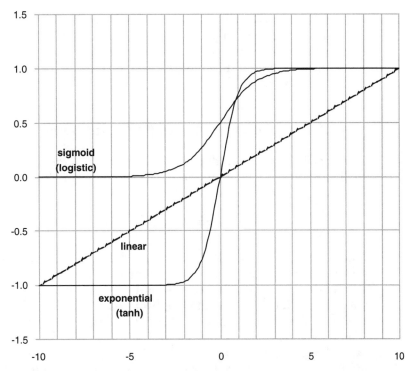

Figure 13.5 Three common transfer functions are the sigmoid, linear, and hyperbolic tangent functions.

By far, the most common transfer function is the S-shaped sigmoid function. Even though it is not linear, the behavior of the sigmoid is appealing to statisticians. When the weights on all the inputs are small, then the result of the combination function is small—say between −1 and 1. Within this range, the sigmoid function is almost linear and the unit (or entire neural network) exhibits almost-linear behavior. Statisticians appreciate linear systems and almost-linear systems are almost as well appreciated. As the weights get larger, the sigmoid gradually saturates to either −1 or 1. This behavior corresponds to a gradual movement from a linear model of the input to a non-linear model. In short, neural networks do a good job of prediction on three types of problems: linear problems, near-linear problems, and non-linear problems.

A network can contain units with different transfer functions. However, the default transfer function in most cases for off-the-shelf tools is the sigmoid. Sophisticated tools sometimes allow experimentation with other combination and transfer functions. Other functions have significantly different behavior from the standard units. It may be fun and even helpful to play with different types of activation functions. If you do not want to bother, though, you can have confidence in the standard functions that have proven successful for many neural network applications.

Sigmoid Function and Ranges for Input Values

The sigmoid function produces values between 0 and 1 for all possible outputs of the summation function. The formula for the sigmoid is:

$$Sigmoid(x) = \frac{1}{1 + e^{-x}}$$

When used in a neural network, the x is the result of the combination function, typically the weighted sum of the inputs into the unit.

Since the sigmoid function is defined for all values of x, why do we insist that the inputs to a network be in the range from 0 to 1? Part of the reason is that the network is laid out so the outputs from some units are the inputs into other units. For simplicity, it is easier for all units to look alike. That is, since some always have inputs between 0 and 1, let's keep everything equal and put this restriction everywhere. Requiring that all inputs be in the same range also prevents one set of inputs, such as the price of a house—a big number in the tens of thousands—from dominating other inputs, such as the number of bedrooms.

The sigmoid function is able to distinguish between values near 0, but as x gets much larger or smaller, the sigmoid value gets closer and closer to 1 or –1. When x is large, small adjustments to the weights on the inputs have almost no effect on the output of the unit making it difficult to train. That is, the sigmoid function can take advantage of the difference between one and two bedrooms, but a house that costs \$10,000 and one that costs \$500,000 would be hard for it to distinguish. Keeping the inputs relatively small enables adjustments to the weights to have a bigger impact. This aid to training is the strongest reason for insisting that inputs lie between 0 and 1.

In fact, even when a feature naturally falls into a range smaller than 0 to 1, such as 0.5 to 0.75, it is desirable to scale the feature so the input to the network uses the entire range from 0 to 1. Using the full range of values from 0 to 1 ensures the best results.

Feed-Forward Neural Networks

Figure 13.6 illustrates how a feed-forward neural network calculates output values from input values. The topology, or structure, of this network is typical of networks used for prediction and classification. The units are organized into three layers. The layer on the left is connected to the inputs, whose values have been massaged to fall between 0 and 1. These units are the *input layer* of the network. Each unit in the input layer is connected to exactly one source. In this example, the input layer does not actually do any work. Each input layer unit copies its input value onto its output. If this is the case, why are we bothering to talk about it here? It is an important part of the vocabulary of

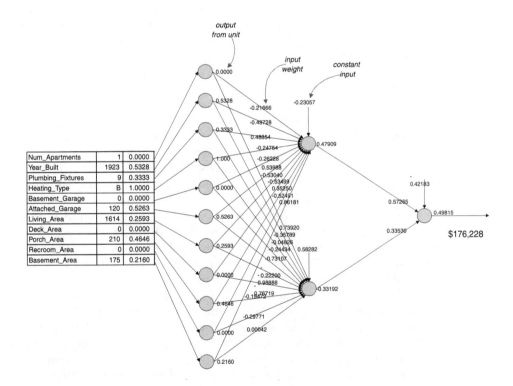

Num_Apartments	1	0.0000
Year_Built	1923	0.5328
Plumbing_Fixtures	9	0.3333
Heating_Type	B	1.0000
Basement_Garage	0	0.0000
Attached_Garage	120	0.5263
Living_Area	1614	0.2593
Deck_Area	0	0.0000
Porch_Area	210	0.4646
Recroom_Area	0	0.0000
Basement_Area	175	0.2160

This is an example of a neural network set up with the real estate appraisal training example described earlier. In this network, the input layer just passes the input values through since they are already massaged. The hidden layer has two units and the output is very close to the actual value of $171,000.

Figure 13.6   The real estate training example in a neural network.

neural networks and in more complicated networks input layers do play a more significant role.

The next layer is called a *hidden layer* because it is connected neither to the inputs nor to the output of the network. Each unit in the hidden layer is fully-connected to all the units in the input layer. Since this network contains standard units, the units in the hidden layer calculate their output by multiplying the value on each input by its corresponding weight, adding these up, and applying the sigmoid function. A neural network can have any number of hidden layers, but in general, one hidden layer is sufficient. The wider the layer (i.e., the more units it contains) the greater the capacity of the network to recognize patterns. This greater capacity has a drawback, though, because the neural network can recognize patterns-of-one by memorizing each of the training examples. *We want the network to generalize on the training set, not to memorize it.* In order for the network to generalize its training data instead of memorizing it, the network should not have too wide a hidden layer.

Notice that the units in Figure 13.6 each have an additional input coming down from the top. This is the constant input and is always set to 1. Like other inputs, it has a weight and is included in the combination function. The constant input acts as a global offset that helps the network better understand patterns. The training phase adjusts the weights on constant inputs just like the other weights in the network.

The last unit on the right is the *output layer* because it is connected to the output of the neural network. It is fully-connected to all the units in the hidden layer. Most of the time, the neural network is being used to calculate a single value, so there is only one unit in the output layer and the value that it produces will lie between 0 and 1. We must unmassage this value to understand the output. For the network in Figure 13.6, we have to convert 0.49815 back into a value between $103,000 and $250,000. It corresponds to $176,228, which is quite close to the actual value of $171,000.

Sometimes the output layer has more than one unit. For instance, a department store chain wants to predict the likelihood that customers will be purchasing products from various departments, like women's apparel, furniture, and entertainment. The stores want to use this information to plan promotions and direct target mailings.

To make this prediction, they set up the neural network shown in Figure 13.7. This network has three outputs, one for each department. The outputs are a propensity for the customer described in the inputs to make his or her next purchase from the associated department.

After feeding the inputs for a customer into the network, the net-

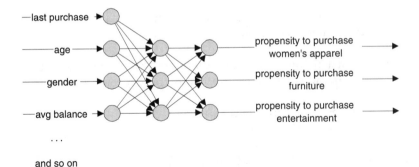

—last purchase

age

gender

avg balance

. . .

propensity to purchase
women's apparel

propensity to purchase
furniture

propensity to purchase
entertainment

and so on

Figure 13.7 A closer look at a network with more than one output used to predict the department where department store customers will make their next purchase.

work will calculate three values. Given all these outputs, how can the department store determine the right promotion or promotions to offer the customer? Some common methods are

- taking the department corresponding to the unit with the maximum value;
- taking the departments corresponding to the units with the top three values;
- taking all departments corresponding to the units that exceed some threshold value; or,
- taking all departments corresponding to units that are some percentage of the unit with the maximum value.

All of these possibilities work well and have their strengths and weaknesses in different situations. There is no one right answer that always works. In practice, you want to try several of these possibilities on the test set in order to determine which works best in your situation.

How Does the Neural Network Learn Using Backpropagation?

Training a neural network is the process of setting the best weights on the inputs of each of the units. The goal is to use the training set to produce weights where the output of the network is as close to the desired output as possible for as many of the examples in the training set as possible. By far the most common technique for doing this is backpropagation, originally developed by John Hopfield. At the heart of backpropagation are the following three steps:

1. The network gets a training example and, using the existing weights in the network, it calculates the output or outputs the example.
2. Backpropagation then calculates the error, by taking the difference between the calculated result and the expected (actual result).
3. The error is fed back through the network and the weights are adjusted to minimize the error.

Using the error measure to adjust the weights inside a single unit is the critical part of this algorithm. Each unit is assigned a specific responsibility for the error. For instance, in the output layer, one unit is responsible for the whole error. This unit then assigns a responsibility for part of the error to each of its inputs, which come from units in the hidden layer, and so on, if there is more than one hidden layer. The specific mechanism is not important. Suffice it to say that it is a complicated mathematical procedure that requires taking partial derivatives of the transfer function.

Given the error, how does a unit adjust its weights? It starts by measuring how sensitive its output is to each of its inputs. That is, it estimates whether changing the weight on each input would increase or decrease the error. The unit then adjusts each weight to reduce, but not eliminate, the error. The adjustments for each example in the training set slowly nudge the weights toward their optimal values. Remember, the goal is to generalize and identify patterns in the input, not to exactly match the training set. Adjusting the weights is like a leisurely walk instead of a mad-dash sprint. After being shown enough training examples, the weights on the network no longer change significantly and the error no longer decreases. This is the point where training stops; the network has learned the input.

This technique for adjusting the weights is called the *generalized delta* rule. There are two important parameters associated with using the generalized delta rule. The first is *momentum*, which refers to the tendency of the weights inside each unit to change the "direction" they are heading in. That is, each weight remembers if it has been getting bigger or smaller, and momentum tries to keep it going in the same direction. A network with high momentum responds slowly to new training examples that want to reverse the weights. This is useful if the training examples are ordered by similarity. If momentum is low, then the weights are allowed to oscillate more freely.

The *learning rate* controls how quickly the weights change. The best approach for the learning rate is to start big and decrease it slowly as the network is being trained. Initially, the weights are random, so large oscillations are useful to get in the vicinity of the best weights. However, as the network gets closer to the optimal solution, the learning rate should decrease so the network can fine-tune to the most optimal weights.

Researchers have invented hundreds of variations on the generalized delta rule. Each of these approaches has its advantages and disadvantages. In all cases, they are looking for a technique that trains networks quickly to arrive at the optimal solution. Some neural network packages offer multiple training methods to allow users to experiment with the best solution for their problems.

One of the dangers with any of the training techniques is falling into something called a local optimum. This happens when the network produces all-right results for the training set and adjusting the weights no longer improves the performance of the network. However, there is some other combination of weights—significantly different from those in the network—that yields a much better solution. This is analogous to trying to climb to the top of a mountain and finding that you have only climbed to the top of a nearby hill. There is a tension between finding the local best solution and the global best solution. Controlling the learning rate and momentum helps to find the best solution.

Training Using Genetic Algorithms

We will learn in Chapter 14 that genetic algorithms are a good method for finding global optima. The use of genetic algorithms to train neural networks is becoming increasingly popular. How can genetic algorithms be adapted to this purpose? The process is actually quite simple.

The first step when using genetic algorithms is to define a *chromosome*. All the weights in the network are gathered together into an array to form a chromosome, as shown in Figure 13.8. The next step is to determine the fitness function for the chromosome. We can evaluate the chromosome for any given training example and determine the error for that example (the error is the absolute value or square of the difference between the calculated value and the actual value). Since the goal is to minimize the error over the training set, we evaluate the network with the chromosome weights over the entire training set and add up all the errors as we go along. The fitness function, then, is the sum of the errors for all the examples in the training set. The genetic algorithm is now let loose to minimize the fitness function using selection, crossover, and mutation.

Genetic algorithms can also play a role in defining the topology.

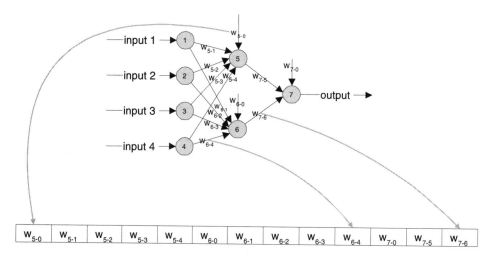

This chromosome represents all the weights in the neural network. Each weight is
represented as a sequence of bits.

Figure 13.8 The weights in the neural network can be gathered into a chromosome for use in genetic algorithms.

For instance, instead of encoding the weights, the chromosome could encode the number of hidden units, momentum, and the learning rate. In this scenario, the network would be trained over a portion of the test set using the parameters in the chromosome. Then, when the network has been trained, it would be evaluated over the evaluation set to calculate the fitness function. Creating new generations in this case is clearly a time-consuming process. However, the result should be close to the best possible feed-forward neural network.

The results from using genetic algorithms are promising and they have been showing up in neural network packages. The use of genetic algorithms is one of many different techniques, some still in research labs, to help neural networks learn faster and more effectively.

CHOOSING THE TRAINING SET

The training set consists of records whose prediction or classification values are already known. Choosing a good training set is critical. A poor training set dooms the network, regardless of any other work that goes into creating it. Fortunately, there are only a few things to consider in choosing a good one.

Coverage of the Values for All the Features

The most important of these considerations is that the training set needs to cover the full range of values for all the features that the network might encounter. In the real estate appraisal example, this means including inexpensive houses and expensive houses, big houses and little houses, and houses with and without garages. In general, it is a good idea to have several examples in the training set for each value of a categorical feature and for a range of values for ordered discrete and continuous features.

The inputs to the neural networks should lie between 0 and 1. This means that the values have to be massaged to get into this range. In some cases, though, it does not mean that the minimum value needs to map to 0 and the maximum value to 1. The range of housing sizes in the appraisal example went from 714 sq. ft. to 4,185 sq. ft. Instead of having 714 map to 0 and 4,185 map to 1, a better approach is to leave some slack around the edges. Map the minimum and the maximum values to 0.1 and 0.9 instead and the network will be able to handle slightly smaller and slightly larger homes, from 280 sq. ft. to 4,619 sq. ft.

The Number of Features

The time needed to train a neural network is directly related to the number of input features used by the network; the more features, the longer it takes for the network to converge. Actually, a bigger problem is that as the number of features increases, the network becomes more likely to converge to an inferior solution. Manually discarding features that are unlikely to have predictive power often significantly increases the predictive power of neural networks.

A hybrid approach is to use another technique to determine which features are likely to be more important for predictive purposes and then to use only the important features for training the network. Statistical correlations are one possible way to prioritize importance. Another is to use decision trees. As discussed in Chapter 12, decision trees do a good job of determining which features are most important. The features higher up in the tree have more predictive power. These features can then be used as the input into the neural network.

The Number of Inputs

The more features there are in the network, the more training examples that are needed to get a good coverage of patterns in the data. Unfortunately, there is no simple rule to express a relationship between the number of features and the size of the training set. However, typically a minimum of 10 to 20 examples are needed to support each feature with adequate coverage; having several hundred is not unreasonable.

The Number of Outputs

In most training examples, there are typically many more inputs going in than there are outputs going out, so good coverage of the inputs results in good coverage of the outputs. However, it is very important that there be many examples for all possible output values from the network. In addition, the number of training examples for each possible output should be about the same. This can be critical when deciding what to use as the training set.

For instance, if the neural network is going to be used to detect rare, but expensive events—failure rates in a diesel engines, fraudulent use of a credit card, or who will respond to an offer for a home equity line of credit—then you need to be sure that the training set has a sufficient number of examples of these rare events. A random sample of available data is not sufficient, since common examples will swamp the rare examples. To get around this, the training set needs to oversample the rare cases. For this type of problem, a training set consisting of 10,000 "good" examples and 10,000 "bad" examples gives better results than a randomly selected training set of 100,000 good examples and 1,000 bad examples. After all, using the randomly sampled training set the neural network would probably assign "good" regardless of the input—and be right 99 percent of the time. This is an exception to the general rule that a larger training set is better.

Available Computational Power

The biggest constraint on the size of the training set is the time available for training. The standard algorithm for training a neural network requires passing through the training set dozens or hundreds of times before the network converges on its optimal weights. For a given network and training set, this is much faster when running on a parallel computer than on a desktop machine with 8 Mbytes of memory. When using a neural network for a given application, though, the effort to train the network once is not the only effort. It is common to iterate through many experiments, varying the features, massaging functions, topology of the network, and learning parameters to look for the best results. Keeping the training set to a size consistent with the work you need to accomplish is important.

TIP

The training set for a neural network has to be large enough to cover all the values taken on by all the features. You want to have at least a few dozen examples for each input feature. For the outputs of the network, you want to be sure that there is an even distribution of values. This is a case where fewer examples in the training set can actually improve results, by not swamping the network with "good" examples when you want to train it to recognize "bad" examples. The size of the training set is also influenced by the power of the machine running the model. A neural network needs more time to train when the training set is very large. That time could perhaps better be used to experiment with different features, massaging functions, and parameters of the network.

PREPARING THE DATA

Preparing the input data is often the most complicated part of using a neural network. Part of the complication is the normal problem of choosing the right data and the right examples for a data mining endeavor. Another part is massaging the data so each feature in the data has a value in the range from 0 to 1—remember, massaging the values to this range helps networks recognize patterns in the input. Some neural network packages facilitate this translation using friendly, graphical interfaces. Since the format of the data going into the network has a big effect on how well the network performs, we are reviewing the common ways to massage data.

Features with Continuous (Floating and Fixed Point) Values

Some features take on continuous values, generally ranging between known minimum and maximum bounds. Examples of such features are:

- Dollar amounts (sales price, monthly balance, weekly sales, income, etc.)
- Averages (average monthly balance, average sales volume, etc.)
- Ratios (debt-to-income, price-to-earnings, etc.)
- Physical measurements (area of living space, temperature, etc.)

In the real estate appraisal example, we saw the most common way to handle continuous features. When these features fall into a predefined range between a minimum value and a maximum value, such as the sales price on the house, then we can easily massage it to have a value from 0 to 1. The specific calculation is:

$$\text{massaged\_value} = \frac{\text{original\_value} - \text{minimum}}{\text{maximum} - \text{minimum}}$$

This works well, but in practice there are some additional considerations. What if the maximum and minimum values are not known? Someone could build a new house in the neighborhood with 5,000 square feet of living space and render the real estate appraisal network useless. There are several ways to approach this:

- Plan for a larger range. The range of living areas in the training set was from 714 square feet to 4185 square feet. Instead of using these values for the minimum and maximum value of the range, allow for some growth, using, say, 500 and 5000 instead.
- Reject out-of-range values. Once we start extrapolating beyond the ranges of values in the training set, we have much less confidence in the results. Only use the network for predefined ranges of input values. This is particularly important when using a network for controlling a manufacturing process; wildly incorrect results can lead to disasters.
- Peg values lower than the minimum to the minimum and higher than the maximum to the maximum. So, houses larger than 4,000 square feet would all be treated the same. This works well in many situations. However, we suspect that the price of a house is highly correlated with the living area. So, a house with 20 percent more living area than the maximum house size (all other things being equal) would cost 20 percent more. In other situations, pegging the values can work quite well.
- Map the minimum value to 0.1 and the maximum value to 0.9 instead of 0 and 1 respectively. To do this, use the following formula instead:

$$\text{massaged\_value} = \frac{(0.9 - 0.1)\,(\text{original\_value} - \text{minimum})}{\text{maximum} - \text{minimum}} = +0.1$$

Figure 13.9 illustrates another problem that sometimes arises with continuous features—skewed distribution of values. In this data, almost all incomes are under $100,000, but the range goes from $10,000 to $1,000,000. Massaging the values as suggested maps a $30,000 income to 0.0303 and a $65,000 income to 0.0657—hardly any difference at all,

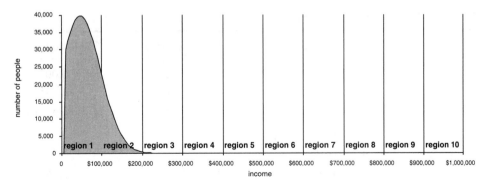

Figure 13.9 Household income provides a good example of a skewed distribution. Almost all the values are in the first 10% of the range (income of less than $100,000).

although this income differential might be very significant for a marketing application. On the other hand, $250,000 and $800,000 become 0.2525 and 0.8081 respectively—a very large difference, though this income differential might be much less significant. The incomes are highly skewed toward the low end and this can make it difficult for the neural network to take advantage of the income field. Skewed distributions can prevent a network from effectively using an important field.

There are several ways to resolve this. The most common is to split a feature like income into ranges. This is called *discretizing* the field. Figure 13.9 illustrates breaking the incomes into 10 equal-sized ranges, but this is not useful at all. Virtually all the values fall in the first two ranges. A better choice of ranges is:

$10,000–$17,999	very low
$18,000–$31,999	low
$32,000–$63,999	middle
$64,000–$99,999	high
$100,000 and above	very high

In doing this, we recognize that we are losing information during this transformation. A household with an income of $65,000 now looks exactly like a household with an income of $98,000. On the other hand, the neural network can more easily handle the ranges.

Another possibility is to filter the values to improve their distribution. A good function to use for filtering income is the logarithm (abbreviated to log). For a power of 10, the logarithm is the exponent, so

Table 13.4 Different Ways to Massage Income

Income	Massaged Income	log(Income)	Massaged log
$10,000	0.0101	4.0000	0.0000
$18,000	0.0182	4.2553	0.1276
$32,000	0.0323	4.5051	0.2526
$63,000	0.0636	4.7993	0.3997
$100,000	0.1010	5.0000	0.5000
$250,000	0.2525	5.3979	0.6990
$800,000	0.8081	5.9031	0.9515
$1,000,000	1.0101	6.0000	1.0000

the log of 10 is 1 ($10 = 10^1$), of 100 is 2 ($100 = 10^2$), of 1000 is 3 ($1000 = 10^3$), and so on. Taking the log of the incomes converts them to the range from 4 to 6. Table 13.4 compares the results using the income versus using the logarithm. We can see from the table that the logarithm filter does a much better job of spreading out the values that we are interested in.

As a final consideration, sometimes we want to derive new features from the existing features. If we are using the neural network to predict prices on the stock market, for instance, we may be very disappointed in its performance trying to make the prediction using raw price quotes. The prediction will improve if we use the network to determine whether the stock is going up or down—and feed it historical *changes* in prices. Use the difference in prices as input into the network instead of the absolute price. Of course, the difference still has to be scaled into the range from 0 to 1.

Features with Ordered, Discrete (Integer) Values

We have seen that continuous features can be discretized into ordered, discrete values. Other examples of features with ordered values include:

> Counts (number of children, number of items purchased, months since sale, etc.)
>
> Age
>
> Ordered categories (low, medium, high)

Like the continuous features, these have a maximum and minimum value. For instance, age usually ranges from 0 to about 100, but the exact range may depend on the data we are using. The number of children may go from 0 to 4, with anything over 4 considered to be 4. Massaging these values is simple. First, we count the number of different values. In this case, there are 5 discrete values: 0, 1, 2, 3, and 4. What we want to do is assign equal spaced values in the interval from 0 to 1 to each of these values. Figure 13.10 shows how to do this for these five values. We get the following mapping: $0 \rightarrow 0.00$, $1 \rightarrow 0.25$, $2 \rightarrow 0.50$, $3 \rightarrow 0.75$, and $4 \rightarrow 1.00$. It is that simple. Notice that mapping the values onto the unit interval like this preserves the ordering, so the massaged value of 1 is less than the massaged values of 2, 3, and 4. When we discretized the income values, we put them into five ranges. Each of these ranges gets assigned a single value in the range as with the example in Figure 13.10. Breaking the income values into ranges preserves the ordering.

Another approach to handling discrete, ordered values is sometimes quite useful. These are called *thermometer codes*:

$$0 \rightarrow 1\,0\,0\,0\,0 \quad = 0.5000$$
$$1 \rightarrow 1\,1\,0\,0\,0 \quad = 0.7500$$
$$2 \rightarrow 1\,1\,1\,0\,0 \quad = 0.8750$$
$$3 \rightarrow 1\,1\,1\,1\,0 \quad = 0.9375$$

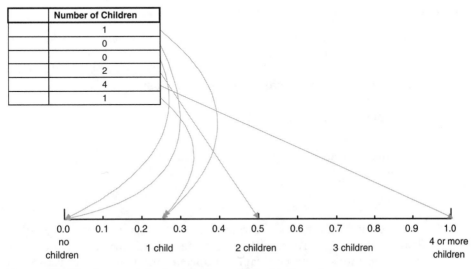

Figure 13.10   An example of massaging a field with five values.

Their name arises because the sequence of 1s always starts on one side and rises to the value, like the mercury in a thermometer. We treat the codes as binary integers, in this case between 1 and 16. To get the decimal value, we divide the code value by 16. Thermometer codes are good for things like academic grades and bond ratings, where the difference on one end of the scale is less significant than differences on the other end. For instance, the difference between a D and an F is considerably different from an A and a B. Using a thermometer code, we would assign the grades A, B, C, D, and F the codes 0.9375, 0.8750, 0.7500, 0.5000, and 0.0000 respectively. Applying a thermometer code to a feature with more than 8 or so values reduces its effectiveness, since the high-end values cluster so close to 1.

Thermometer codes are one way of including prior information into the coding scheme. They keep codes close together because you have a sense that the code values should be close. This type of knowledge can improve the results from a neural network—don't make it discover what you already know. Feel free to map values onto the unit interval so that codes close to each other match your intuitive notions of how close they should be.

Thermometer codes and scaling are sufficient for most applications with categorical features that have up to a few dozen possible values. When there are more than a hundred or so values, then treating a discrete ordered feature as a continuous feature works just as well.

Features with Categorical Values

Features with categories are unordered lists of values. These are different from ordered lists, because there is no ordering to preserve and introducing an order may be inappropriate. There are typically many examples of categorical values in data, such as:

gender, marital status, etc.;

status codes;

product codes;

ZIP codes;

and so on.

Although ZIP codes are represented as numbers (in the United States), they really represent discrete geographic areas and the codes themselves give little geographic information. There is no reason to think that 10014 is more like 02116 than it is like 95407, even though the numbers are much closer. Since their ordering has little significance, ZIP codes are categorical instead of ordered, discrete even though they look like numbers.

There are two fundamentally different ways of handling categorical features. The first is to treat the codes as discrete, ordered values, then assign them values using the methods discussed in the previous section. Unfortunately, the neural network does not understand that the codes are unordered. So, if we are trying to massage the codes for marital status, "single," "divorced," "married," "widowed," and "unknown," then these codes map to 0.00, 0.25, 0.50, 0.75, and 1.00 respectively. From the perspective of the network, "single" and "unknown" are very far apart whereas "divorced" and "married" are quite close. For most input fields, this implicit ordering does not have much of an effect. In other cases, the values have some relationship to each other and the implicit ordering might confuse the network.

The second way of handling categorical features is to break the categories into flags, one for each value. Assume that there are three values for gender (male, female, and unknown). We can break this into three flags that take the values 0.0000 or 1.000, shown in Table 13.5.

This is an example of *1 of N coding*. In fact, though, we can be a little smart about this and eliminate the gender-unknown flag. The gender is unknown when it is neither male nor female. This slight modification is known as *1 of N-1 coding* and results in Table 13.6.

Why would we want to do this? We have now multiplied the number of input variables and this is generally a bad thing for a neural network. However, these coding schemes are the only way to eliminate implicit ordering among the values.

There are three almost equivalent options for coding a field like gender that has three values (male, female, and unknown):

- 1-of-N coding generating three massaged features
- 1-of-N-1 coding generating two massaged features
- massage gender using male $\rightarrow$ 0.00, unknown $\rightarrow$ 0.50, and female $\rightarrow$ 1.00

Table 13.5 Handling Gender Using Flags (1 of N Coding)

Gender	Gender Male Flag	Gender Female Flag	Gender-Unknown-Flag
Male	1.000	0.000	0.000
Female	0.000	1.000	0.000
Unknown	0.000	0.000	1.000

Table 13.6 Modification of Gender Flags (1 of N-1 Coding)

Gender	Gender Male Flag	Gender Female Flag
Male	1.000	0.000
Female	0.000	1.000
Unknown	0.000	0.000

By putting "unknown" between "male" and "female," the last choice minimizes the effect of implicit ordering. When there are more categories, then 1-of-N coding eliminates implicit ordering.

Other Types of Features

Some of the features you might want to use for your neural network do not fit directly into any of the three categories previously described. For complicated features, what you want to do is extract the meaningful information and use one of the above techniques to represent the result. Remember, the input to a neural network consists of inputs whose values should be in the range from 0 to 1.

Dates are a good example of data that you may want to handle in special ways. Any date or time can be represented as the number of days or seconds since a fixed point in time, allowing them to be massaged and fed directly into the network. However, if the date is for a transaction, then the day of the week and month of the year may be more important than the actual date. For instance, the month would be important for detecting seasonal trends in data. You might want to extract this information from the date and feed it into the network instead of, or in addition to, the actual date.

The address field—or any text field—is similarly complicated. Generally, addresses are useless to feed into a network, even if you could figure out a good way to massage a free-text field. However, the address may contain a ZIP code, city name, state, and apartment number. All of these are useful features by themselves, even though the address field taken as a whole is usually useless.

INTERPRETING THE RESULTS

The techniques used for massaging the inputs into the neural network all have inverses for interpreting the outputs. For instance, the network might be used to calculate the value of a house and, in the training set, the output value is set up so that \$103,000 maps to 0.1 and \$250,000 maps to 0.9. If the model is later applied to another house and the output is 0.5, then we can figure out that this corresponds to \$176,500—halfway between the minimum and the maximum values. This inverse transformation makes neural networks particularly easy to use for predicting continuous values.

On the other hand, if the network is trying to predict something with binary or categorical values—such as whether a customer should be included in a mailing or whether a stock should be sold—then interpreting the results is more difficult because the network produces continuous values. When using a network for this purpose, the output needs to be calibrated to determine what ranges correspond to which values. Ideally, the network would also produce an output of 0 (or 0.1) for the low value and 1 (or 0.9) for the high value. Unfortunately, for some inputs, the network will always produce intermediate values that are more difficult to interpret. So, what can we do?

The naïve approach is to arbitrarily say that any value under 0.5 corresponds to one value and any value above 0.5 corresponds to the other value (and exactly 0.5 can go either way). This is simple to implement and understand, but it may not be the best solution. Another approach might be to divide the interval into thirds, with any less than 0.33 being assigned to one category, anything greater than 0.67 going into the other, and the rest being declared "unknown."

Yet another approach is to assign a confidence level along with the value. This would result in the following interpretations, shown in Table 13.7.

All these possibilities work in some cases but they are ad hoc, meaning that we are trying to guess at the best interpretation. Is there a better approach? In fact, there is. In Chapter 5, we introduced the test set and evaluation set along with the training set. Figuring out

Table 13.7 Categories and Confidence Levels for NN Output

Output Value	Category	Confidence
0.0	A	100%
0.2	A	80%
0.49	A	51%
0.51	B	51%
0.8	B	80%
1.0	B	100%

how to interpret the results from a neural network is a good job for the test set. Figure 13.11 shows some typical results from applying a neural network on the test set. In this case, the network is classifying data into two classes. Most of the members of class A cluster at the low end and most of the members of class B cluster at the high end. However, there are some exceptions. From the data, we can see that anything less than 0.62 should be in class A and that anything greater than 0.64 should be in class B—then decide that a cutoff of 0.63 is the right cutoff. Notice that in this case, a cutoff of 0.5 might be missing an important cluster of As whose results are slightly higher than 0.50.

Another approach for binary values is to use a network that produces two outputs, one for class A and one for class B. For members of the training set in class A, the network would be trained so the class A detector is 1 and the class B detector is 0. For members in class B, the class B detector would be 1 and the class A detector is 0. We can interpret the results so each of these values is a confidence level. So, if the

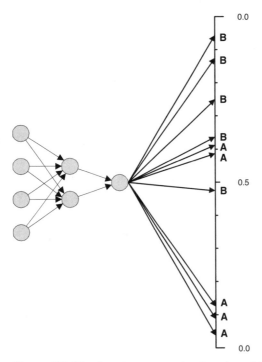

Figure 13.11 Running a neural network on 10 test examples from the test set can help determine how to interpret results.

outputs were 0.8 and 0.2, then we would say that the example has an 80 percent chance of being in class A and a 20 percent chance of being in class B.

This works well, until an example gives results of 0.1 for the A detector and 0.3 for the B detector. Do we assign it to class B with a 30 percent confidence? Or, do we say that it is three times more likely to be class B than class A, and give it a 75 percent confidence? Once again, the test set can help determine which range of values on the detector outputs gives the best results. By running the network over the test set, we understand the accuracy of its results.

TIP

Because neural networks produce continuous values, the output from a network can be difficult to interpret for categorical results (used in classification). The best way to calibrate the output is to run the network over a test set, entirely separate from the training set, and to use the results from the test set to calibrate the output of the network to categories. In many cases, the network can have a separate output for each category; that is, a *propensity* for that category. Even with separate outputs, the test set is still needed to calibrate the outputs.

The approach is similar when there are more than two options under consideration. For example, consider a long distance carrier trying to target a new set of customers with three targeted service offerings:

- discounts on all international calls;
- discounts on all long distance calls that are not international; and,
- discounts on calls to a predefined set of customers.

The carrier is going to offer incentives to customers for each of the three packages. Since the incentives are expensive, the carrier needs to choose the right service for the right customers in order for the campaign to be profitable. Offering all three products to all the customers is expensive and, even worse, may confuse the recipients, reducing the response rate.

The carrier test markets the products to a small subset of customers who receive all three offers but are only allowed to respond to one of them. It intends to use this information to build a model for predicting the response rate for each of the offerings. The training set from the test marketing campaign uses the following coding: no response → 0.00, international → 0.33, national → 0.67, and specific numbers → 1.00. After training a neural network with information about the customers, the carrier starts applying the model.

But, applying the model does not go as well as planned. Many customers cluster around the four values used for training the network. However, apart from the non-responders (who are the majority), there are many instances when the network returns intermediate values like 0.5 and 0.83. What can be done?

First, the carrier should use a test set to understand the output values. By interpreting the results of the network based on what happens in the test set, it can find the right ranges to use for transforming the results of the network back into marketing segments. This is the same process shown in Figure 13.11.

Another observation in this case is that the network is really being used to predict three different things, whether a recipient will respond to each of the campaigns. This strongly suggests that a better structure for the network is to have three outputs: a propensity to respond to the international plan, to the long distance plan, and to the specific numbers plan. The test set would then be used to determine where the cutoff is for non-respondents.

NEURAL NETWORKS FOR TIME SERIES

In many data mining problems, the data naturally falls into a time series. An example of such a series is the closing price of IBM stock or the daily value of the Swiss Franc to U.S. Dollar exchange rate. Someone who is able to predict the next value, or even whether the series is heading up or down, has a tremendous advantage over other investors. Although predominant in the financial industry, time series appear in other areas, such as using transaction history to determine when a customer is likely to attrite or using a series of physical measurements to determine when an engine is going to break down. Financial time series, though, are the most studied since a small advantage in predictive power translates into big profits.

Neural networks are easily adapted for time-series analysis. Figure 13.12 illustrates how this is done. The network is trained on the time-series data, starting at the oldest point in the data. The training then moves to the second oldest point and the oldest point goes to the next set of units in the input layer, and so on. The network trains like a feed-forward, backpropagation network trying to predict the next value in the series at each step.

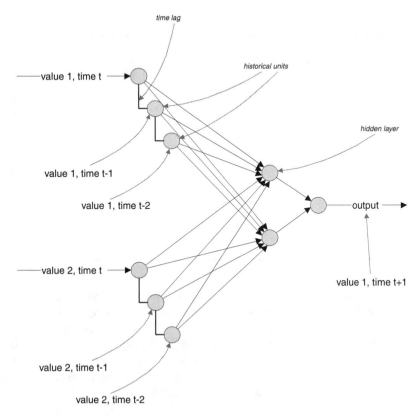

Figure 13.12 A time-delay neural network remembers the previous few training examples and uses them as input into the network. The network then works like a feed-forward, backpropagation network.

Notice that the time-series network is not limited to data from just a single time series. It can take multiple inputs. For instance, if we were trying to predict the value of the Swiss France to U.S. Dollar exchange rate, we might include other time-series information, such as the volume of the previous day's transactions, the U.S. Dollar to Deutsch Mark exchange rate, the closing value of the stock exchange, and the day of the week. We might even include non-time-series data such as the reported inflation rate in the countries over the period of time under investigation.

The number of historical units controls the length of the patterns that the network can recognize. For instance, keeping 10 historical units on a network predicting the closing price of a favorite stock will allow the network to recognize patterns that occur within two-week

Table 13.8 Time Series

Data Element	Day-of-Week	Closing Price
1	1	$40.25
2	2	$41.00
3	3	$39.25
4	4	$39.75
5	5	$40.50
6	1	$40.50
7	2	$40.75
8	3	$41.25
9	4	$42.00
10	5	$41.50

time periods. Relying on such a network to predict the value three months in the future is not a good idea and not recommended.

Actually, you can get the same effect of a time-delay neural network using a regular feed-forward, backpropagation network by modifying the input data. Say that we have the following time series, shown in Table 13.8 with 10 data elements and we are interested in two features: the day of the week and the closing price.

Table 13.9 Time Series with Time Lag

Data Element	Day-of-Week	Closing Price	Previous Closing Price	Previous-1 Closing Price
1	1	$40.25		
2	2	$41.00	$40.25	
3	3	$39.25	$41.00	$40.25
4	4	$39.75	$39.25	$41.00
5	5	$40.50	$39.75	$39.25
6	1	$40.50	$40.50	$39.75
7	2	$40.75	$40.50	$40.50
8	3	$41.25	$40.75	$40.50
9	4	$42.00	$41.25	$40.75
10	5	$41.50	$42.00	$41.25

To create a time series with a time lag of three, we just add new features for the previous values. We do not need to copy the day-of-the-week over three times, since this is redundant. The result is Table 13.9. This data can now be input into a feed-forward, backpropagation network without any special support for time series.

HEURISTICS FOR USING FEED-FORWARD, BACKPROPAGATION NETWORKS

Even with sophisticated neural network packages, getting the best results from a neural network takes some effort. This section covers some heuristics for setting up a network to obtain good results.

Probably the biggest decision is the number of units in the hidden layer. The more units, the more patterns the network can recognize. This would argue for a very large hidden layer. However, there is a drawback. The network might end up memorizing the training set instead of generalizing from it. In this case, more is not better. Fortunately, you can detect when a network is overtrained. If the network performs very well on the training set, but does much worse on the test set, then this is an indication that it has memorized the test set.

How large should the hidden layer be? One rule of thumb is that it should never be more than twice as large as the input layer. A good place to start is to make the hidden layer the same size as the input layer. If the network is overtraining, reduce the size of the layer. If it is not sufficiently accurate, increase its size. When using a network for classification, the network should start with one hidden unit for each class.

Another decision is the size of the training set. The training set must be sufficiently large to cover the ranges of inputs available for each feature. In addition, you want several training examples for each weight in the network. For a network with s input units, h hidden units, and 1 output, there are $n*(s+1)+h+1$ weights in the network. For instance, if there are 15 input features and 10 units in the hidden network, then there are 162 weights in the network. You want at least 5 to 10 examples in the training set for each weight. So, the training set should have at least 810 examples.

Finally, the learning rate and momentum parameters are very important for getting good results out of the network. Initially, the learning should be set high to make large adjustments to the weights. As the training proceeds, the learning rate should decrease in order to fine-tune the network. The momentum parameter allows the network to move toward a solution more rapidly, preventing oscillation around less useful weights.

HOW TO KNOW WHAT IS GOING ON INSIDE A NEURAL NETWORK

Neural networks are opaque. Even knowing all the weights on all the units throughout the network does not give much insight into why the network works. This lack of understanding has some philosophical appeal—after all, we do not understand how human consciousness arises from the neurons in our brains. As a practical matter, though, opaqueness impairs our ability to understand the results that the network produces.

If only we could ask the network to tell us how it is making its decision in the form of rules. . . . Unfortunately, the same non-linear characteristics of units that make them so powerful also make them unable to produce simple rules. Eventually, research into rule extraction from networks may bring unequivocally good results. Until then, the trained network itself is the rule, and other methods are needed to peer inside to understand what is going on.

Fortunately, a technique called *sensitivity analysis* can be used to understand how opaque models work. Sensitivity analysis does not provide explicit rules, but it does indicate the relative importance of the inputs to the result of the network. Sensitivity analysis uses the test set to determine how sensitive the output of the network is to each input. The following are the basic steps:

1. Find the average value for each input. Because the distribution of values in the test set is not uniform, the average value will generally not be exactly 0.5. We can think of this average value as the center of the test set.
2. Measure the output of the network when all inputs are at their average value.
3. Measure the output of the network when each input is modified, one at a time, to be at its minimum and maximum values (usually 0 and 1 respectively).

For some inputs, the output of the network changes very little for the three values (minimum, average, and maximum). The network is not *sensitive* to these inputs. Other inputs have a large effect on the output of the network. The network is *sensitive* to these inputs. The amount of change in the output measures the sensitivity of the network for each input. By using these measures for all the inputs, you can create a relative measure of the importance of each feature.

There are variations on this procedure. It is possible to modify the values of two or three features at the same time to see if combinations of features have a particular importance. Sometimes, it is useful to start from a location other than the center of the test set. For instance, the analysis might be repeated for the minimum and maximum values of the features to see how sensitive the network is at the extremes. If sensitivity analysis produces significantly different results for these three situations, then there are higher order effects in the network that are taking advantage of combinations of features.

When using a feed-forward, backpropagation network, sensitivity analysis can take advantage of the error measures usually used during the learning phase instead of having to test each feature independently. The test set is fed into the network to produce the output and the output is compared to the predicted output to calculate the error. The network then propagates the error back through the units, not to adjust any weights but to keep track of the sensitivity of each input. The error is a proxy for the sensitivity, determining how much each input affects the output in the network. Accumulating these sensitivities over the entire test set determines which inputs have the larger effect on the output.

TIP

Neural networks do not produce easily understood rules that explain how they arrive at a given result. Even so, it is possible to understand the relative importance of inputs into the network by using sensitivity analysis. Sensitivity can be a manual process where each feature is tested one at a time relative to the other features. It can also be more automated by using the sensitivity information generated by backpropagation. In many situations, understanding the relative importance of inputs is almost as good as having explicit rules.

USING NEURAL NETWORKS FOR UNDIRECTED DATA MINING

Neural networks can also be used for undirected data mining. Self-organizing maps (SOMs), also called Kohonen Feature maps, were invented by the Finnish researcher Dr. Tuevo Kohonen. Although used originally for images and sounds, these networks can also recognize clusters in data. They are based on the same underlying units as feed-forward, backpropagation networks, but SOMs are quite different in two respects. They have a different topology and the backpropagation method of learning is no longer applicable. They have a different method for training.

What Is a Self-Organizing Map?

The *self-organizing map* (SOM), an example of which is shown in Figure 13.13, is a neural network that can recognize unknown patterns in the data. Like the networks we've already looked at, the basic SOM has an input layer and an output layer. Each unit in the input layer is connected to one source, just as in the feed-forward, backpropagation

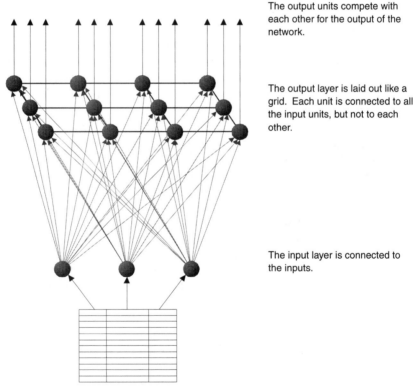

The output units compete with each other for the output of the network.

The output layer is laid out like a grid. Each unit is connected to all the input units, but not to each other.

The input layer is connected to the inputs.

Figure 13.13 The Self-Organizing Map is a special kind of neural network that can be used to detect clusters.

networks. Also, like those networks, each unit in the SOM has an independent weight associated with each in-coming connection (this is actually a property of all neural networks). However, the similarity between SOMs and feed-forward, backpropagation networks ends here.

The output layer consists of many units instead of just a handful. Each of the units in the output layer is connected to all of the units in the input layer. The output layer is arranged in a grid, as if the units were in the squares on a checkerboard. Even though the units are not connected to each other in this layer, the grid-like structure plays an important role in the training of the SOM, as we will see shortly.

How does an SOM recognize patterns? Imagine one of the booths at a carnival where you throw balls at a wall filled with holes. If the ball lands in one of the holes, then you have your choice of prizes. Training an SOM is like being at the booth blindfolded and initially the wall has no holes, very similar to the situation when you start looking for patterns in large amounts of data and don't know where to start. Each time you throw the ball, it dents the wall a little bit. Eventually, when enough balls land in the same vicinity, the indentation breaks through the wall, forming a hole. Now, when another ball lands at that location, it goes through the hole. You get a prize—at the carnival, this is a cheap stuffed animal; with an SOM, it is an identifiable cluster.

Figure 13.14 shows how this works for a simple SOM. When a member of the training set is presented to the network, the values flow forward through the network to the units in the output layer. The units in the output layer compete with each other and the one with the highest value "wins." The reward is to adjust the weights leading up to the winning unit to strengthen in the response to the input pattern. This is like making a little dent in the network.

There is one more aspect to the training of the network. Not only are the weights for the winning unit adjusted, but the weights for units in its immediate neighborhood are also adjusted to strengthen their response to the inputs. This adjustment is controlled by a *neighborliness* parameter that controls the size of the neighborhood and the amount of adjustment. Initially, the neighborhood is rather large and the adjustments are large. As the training continues, the neighborhoods and adjustments decrease in size. Neighborliness actually has several practical effects. One is that the output layer behaves more like a connected fabric, even though the units are not directly connected to each other. Clusters similar to each other should be closer together than more dissimilar clusters. More importantly, though, neighborliness allows for a group of units to represent a single cluster.

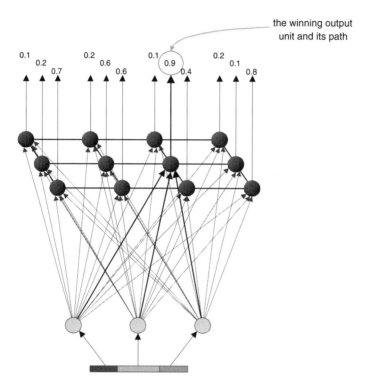

Figure 13.14 An SOM finds the output unit that does the best job recognizing a particular input.

Without this neighborliness, the network would tend to find as many clusters in the data as there are units in the output layer—introducing bias into the cluster detection.

Typically, an SOM identifies fewer clusters than it has output units. This is inefficient when using the network to assign new records to the clusters since the new inputs are fed through the network to unused units in the output layer. To determine which units are actually used, we apply the SOM to the test set. The members of the test set are fed through the network, keeping track of the winning unit in each case. Units with no hits or with very few hits are discarded. Eliminating these units increases the run-time performance of the network by reducing the number of calculations needed for new instances.

Once the final network is in place—with the output layer restricted only to the units that identify specific clusters—it can be applied to new instances. An unknown instance is fed into the network and is assigned to the cluster at the output unit with the largest weight. The network has identified clusters, but we do not know anything about them. We will return to the problem of identifying clusters a bit later.

The original SOMs used two-dimensional grids for the output layer. This was an artifact of earlier research into recognizing images in images, composed of a two-dimensional array of pixel values. The output layer can really have any structure—with neighborhoods defined in three dimensions, as a network of hexagons, or laid out in some other fashion.

Case Study: Finding Clusters

A large bank is interested in increasing the number of home equity loans that it sells. It is decided that the bank needs to understand the customers that currently have home equity loans to determine the best strategy for increasing its market share. To start this process, demographics are gathered on 5,000 customers who have home equity loans and 5,000 customers who do not have them.

The data that is gathered has fields like the following:

- Appraised value of house
- Amount of credit available
- Amount of credit granted
- Age
- Marital status
- Number of children
- Household income

This data forms a good training set for clustering. The input values are massaged so they all lie between 0 and 1; these are used to train an SOM. The network identifies five clusters in the data, but it does not give any information about the clusters. What do these clusters mean?

What we need is a way to compare the different clusters. A common technique that works particularly well with neural network techniques is the *average member* technique. What we want to do is determine the most average member of each of the clusters—the center of the cluster. This is similar to the approach we used for sensitivity analysis. To do this, we find the average value for each feature in each cluster.

For example, say that half the members of a cluster are male and half are female, and that male maps to 0.0 and female to 1.0. The average member for this cluster would have a value of 0.5 for this feature. In another cluster, there may be nine females for every male. For this cluster, the average member would have a value of 0.9. This averaging works very well with neural networks since all inputs have to be massaged into a numeric range.

TIP

Neural networks can identify clusters but they do not identify what makes the members of a cluster similar to each other. A powerful technique for comparing clusters is to determine the center or average member in each cluster. Using the test set, you calculate the average value for each feature in the data. These average values can then be displayed in the same graph to determine the features that make a cluster unique.

These average values can then be plotted together as in Figure 13.15, which shows the centers of the five clusters identified in the banking example. We can see the features that define a particular cluster. In this case, the bank noted that one of the clusters was particularly interesting, consisting of married customers in their forties with children. A bit more investigation revealed that these customers also had children in their late teens.

The marketing department of the bank concluded that these people were taking out home equity loans to pay college tuition fees. The department arranged a marketing program designed specifically for this market, selling home equity loans as a means to pay for college education. The bank measured the results from this campaign and were disappointed. The marketing program was not successful.

Since the marketing program failed, it may seem as though the clusters identified by the SOM did not live up to their promise. In fact, the problem lay elsewhere. The bank had initially only used general customer information. It had not combined information from the many different systems servicing its customers. The bank returned to the problem of identifying customers, but this time it included more information—from the deposits system, the credit card system, and so on.

The basic methods remained the same, so we will not go into detail about the analysis. With the additional data, the bank discovered that the cluster of customers with college-age children did actually exist, but a fact had been overlooked. When the additional data was included, the bank learned that the customers in this cluster also tended to have business accounts as well as personal accounts. This led to a new line of thinking. When the children leave home to go to college,

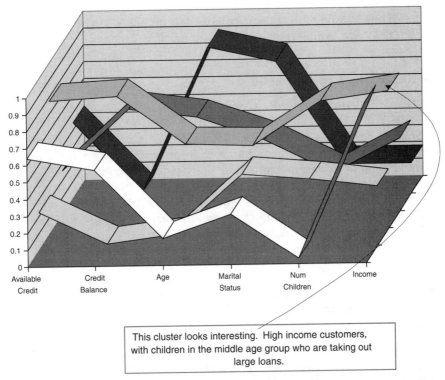

The centers of five clusters are compared on the same graph.

This cluster looks interesting. High income customers, with children in the middle age group who are taking out large loans.

Figure 13.15 The centers of five clusters are compared on the same graph. This simple visualization technique helps identify interesting clusters.

the parents now have the opportunity to start a new business by taking advantage of the equity in their home.

With this insight, the bank created a new marketing program targeted at the parents on starting a new business in their empty nest. This program succeeded and the bank saw improved performance from its home equity loans group. The lesson of this case study is that, although SOMs are powerful tools for finding clusters, neural networks really are only as good as the data that goes into them.

STRENGTHS OF ARTIFICIAL NEURAL NETWORKS

The strengths of neural networks are:

- They can handle a wide range of problems.
- They produce good results even in complicated domains.

- They handle both categorical and continuous variables.
- They are available in many off-the-shelf packages.

Neural Networks Are Versatile

Neural networks provide a very general way of approaching problems. When the output of the network is continuous, such as the appraised value of a home, then it is performing prediction. When the output has discrete values, then it is doing classification. A simple rearrangement of the neurons and the network becomes adept at detecting clusters.

The fact that neural networks are so versatile definitely accounts for their popularity. The effort needed to learn how to use them and to learn how to massage data is not wasted, since the knowledge can be applied wherever neural networks would be appropriate.

Neural Networks Can Produce Good Results in Complicated Domains

Neural networks produce good results. Across a large number of industries and a large number of applications, neural networks have proven themselves over and over again. These results come in complicated domains, such as analyzing time series and detecting fraud, that are not easily amenable to other techniques. The largest neural network in production use is probably the system that AT&T uses for reading numbers on checks. This neural network has hundreds of thousands of units organized into seven layers.

As compared to standard statistics or to decision-tree approaches, neural networks are much more powerful. They incorporate non-linear combinations of features into their results, not limiting themselves to rectangular regions of the solution space. They are able to take advantage of all the possible combinations of features to arrive at the best solution.

Neural Networks Can Handle Categorical and Continuous Data Types

Although the data has to be massaged, neural networks have proven themselves using both categorical and continuous data, both for inputs and outputs. Categorical data can be handled in two different ways, either by using a single unit with each category given a subset of the range from 0 to 1 or by using a separate unit for each category. Continuous data is easily mapped into the necessary range.

Neural Networks Are Available in Many Off-the-Shelf Packages

Because of the versatility of neural networks and their track record of good results, many software vendors provide off-the-shelf tools for neural networks. The competition between vendors makes these packages easy to use and ensures that advances in the theory of neural networks are brought to market.

Many of these packages, though, are for the desktop. Although desktop processors are becoming faster and faster, the data still resides on larger systems, usually either mainframes or relational database systems. Increasingly, vendors are announcing neural networks that work on data inside relational databases and inside common analysis platforms like SAS.

WEAKNESSES OF ARTIFICIAL NEURAL NETWORKS

Neural networks have some weaknesses:

- They require inputs in the range from 0 to 1.
- They cannot explain their results.
- They may converge prematurely to an inferior solution.

All Inputs and Outputs Must Be Massaged to [0,1]

The inputs to a neural network must be massaged to be in a particular range, usually between 0 and 1. This requires additional transforms and manipulations of the input data that require additional time, CPU power, and disk space. In addition, the choice of transform can affect the results of the network. Fortunately, tools try to make this massaging process as simple as possible. Good tools provide histograms for seeing categorical values and automatically transform numeric values into the range. Still, skewed distributions with a few outliers can result in poor neural network performance.

The requirement to massage the data is actually a mixed blessing. It requires analyzing the training set to verify the data values and their ranges. Since data quality is the number one issue in data mining, this additional perusal of the data can actually forestall problems later in the analysis.

Neural Networks Cannot Explain Results

This is the biggest criticism directed at neural networks. In domains where explaining rules may be critical, such as denying loan applications, neural networks are not the tool of choice. They are the tool of choice when acting on the results is more important than understanding them.

Even though neural networks cannot produce explicit rules, sensitivity analysis does enable them to explain which inputs are more important than others. This analysis can be performed inside the network, by using the errors generated from backpropagation, or it can be performed externally by poking the network with specific inputs.

Neural Networks May Converge on an Inferior Solution

Neural networks usually converge on some solution for any given training set. Unfortunately, there is no guarantee that this solution provides the best model of the data. Use the test set to determine when a model provides good enough performance to be used on unknown data.

WHEN TO APPLY NEURAL NETWORKS

Neural networks are a good choice for most classification and prediction tasks when the results of the model are more important than understanding how the model works. Because they are opaque, it is difficult to extract rules from them.

Neural networks can also be used for undirected data mining tasks, like clustering. In this case, the network will identify clusters of records that are similar to each other, but it does not explain how they are similar. Other techniques, such as comparing the centers of clusters graphically provide this information.

The only time neural networks do not work well is when there are many hundreds or thousands of input features. Large numbers of features make it more difficult for the network to find patterns and can result in long training phases that never converge to a good solution. Here, neural networks can work well with decision-tree methods. Decision trees are good at choosing the most important variables—and these can then be used for training a network.

Genetic Algorithms

14

Like memory-based reasoning and neural networks, genetic algorithms are based on an analogy to biological processes. Evolution and natural selection have, over the course of millions of years, resulted in adaptable, specialized species and individuals that are highly suited to their environment. These processes serve to optimize the fitness of individuals over succeeding generations by propagating the genetic material in the most fit individuals of one generation to the next generation. Genetic algorithms apply the same idea to problems where the solution can be expressed as an "individual" and the problem is to maximize the "fitness" of individuals. For instance, one application of genetic algorithms is to the training of neural networks. An individual would be the set of weights inside the network, and the fitness of an individual would be the predictive ability of the neural network based on the weights applied to the training set. Like evolution, genetic algorithms proceed by having more fit individuals propagate their genetic material to succeeding generations. Less fit individuals—and their genetic material—do not survive. Although chance plays a significant role in the survival of any individual, over a larger population the rule of large numbers prevails and natural selection serves to propagate the genetic material that produces the most fit individuals.

In the past few years, genetic algorithms have been applied to three areas with promising results: training neural networks, generating scoring functions for MBR, and as embedded optimization engines in scheduling packages. By far the most common application has been for training neural networks. Many neural network packages now incorporate genetic algorithms as an option for training.

The first work on genetic algorithms dates to the late 1950s when biologists and computer scientists worked together to model the mechanisms of genetics on early computers. A bit later, in the early 1960s, John Holland and his colleagues at the University of Michigan applied this work on computerized genetics—chromosomes, genes, alleles, and fitness functions—to the optimization of a large range of functions. In 1967, one of Holland's students, J. D. Bagley, coined the term *genetic algorithms* in his graduate thesis to describe the optimization technique. However, researchers were uncomfortable with genetic algorithms because of their dependence on random choices; these choices seemed arbitrary and unpredictable. In the 1970s, John Holland developed a solid theoretical foundation for the technique. His theory of schemata gives insight into why genetic algorithms work—and intriguingly why genetics itself creates successful, adaptable creatures such as ourselves.

In the world of data mining and data analysis, the use of genetic algorithms has not been as widespread as the use of other techniques. Data mining focuses on tasks at hand, like classification and prediction, instead of optimization. Although many data mining problems can be framed as optimization problems, this is not the usual description. For instance, a typical data mining problem might be to predict the level of inventory needed for a given item in a catalog based on the first week of sales, characteristics about the items in the catalog, and its recipients. Rephrasing this as an optimization problem turns it into something like "what function best fits the inventory curve for predictive purposes." Applying statistical regression techniques is one way to find the function. Feeding the data into a neural network is another way of estimating it. Using genetic algorithms offers another possibility.

Few commercial products currently incorporate genetic algorithms. However, they are still an important and active area of research for investigators studying machine learning—figuring out how computers can learn about their environment the way that people do. The continued interest in genetic algorithms as a topic of active research leads us to believe that they will play an increasingly important role in future data mining products and as embedded engines in other products.

HOW THEY WORK

The power of genetic algorithms comes from their foundation in biology where genetics has proven capable of adapting life to a multitude of environments. Genetics is a rapidly expanding field where new results occur almost every month. The human genome project is just one example of where it is advancing. This endeavor seeks to map all the genes encoded in human DNA as a basis for future advancements in medicine, genetics, and biochemistry. As knowledge about genetics grows, so do the complexities and subtleties. Although interesting, these are fortunately beyond the scope of knowledge needed to understand genetic algorithms. The language used to describe the computer technique borrows heavily from the biological model. The following section provides a very basic overview of the genetics needed to understand the technique.

Simple Overview of Genetics

Life depends on proteins, which consist of sequences of 20 basic units called amino acids. The chromosomes in the nucleus of a cell are strands of DNA (deoxyribonucleic acid) that carry the blueprints for the proteins needed by the cell. The DNA encodes these blueprints for the amino acids sequences using strands of nucleotides. These nucleotides comprise the four letters of the genetic alphabet:

A, adenosine

C, cytosine

G, guanine

T, thymine

Triplets of nucleotides represent the 20 amino acids. For instance, the amino acid called methionine corresponds to the triplet ATG. Another amino acid, lysine, has two "spellings": AAA and AAG. So, if a strand of DNA contains the following letters

TGGAAGTGGCGA

then it decodes into a protein containing four amino acids: methionine, TGG; lysine, AAG; methionine, TGG; followed by arginine, CGA (see Figure 14.1). This description intentionally glosses over the details of the actual biochemical mechanism that turns the blueprints into proteins, but it provides a high-level outline of the mapping from genetic information in DNA to the building blocks of proteins.

In this simplified model, the process of evolution works as follows. The proteins produced by the representations in the DNA express themselves as features of the living organism, such as blue eyes, five fingers, the structure of the brain, a long trunk and so on. Genes can express themselves in damaging ways, causing the resulting organism to die. Healthy organisms survive to produce offspring and pass their DNA to the next generation. In higher-level animals, the DNA is actually mixed with the DNA from another survivor during sexual replication, using a technique called crossover (we'll get back to this later). Sometimes, mistakes are made in passing genes from one generation to the next—these are mutations. The combination of all these processes over the course of many generations results in organisms highly adapted to their environment: the process of evolution.

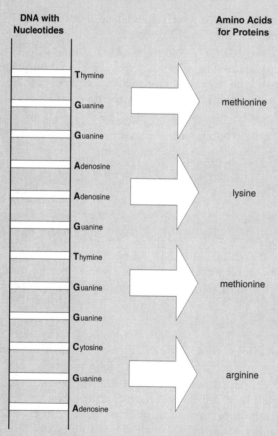

Figure 14.1 A biological example of encoding is the mapping from nucleotides in DNA to amino acids in protein.

Genetics on Computers

A simple example will help illustrate how genetic algorithms work: trying to find the maximum value of a simple function with a single parameter p in the range from 0 to 31. The function for this purpose is $31p - p^2$ where p varies between 0 and 31 (see Figure 14.2). The genetic material is called a genome, which, in this case, contains only a single five-bit gene for the parameter p (five bits are needed to represent the numbers from 0 to 31). This function peaks at the values 15 and 16, represented as *01111* and *10000* respectively. This example shows that genetic algorithms are applicable even when there are multiple, dissimilar peaks.

Genetic algorithms work by evolving successive generations of genomes that get progressively more and more *fit*. The goal is to maximize the fitness of the genomes in the population. In nature, fitness is simply whether an organism survives to reproduce. On a computer, there is much more flexibility. We choose the fitness function to solve the problem. For this example, the appropriate fitness function is $31p - p^2$. The technique consists of applying the following steps:

1. Identify the genome and fitness function, and create an initial generation of genomes.
2. Modify the initial population by applying selection, crossover, and mutation.
3. Repeat step 2 until the fitness of the population no longer improves.

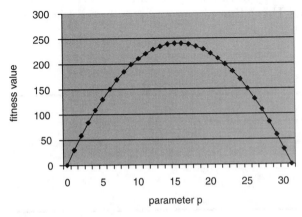

Figure 14.2 This simple function will help illustrate genetic algorithms.

The first step in using genetic algorithms is setting up the problem. The genome, as previously mentioned, consists of a single, five-bit gene for the parameter p. Over the course of generations, the fitness function is going to be maximized; it processes a genome and produces a single fitness value. For this example, shown in Table 14.1, the initial generation consists of four genomes, randomly produced. A real problem would typically have a population of hundreds or thousands of genomes, but that is impractical for illustrative purposes. Notice that in this population, the average fitness is 117.75—pretty good, but genetic algorithms will improve it.

The basic algorithm modifies the initial population using three operators—selection, then crossover, then mutation—as illustrated in Figure 14.3.

Selection is similar to natural selection where only the fittest individuals in the population survive to pass their genetic material on to the next generation. Unlike nature, though, the size of the population usually remains constant from one generation to the next, so there is no chance of the population becoming extinct. The chance of a genome surviving to the next generation is proportional to its fitness value—the higher the value relative to other genomes, the more copies that survive to the next generation. Table 14.2 shows the ratio of the fitness of the four genomes to the population fitness. This ratio determines the number of copies of each genome expected in the next generation.

The expected number of copies is a fraction, but the number of genomes in the population is never fractional. Survival is based on choosing the genomes in a random way proportional to their fitness. Figure 14.4 illustrates the roulette wheel or spinner approach to selection. A spinner is set up with each genome having an area proportional to its fitness. It is spun randomly, landing at a spot pointing to a particular genome. Using the spinner converts the fractional probabilities to whole number approximations.

Table 14.1 Four Randomly Generated Genomes

Genome	p	Fitness
10110	22	176
00011	3	87
00010	2	58
11001	25	150

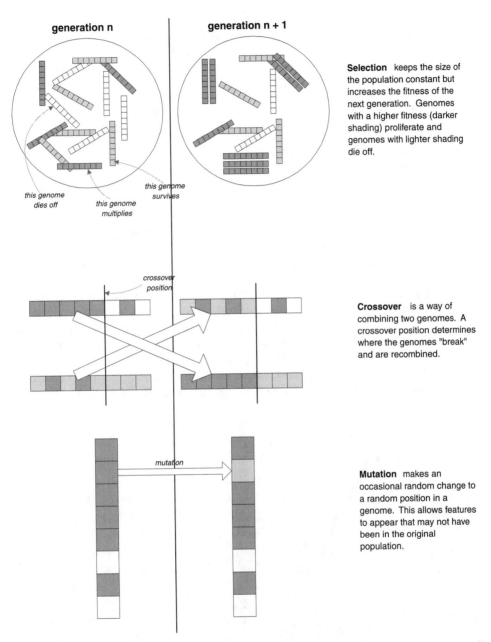

Selection keeps the size of the population constant but increases the fitness of the next generation. Genomes with a higher fitness (darker shading) proliferate and genomes with lighter shading die off.

Crossover is a way of combining two genomes. A crossover position determines where the genomes "break" and are recombined.

Mutation makes an occasional random change to a random position in a genome. This allows features to appear that may not have been in the original population.

Figure 14.3 The basic operators in genetic algorithms are selection, crossover, and mutation.

Table 14.2 Using Fitness for Selection

Genome	Fitness	% of Total Population Fitness	Expected Copies
10110	176	37.4%	1.50
00011	87	18.5%	0.74
00010	58	12.3%	0.49
11001	150	31.8%	1.27

Applying selection to the original four genomes yields the following survivors, shown in Table 14.3. Notice that in general this procedure produces more copies of the fittest genomes and fewer of the less fit. One of the less fit, *00011*, has not survived this round of selection, but there are two copies of *10110*, the fittest. And, the average fitness of the population has increased from 117.75 to 140.

The next operator applied to the surviving genomes is crossover. Crossover, which occurs in nature, creates two new genomes from two existing ones by gluing together pieces of each genome. As shown in Figure 14.3, crossover starts with two genomes and a random position. The first part of one genome swaps places with the first part of the sec-

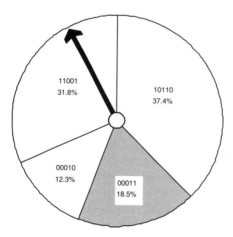

Figure 14.4 Selecting the genomes for the next generation is like spinning a spinner where each genome has an area on the spinner proportional to its fitness.

Table 14.3   The Population After Selection

Genome	Fitness
10110	176
11001	150
00010	58
10110	176

ond. For instance, starting with the two genomes *10110* and *00010* and using a crossover position between the second and third position works as follows:

```
10|110
00|010
```

The result of crossover is (the genes from the second genome are underlined):

```
10|010
00|110
```

The resulting genomes, called children, have a piece inherited from each of their parents. Applying crossover to the population proceeds by selecting pairs of genomes and flipping a coin to determine whether they cross over. This probability is the crossover probability, often denoted by p_c. If they do cross over, then a random position is chosen and the children of the original genomes replace them in the next generation. A value of 0.5 for the crossover probability (corresponding to a coin toss) generally produces good results. In the example, the two genomes *10110* and *00010* are chosen for crossover and the position is between the second and third genes (Table 14.4). After selection and crossover, notice that the average fitness of the population has gone from 117.75 to 178.5. This is a significant improvement after only one generation.

The final operation is mutation. Mutation rarely occurs in nature and is the result of a miscoded genetic material being passed from a parent to a child. The resulting change in the gene may represent a significant improvement in fitness over the existing population, although more often than not, the results are harmful. Selection and

Table 14.4 The Population After Selection and Crossover

Genome	p	Fitness
10010	17	238
11001	25	150
00110	6	150
10110	22	176

crossover do a good job of searching the space of possible genes, but they depend on initial conditions and randomness that might conspire to prevent certain valuable combinations from consideration in succeeding generations. Mutation provides the additional input. The mutation rate is quite small in nature and is usually kept quite low for genetic algorithms—no more than one mutation or so per generation is a reasonable bound. For the example at hand, when a mutation occurs, the bit changes from a 0 to a 1 or from a 1 to a 0.

Assume that there is one mutation in this generation, occurring in the second genome at position 3. Table 14.5 shows the population of genomes after such a mutation. Notice that this mutation, like many mutations, is destructive: The fitness of the genome affected by the mutation decreased from 150 to 58, the average fitness of the population decreased from 178.5 to 155.5, and the resulting genome is unlikely to survive to the next generation. This is not unusual. The primary modus operandi of genetic algorithms is selection and crossover. Mutation is very much a second-order effect that helps avoid premature convergence to a local optimum. When the initial population provides good coverage of the space of possible combinations, then succeeding generations will move quickly toward the optimal solution

Table 14.5 The Population After Selection, Crossover, and Mutation

Genome	p	Fitness
10010	17	238
11101	29	58
00110	6	150
10110	22	176

by means of selection and crossover. Changes introduced by mutation are likely to be destructive and will not last for more than a generation or two. Yet, even though the mutation is harmful in the example, the second generation is a considerable improvement over the original population.

The basis of genetic algorithms is the continual improvement of the fitness of the population by means of selection, crossover, and mutation as genes are passed from one generation to the next. After a certain number of generations—typically several dozen or hundred—the population evolves to a near-optimal solution. Genetic algorithms do not always produce the exact optimal solution, but they do a very good job of getting close to the best solution quite quickly. As a data mining tool, where exact solutions may not be feasible, being close to the best solution still yields actionable results.

Representing Data

The previous example illustrated the basic mechanisms of applying genetic algorithms to the optimization of a simple function, $31p - p^2$. Since the example was trying to maximize a function, the function itself served as the fitness function. The genomes were quite easy to create, because the function had one parameter, an integer that varied between 0 and 31. This genome contained a single gene, representing the parameter, and consisting of a sequence of five binary bits. The choice of representation using binary sequences is not accidental. As we will explain later in the section on schemata, genetic algorithms work best on binary representations of data—a highly convenient circumstance since computers themselves work most efficiently on binary data.

Genetic algorithms are different from other data mining and optimization techniques in that they manipulate the patterns of bits in the genomes and do not care at all about the values represented by the bits—only the fitness function knows what the patterns really mean. One requirement for the fitness function is that it is able to transform any genome into a fitness value. This requirement does not seem particularly onerous. After all, integers and floating-point numbers are easily represented as sequences of bits. And, since we are working with bit representations, we can adjust the number of bits to fit our needs. For instance, in a normal database or compute language, we would represent the age of a person using 8, 16, or 32 bits. However, since the range of ages is pretty well-defined, we really only need 7 bits to cover the ages from 0 to 127. This allows us to use other bits to represent other data and eliminates the possibility that a mutation will create a genome with an age of 254. Similarly, floating-point data can be represented using standard floating-point representations or using a fixed-point representation, depending on the range.

This solves the problem for numeric data types. What about categorical (or discrete types)? To represent a discrete set of categories, simply map the categories to the integers, such as:

male → 0
female → 1

If there are unknown values, than an additional bit is needed to indicate "unknown":

male → 00
female → 11
unknown → 01

But now there is a problem. The mechanisms of crossover and mutation can create arbitrary bit patterns in the genome, so we have to be sure that all bit patterns represent something significant to the fitness function. What happens if a gene representing a female (*11*) crosses over with a male (*00*) and the crossover position is between the two bits? One child has the representation *01*, indicating "unknown." The other is *10*, which, according to our mapping, has no meaning. The fitness function that uses gender information is undefined, because the bit pattern is undefined. In this case, the solution is rather simple: We need to complete the representation by extending the "unknown" classification to include both patterns, *01* and *10*. The general rule here is to include an "unknown" classification to ensure that the fitness function can understand any bit patterns created by repeated applications of crossover and mutation.

TIP

The fitness function is defined on the genome, a sequence of bits. It must be able to understand any pattern of 1s and 0s in the bits, since selection, crossover, and mutation may generate any arbitrary pattern. When a particular pattern of bits does not make sense, then the fitness function should return a very low value—so the pattern does not get passed on to succeeding generations.

CASE STUDY: USING GENETIC ALGORITHMS FOR RESOURCE OPTIMIZATION

One area where genetic algorithms have proven quite successful is in problems involving scheduling resources subject to a wide range of constraints. These types of problems involve competition for limited resources while adhering to a complex set of rules that describe relationships. The key to these problems is defining a fitness function that incorporates all the constraints into a single fitness value. Although these problems are outside the range of what we have been considering as data mining problems, they are interesting and do illustrate the power of genetic algorithms.

An example of such a problem is the assignment of forty medical residents to an outpatient clinic, as faced by Dr. Ed Ewen at the Medical Center of Delaware. The clinic is open seven days a week and the residents are assigned to one particular day of the week through an entire year, regardless of their other duties. The best assignment balances several different goals:

- The clinic must have staff at all times.
- The clinic should have a balance of first-, second-, and third-year residents.
- Third-year residents see eight patients per day, second-year residents see six, and first-year residents see four.

So far, this problem is not so complicated. However, each resident spends four weeks on a rotation in a given part of the hospital, such as the intensive care ward, the oncology unit, or a community hospital. These rotations impose some other constraints:

- Senior residents do not go to clinic when they are working at the medical intensive care rotation, but all other residents do.
- Junior residents do not go to clinic when they are working at the cardiac care rotation, but all other residents do.
- No more than two residents can be assigned to the clinic on the same day from the intensive care unit rotation.
- No more than three residents can be assigned to the clinic on the same day from other rotations.

As an example of problems that may arise, consider that during one rotation, five residents are assigned to the clinic on a particular day. During the next rotation, the senior is on the medical intensive care rotation and the two juniors are on the cardiac care rotation. Now there are only two residents left at the clinic—and this is insufficient for clinic operations.

The genetic algorithms approach recognizes that there is probably no perfect solution to this problem, but that some assignments of residents to days of the week are clearly better than others. Dr. Ewen recognized that he could capture the "goodness" of a schedule using a fitness function. Actually, the function that Dr. Ewen used was an anti-fitness function—the higher the value, the worse the schedule. This function imposed penalties for violating the constraints:

- For each day when the clinic has fewer than three residents, an amount is added—a larger amount for the bigger the size of the deficit.
- For each day when there are no seniors in the clinic, a small amount is added.
- For each day when fewer than three residents are left on a rotation, a large amount is added to the fitness function.
- And so on.

Setting up a spreadsheet with these functions, Dr. Ewen tried to minimize the functions to get the best assignment. His initial assignments had scores in the range of 130 to 140. After several hours of work, he was able to reduce the score to 72. Pretty good.

However, he had a genetic algorithms package from the Ward Systems Group (that plugs into Excel spreadsheets) available to work on this problem. He started with a population of 100 randomly generated assignments (none of which were very good). After 80 generations, the package lowered the score to 21—considerably better than he was able to do by hand.

This example gives a good flavor for optimization problems where genetic algorithms are applicable. They differ from data mining problems because they are more rule-oriented than data-oriented. The key to solving these problems is to incorporate the constraints into a single fitness function to be optimized (either by finding a maximum or a minimum). The resulting fitness function might be highly non-linear, making it difficult to optimize using other techniques. As we will see, the same techniques adapt to situations on large amounts of data.

Genetic algorithms are a good tool when there are more rules than data in the problem (although they are useful in other areas as well). These types of scheduling problems often involve competition for limited resources subject to complex relationships that describe the resources and their users. The key is to define a fitness function that captures the goodness of a particular resource assignment. If the fitness function can be described in a spreadsheet, such as Excel, then genetic algorithms packages, such as GeneHunter from the Ward Systems Group, can find the optimal solution.

SCHEMATA: WHY GENETIC ALGORITHMS WORK

At first sight, there is nothing sacrosanct in the selection, crossover, and mutation operators introduced earlier in this chapter. Why, for instance, does crossover choose only one intermediate point instead of two or more? Why does the mutation rate stay so low? The fact that nature behaves this way is not sufficient justification if multiple crossover points result in better results more quickly or if a high mutation rate gives better results.

For solving problems that yield actionable results, the fact that genetic algorithms have worked well in practice may be sufficient justification for continuing to use them as they are. However, it is still comforting to know that the technique has a solid theoretical foundation. John Holland developed his theory of schemata processing in the early 1970s to explain why selection, crossover, and mutation work so well in practice. Readers interested in using genetic algorithms for some of their problems are particularly well advised to understand schemata, even if the genetic algorithms are buried inside tools they are using, since this understanding explains both the power and the limits of the technique.

A *schema*, which comes from the Greek word meaning "form" or "figure," is simply a representation of the patterns present in a genome. Schemata (the plural is formed from the Greek root) are represented as sequences of symbols. The *1*s and *0*s (called the *fixed positions*) of genomes are augmented by an asterisk, *, that matches either a *0* or a *1*. The relationship between a schema and a genome is simple. A genome matches a schema when the fixed positions in the schema match the corresponding positions in the genome. An example should make this quite clear; the following schema

10**

matches all of the following four genomes because they all have four symbols, beginning with a *1* followed by a *0*:

1 0 0 0
1 0 0 1
1 0 1 1
1 0 1 0

The *order* of a schema is the number of fixed positions that it contains. For instance, the order of *1*10111* is 6, of ****1010**1* is 5, and of *0*************** is 1. The *defining length* of a schema is the distance between the outermost fixed positions. So, the defining length of *1*10111* is 6 (7 − 1), of ****1010**1* is 6 (10 − 4) and of *0*************** is 0 (1 − 1).

Now, let us look at fitness functions in terms of schemata. If the genome *000* survives from one generation to the next, then the schema *0** has also survived, as have **0*, ***0, **00, 0*0, 00**, and ****. The fitness of a particular schema, then, is the average fitness of all the genomes that match the schema in a given population. For instance, the fitness of the schema *0** is the average fitness of the genomes *000, 001, 010*, and *011* since the schema survives when these genomes survive, at least considering only the selection operator. Consider two schemata from the previous example using the fitness function $31p - p^2$, *10***, and *00***. One genome in the initial population matches *10***, so its fitness is 176. The two genomes matching *00**** have fitness values of 87 and 58. The first schema is fitter than the second. And, in fact, in the next generation there is only one genome matching *00**** and there are two matching *10***. The fitter schema has survived and proliferated; the less fit is disappearing.

A geometric view of schemata is sometimes helpful for understanding them. Consider the eight possible genomes of length three: *000, 001, 010, 011, 100, 101, 110*, and *111*. These lie at the corners of a unit cube, as shown in Figure 14.5. Schemata then correspond to the edges and faces of the cube. The edges are the schemata of order 2 and the faces of order 1. As genetic algorithms are processing different genomes; they are also processing schemata, visualized by these features on a cube. The population covers pieces of the cube trying to find

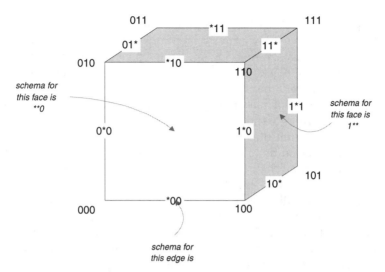

Figure 14.5 A cube is a useful representation of schemata on three bits. The corners represent the genes, the edges represent the schemata of order 2, the faces, the schemata of order 1, and the entire cube, the schema of order 0.

the corners with the best fitness. This geometric perspective generalizes to higher dimensions, where the selection, crossover, and mutation operators correspond to cuts through hypercubes in some higher dimension space, but it is harder to visualize these higher dimensions.

Consider the schema, *1***1*. This is also quite fit in the original population, with a fitness of 150. There is one genome that matches it in the original population and the same one in the next generation. This schema has survived only because the genome containing it did not cross over with another genome. Almost any crossover would have destroyed it. Compare this to *10*** that survived a crossover. The shorter the defining length of a schema, the more likely it will be to survive from one generation to another. So, even longer schemata that are very fit are likely to be replaced by shorter, but fit, cousins. Using more complicated crossover techniques, such as making two cuts, changes the behavior entirely. With more complicated techniques, the defining length is no longer useful and Holland's results on schemata do not necessarily hold.

Holland rigorously proved these two observations and summed them up in the Schema Theorem (also called the Fundamental Theorem of Genetic Algorithms): short, low-order schemata with above-average fitness increase in population from one generation to the next. In other words, short, low-order schemata are the building blocks that genetic algorithms are working on. From one generation to the next, the fittest building blocks survive and mix with each other to produce fitter and fitter genomes.

The Schema Theorem explains that genetic algorithms are really searching through the possible schemata to find fit building blocks that survive from one generation to the next. A natural question is how many building blocks are typically being processed? We will spare the reader the details, but Holland showed that the number of schemata being processed by a population of n genomes is proportional to n^3 (Goldberg explains this well). This means that each generation is really evaluating n^3 different schemata, even though it is only doing work on n different genomes. Holland calls this property *implicit parallelism*. The computational effort for a genetic algorithm is proportional to the size of the population, but in this effort, the algorithm is usefully processing a number of schemata proportional to n^3. The property of implicit parallelism should not be confused with explicit parallelism that is available when running genetic algorithms on a distributed network of workstations or on a computer with multiple processors.

The Schema Theorem gives us insight into why genomes work better when there are only two symbols (*0*s and *1*s) in the representation. Finding the best building blocks requires processing as many schemata as possible from one generation to the next. For two symbols, the number of different genomes of a given length is 2^{length} and the number of different schemata is 3^{length}. Roughly, the number of unique schemata being processed by a single genome is about 1.5^{length}. Now, what happens if there are more symbols in the alphabet, say by adding *2* and *3*? Now the number of genomes of a given length is 4^{length}, but the number of different schemata is 5^{length}. Although there are more schemata, the number of schemata corresponding to a given genome is only 1.25^{length}. As the number of symbols increases, the relative number of schemata decreases. Another way of looking at this is to consider the schema **00*. If there are only two letters in the alphabet, then only two genomes process this schema, *000* and *100*. If there are four letters, then there are four genomes: *000, 100, 200*, and *300*. Since genetic algorithms are trying to find the best schemata using a given population size, the additional genomes do not help the search.

Schemata are the building blocks of the solutions, and using only two symbols allows the maximum number of schemata to be represented in a given population size. These estimates are not exact, but they are suggestive. More rigorous treatment confirms the result that an alphabet of two symbols is optimal from the point of view of processing schemata.

APPLICATION TO NEURAL NETWORKS

One of the strengths of genetic algorithms is their ability to work on *black boxes*—that is, on problems where the fitness function is available but the details of the calculations are not known. The use of genetic algorithms to train neural networks is probably their most common application. Without explaining the inner working of neural networks, we can explain the use of genetic algorithms.

Figure 14.6 illustrates a simple neural network with three input

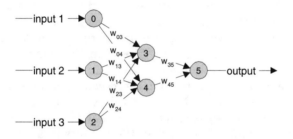

Without really even understanding how a neural network works, the weights can be gathered into a genome so a genetic algorithm can optimize them.

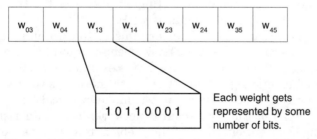

Figure 14.6 A neural network is described by weights that genetic algorithms can optimize.

nodes, a hidden layer with two nodes, and a single output node. The key to making the network work well is to adjust the weights on its edges so that the output produces the right answer for appropriate inputs. Chapter 13 discusses what the functions are inside the nodes and how standard training algorithms proceed. For now, all we need is that the network can produce an output for any given set of weights and inputs. The weights are real numbers between 0 and 1 and that there is a training set that includes inputs and the corresponding correct output.

The first problem faced is to determine what a genome looks like. The genome consists of all the weights in the network glommed together. Each weight varies between 0 and 1. One way to represent the weights is as 8-bit integers that vary between 0 and 225. To convert each span of 8 bits to a weight in the network requires dividing the integer by 255.

What is the fitness function? Comparing this predicted output to the actual output for the training set provides the basis for a fitness function. A good comparison is the error of the network on the training set. This is measured by taking the sum of the absolute value of the differences between the actual output of the network and the correct value. Actually, this produces an anti-fitness function, since the error is 0 when the network perfectly predicts the outputs (which is the desired result). The genetic algorithms can proceed by minimizing this function or, alternatively, by subtracting this value from a suitably large number to create a fitness function to maximize.

Now a 64-bit genome represents all the weights in a neural network. The fitness function determines how closely these weights perform on the training set. To proceed with training using genetic algorithms requires generating an initial population, then applying selection, crossover, and mutation. The end result will be a neural network that does a good job of predicting outputs over the training set (and presumably over other inputs as well).

This application of genetic algorithms to the training of neural networks works so well that it has now been incorporated into several commercial neural network packages. This example demonstrates the versatility of genetic algorithms. The neural networks themselves remain a black box, which makes the technique practical for many different variations of the basic neural network. The main issues are determining the right encoding of the problem into genomes and finding the right fitness function.

BEYOND THE SIMPLE ALGORITHM

Researchers have been pushing the bounds on genetic algorithms in several directions. Some of these enhancements are refinements to the basic algorithm; others modify the algorithm to provide a better model of genetic activity in the natural world. This work is often under the guise of machine learning, an area of current artificial intelligence research that aims to enable computers to learn in ways analogous to humans. We are confident that, like neural networks, expert systems, and memory-based reasoning, today's research will soon find profitable applications in data mining, so it is worth reviewing modifications to the current paradigm.

The simple genetic algorithm previously described offers several areas of improvement. One of the inefficiencies in the algorithm is the fact that entire populations are replaced from one generation to the next. This is a gross oversimplification of what happens in nature. Instead of replacing an entire population, some researchers have worked with overlapping populations that can grow in size. They have introduced the notion of *crowding* to determine which existing members should be targeted for replacement. When applied naively, this tends to result in very fast convergence, often to suboptimal solutions, because all the less fit genomes are replaced before they have an opportunity to reproduce—and often the less fit genomes have something to offer. To get around this, the targets for replacement often come from subsets of the population that exhibit high degrees of similarity.

The issue of overly fast convergence is actually a problem for the simple genetic algorithm because the goal of finding the globally optimal solution conflicts with locally optimal solutions that are nearer by. Overly fast convergence often suggests that the search is being limited. To get around this, the various probabilities for crossover and mutation are often set high initially, then slowly decreased from one generation to the next.

The genomes discussed so far consist of only a single strand of genes. Didn't we learn back in high school that DNA consists of two intertwining strands in a helix structure? What happened to those other concepts buried back in this high school past, like recessive and dominant genes? The genetics used so far is based on the simplest chromosomes found in nature, single-stranded or *haploid* chromosomes. These tend to be found in uncomplicated, single-cell organisms. In more complex organisms, the chromosomes are two-stranded or *diploid*, as in our own DNA.

The algorithmic characteristics of diploid chromosomes are much the same as haploid chromosomes. They are two chromosomes tied together. The actual algorithm proceeds in much the same way: Selection, crossover, and mutation are the same. The difference is that now there are two alleles for each gene (two possible values) instead of one. When they match, there is no problem. When they do not, which does the fitness function use? In the language of genetics, this is asking which of the alleles gets *expressed*. For instance, when an allele for blue eyes pairs up with an allele for brown eyes, the brown eyes "win"; that is, it gets expressed instead of the blue eyes. Researchers have solved this problem by including information about dominance into the alleles themselves. The details of this mechanism are beyond the scope of this book. The interested reader is referred to Goldberg's classic book *Genetic Algorithms*.

What is interesting is why we would care about diploid structures? Geneticists have long wondered why two-stranded chromosomes predominate in nature, when single-stranded ones are simpler. They believe that the two-stranded structure allows an organism to "remember" a gene that was useful in another environment, but has become less useful in the current environment. In terms of GA, this suggests that these are useful in cases where the environment—or fitness function—is changing over time. In the real world, this may prove to be quite useful. An example of a changing fitness function would be a function that tried to determine the price of bonds over time. The goodness of a given bond price depends on factors not under control of the algorithm, such as the rate of inflation. The "fitness" function can take this into account by changing over time to incorporate estimates of inflation.

STRENGTHS OF GENETIC ALGORITHMS

The strengths of genetic algorithms are:

- Produce explainable results
- Easy to apply the results
- Able to handle a wide range of data types
- Applicable to optimization
- Integrate well with neural networks

Produce Explainable Results

Genetic algorithms produce results that are as explainable as the genes contained in the genome. Since these are generally well understood parameters in the fitness function, they are as simple to explain as the fitness function itself. In some circumstances, such as when genetic algorithms are used in conjunction with neural networks, the fitness function may not be transparent. On the other hand, genetic algorithms do not do a good job of explaining why a particular set of genomes is useful. By watching the fitness of the generations improve over time and monitoring the best individual in each generation, it is possible to get a feel for the evolutionary path being taken.

Easy to Apply the Results

The results of genetic algorithms are easy to apply because they take the form of parameters in the fitness function. In many cases, genetic algorithms are used for finding optimal values. The values themselves or the result of the fitness function may be actionable. In other cases, they are used for setting parameter values on the fitness function based on a training set. The fitness function can then be applied as easily to new instances as to the training set. Simple parameterized fitness functions can even be expressed in SQL and run directly on a relational database.

Able to Handle Wide Range of Data Types

Genetic algorithms are not inherently limited in the types of data that they need. So long as the data can be represented as a string of bits of a fixed length, then it can be handled by genetic algorithms.

Applicable for Optimization

In many cases, the information needed from data is the optimal value of one or more parameters—how many clerks to hire, what price to set, and so on. In these circumstances, genetic algorithms provide a flexible and powerful way to search for optimal values. This technique is subject to fewer constraints than other methods and can be applied to arbitrarily complex functions. In fact, the function does not even have to be known for genetic algorithms to produce good results. It can be a black box, whose details are hidden from the technique, such as the training of a neural network.

Integrate Well with Neural Networks

The most common application of genetic algorithms is in combination with neural networks. They are applicable in several areas. In this chapter, we discussed how genetic algorithms could be applied to the training of neural networks. They can also be used for determining the best topology and reducing the number of inputs to the most important ones. When used with neural networks, genetic algorithms are often incorporated directly into the commercial packages and the details of the algorithms are hidden from users.

WEAKNESSES OF GENETIC ALGORITHMS

The weaknesses of genetic algorithms are:

- Difficulty in encoding many problems
- No guarantee of optimality
- Computationally expensive
- Available in few commercial packages

Difficulty in Encoding Many Problems

The biggest problem in using genetic algorithms is that the given problem must be encoded so it can be represented as fixed-length genomes being optimized by a fitness function. Although many problems fall naturally into this category, the details of encoding affect the goodness of the results. We discussed how genetic algorithms work in terms of creating small and fit building blocks. The encoding of a problem needs to support these building blocks in order for the technique to be effective.

No Guarantee of Optimality

Genetic algorithms are a global optimization technique. As such, they can potentially suffer from problems suffered by global optimization. In particular, they may get stuck on local optima and never find the best solution. This happens often when the generations converge too rapidly to a solution. Also, the genetic algorithms may find the area where the best solution lies, but may settle on a nearby solution. In some cases, genetic algorithms are combined with other techniques, such as hill climbing, to get around this problem. This proceeds by changing each bit in the solution to see if a better solution appears.

Computationally Intensive

Genetic algorithms can be quite computationally intensive. This is especially true when the fitness function comprises multiple functions evaluated over a training set. On the other hand, genetic algorithms are prime candidates for explicit parallelism and the authors expect parallel implementations to be appearing on the market in the near future.

Available in Few Commercial Packages

Apart from their use in neural network packages, genetic algorithms are available from only a handful of vendors. As of this writing, all the commercial code runs on desktops so does not take advantage of more computationally powerful platforms. Public domain code is available, however, for interested readers who wish to experiment with their own applications.

WHEN TO APPLY GENETIC ALGORITHMS

Genetic algorithms are often incorporated into other packages. In particular, neural network packages are increasingly using the power of genetic algorithms under the hood to improve performance of the neural network. In this application, the genetic algorithms are applied without much intervention from the user.

When not incorporated into existing packages, genetic algorithms are best applied to optimization problems. The easiest problems are those where there are specific parameters to optimize in a known fitness function. However, by cleverly coding problems, many different problems are amendable to genetic algorithms.

Data Mining and the Corporate Data Warehouse

15

Since the introduction of computers into data processing centers in the 1960s, virtually every operational system in business has been automated. These systems run companies, creating large amounts of data along the way. This automation has changed how we do business and how we live: ATM machines, adjustable rate mortgages, just-in-time inventory, credit cards, overnight deliveries, and frequent flier/buyer clubs are a few examples of how automation has opened new markets and revolutionized existing ones. In a typical company, this automation has resulted in scads of data residing in dozens of disparate systems, from automated general ledgers to sales force automation systems, from inventory control to electronic data interchange (EDI), and so on. The data about specific parts of a business is there—lots and lots of data, somewhere, in some form.

That is, data is available but not information—*and not the right information at the right time*. This is the goal of the data warehouse. Data warehousing is the process of bringing together disparate data from throughout an organization for decision-support purposes. Decision support, as used here, is intentionally ambiguous. It can be as rudimentary as getting reports on production to front-line managers every week. It can be as complex as sophisticated modeling of prospective customers using neural networks to determine to whom to extend offers of credit. It can be and is just about everything in between.

This definition is a natural ally of data mining. Data mining seeks to find actionable patterns in data and therefore has a hard requirement for clean and consistent data. A data mining endeavor includes the effort to identify, acquire, and cleanse data. When a well-designed corporate data warehouse is available, the warehouse can often supply the necessary data. Better yet, if the design of the data warehouse includes support for data mining applications, the warehouse facilitates and catalyzes the data mining efforts. The two technologies work together to deliver value. Data mining fulfills much of the promise of data warehousing by converting an essentially inert source of data into actionable information.

Relational database management systems (RDBMS)—the heart of the data warehouse—are increasingly providing built-in support for more advanced access to the data than provided by SQL, the standard interface to RDBMSs. For instance, on-line analytic processing (OLAP), discussed in more detail in the next chapter, now finds built-in support for its data structures. The engines are also starting to support the structures needed for data mining, as database vendors partner with tools vendors to create relational data mining environments.

As useful as a data warehouse is, it is not prerequisite for data mining and data analysis. Statisticians, actuaries, and analysts have been using statistical packages for decades—and achieving good results with their analyses—without the benefit of a centralized warehouse. This process can continue to be useful, but increasingly a data warehouse is becoming an imperative for any kind of decision support or information analysis. There are several forces driving the need for data warehousing:

- Acquisitions and mergers have created very diverse computer systems within large corporations. Larger banks, for instance, often have dozens of systems performing the same function, such as deposit and loan systems, due to consolidation in the banking industry.
- The automation of all parts of a business has left unmerged, unacquired companies with dozens of systems running different parts of the business. Like the blind man describing the elephant, each of these systems tells only a piece of the story.
- Flexibility in the marketplace has replaced mass production. Mass marketing is out. Mass customization and 1-to-1 marketing are in. The trend is toward gathering and using information. Competitive advantage resides in knowledge—especially knowledge about the

customer, but also about the products, the market, and competitors. Data residing in operational systems is often the cheapest way to gather knowledge about customers.

- The increased focus on service instead of product has created communication gaps. These gaps result in very different views of the business that, unless explained and rectified, can damage strategic initiatives. Everyone in an organization can agree on what earth-moving equipment is and how many units are sold when. But a marketing department in a bank may have a very different definition of "consumer loans" (how the loan is used) than risk management (the conditions of the loan)—so the reports describing sales of consumer loans may differ markedly from reports detailing the outstanding risk for supposedly the same product.

- Technology can support data warehousing. Competition in the mainframe and midrange markets has significantly lowered computing and storage costs. At the same time, new parallel technologies have made multi-terabyte (millions of megabytes!) databases a reality.

- Tools are becoming more versatile and user-friendly. Data cleansing tools, relational databases, metadata tools, statistical packages, OLAP engines, query generation tools, and data mining packages are available and ready to use. Building a data warehouse is still a big systems integration task, but the components are increasingly commercial off-the-shelf (COTS) packages.

This chapter tries to focus on data warehousing as part of the virtuous cycle of data mining, as a valuable and often critical component in supporting all four phases of the cycle: identifying opportunities, analyzing data, applying information, and measuring results. It is not a how-to guide for building a warehouse—there are many books already devoted to that subject.

First, the architecture of data and its different forms inside an organization are discussed. Then there is a discussion on a comprehensive architecture for a data warehouse. The multitiered architecture reflects the fact that needs for data span a range, from the most detailed transactions to highly summarized reports and models. This architecture provides the full complement of functionality needed for decision support. Next is a discussion of the important elements of this architecture from the perspective of data mining and data analysis. Finally, the important considerations are summarized into a list.

THE ARCHITECTURE OF DATA

Data is the heart of both data warehousing and data mining and it can be described in many different ways. One way is simply differentiating between internal data and external data; that is, between data generated inside the business and data generated outside. On first glance, this seems quite useful. However, on deeper analysis, the distinction gets very blurry. Does the data purchased by a credit card company from a bureau count as internal data or external data? Does the data generated by an outsourced call center count as internal data? Outsourced billing? Householding done on in-house systems but using a vendor's proprietary system? Answering these questions is not worth the effort. Data is data and the internal versus external distinction is not always useful.

A more useful way of looking at data is in terms of abstraction, as shown in Figure 15.1. The different levels of abstraction show that data exists on several interdependent levels and help determine how much investment needs to be made to support different levels. These levels of abstraction are:

- Operational data
- Summary data
- Schema
- Metadata
- Business rules

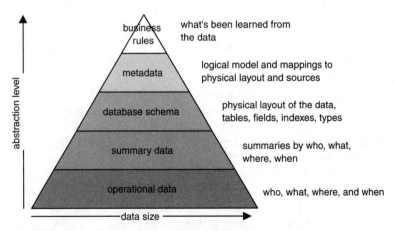

Figure 15.1 A hierarchy of data and its descriptions helps users navigate around a data warehouse. As data gets more abstract, it generally gets less voluminous.

Operational data is the most basic form of data. Every product purchased by a customer, every bank transaction, every credit card purchase, every flight segment, every package, every telephone call gets recorded in some operational system. Typically these systems lead to billing, inventory, and similar systems that discard the transactions at the first opportune moment. Changes to operational data are quite common. Maintenance is constant, caused by the introduction of new products, expanding numbers of customers, and new technology. The fact that operational data changes has to be part of any robust data warehousing approach.

The amount of data gathered from these systems can be enormous. A typical fast food restaurant sells hundreds of thousands of meals over the course of a year. A chain of food markets can have tens or hundreds of thousands of transactions a day. A large bank processes millions of checks and credit card purchases a day. A regional bell in the United States completes hundreds of millions of telephone calls every day. Even with the price of disk falling, storing all these transactions requires a significant investment.

Summary data is the first level of abstraction. It is derived from operational data and is the most common way that users interact with data. Summary data results in the bottom line in billing systems. Summary data is the data in reports that provide static views of the business. It is very valuable—condensing, summarizing, and aggregating data is necessary for us to understand it and the dimensions used for summarization such as region and product often represent actionable areas in a business. However, today's summary data may not be important in the future, as markets, customers, and products evolve. Similarly, it may be difficult to compare today's summary data to last year's or next year's because the underlying operational data has changed. Being able to stabilize summary data is one effect of a well-designed data warehouse.

The next level of abstraction is data about the data itself. This most basic level is the physical layout of the operational data and the summary data. The layout is important. It tells us what we have and therefore what we can know. Do we know the telephone numbers of customers? If so, then there is some telephone number field somewhere in the data. Can we determine sales trends for products in different regions? If so, then there are tables with historical sales data for products in different regions or tables with operational data that can be used to create the appropriate summaries.

The abstraction level above the physical schema is metadata. Metadata differs from the physical layout by defining the data in business terms. The basis of the metadata is a logical data model that defines the data in terms of entities, attributes, and relationships meaningful on the business level. This level describes the product hierarchy, the attributes of a customer, and the relationship between the business and its various partners. It can also describe other attributes of data, such as when it is available, where it is available, what applications use it, and so on. This level has to be quite flexible to changes, since external changes that do not affect the data—like spinning off a department into a wholly owned subsidiary or regulatory changes–do affect the metadata.

TIP

THE IMPORTANCE OF METADATA

Metadata provides the key link between the business users and the data. It describes the data in business terms. A good metadata system gives users the ability to browse through the metadata on their desktops and, perhaps, even gives them limited ability to update certain fields. To be successful, the metadata has to be accurate and accessible. Having to keep the metadata up-to-date is also beneficial because it imposes a discipline on the data warehouse—changes are documented and communicated back to the users. A successful metadata component makes users more comfortable with the data warehouse and encourages them to take full advantage of it.

The highest level of abstraction is the business rules. Business rules not only describe the structure of the data—this is the role of metadata—but they also describe why relationships exist and how they are applied. Business rules are difficult to capture and often lie buried deep inside code fragments and old memos. No one may remember why the fraud detection system ignores claims under $500. Presumably there was a good business reason, but the reason, the business rule, is often lost once the rule is embedded in the computer system.

Business rules have a close relationship to data mining. Some data mining techniques, such as market basket analysis and decision trees, produce explicit rules, which should be captured as business rules. Even more generally, the process of using data mining should be captured as business rules as well as specific results.

THE CURRENT STATE

Data warehousing has become the information systems project of the 1990s. When the decade began, the term had hardly been invented. Now, virtually every large corporation has at least one data warehouse and is working on its next one. Many data warehouses are already on their third- and fourth-generations. Hundreds of vendors, from systems integrators to relational databases to OLAP vendors to middleware and tools vendors, claim to have the data warehousing solution. What is the current state of data warehousing and how does this affect data mining efforts? As with anything that has become so widespread so quickly, "data warehouse" refers to many different types of systems that have little in common other than the fact that they contain data (see Figure 15.2). Some common types of systems are:

- Middleware tools provide a single interface to a distributed network of source systems departmental data warehouses or operational data stores. Distributed data warehousing seems like a good idea; that is, until someone runs a query. The disparate source systems do not talk to each other easily, do not contain compatible data, and are not designed for the complex queries needed for decision support.
- Departmental data warehouses store summarized representations of interest to a single application area. These are useful systems, often implemented using OLAP tools or custom-built applications. They deliver value to the end user, but do not solve the data integrity problem. A proliferation of departmental data warehouses can create more problems than it solves by increasing the number of incompatible systems dependent on inconsistent data.
- Interdepartmental staging areas cleanse data but maintain no history and do not have a logical data model. These systems feed downstream applications and help solve the data cleansing problem, so downstream systems are at least using somewhat similar data.
- Operational data stores take the data from one or a set of related operational systems and put it in a relational database. This makes it easier to cleanse and access the raw data for the data warehouse, but it does not necessarily bring disparate data sources together in one place.

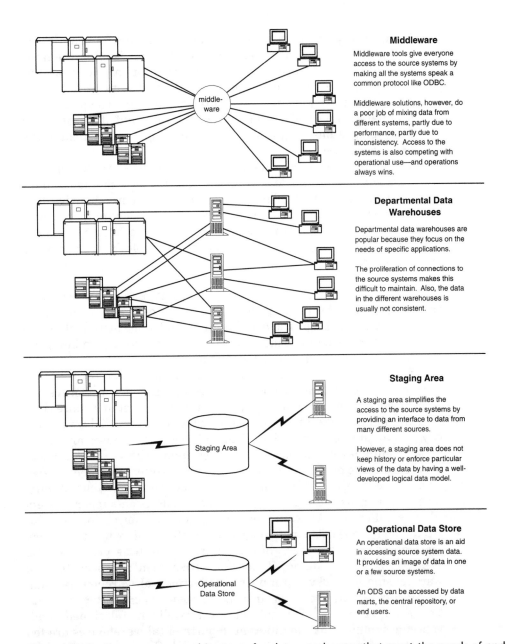

Middleware

Middleware tools give everyone access to the source systems by making all the systems speak a common protocol like ODBC.

Middleware solutions, however, do a poor job of mixing data from different systems, partly due to performance, partly due to inconsistency. Access to the systems is also competing with operational use—and operations always wins.

Departmental Data Warehouses

Departmental data warehouses are popular because they focus on the needs of specific applications.

The proliferation of connections to the source systems makes this difficult to maintain. Also, the data in the different warehouses is usually not consistent.

Staging Area

A staging area simplifies the access to the source systems by providing an interface to data from many different sources.

However, a staging area does not keep history or enforce particular views of the data by having a well-developed logical data model.

Operational Data Store

An operational data store is an aid in accessing source system data. It provides an image of data in one or a few source systems.

An ODS can be accessed by data marts, the central repository, or end users.

Figure 15.2 Four common architectures for data warehouses that meet the needs of end users but do not solve all the problems that data warehousing should be addressing.

- Overgrown prototypes of large relational databases contain the data but not in a format easily accessible. This is often the first-generation data warehouse—a demonstration project that has evolved into a complicated amalgamation of data and systems that just barely work together. Often the one or two applications originally supported by the system do work, but it is easier for new applications to go back to the source systems instead of the data warehouse.
- The multitiered approach has a fairly normalized relational database with consistent logical model that supports metadata, data marts, and end users. This is the direction for comprehensive data warehousing solutions. We will discuss this model in more detail in the next section. Only recent advances in technology (and decreases in prices) have made this option viable in the corporate environment.

The last of these systems focuses on the data and how it is used in the organization. It is the best sort of system for data mining purposes, especially when it keeps the detail data available for historical analyses. The other systems are more or less useful, depending on how good a job they do in gathering and cleaning data.

Since data warehousing is such a good idea, large corporations often have several data warehouses. A proliferation of warehouses can be as useless as not having any at all, unless the systems share common attributes—like the definition of customer, the product hierarchy, and all are kept up-to-date. Many of these warehouses are at the departmental level and may be useful for applications in that particular area. On the other hand, these systems are often designed for specific applications and the data may not be useful for data mining purposes. For instance, a retailer may have a decision-support system (that is called a data warehouse) to maintain information summarized along shop-SKU-time dimensions. If the retailer wants to learn more about its customers, this summarized database provides little value. It has no customer dimension. A common approach to data warehousing is to develop multiple departmental warehouses using OLAP cubes, then to standardize on dimensions across the organization (see Figure 15.3). This solution works well when designed in advance, assuming that the different departmental warehouses are fed equivalent source data. If not designed well, this system leads to a proliferation of unrelated systems and places more burdens on decision support.

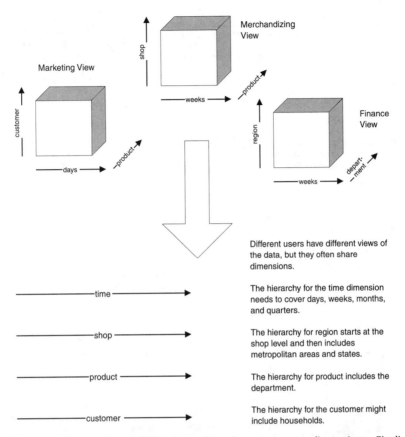

Figure 15.3 Different views of the data often share common dimensions. Finding the common dimensions and their base units is critical to making data warehousing work well across an organization.

THE MULTITIERED ARCHITECTURE FOR A DATA WAREHOUSE

The multitiered approach to data warehousing recognizes that data needs come in many different forms. It provides a comprehensive solution for managing data for decision support. The major components of this architecture (see Figure 15.4) are:

- *Source systems* are where the data comes from.
- *Data Transport and Cleansing* move data between different data stores.

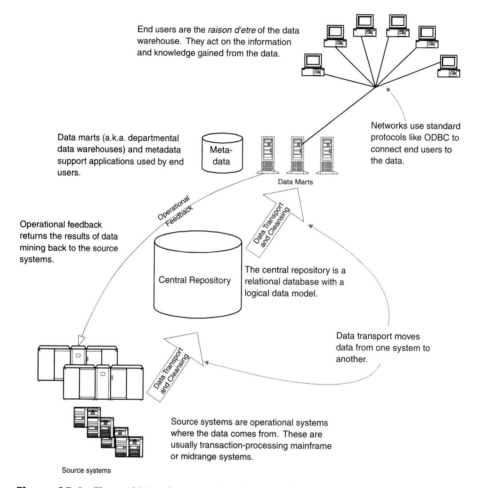

Data marts (a.k.a. departmental data warehouses) and metadata support applications used by end users.

End users are the *raison d'etre* of the data warehouse. They act on the information and knowledge gained from the data.

Networks use standard protocols like ODBC to connect end users to the data.

Data Marts

Operational feedback returns the results of data mining back to the source systems.

The central repository is a relational database with a logical data model.

Data transport moves data from one system to another.

Central Repository

Source systems are operational systems where the data comes from. These are usually transaction-processing mainframe or midrange systems.

Source systems

Figure 15.4 The multitiered approach to data warehousing includes a central repository, data marts, and end-user tools.

- The *Central Repository* is the main store for the data warehouse.
- The *Metadata* describes what is available and where.
- *Data Marts* provide fast, specialized access for end users and applications.
- *Operational Feedback* integrates decision support back into the operational systems.
- *End users* are the reason for developing the warehouse in the first place.

One or more of these components exist in virtually every system called a data warehouse. They are the building blocks of decision support throughout an enterprise. The following discussion of these components follows a data-flow approach. The data is like water. It originates in the source systems and flows through the components of the data warehouse ultimately to deliver information and value to end users.

The components of the data warehouse rest on a technological foundation consisting of hardware, software, and networks. When implementing a data warehousing solution, investments in all three areas are usually needed, since the needs of decision-support systems are quite different from those of operational systems.

Source Systems

Source systems are the operational systems inside the organization, providing the lowest level of data (in terms of abstraction). They were designed for operational use, not for decision support, and the data reflects this fact. The data is highly specialized. For example, a retail point-of-sales system might have a "returned dollars" field containing the dollar amount for returned merchandise when a customer makes a return. However, when customers make purchases and returns at the same time, then the field has no value. Instead, there is a negative value in the "dollar amount sold" field, indicating that the amount was subtracted from the sales total (and wreaking havoc on reports that use this data). A telephone switching system breaks up telephone calls longer than 48 hours into 24-hour increments to support the billing system. A zero in the amount withdrawn field in a deposit system indicates a balance inquiry. A telephone number with alphabetic characters indicates a calling card call, and so on. Each system has its own peculiarities. Although well-designed when built, operational systems respond to changes in the business environment, evolving over time away from their original design.

When dealing with multiple systems, the data issues multiply quickly. Four deposit systems have four different, incompatible codes for account status. Product descriptions depend on which system contains the code. Different systems use their own versions of account numbers and customer ids. In one system, "shipping date" means planned shipping date and in another it means actual shipping date. Once again, the systems perform the function they were designed to perform and have evolved over time to continue performing the function. Gathering the data together for decision support stresses the operational systems since these systems were originally designed for transaction processing and are usually quite successful doing their intended function. Bringing the data together in a consistent format is almost always the most expensive part of implementing a data warehousing solution.

The source systems offer other challenges to gathering data for a data warehouse—or directly into a data mining environment. They generally run on a wide range of hardware and much of the software is built in-house or highly customized. These systems are mainframe and midrange systems and generally use complicated and proprietary file structures. Mainframes were designed to hold and process data, not to share it. Although they are becoming more open, getting access to the data is always an issue, especially when different systems are supporting very different parts of the organization. And, the systems may be geographically dispersed, further contributing to the difficulty of gathering the data.

Data Transport and Cleansing

Data transport and cleansing tools refer to the software used to move data from the source systems to the warehouse or analysis environment (or between source systems, but that is not a concern here). Traditionally, data movement and cleansing have been the responsibility of programmers writing special purpose code as the need for data arose. This process is not scalable to the gigabytes of data needed to support a data warehouse, especially when combined with the constant changes in the data sources and the growing proliferation of decision-support systems dependent on the data.

Several products are now available to facilitate data movement and data cleaning. These tools offer graphical user interfaces to describe the mapping from one source system to another and offer error checking and verification of out-of-bounds conditions on the data. Transformation rules, such as "change all numeric state codes to two character abbreviations," are then expressed in COBOL, RPG, or some scripting language that gets compiled and run automatically. More advanced tools support aggregation, conditionals, and table lookups during the cleansing process.

The goal of these tools is to describe where data comes from and what happens to it—not to write the procedure code that modifies the data. Standard procedural languages, such as COBOL and RPG, focus on the "how" instead of the "what," making it difficult to reuse code developed for a specific purpose. Often these tools provide a metadata interface, so end users can understand what is happening to "their" data during the loading of the central repository. Being able to capture the transformation rules for informational purposes is a valuable feature.

Central Repository

The central repository is the most technically advanced part of the data warehouse. This is the database containing the data. It has three key features:

- Scalable hardware
- Relational database system
- Logical data model

Scalable hardware refers to the ability of the hardware to grow virtually without limit. The same hardware supports more users, more data, more processing power. In the past few years, improvements in parallel technology have made this possible at the hardware level (see Figure 15.5). Parallel machines can grow by adding more disk, more memory, more processing units, or more bandwidth between processors—all while taking advantage of the existing investment in technology, training, and operational support. This is particularly important for data warehouses where the amount of data can quickly grow into the hundreds of gigabytes or terabytes of data, requiring dozens of processors and hundreds of disks for the system.

Relational databases have now matured to take advantage of scalable hardware platforms for all the data-intensive operations: loading data, building indexes, backing up the database, and processing queries. A plethora of tools and applications are available for relational databases as well. Every RDBMS speaks the open database connectivity standard (ODBC), used by virtually every desktop tool, as well as other vendor-specific standards. IBM, Oracle, Informix, Sybase, and Tandem, the leading vendors of relational technology on scalable platforms, are enhancing their products to support more complex data types and more advanced methods of accessing the data than rote SQL. Performance of these systems, even on very large databases, has improved to the point where systems viable for decision support are available at a reasonable cost.

The final key component in the central repository is a logical data model. A data model describes the structure of the data inside a database. Often, the data model is confused with the physical layout (or

Uniprocessor

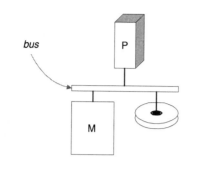

A simple computer follows the architecture laid out by Von Neumann. A Processing Unit communicates to Memory and Disk over a local bus. (Memory stores both data and the executable program.) The speed of the processor, bus, and memory limits performance and scalability.

SMP

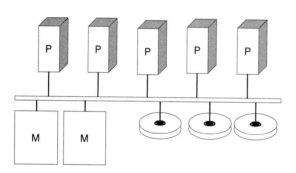

The symmetric multiprocessor (SMP) has a shared-everything architecture. It expands the capabilities of the bus to support multiple processors, more memory, and more disk. The capacity of the bus limits performance and scalability. SMP architectures usually max out with fewer than 20 processing units.

MPP

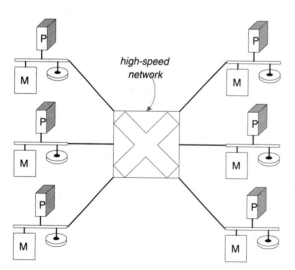

The massively parallel processor (MPP) has a shared-nothing architecture. It introduces a high-speed network (also called a switch) that connects independent processor/memory/disk components. MPP architectures are very scalable, but fewer software packages can take advantage of all the hardware.

Figure 15.5 Parallel computers build on the basic Von Neumann uniprocessor architecture. SMP and MPP systems are scalable because more processing units, disk, and memory can be added into the system.

Parallel Technology: A Comparison of SMP and MPP

Parallel technology is the key to scalable hardware and it comes in two flavors: symmetric multiprocessing systems (SMPs) and massively parallel processing systems (MPPs). An SMP machine is centered on a *bus*, a special network present in all computers that connects processing units to memory and disk units. The bus acts as a central communication device, so SMP systems are also called *shared everything*. Every processing unit can access all the memory and all the disk units. This form of parallelism is quite popular because an SMP box supports the same applications as uniprocessor boxes—and many times the applications can take advantage of the additional hardware with minimal changes to the code. However, SMP technology has its limitations because it places a heavy burden on the central bus, which gets saturated as the processing load increases. Contention for the central bus is often what limits the performance of SMPs. They tend to work well when they have fewer than 10 to 20 processing units.

MPPs, on the other hand, behave like separate computers connected by a very high-speed network (also called a switch). Each processing unit has its own memory and its own disk, so the bus connecting the processing unit to memory and disk never gets saturated. However, one drawback is that some memory and some disk are now local and some are remote—a distinction that can make MPPs harder to program. Programs designed for one processor can always run on one processor in an MPP, but they require modifications to take advantage of all the hardware. MPPs are truly scalable so long as the network connecting the processors can supply more bandwidth and the network technology used in these machines is very fast. The MPP architecture has supported systems with thousands of nodes and thousands of disks.

Both SMPs and MPPs have their advantages. Recognizing this, the vendors of these boxes are making them more similar. SMP vendors like DEC, Sun Microsystems, and Hewlett Packard are connecting their SMP boxes together in clusters—that is, with specialized high-speed scalable networks based on fiber optics and asynchronous transfer mode technology. At the same time, MPP vendors, like IBM and NCR, are replacing their single-processing units with SMP processing units, creating a very similar architecture.

schema) of the database. However, there is a critical difference. The purpose of the physical layout is to maximize performance and to inform database administrators (DBAs). The purpose of the logical data model is to communicate the contents of the database to a wider audience. The business user must be able to understand the logical data model—entities, attributes, and relationships. The physical layout is an implementation of the logical data model, making compromises and choices along the way to optimize performance.

When embarking on a data warehousing project, many organizations feel compelled to develop a comprehensive, enterprise-wide data model. That is, they want to model everything inside the organization. These efforts are often surprisingly unsuccessful. The logical data model for the data warehouse does not have to be quite as uncompromising as an enterprise-wide model. For instance, a conflict between product codes in the logical data model for the data warehouse can be (but not necessarily should be) resolved by including both product hierarchies—a decision that takes 10 minutes to make. In an enterprise-wide effort, resolving conflicting product codes can require months of investigations and meetings.

Metadata

Metadata is an often overlooked component of the data warehousing environment. In the narrowest sense, metadata simply means "data about data." The basic metadata is the database schema; that is, the physical layout of the data in tables. When used correctly, though, metadata is much more. It answers questions posed by end users about the availability of data, gives them tools for browsing through the contents of the data warehouse, and gives everyone more confidence in the data. This confidence is the basis for new applications and an expanded user base.

A good metadata system should include the following pieces:

- The annotated logical data model. The annotations should explain the entities and attributes, including valid values.
- Mapping from the logical data model to the source systems.
- The physical schema.
- Mapping from the logical model to the physical schema.
- Common views and formulas for accessing the data. What is useful to one user may be useful to others.
- Load and update information.
- Security and access information.

In any data warehousing environment, each of these pieces of information is available somewhere—in scripts written by the DBA, in email messages, in documentation, in the system tables in the database, and so on. Metadata makes this information available to the users, in a format they can readily understand. The key is giving users access so they feel comfortable with the data warehouse, with the data it contains, and with knowing how to use it.

Data Marts

There are typically hundreds or thousands of users that can make use of the data inside a data warehouse. Different users have different needs, ranging from simple canned reports to ad hoc queries to advanced analysis. Meeting the needs of all the users with a single centralized system is not always feasible and not always wise:

- A single centralized system centralizes control over the data and the system. End users may want to exert more control over their information environment.
- A single centralized system is subject to delays and preemption when new data sources and new capabilities are put on-line—delays that affect everyone using the data even if they do not benefit from the enhancements.
- To satisfy a wide range of requests, the design has to sacrifice performance in all areas, making it more expensive to achieve desired levels of performance.
- Breaking out the costs for a centralized system supporting many different departments is difficult from a charge-back and accounting perspective.

The solution to these problems is the data mart, also called a departmental data warehouse. A data mart is a specialized system that brings together the data needed for a department or related applications. There are several different varieties of data marts.

Data marts can be implemented within the central repository by creating special, application-specific *views* on the data in the base tables. A view is a built-in query that presents the users with the data they need access to. A view can be as simple as the subset of data for all business customers in Florida or more complicated like a roll-up of buying habits for customers or sales trends for products. The data in a view can combine data from multiple base tables. Users then access the view that, at the time they issue the query, gets resolved using the underlying tables in the database. Views are flexible, easily changed, and occupy no space in the database, but they are expensive at run-time.

Another approach is the *instantiated view*. This is an optimization of the view where the data for a particular view is placed into another table and kept up-to-date with the original data. Instantiated views duplicate storage to improve performance. The physical storage for an instantiated view can co-reside with the central repository or it can be on another machine. Keeping the instantiated view in sync with the base tables requires using database replication mechanisms or triggers. Or, the instantiated view can be recreated at fixed intervals, such as once a week.

More interesting data marts are those that use different representations of the data. This includes OLAP engines, that are becoming increasingly popular for giving business users access to most of the data they need (these are discussed in more detail in Chapter 16). It also includes data sets for analysis, using statistical tools and data mining tools. The advantage to using the central repository as a common source for data in these systems is to guarantee the consistency of the data used for analysis and reporting purposes. The decision-support systems need to share data but not necessarily software systems and hardware platforms.

Finally, not all the data in data marts needs to come from the central repository. Often specific applications have an exclusive need of data. The real estate department, for instance, might be using geographic information in combination with data from the central repository. The marketing department might be combining zip-code demographics with customer data from the central repository. The central repository only needs to contain data that is likely to be shared among different applications, so it is one data source—usually the dominant one—for data marts.

Operational Feedback

Operational feedback systems integrate data-driven decisions back into the operational systems. The most common examples are the electronic data interchange (EDI) systems common among large- and medium-size retailers. These systems keep track of inventory and can automatically place orders when inventory reaches certain levels. Using EDI, the stocking of shelves has become paperless, much less costly, and much more efficient. The orders emanate automatically from the retailer and go to the wholesaler, manufacturer, or distributor over computer networks.

Operational feedback systems are also valuable wherever a corporation interacts with customers. For instance, a call center can customize its scripts and prioritize incoming calls by using information gathered from the central repository. The desktop customer service system in retail banking can offer new products to existing customers—products determined perhaps by data mining analyses to predict what each customer would be interested in. Sales associates in catalog companies can keep abreast of what items, colors, and styles are likely to sell together, based on data in the warehouse, and use this information to customize the products they push to customers placing orders.

Operational feedback offers the capability of completing the virtuous cycle of data mining very quickly. Once a feedback system is set up, intervention is only needed for monitoring and improving it—letting computers do what they do best (repetitive tasks) and letting people do what they do best.

End Users and Desktop Tools

The final and perhaps most important component in any data warehouse is the end users. This refers to analysts who use the data warehouse in a specialized way—such as searching for information using advanced algorithms—application developers, and business users who act on the information.

Analysts

Analysts want to access as much data as possible to discern patterns. They use special-purpose tools, such as statistics packages and data mining tools. Often, these are considered to be the primary audience for a data warehouse.

Usually, though, there are just a few technically sophisticated people who fall into this category. Although the work that they do is often highly leverageable, it is difficult to justify the expense of an investment in a data warehouse based on increases in their productivity. The virtuous cycle of data mining comes into play here. The purpose of the data warehouse—or data mining environment—is to create value. A data warehouse brings together data in a cleansed, meaningful format. The purpose, though, is to spur creativity, a very hard concept to measure. Later in this chapter we will return to the subject of using a data warehouse for data mining.

Application Developers

Much of the software that runs on a data warehouse is customized or custom-developed for the particular environment. These systems range from executive information systems (EIS) that provide high-level summaries with limited drill-down capability to risk management systems and sales forecasting systems. In order to develop stable and robust applications, developers have some specific needs from the data warehouse.

First, the applications they are developing need to be shielded from changes in the structure of the data warehouse. That is, new tables, new attributes in tables, and reorganizing the structure of existing tables should have a minimal impact on existing applications. Special application-specific views on the data help provide this assurance. In addition, open communication and knowledge about what applications use which attributes and entities can prevent development gridlock.

Second, the developers need access to valid field values and to know what the values mean. This is the purpose of the metadata, which provides documentation for the structure of the data. By setting up the application to verify data values against expected values in the metadata, developers can circumvent problems that more often appear only after applications have rolled out.

The developers also need to provide feedback on the structure of the data warehouse. This is one of the principle means of improving the warehouse, by identifying new data that needs to be included in the warehouse. Since real business needs are driving the development of the applications, the needs of developers are important to ensure that a data warehouse contains the data it needs to deliver business value.

The data warehouse is going to change and applications are going to continue to use it. The key to delivering success is controlling and managing the changes. The applications are a product for the end users. The data warehouse is there to support their data needs—not vice versa.

Business Users

Business users are the ultimate devourers of information derived from the corporate data warehouse. Their needs drive the development of applications, the architecture of the warehouse, the data it contains, and the priorities for implementation.

Many business users may only interface to the warehouse through printed reports, the same way they have been gathering information since before computers. Even these users will experience the power of having a data warehouse as the reports become more accurate, more consistent, and easier to produce.

More important, though, are the people who use the computers on their desks and are willing to take advantage of direct access into the data warehousing environment. Typically, these users access intermediate data marts to satisfy the vast majority of their information needs using friendly, graphical tools that run in their familiar desktop environment. These tools include off-the-shelf query generators, custom applications, OLAP interfaces, and report generation tools. On occasion, they may drill down into the central repository to explore particularly interesting things they find in the data. More often, they will contact an analyst to do the heavier analytic work.

Business users also have applications built for specific purposes. These applications may even incorporate some of the data mining techniques discussed in the last seven chapters. For instance, a resource scheduling application might include an engine that optimizes the schedule using genetic algorithms. A sales forecasting application may have a built-in neural network. When embedded in an application, the data mining algorithms are usually quite hidden from the end user, who cares more about the results than the algorithms that produced them.

WHERE DATA MINING FITS IN

Data mining plays an important role in the data warehouse environment. The initial returns from a data warehouse come from automating existing processes, such as putting reports on-line and giving existing applications a clean source of data. The bigger returns are the improved access to data that can spur innovation and creativity—and these come from new ways of looking at and analyzing data. This is the role of data mining—to provide the tools that improve understanding and inspire creativity based on observations in the data.

A good data warehousing environment serves as a catalyst for data mining. The two technologies work together as partners:

- Data mining wants to work on large amounts of data and the more detailed the data, the better—data that comes from a data warehouse.
- Data mining thrives on clean and consistent data—capitalizing on the investment in data cleansing tools.

- The data warehouse environment enables hypothesis testing and simplifies efforts to measure the effects of actions taken—enabling the virtuous cycle of data mining.
- The scalable hardware and relational database software can also be put to use to support data mining techniques—doubling the value of the investment in these technologies.

The benefits of having a data warehouse when approaching data mining are discussed in more detail in the following sections.

Lots of Data

The traditional approach to data analysis generally starts by reducing the size of the data. There are three common ways of doing this: summarizing detailed transactions, taking a subset of the data, and only looking at certain attributes. The purpose in reducing the size of the data has been to make it possible to analyze the data on the available hardware and software systems. When properly done, the laws of statistics come into play and it is possible to choose a subset of the data that behaves roughly like the rest of the data.

Data mining, on the other hand, is searching for trends in the data and for valuable anomalies. It is often trying to answer different types of questions, such as "what product is this customer most likely to purchase next?" Answering a question like this requires having lots of data about that customer and, presumably, about every customer since you want to answer the same question about everyone. This is often the motivation for needing detailed, transaction-level data. This is the data that pushes the size of data warehouses into the terabytes—every credit card purchase, every ATM transaction, every telephone call, every package delivery, every purchase, every flight reservation made by every customer.

When the traditional approach of summarizing data hits the data warehouse, it often results in the following hybrid structure:

- Summarized data for all customers
- Detailed data for customers in one market
- Detailed data for a random subset of customers

This approach seems like a reasonable compromise but it is actually rather expensive. It incurs additional overhead in deciding which detailed data to keep and which not to keep. The biggest drawback is at the summary level for all customers. The decision on what gets summarized happens 6 to 12 months before the data is available to the business users. How can the designer know what the business will need in the future? Once data has been summarized, the detail level is often not available at all, or very expensive to retrieve from tapes archived in deep, dark, inaccessible vaults.

Another problem is applying the results. The detailed transaction data may contain actionable and profitable information on trends or customer segmentation. Unfortunately, the data is only available on a few customers—the ones specially chosen to have their detail data stored. By the time the relevant data is gathered for other customers, the analysis may no longer be valid.

Data mining algorithms, fortunately, are often able to take advantage of large amounts of data. When looking for patterns that identify rare events—such as the most profitable customers—large amounts of data ensure that there is sufficient data for analysis. A subset of the data might be statistically relevant in toto, but when you try to decompose it into other segments (by region, by product, by customer segment), there is too little data to produce statistically meaningful results.

Data mining algorithms like to have lots of data. CART, one of the algorithms for producing decision trees works very well, even when there are dozens or hundreds of attributes on each record. Link analysis requires a full complement of the data to create a graph. Neural networks can train on millions of records at a time. And, even though the algorithms often work on summaries of the detailed transactions (especially at the customer level), what gets summarized can change from one run to the next. Prebuilding the summaries and discarding the transaction data locks you into only one view of the data.

TIP

ON SAMPLING AND SUMMARIZATION IN THE DATA WAREHOUSE

In the data warehousing environment, very few users, if any, think they need access to the detailed, transaction-level data. At first sight, summarizing the detail data to reduce its size or using a subset of the data both seem like good ways to reduce the size (and cost) of the data warehouse while still meeting the needs of all users.

This approach introduces more problems than it solves:

- Summarizations and subsets of the data that seem useful today probably will not meet future business needs.
- Summarizing the data introduces dependencies, such as on the definition of a customer or the regional sales hierarchy, that make the data warehouse brittle. That is, the data warehouse will not be able to respond to changes in the business environment.
- Many analyses of the data thrive on detail. Some arcane summarization of the data—discovered serendipitously or by data mining—may prove to have powerful predictive capabilities.

It is better to store the detail data and to derive all summarizations and subsets from the same master source—the central repository. Summarization and subsets of data play an important role in exploiting data. They are best used in the data marts.

Consistent, Clean Data

Data mining algorithms are often working on gigabytes of data combined from several different sources. Much of the work in looking for actionable information actually takes place when bringing the data together—often 80 percent or more of the time is spent bringing the data together when a data warehouse is not available. Subsequent problems, such as matching account numbers, interpreting codes, and applying households, further delay the analysis. Finding interesting patterns is often an iterative process that requires going back to the data to get different data elements. Finally, when interesting patterns are found, it is often necessary to repeat the process on the most recent data available.

A data warehouse solves these problems. Data is cleaned once, when it is loaded into the data warehouse. The meaning of fields is well-defined and available through the metadata. Incorporating new data into analyses is as easy as finding out what data is available through the metadata and retrieving it from the warehouse. A particular analysis can be reapplied on more recent data, since the warehouse is kept up-to-date.

In short, a data warehouse moves the cleansing and upkeep of the data to a special group charged with this responsibility. It is no longer a partial responsibility of the analysts or of the IS group to support data cleansing. The end result is that the data is cleaner and more available—and that the analysts can spend more time applying powerful tools and insights instead of moving data and pushing bytes.

Hypothesis Testing and Measurement

The data warehouse facilitates two other areas of data mining. Hypothesis testing is the verification of educated guesses about patterns in the data. Do tropical colors really sell better in Florida than elsewhere? Do people tend to make long distance calls after dinner? Are the users of credit cards at restaurants really high-end customers? All of these can be expressed rather easily as queries on the appropriate relational database. Having the data available makes it possible to ask questions and find out quickly what the answers are.

WARNING

One caveat about hypothesis testing is that these queries can be quite expensive to run. Typical operational systems may require days of elapsed time to run an interesting decision-support query—and then only if the machine does not run out of system resources. Even in a data warehouse, queries like this sometimes fall into the "killer query" category. However, on a scalable platform using a database with a good optimizer, most queries can be readily answered.

Measurement is the other area where data warehouses have proven to be very valuable. Often marketing efforts, product improvements, and so forth take place and feedback on the success is very limited. A data warehouse makes it possible to see the results much quicker and to find related effects. Did sales of other products improve? Did customer attrition increase? Did calls to customer service decrease? And so on. Having the data available makes it possible to understand the effects of actions, whether the action was spurred by data mining results or by something else. Measurement enables an organization to learn from its mistakes and to build on its successes.

Scalable Hardware and RDBMS Support

The final synergy between data mining and data warehousing is on the systems level. The same scalable hardware that makes it possible to store and query large databases also makes it possible to run advanced analysis algorithms on large amounts of data. Of course, the software being used must be able to run in the scalable environment. Parallel software is increasingly available for this purpose, especially for neural networks, decision trees, and market basket analysis.

Perhaps a more interesting area is the increased support of data mining algorithms inside relational databases. The relational model is a good model for representing data and for issuing many types of queries. However, there are some types of analysis that are difficult to express in SQL (the language of relational databases). Database vendors are working with tool vendors to include support in their products for these algorithms. This is often done as an extension of customizations already being made to support relational OLAP tools.

Some vendors have taken the lead in this area. Pilot Software's Lightship product, released in the fall of 1996, was the first tool that used a relational database to run its data mining code. Its user interface supports common algorithms and decision trees. However, the implementation is inside the database using *stored procedures* and on the database platform using special server processes. Stored procedures are a language inside databases that can access the data directly, without going through the expensive mechanisms of moving data into and out of the database system. More tool vendors are moving in this direction and the database vendors are adding features to make these efforts perform better.

CONSIDERATIONS FOR BUILDING A DATA WAREHOUSE TO SUPPORT DATA MINING

Data warehouses provide a natural support for data mining applications. There are some things to keep in mind, though, when building a data warehouse for this purpose.

First, the data warehouse should contain a central repository that contains detailed data, the kind of data needed by data mining algorithms. Often, an OLAP engine is called a data warehouse. Without a drill-down database, it is not very useful for data mining.

Second, the hardware investment for the central repository should support additional tools. Being able to use the same hardware—even a separate, disjoint partition of a parallel machine—facilitates moving data from the warehouse to the data mining tool. It is also a good way to incorporate advanced data mining tools that can take advantage of the parallel platforms to process more data and improve results.

Third, the data warehouse should be used regularly to measure the effectiveness of campaigns, especially those based on results from data mining. This measurement completes the virtuous cycle. It also means that the data needed for measurement should be incorporated into the warehouse.

16

Where Does OLAP Fit In?

In the past few years, on-line analytic processing (OLAP) tools have emerged as the "answer" for accessing large databases, whether the data resides in a single centralized data warehouse, in virtual distributed warehouses, or on operational systems. The hype around OLAP suggests that it is a substitute for data mining. This is not true. OLAP tools are powerful and fast tools for *reporting* on data, in contrast to data mining tools that focus on *finding patterns* in data. OLAP and data mining are complementary; both are important parts of exploiting data. OLAP is a presentation tool that can enable manual knowledge discovery; fundamentally, though, it depends on human intelligence for the knowledge discovery piece. Even though it may not formally be part of data mining, it is part of the solution to handling data in the business environment. Data mining can take advantage of the analysis needed to implement an OLAP solution. We have included a chapter on OLAP to show when and how these tools are useful, and how they can be successfully used to complement data mining solutions.

The business world has been generating reports to meet business needs for many decades. Figure 16.1 shows a range of common reporting capabilities. The oldest manual methods are the mainframe report-generation tools whose output is traditionally on green-bar paper or green screens. These mainframe reports automate paper-based methods that preceded computers and are very resource-intensive to

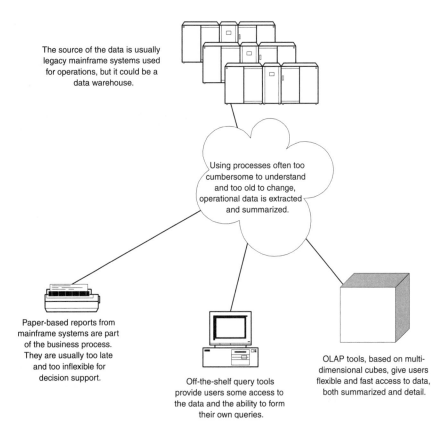

The source of the data is usually legacy mainframe systems used for operations, but it could be a data warehouse.

Using processes often too cumbersome to understand and too old to change, operational data is extracted and summarized.

Paper-based reports from mainframe systems are part of the business process. They are usually too late and too inflexible for decision support.

Off-the-shelf query tools provide users some access to the data and the ability to form their own queries.

OLAP tools, based on multi-dimensional cubes, give users flexible and fast access to data, both summarized and detail.

Figure 16.1 Reporting requirements on operational systems are typically handled the same way they have been for decades. Is this the best way?

generate. Producing them is often the primary function of IS departments. Even minor changes to the reports require modifying code that sometimes dates back 10 or 20 years. The result is a lag between the time a user requests changes to the time he or she sees the new information that measures in weeks and months. This is old technology that organizations are generally trying to move away from except for the lowest level reports that summarize specific operational systems.

In the middle are off-the-shelf query generation packages that have become popular for accessing data in the past decade. These generate queries in SQL and can talk to local or remote data sources using a standard protocol, such as Microsoft's Open Database Connectivity

standard (ODBC), Sybase's Open Server standard, or IBM's Distributed Remote Data Access (DRDA) standard. These tools are available
from dozens of vendors and have flexible graphical user interfaces.
With a day or so of training, business analysts can usually generate
the reports that they need. Of course, the report itself is often running
as an SQL query on an already overburdened database, so response
times measure in minutes or hours when the queries are even allowed
to run to completion. These response times are much faster than the
older report-generation packages, but they still make it difficult to exploit the data. The goal is to be able to ask a question and to be able to
remember the question when the answer comes back.

TIP

Long response times usually come from running queries on overburdened operational systems and less often on saturated networks. Although the answer may come back, it may be too late. The user may
have forgotten the question, why it was important, or moved on to
some other task while waiting hours for the answer set. The situation
is even worse when users have to go through an intermediary, such as
the IS department, in order to create a report. Interactive response
times (in the 3–5 second range) are a requirement for convincing business users to exploit data on a daily basis.

OLAP is the next advance in giving end users access to data.
These are client-server tools that have an advanced graphical interface talking to a powerful and efficient representation of the data,
called a cube. The cube is ideally suited for queries that allow users to
slice-and-dice data in any way they see fit. The cube itself is stored either in a relational database, typically using a star schema, or in a special multi-dimensional database that optimizes OLAP operations.
OLAP tools have very fast response times, measured in seconds. SQL
queries on standard relational databases would require hours or days
in many cases to generate the same information. In addition, OLAP
tools provide handy analysis functions that are difficult or impossible
to express in SQL.

Setting up the cube requires analyzing the data and the needs of
the end users—generally done by specialists familiar with the data
and the tool. Although designing and loading the cube may initially
take days or weeks, the result provides informative and fast access to

end users, generally much more helpful than the results from a query-generation tool. Response times, once the cube has been built, are almost always measured in seconds, allowing users to explore data and drill down to understand interesting features that they encounter.

AN OLAP EXAMPLE

OLAP allows users to slice-and-dice data to find the information they need. OLAP has proven successful in virtually every industry. For a simple example, though, we will be using the moviegoers database introduced in Chapter 5. Table 16.1 shows some sample rows from the moviegoer database.

The representation of the database mirrors how it was gathered, using surveys. However, it differs from the schema shown in Chapter 5 that has four tables. All the information for each person viewing a given movie is in a single row. Multiple rows repeat the same information, such as the source of the record. This structure for the data is called *denormalized* and is anathema to database administrators used to transactional systems where updates to data are common. Updating information in a denormalized database is a nightmare because a single change, like updating the name of a movie, requires updating every row that has the name. Relational databases are usually *normalized*, so only one row has to be updated for any such change. In addition, storing multiple copies of the same row is inefficient since the repetition of data in multiple rows takes up additional disk space.

Table 16.1 Moviegoers Database

Moviegoers name	sex	age	source	Movie name
Amy	f	27	Oberlin	Independence Day
Andy	m	34	Oberlin	The Birdcage
Bob	m	51	Pinewoods	Schindler's List
Cathy	f	39	124 Mt. Auburn	The Birdcage
Curt	m	30	MRJ	T2 Judgment Day
David	m	40	MRJ	Independence Day
Erica	f	23	124 Mt. Auburn	Trainspotting

Star Schema

This denormalized way of representing data has become one of the standard ways to represent data for decision-support purposes. Ralph Kimball, one of the founders of Red Brick (a database company that specializes in decision-support databases), developed the *star schema* for representing data in this fashion. The star schema is similar in many ways to the cube used in OLAP. In fact, cubes are usually represented as star schema for OLAP tools that use relational database engines.

A star schema starts with a *central fact table* that corresponds to facts about a business. These can be at the transaction level but are more often low-level summaries of transactions. In the moviegoers database, this fact table contains the person, the movie, and the source of the information. For retail sales, the central fact table might contain daily summaries of sales for each product in each store (shop-SKU-time). For a credit card company, the central fact table might contain rows for each transaction by each customer. For a database of frequent fliers, it contains information about each flight segment. For a diesel engine manufacturer interested in repair histories, it might contain each repair made on each engine or a daily summary of repairs at each shop.

Each row in the central fact table contains some combination of keys that make it unique. For the moviegoers, this is the person, the movie, and the source. For other databases using a star schema, it is usually something like the product, location, and time of the event; sometimes customer is also included. These keys are called *dimensions*. The central fact table also has other columns that typically contain numeric information specific to each row, such as the amount of the transaction, the number of transactions, and so on. Unfortunately, there is no such additional data in the moviegoers database, but we could imagine the cost of the movie, the time of the showing, or the amount each person spent on refreshments as good candidates for additional columns in the central fact table.

Associated with each dimension are auxiliary tables called *dimension tables* that contain information specific to the dimensions. For instance, the dimension table for a time dimension might specify the day of the week for a particular date, its month, year, and whether it is a holiday. In the moviegoers database, all the information we have about a person, like the gender, age, and name, are candidates for dimension tables.

In diagrams, the dimension tables are connected to the central fact table, resulting in a shape that resembles a star. Figure 16.2 illustrates what a star schema looks like for the moviegoers database. Notice that the keys in the central fact table are indexes into the dimension tables. This example is very simple. It only has three dimensions. A real example of a star schema looks more like Figure 16.3.

Increasingly, relational database vendors are providing more support for star schema. With a typical architecture, any query on the central fact table would require multiple joins back to the dimension tables. By applying standard indexes, and creatively enhancing indexing technology, relational databases can handle these queries quite well.

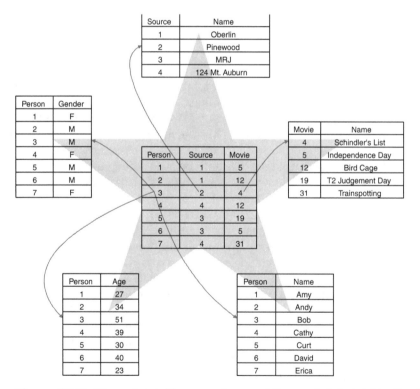

Figure 16.2 Dimension tables spread around the central fact table like the points of a star.

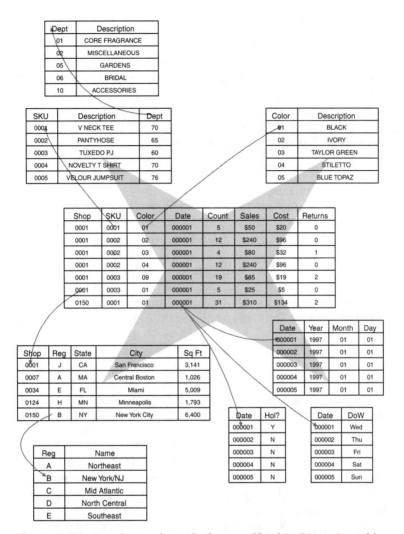

Figure 16.3   A real star schema looks more like this. Dimension tables are nested and there may be more than one dimension table for a given dimension.

From the perspective of OLAP, there are two types of columns in the denormalized data. *Dimension columns* contain information used for summarizations. These columns take a fixed number of values, such as location, product codes, and dates. Often, the value in the column is part of a hierarchy, such as a location code that also supports zip-code, state, and region. *Aggregate columns* are calculated amounts, like counts, averages, and sums. These are often numeric values, such as dollar amounts or cash.

Figuring out which columns should be dimensions and which aggregate is not always as simple as looking at the type of data in the column. The best way is to consider sample reports that users might want to run on the data. Sometimes, such reports already exist, providing a good starting point. For the moviegoers database, we might determine that the follow reports are interesting:

- The number of times each movie was seen for movies seen more than five times.
- For what movies is the average age of the viewers over 30?
- The number of people and their ages by source.
- The number of people from each source by gender.

These four reports (see Figure 16.4) suggest that the name of the movie, the gender of moviegoers, and the source of information, would be good candidates for dimensions. Candidates for aggregation are the number of times that each movie was seen and the average age of the moviegoers.

We are now well on the way to forming a cube. Each dimension corresponds to an axis of the cube, as shown in Figure 16.5. One dimension corresponds to the gender of the people responding. The gender axis is split in half, one for male and the other for female. Similarly, the source-of-information axis is split into four parts for each source, and the movie axis is split into 35 pieces, one for each movie.

The larger cube contains 2*4*35 = 280 subcubes. Notice that the number of subcubes is fixed regardless of the number of people in the original survey, assuming that the sizes of the dimensions do not change. We could have gathered information from 50 people or 50 million people and, assuming they came from the same four sources, the same two genders, and saw the same 35 movies, the cube would contain the same number of subcubes.

Each subcube contains aggregate information about the data that lands in it:

- The key (movie id, source, gender)
- The number of rows
- The sum of the ages of people in the rows (to calculate the average)

The subcubes are the building blocks of reports. Say we want to know the number of different movies seen by women from 124 Mt. Auburn.

What are the number of people
and their ages by source?

Source	Number	Average Age
1	103	31.34
2	23	39.35
3	54	35.04
4	28	33.43

The number of people from
each source by gender.

Source	Gender	Count
1	Female	55
1	Male	48
2	Female	16
2	Male	7
3	Female	14
3	Male	40
4	Female	28
4	Male	0

Movie ID	Average Age
110	50.00
48	46.00
30	46.00
23	45.13
25	44.80
107	44.00
89	41.00
17	40.00
26	39.67
114	39.00
6	39.00
9	38.50
69	38.00
84	37.00
1	34.65
80	32.00
97	32.00
22	31.67
32	31.50
57	31.00
21	30.00
44	30.00
54	30.00
73	30.00

For what movies is
the average age of
the viewers over
30?

The number of times
each movie was seen for
movies seen more than
five times.

Movie ID	Count
1	34
13	14
26	12
60	11
32	10
22	9
90	9
31	8
23	8
9	8

Figure 16.4 Four typical reports that provide information from the moviegoers database.

How does the cube help? The subcubes corresponding to women are in the front face of the cube. The subcubes corresponding to 124 Mt. Auburn are on the top face. So, the subcubes in the top, front edge contain all the information we need to answer this query. We only care about subcubes whose count is greater than zero—meaning that at least one woman from 124 Mt. Auburn has seen the movie referred to in the key for that subcube. We add up the number of such subcubes and, voila, arrive at the answer (see Figure 16.6). This process is much simpler than trying to generate and run this request in SQL. Plus, available OLAP tools make it very easy to express such a query.

OLAP tools also have the ability to answer the "how come" question. Sometimes the reports built up from the subcubes only whet your

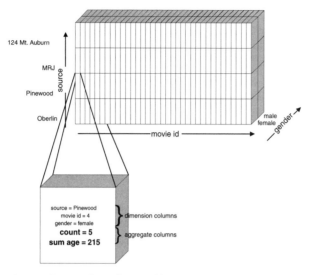

Figure 16.5   The cube used for OLAP is divided into subcubes. Each subcube contains the key for that subcube and summary information for the data falls into that subcube.

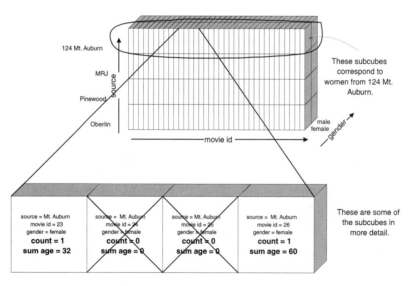

Figure 16.6   How to use a cube to determine the number of different movies seen by women from 124 Mt. Auburn.

appetite for information. You want to see which records that have landed in the subcubes correspond to the reports. This capability is called *drilling down* into the database. It allows you to look at the original records that constitute an OLAP report. Almost all OLAP tools provide drill-down capabilities back to the original database.

What It Looks Like in SQL

The question "How many different movies were seen by women from 124 Mt. Auburn?" can be answered using SQL on a relational database using the normalized schema presented in Chapter 4. The corresponding SQL looks like:

```
SELECT COUNT DISTINCT (*)
FROM moviegoers g, sources s
WHERE g.source_ID = s.source_ID
  AND g.sex = 'f'
  AND s.source = '124 Mt. Auburn';
```

The drill-down capability of OLAP tools generates SQL to run on the relational database representing the data. This is not magic. It is fairly easy to express the contents of a subcube as an SQL query. For instance, the subcube with the key (source=Pinewood, movieid=6, sex=Female) has the corresponding query:

```
SELECT s.source, m.name, g.sex, COUNT(*),
SUM(g.age)
FROM moviegoers g, sources s, movies m
WHERE g.source_ID = s.source_ID
  AND g.movie_ID = m.movid_ID
  AND m.sex = 'f'
  AND s.source = 'Pinewood'
  AND m.name = 'XXX'
GROUP BY 1, 2, 3;
```

Some minor modifications to this query can retrieve all the rows in the subcube instead of their summarized information (eliminating the GROUP BY and changing the SELECT). Using a standard protocol like ODBC, OLAP tools can drill down into any relational database to fetch the rows corresponding to any subcube.

WHAT'S IN A CUBE?

The preceding example introduced OLAP by structuring the movie-goers database as a cube, more formally known as a multidimensional database (MDD). Let us look at the properties of multidimensional databases to help us better understand OLAP and its role in data mining.

The cube in the moviegoers example was quite simple, having three flat dimensions (this made it easier to use for illustration). In general, cubes for interesting problems have more dimensions, often on the order of 5 to 20 dimensions and the dimensions themselves have a structure. Such cubes are not easily drawn; tools get around this problem by permitting views of two- and three-dimensional slices of the cube.

An MDD is a way of representing data that comes in tabular form (that is, data that has rows and columns). An MDD has a set of dimensions, each of which is divided into discrete values. A subcube is the region of the MDD where all dimensions have fixed values. Inside a subcube are calculations, counts, and aggregations of all the records that land in it. In a well-formed cube, each record lands in exactly one subcube. This is the cardinal rule of multidimensional databases.

TIP

When choosing the dimensions for a cube, be sure that each record lands in exactly one subcube. If you have redundant dimensions—such as one dimension for date and another for day of the week—then the same record will land in two or more subcubes. If this happens, then the summarizations based on the subcubes will no longer be accurate.

Apart from the cardinal rule that each record inserted into the cube should land in exactly one subcube, there are three other things to keep in mind when using cubes:

- Handling continuous values
- Hierarchical dimensions
- Dimensions that span multiple fields

These three issues arise when trying to develop cubes, and resolving them is important to making the cubes useful for analytic purposes.

Handling Continuous Values

Data contains values that are continuous. Putting continuous values into a cube is usually quite inefficient and makes the cube less useful for decision support. Often, the continuous values are appropriate for the aggregate columns instead of the dimension columns. For instance, in the moviegoer database, we did not need to include *age* as a dimension, but we did include the *sum of the ages* as an aggregate. This cube cannot be used to answer a question like "what age group sees the most movies." To answer this question, *age* would have to be a dimension. However, age is basically a continuous dimension. (Actually, *age* is not the best example for this purpose since it takes on few values—fewer than 100. There are many examples in the real world where the number of values is much larger, such as distance between two cities, dollar amount of purchase, price, and so on.)

The solution to this problem is to discretize the continuous dimension by defining ranges, such as "high" and "low," for the data. For age, we would bin the age into different ranges, such as 0 to 15, 15 to 25, and so on. Even though age is used as a dimension, we can still keep it as an aggregate.

Consider a database that includes an estimate of the lifetime customer value (LCV) for each customer. End users may want to use the cube to answer questions like "how do customers with a high LCV differ from customers with a low LCV?" To answer a question like this, the corresponding cube needs to include LCV along a dimension.

The estimate of LCV is an example of a continuous value. Say it ranges from –200 to 1,000, where –200 means the customer is costing money and 1,000 is a very valuable customer. The solution is range binning, dividing the customers into 10 bins, or deciles, each with about the same number of customers. We select ranges for the dimension, like –200 to 0 in bin #1, 0 to 20 in bin #2, and so on. Each record lands in exactly one bin. Now we use the bins as one of the dimensions for the MDD. Most OLAP tools provide utilities to help with discretizing dimensions in this manner.

Hierarchical Dimensions

Sometimes, a single column seems appropriate for multiple dimensions. For instance, OLAP is a good tool for visualizing trends over time, such as for sales or financial data. A specific date in this case potentially represents information along several dimensions:

Day of the week

Month

Quarter

Calendar year

One approach is to represent each of these as a different dimension. In other words, we would introduce four new dimensions, one for the day of the week, one for the month, one for the quarter, and one for the calendar year. If we want to know about the data for January 1996, then we would look at the subcube where the January dimension intersects the 1996 dimension.

This can become expensive. If we have three years of historical data, then we have:

7 days of the week (Monday, Tuesday, etc.)

12 months of the year (January, February, etc.)

4 quarters (Q1, Q2, etc.)

3 years (1995, 1996, etc.)

These dimensions contribute 1,008 subcubes! Dimensions multiply quickly and we have not included location codes, product codes, and so on.

Can anything be done? Well, if we look closely at these dimensions we notice that there is a lot of redundancy. If we want to know about Q1, couldn't we just use the data in the January, February, and March subcubes? Of course we can. The dimensions overlap; they do not contain new information. In fact, the summaries for Q1 are going to land in three cubes, one each for January, February, and March. This is a bad thing and violated the cardinal rule of building cubes. Some things we want to put into a dimension are really combinations of subcubes along another dimension, as shown in Figure 16.7.

The problem of redundant dimensions is arising because the dimensions do not have any internal structure. Most OLAP tools let you describe a dimension as a hierarchy. For instance, a time dimension could be described as having a month, quarter, and year. In fact, in some cases, the dimensions can have other properties that allow the same dimension to be used for day-of-the-week. To handle this, the tools include a mechanism for describing dimension schema, descriptions of hierarchies of information, and other properties within a dimension. This ability is a powerful feature that is also frequently applied to geography, product codes, and stockkeeping units (SKUs) as well.

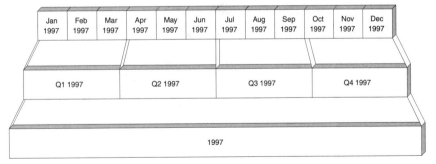

When specific months are kept along a dimension (both the month and the year), then quarters and years are redundant dimensions. They should be built as hierarchies on the month dimensions.

Figure 16.7 Potential new dimensions can represent hierarchies of existing dimensions.

WARNING

Beware of redundant dimensions. Often it is useful to split a large dimension, like date, into more useful pieces, like month and year. However, be sure that each record will always land in exactly one subcube so the overall cube remains consistent. Violations of the cardinal rule of building cubes (see Figure 16.8) arise when dimensions overlap, such as separate dimensions for month and quarter, or for county and state, or state and region. Avoiding redundant dimensions ensures that record counts summed across all the subcubes in the entire cube will be equal to the number of records inserted into the cube.

Is *year* a redundant dimension? That depends on whether the *month* dimension is for a specific month (like "January 1997") or for the same month in many years ("January"). If *month* is specific, then *year* is redundant since the information for a specific year (say 1997) can be obtained from the 12 subcubes corresponding to "January 1997" through "December 1997." If *month* is not specific, then there is no "January 1997" subcube. The "January" subcube contains information from multiple years. The *year* dimension is needed in this case.

A good baseline for analyzing the dimensions is the number of distinct values in the column. Three years have 1,095 or 1,096 days. If a cube were built with all the following dimensions, it would have over a million subcubes:

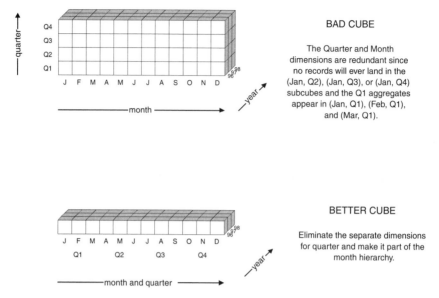

Figure 16.8 Eliminate redundant dimensions by incorporating them into hierarchies on other dimensions.

Day of the week (7)

Day of the month (31)

Day of the year (366)

Month of the year (12)

Year (3)

This is highly inefficient. In this case, building hierarchies on date (1,096 different values) is a major simplification (see Figure 16.9). Different tools have different ways of expressing these hierarchies.

Dimensions that Span Multiple Fields

Sometimes multiple columns in the input correspond to a single dimension. A simple example of this is when the date field is stored as separate fields for month, day, and year. When creating the dimension (or dimensions) for date, we want to consider these three columns in a single dimension.

Another example comes from a major bank where the database of accounts has four different codes for account status. Including all four columns as separate dimensions is cumbersome and makes the MDD

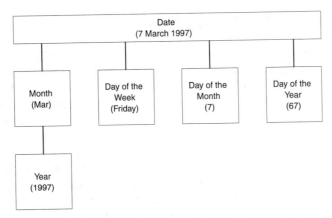

Figure 16.9 There are multiple hierarchies for dates.

more difficult for end users. These columns need to collapse down into a single dimension, since the flag really does not need four different code sets. This requires a preprocessing step to consolidate the codes. In the case of account codes, the first thing to do is to determine which account status codes are of interest to end users. Perhaps one set of codes dominates the others. Perhaps there is useful information in all available codes. Once the set the users are interested in is known, you need to map the existing codes to the new codes. These new codes become the dimension in the MDD.

TIP

When defining the dimensions for an MDD, there are three things to keep in mind:

- Columns with continuous data or with many values need to be discretized. You do this by determining a number of bins and assigning each bin a range of values on the column.
- Some columns may want to be split into multiple dimensions. This can be useful and intuitive for users, but be sure that each record only lands in a single subcube.
- Some columns may want collapse into a single dimension. This is a standard dirty data problem and is usually handled by preprocessing the data.

Fortunately, many OLAP tool vendors have developed solutions for these issues that they have incorporated into their products.

THE BIG DEBATE: MOLAP VERSUS ROLAP

ROLAP (Relational OLAP) tools store the cube inside a relational database management system, taking advantage of the database for many features, like security, concurrent access, and importing data. MOLAP (multidimensional OLAP) tools store the cube in a proprietary multidimensional database designed specifically for the features and performance needs for OLAP. This choice between storage architectures has been amplified by marketing departments of OLAP tool vendors far beyond its real significance. In fact, there are some advantages to ROLAP and some advantages to MOLAP; some vendors provide both solutions. The debate about the underlying storage architecture is not the point. More important considerations about features, performance, and ongoing costs are what determine the best tool for the job. However, the debate is instructive for understanding some of the details of an OLAP solution and the types of features that make one solution more attractive than another.

OLAP tools that use relational technology store the base data as a star schema. The use of the star schema makes it very unlikely that the OLAP tool can take advantage of existing databases, especially operational systems that are likely to be highly normalized. In addition to the central fact table and dimension tables, a ROLAP tool also keeps aggregate tables that have summarizations of the data along different dimensions. Queries on the cube are standard SQL, using the summarization tables for performance where possible. One of the main advantages of ROLAP tools is that they leverage the relational experience that already exists inside an organization, particularly when the underlying relational database system is an accepted standard. Security standards, database administrators, and approval processes for new tools can be avoided.

At first glance, the argument for ROLAP is quite convincing. Relational database technology has proven its robustness and applicability to business problems since the early 1980s. Skilled personnel are readily available who understand the technology. Relational databases use industry-standard interfaces and run on a wide variety of platforms, including the scalable parallel platforms that are becoming increasingly popular for large databases. Multi-user concurrent access comes for free and updates to the base table can occur at any time, cascading through the summary tables. And, in many cases, data warehouses based on relational databases are the source for OLAP as well as data mining applications, facilitating the integration of the data with the decision-support applications. This is especially true in midrange environments, where the operational system, data warehouse and cubes all use the same hardware and software vendors.

However, there is a strong case to be made that the needs of OLAP are different from relational databases. Even though an MDD can be represented in a tabular, relational format—and some would say you have to coerce the data in order to do it—that does not mean it is the best format. After all, relational databases have been designed to support large numbers of individual transactions and not the complicated queries with many joins required for OLAP. Summary tables, triggers, stored procedures, and other optimizations are really workarounds because the underlying relational technology was designed for other purposes.

This is a strong argument as well. MDDs resolve the queries needed for OLAP quickly and efficiently without passing through the relational layer. They do not suffer from the overhead needed in a relational database to support transaction processing. The security mechanisms used for relational databases are cumbersome to apply to multidimensional databases, since the data for a given dimension is spread through many tables (due to the summarizations). Using an MDD makes it much easier to add new dimensions and hierarchies within a dimension. In addition, MDDs can resolve a broader range of OLAP queries more quickly and more consistently by incorporating features and functions not found in SQL. Performance is one of the driving forces for using OLAP technology, so don't MDDs make sense?

In the end, the debate about ROLAP and MOLAP really boils down to the choice of OLAP vendor and the environment where the tool will have to operate. Each site and each situation place different relative requirements on the OLAP product, on the ability to quickly update dimension schema versus the ability to insert new data, on the performance for typical queries, on extended features, on the use of already approved software, and so on. And, as the market matures, the differences between ROLAP and MOLAP will gradually disappear.

OLAP AND DATA MINING

Data mining is about the successful exploitation of data for decision-support purposes. The virtuous cycle, described in Chapter 2, reminds us that success depends on more than advanced pattern recognition algorithms. We need to provide feedback to people and use the information from data mining to improve business processes. We need to enable people to provide input, in the form of observations, hypotheses, and hunches about what results are important and how to use those results.

In the larger solution to exploiting data, OLAP clearly plays an important role as a means of broadening the audience with access to data. Decisions once made based on experience and educated guesses can start to be based on data and patterns in the data. Anomalies and outliers can be identified for further investigation, including applying data mining techniques. For instance, a user might discover that a particular item sells better at a particular time during the week by use of an OLAP tool. This might lead to an investigation using market basket analysis to find other items purchased with that item. Market basket analysis might suggest an explanation for the observed behavior—more information and more opportunities for exploiting the information.

There are other synergies between data mining and OLAP. We learned in Chapter 12 that one of the characteristics of decision trees is their ability to identify the most informative features in the data relative to a particular outcome. That is, if we are trying to predict attrition using a decision tree, then the upper levels of the tree will have the features that are the most important predictors for attrition. Well, these predictors would probably be a good choice for dimensions using an OLAP tool. Such analysis helps build better, more useful cubes.

Another problem when building cubes is determining how to make continuous dimensions discrete. We make a dimension discrete by assigning bins to ranges of values on that dimension. This begs the question of how to choose the ranges. In this chapter, we talked about using equal-sized bins, such as deciles. The information from the decision tree is useful here, too. The nodes of a decision tree determine the best breaking point for a continuous value. This information can be fed into the OLAP tool to improve the dimension.

One of the problems with neural networks is the difficulty of understanding the results. This is especially true when using them for undirected data mining, such as a clustering algorithm using SOM networks. We might use SOMs to find clusters of people who are no longer using their credit cards. The inputs into the network might be account balances in the months before they left, the types of purchases made with the card, and some demographic and credit information. The SOM identifies clusters, but we do not know what they mean.

OLAP to the rescue! We have a set of data that is now enhanced with a predicted cluster and we want to visualize it better. This is a good application for a cube. By using OLAP on the same data—with information about the clusters included as a dimension—we can determine the features that distinguish clusters. The dimensions used for the OLAP tool are the inputs to the neural network along with the cluster identifier. There is a tricky data conversion problem because the neural networks require continuous values scaled between 0 and 1, and OLAP tools require discrete values. For values that were originally discrete, this is no problem. For continuous values, we can use the binning technique based on ranges.

As these examples show, OLAP and data mining complement each other. Data mining can help build better cubes by defining appropriate dimensions, and further by determining how to break up continuous values on dimensions. OLAP provides powerful visualization to better understand the results of data mining, such as clustering and neural networks. Used together, OLAP and data mining reinforce each other's strengths and provide more opportunities for exploiting data.

STRENGTHS OF OLAP

OLAP has several strengths for analyzing data:

- It is a powerful visualization tool.
- It provides fast, interactive response times.
- It is good for analyzing time series.
- It can be useful to find some clusters and outliers.
- Many vendors offer OLAP products.

OLAP Is a Powerful Visualization Tool

The biggest strength of OLAP is its ability to visualize data in a way readily understandable to business users. It is particularly appropriate when the data represents repeated transactions that contain readily identifiable dimensions. OLAP can be applied across a wide variety of domains, to represent sales in retail stores, charges on a credit card, drugs prescribed to patients, repairs to diesel engines, and so on. This format is related to the star schema mechanism popular among some database vendors for some decision-support applications.

A good choice of dimensions provides a solid and flexible framework for presenting data. Dimensions can model hierarchies of data that are readily apparent in a particular domain. Geography is a good example, where sites, counties, states, and regions are all interesting for data analysis purposes, and OLAP tools can represent all along a single dimension. Other uses for complex dimensions are time and product codes.

OLAP Provides Fast Response

OLAP's ability to analyze data is useful because it can respond to user queries quickly, with response times on large databases measured in seconds. This is a result of precalculating summaries of the data that are suggested by the dimensions on the cube.

This response time is valuable, especially when using the OLAP tools to drill-down into the data to find patterns. Whether the cube is implemented as an MDD or in a relational database, you can usually find the specific data items used to generate a particular report. This yields much better productivity for analysis. And, because of the fast response time, gives users increased confidence in the data and in their ability to use it.

OLAP Is Good for Time Series

Time series are difficult for most tools to handle, but they fit quite well into OLAP. When using time as a dimension, support for hierarchies on the dimensions is important. Complex dimensions can support looking at dates by quarter, month, or day of the week all at the same time.

Some OLAP tools provide broader support for time series by supporting features specific to series. For instance, they can help calculate the ratio between adjacent values, to find, for instance, the rate of growth from one quarter to the next. Trying to create a similar query on a relational database is cumbersome and expensive because SQL does not readily support such inter-row calculations.

OLAP Finds Clusters and Outliers

As an aid for analysis, OLAP provides the ability to identify clusters in the data by being able to look at the data along several dimensions at the same time. For instance, a cluster of drugs prescribed by a particular physician group can be identified using the slicing and dicing features of OLAP tools. This cluster can then suggest ways to sell more drugs to this particular group. Or, using a technique like memory-based reasoning, similar physician groups might be identified for targeted sales.

Once upon a time, special reports had to be coded to identify trends and find outliers. With an OLAP tool, outliers along many dimensions can be identified quickly by business users familiar with the domain in which they are working.

OLAP Is Supported by Many Vendors

Another major strength of OLAP is that there are many vendors supporting OLAP tools—probably almost as many for this single application as for data mining in general. OLAP tools are maturing and popular features are appearing in all the best tools. In addition, training is available for end users and interfaces to data sources are getting simpler and simpler.

WEAKNESSES OF OLAP

OLAP has some weaknesses as well:

- Setting up a cube can be difficult.
- It does not handle continuous variables well.
- Cubes can quickly become out-of-date.
- It is not data mining.

Setting Up a Cube Is Difficult

Not all domains are appropriate for setting up a cube. Sometimes the number of dimensions gets out of control. For instance, a simple retail model might have individual customer transactions as the base data. However, the market may be split between business and retail customers, have international franchises, and different approaches in up-market and down-market areas. It only becomes more complicated if you want to include the method of payment (cash, credit card, store credit, check), use of coupons, SKUs, bundled products, and promotions by manufacturers. Choosing the right dimensions for the cube is critical and decision trees can be helpful.

When setting up dimensions on a cube, the values for the different dimensions need to be comparable between records. For instance, a customer that carries an average monthly balance of $700 on a credit card but has a credit limit of $5,000 is different from a customer with the same average monthly balance but with a credit limit of $750. A better choice might be percent of available credit.

The cube needs to be informative to the end users. Selecting the dimensions and choosing the data for the cube are most of the work that needs to be done.

OLAP Does not Handle Continuous Values

All the dimensions for OLAP are necessarily discrete, meaning that they take on a fixed list of values. This requires discretizing continuous variables in a process called binning. So, a continuous variable like monthly balance on a credit may be split into several bins: "no monthly balance," "small monthly balance," "typical monthly balance," "high monthly balance," and "very high monthly balance."

There are many ways to discretize values, such as graphing the values for many records and "eye-balling" the result, choosing bins with equal numbers of records, and running a decision-tree method like CART to propose breaking points. All of these methods are feasible but add to the complexity of creating a good cube.

Cubes Become Out-of-Date Quickly

The creation of a cube involves several types of information and data:

- Specific base data that goes into the cube
- Definitions of dimensions and hierarchies on the dimensions
- Methods to make continuous data discrete

In a rapidly changing market, all of these can change quickly. The introduction of new product lines, reorganization geographic regions, and changes in pricing structures rapidly conspire to make current data difficult to compare to historical data. This is a common problem in data mining, but is exacerbated by all the choices that explicitly go into making a cube.

By taking advantage of relational database technology, ROLAP tools make it fairly easy to incorporate new base data into a cube. In fact, updates to the cube can happen at the same time that users are analyzing data. However, MOLAP tools are better for changes in the structure of dimensions, since ROLAP tools have to modify all the summarization tables. Adding a new hierarchy to a geography dimension, or a new definition of products, is simpler in a tool based on multidimensional databases.

OLAP Does not Automatically Find Patterns

As we have pointed out throughout this chapter, OLAP complements data mining. It is not a substitute for it. It provides better understanding of data, and the dimensions developed for OLAP can make data mining results more actionable. However, OLAP does not automatically find patterns in data.

WHEN TO APPLY OLAP

OLAP is a powerful way to distribute information to many end users for advanced reporting needs. It provides the ability to let many more users base their decisions on data, instead of on hunches, educated guesses, and personal experience. OLAP complements undirected data mining techniques such as SOM networks. When using SOM networks for finding clusters, OLAP can provide the insight needed to find the business value in the identified clusters. It also provides a good visualization tool to use with other methods, such as decision trees and memory-based reasoning.

17

Choosing the Right Tool for the Job

Having read this far, you now know all about market basket analysis, memory-based reasoning, genetic algorithms, automatic cluster detection, link analysis, decision trees, artificial neural networks, and OLAP. With such a large collection of tools and techniques to choose from, it can be difficult to select the ones best suited to a particular application. In this chapter, we offer some guidelines and issue a report card showing the strengths and weaknesses of all the techniques on a variety of data mining tasks and judged by a variety of criteria.

In the commercial world, the choice of data mining techniques is often tied to the choice of commercial products. When choosing between actual software products rather than abstract algorithms, new criteria such as price, availability, scalability, support, vendor relationships, compatibility, and platform-independence intrude on the selection process. The data mining market place is evolving too rapidly for us to be able to compare the merits of particular products in a book that is meant to remain useful for many years. We do, however, provide a checklist of features to look for and questions to ask when selecting software for data mining.

For up-to-date product news and a wealth of pointers to other services of data mining information, see our Worldwide Web page at http://www.data-miners.com.

CHOOSING THE RIGHT DATA MINING TECHNIQUES

Because the data mining process is iterative, there usually is a series of tasks to perform. These tasks tend to alternate between hypothesis testing and knowledge discovery. The hypothesis testing phase of the cycle calls for on-line analytic processing (OLAP) and other query tools, cross tabulation, directed market basket analysis, and standard statistics. The knowledge discovery phase is best supported by clustering, decision trees, neural networks, link analysis, memory-based reasoning, and undirected market basket analysis.

The choice of what data mining techniques to apply at a given point in the cycle depends on the particular data mining *task* to be accomplished and on the *data* available for analysis. Our approach to selecting data mining techniques has two steps:

> Translate the business problem to be addressed into a series of data mining tasks.

> Understand the nature of the available data in terms of the content and types of the data fields, and the structure of the relationships between records.

Formulate the Business Problem as a Data Mining Task

The first step is to take a business goal such as "improve retention" and turn it into one or more of the data mining tasks from Chapter 4. As a reminder, the six basic tasks addressed by the data mining techniques discussed in this book are:

- Classification
- Estimation
- Prediction
- Affinity Grouping
- Clustering
- Description

To continue with the retention example, assume that our strategy is to identify subscribers who are likely to cancel, figure out why they are likely to drop the service, and make them some kind of special offer that will address their concerns. For the strategy to be successful, we need not only to identify the subscribers who are likely to cancel, but also to assign them to groups according to their presumed reasons for leaving. Based on these presumed reasons, we will construct telemarketing scripts to be used with each group.

The first task is clearly classification. Using a training dataset that contains examples of customers who have canceled along with examples of those who have not, we will build a model capable of labeling each customer as "loyal" or "churn prone." Many of the data mining techniques discussed in this book can be applied to classification tasks of this sort. How do we choose between memory-based reasoning, genetic algorithms, link analysis, decision trees, and neural networks?

In this case, we can be guided by the requirements of the second task: to identify separate groups of subscribers at risk and understand what motivates each group to leave. By using a decision tree to perform the first task, we will have accomplished most of the second task as well. Each leaf of the decision tree will be labeled loyal or churn prone. Each of the churn prone leaves will include its own group of churn prone subscribers and the path to that leaf will be a rule governing who ends up there. With luck and skill, an analyst can turn these mechanistic rules into comprehensible reasons for leaving that, once understood, can be counteracted. It is likely that there will be more leaves than desired for the purpose of developing special offers and telemarketing scripts. Leaves will need to be combined into larger clusters. This can be done taking whole branches of the tree as the clusters, rather than single leaves.

If some other method were chosen for performing the initial classification, the next step might be to apply a clustering algorithm to divide the subscribers judged at risk for attrition into self-similar groups that could be studied further, perhaps by interviewing samples from each cluster.

Note that our preference for decision-tree methods in this case stems from the desire to understand the reasons for attrition and our desire to treat subgroups differentially. If our goal were simply to do the best possible job of predicting which subscribers were at risk, without worrying about the reasons, we might select an approach based on neural networks, memory-based reasoning, or standard statistics. If the goal were instead to estimate next month's minutes of use for each subscriber, neural networks or statistical regression would be better choices (see Table 17.1).

Determine the Characteristics of the Data to Be Mined

Once the data mining tasks have been identified and used to narrow the range of data mining methods under consideration, the characteristics of the available data can help to further refine the selection. In

Table 17.1 Which Techniques to Use for Which Tasks

Technique	Classification	Estimation	Prediction	Affinity Grouping	Clustering	Description
Standard Statistics	√	√	√	√	√	√
Market Basket Analysis			√	√	√	√
Memory-Based Reasoning	√		√	√	√	
Genetic Algorithms	√		√			
Cluster Detection					√	
Link Analysis	√		√	√		
Decision Trees	√		√		√	√
Neural Networks	√	√	√		√	

general terms, the goal is to select the data mining technique that minimizes the number and difficulty of the data transformations that must be performed in order to coax good results from the data.

As we saw in Chapter 5, some amount of data transformation is always part of the data mining process. The raw data may need to be summarized in various ways, missing values must be dealt with, data encodings must be rationalized, and so forth. These kinds of transformations are necessary regardless of the technique chosen. However, some kinds of data pose particular problems for some data mining techniques.

The following is a list of data characteristics that will influence your choice of a data mining approach:

- A preponderance of categorical variables
- A preponderance of numeric variables
- A large number of fields (independent variables) per record

- Multiple target fields (dependent variables)
- Variable-length records
- Time-ordered data
- Free-text data

In the following subsections, we discuss the implications of these data characteristics for different data mining techniques.

Categorical Variables

Categorical variables are fields that take on values from a limited and predetermined set of values. Usually, there is no particular order to the categories. Postal code, car model, marital status, and birth stone are examples of categorical variables. Because categorical variables are not intended to be summed or sorted, they are often represented by character codes but, like zip codes and area codes, may also be represented using numbers.

Data mining tools vary in the ease with which they deal with categorical variables. Market basket analysis and link analysis work *only* with categorical variables. If the data mining task is finding links or affinity groups or finding a pattern over time, and the data consists mainly of categorical variables, market basket analysis is an obvious choice.

Decision trees can be built from categorical variables quite easily as well, but there is a caveat. If the number of categories is large relative to the number of records, so that each value appears only a few times, some decision-tree algorithms will perform poorly. A decision-tree algorithm that creates a new branch for each value taken on by a categorical variable in the training dataset will create a very bushy decision tree that will not perform well. The training set records are spread over so many nodes that most nodes do not receive enough records to make meaningful further splits. Some decision-tree tools allow the user to restrict the tree's branching factor. Others, including CART, always create binary trees and so do not suffer from this problem. So long as there is a way to impose a conservative branching factor, tree methods do well with categorical data.

Categorical variables are especially problematic for neural networks. Recall that the inputs to a neural network are all continuous variables with values ranging from 0 to 1. It is generally not a good idea to convert a categorical variable to a continuous variable by simply assigning a unique value between 0 and 1 to each category, because that creates an implicit ordering that can confuse the neural network. For example, North American telephone area codes can be scaled to the range 0 to 1 by dividing them by 1,000, but this would suggest that Connecticut (203) is very close to Manitoba (204) while Manhattan (212) is quite far from the other boroughs of New York City (718). The alternative is to have a separate input node for each possible value of the categorical variable; but, when there are many categorical variables or some variables take on many different values, this approach greatly increases the size of the neural network increasing both the training time and the minimum acceptable size of the training set.

WARNING

Deciding whether a variable should be treated as numeric or categorical may require some thought. There is a tendency to treat all numeric data as continuous and ordered, but it is important to recognize situations where that is not appropriate. When numeric codes are assigned in an arbitrary manner (zip codes and telephone area codes, for example) they should be treated as categorical variables. But be careful about assuming that assigned codes have no meaningful order; employee numbers, to take one example, are often a proxy for date of hire and length of service.

There are also situations where apparently categorical variables are actually ordered. (Admiral > Rear Admiral > Captain > Commander > Lieutenant > Ensign).

Cyclical variables such as month and day of the week share characteristics of both categorical and ordered numeric variables. In some contexts, it is important to know that May comes between April and June, but at other times we may want to examine all Tuesdays, all Virgos, or all customers born in the year of the rat.

Nearly all datasets contain some categorical variables and neural networks are able to cope with them after the appropriate data transformations have been made. But, when categorical variables make up the majority of the fields, it is best to choose a different data mining technique.

Numeric Variables

Numeric variables of the kind that can be summed and sorted play to the strengths of the data mining techniques that are based on these and other mathematical operations. Age, call duration, price, salary, inseam length, altitude, and temperature are typical examples of numeric variables that might be found in a database.

Neural networks expect all inputs and outputs to be floating-point values between 0 and 1. It is a simple matter to scale any numeric data to this range, although some care must be taken to ensure that not too much information is lost when collapsing a large range into this small interval. Depending on the way the data is dispersed, logarithms or some other non-linear function may be more appropriate than simple division.

Memory-based reasoning and automatic cluster detection depend on distance measures that are generally more straightforward for numeric data than for other types. Decision-tree methods also handle numeric data easily by automatically transforming numeric values into two or more ranges by finding a splitter value. The ranges are then treated in the same way as categorical variables.

Numeric data causes problems for data mining methods that depend on finding exact matches. Market basket analysis and link analysis are the techniques discussed here that share that trait. Integer variables that only take on a few distinct values are not a cause for concern. In a database of high school students, year of birth will only take on a handful of values and it is likely to be a strong component of association rules for classes like Calculus or A.P. English. The problem comes with continuous variables, like temperature or price/earnings ratio, that can take on infinitely many values, and discrete variables, like price to the penny, that take on far too many values for any rule based on a particular value to have much support in the data.

Before applying market basket analysis, all numeric fields that take on more than a handful of values must be converted into categorical variables like "high," "medium," and "low." This is not as simple as it sounds because the choice of how many ranges and where to draw the range boundaries has a large, but hard-to-predict, effect on the rules discovered.

Many Fields per Record

In most data mining applications, there is a single target field or dependent variable and all the other fields, except those that are either clearly irrelevant or clearly dependent on the target field, are treated as input fields or independent variables. Data mining methods vary in their ability to successfully process large numbers of input fields. This can be a factor in deciding on the right technique for a particular application.

In general, techniques which rely on adjusting a vector of weights that has an element for each input field run into trouble when the number of fields grows very large. Neural networks and memory-based reasoning share that trait. Market basket analysis runs into a different problem. It involves looking at all possible combinations of the inputs; as the number of inputs grows, that quickly becomes impossible to do in a reasonable amount of time.

Decision-tree methods are much less hindered by large numbers of fields. As the tree is built, the decision-tree algorithm identifies the single field that contributes the most information at each node and bases the next segment of the rule on that field alone. Dozens or hundreds of other fields can come along for the ride, but won't be represented in the final rules unless they contribute to the solution.

TIP

When faced with a large number of fields, it is a good idea to start by building a decision tree, even if the final model is to be built using a different method. The decision tree will identify a good subset of the fields to use as input to a second technique that might be swamped by the original set of input variables.

Multiple Dependent Variables

Sometimes we want to predict several different outputs based on the same input data. For example, before making an offer of credit, a bank might want to gather all available information on the prospect, then use it to predict:

1. The likelihood of a response
2. The projected first year revenue from this customer
3. The risk of the new customer defaulting

One approach is to model each of these variables separately; there may be good reason for doing so (see the section entitled *Consider Hybrid Approaches* later in this chapter). But if we want the convenience of building and applying a single model that predicts all three variables, then neural nets are the obvious choice. Each target variable will be represented by its own node in the output layer of a neural network. As the values of the input nodes change, all three outputs will be affected.

Simulation

A special case of multiple outputs is simulation. At each step in a simulation, the values of all fields for time *t* are updated based on the values of all fields at time *t – 1*. In Chapter 12 we saw an example of a simulator for industrial process control that used a forest of decision trees. Each tree predicted the future state of a single field based on the state of all fields at the previous time step. This can also be done with neural networks.

Variable-Length Records

While it is always possible to define transactions at a low enough level that they become atomic, in many situations the most natural focus is on *sets* of items or transactions. A shopping cart contains many purchases, a credit card holder makes a number of charges over the course of a month, a catalog order comprises several items, and a telephone subscriber makes multiple calls.

The operational systems that process data of this kind are usually set up to deal with variable-length records. An order, for instance, contains some header information identifying the customer followed by a variable-number item number. Of the data mining techniques discussed in this book, only market basket analysis and link analysis deal naturally with variable-length records. To use any of the other techniques, the data must be transformed in one of two ways, both of which involve some loss of information.

The first solution is summarization. The variable-length records are collapsed into fixed-length records that include fields like `item_count`, `total_price`, `average_price`, and so on. The second method, which is the one usually found in relational databases, is to keep each individual transaction and give it a compound key such as (`order_number`, `item_number`). This is fine for retrieval and reporting purposes, but most data mining techniques are not sophisticated enough to understand the relationships implied by a database schema. Indeed, although relational data mining tools are starting to appear, most data mining tools today require their input as a single denormalized table or "flat file." The tools are unable to look at groups of records together, so the information that several items were part of the same order, or that hundreds of calls to 411 were from the same phone, gets lost.

We saw this problem with the moviegoers sample database. Respondents had seen varying numbers of movies and so accounted for varying numbers of records in the training data. One consequence of this arrangement is that in the denormalized form of the data, a respondent's age, sex, and other data are repeated on several records—one for each movie seen. Without aggregating on the `moviegoer_id` field, there is no way of telling the difference between one 19-year-old male who saw five movies and five 19-year-old males who saw one movie each.

TIP

If the number of individual items that might appear in the variable-length portion of a record is known not to exceed some reasonable maximum, it can be very useful to create a fixed-length record that contains a flag for the presence or absence of each item. Depending on the computer implementation used, each flag may take up only a single bit (which means that 32 flags fit in the space used by an ordinary number). The bit patterns form signatures in the sense that every possible combination of items has its own pattern. These patterns can be interpreted as numbers for testing equality. If the moviegoers data had been encoded in this fashion, there would be only one record per respondent, and any respondents who had seen exactly the same set of movies would have identical "viewer history signatures."

Time-Ordered Data

Time ordered data presents difficulties for all of the techniques and generally requires some augmentation of the test data with time stamps or windowing, difference variables, and so on. Fortunately, there are a few data mining tools that are designed specifically for sequential pattern analysis. These tools are based on modifications to the data mining algorithms that build the concept of time right into the model so that fewer data transformations are required.

The most common of these modified techniques is the time-delay neural network. In a time-delay neural network, each network node receives the last several values calculated by its predecessor. Its output is therefore a function of the last several time steps. The time delays are inserted automatically as part of the algorithm, so no special preparation of the data is required except to feed it to the input nodes in the proper order.

As described in Chapter 8, market basket analysis can be used to generate association rules from time-ordered data as well, but this requires grouping events that happened within the time intervals of interest into baskets or transactions. As we saw in the coffee roaster simulation discussed in Chapter 12, decision trees can be used successfully with time-ordered data, but tend to require many data transformations.

Free-Form Text

Most data mining techniques are incapable of directly handling free-form text. But clearly, text fields often contain extremely valuable information. When analyzing warranty claims submitted to an engine manufacturer by independent dealers, the mechanic's free-form notes explaining what went wrong and what was done to fix the problem are at least as valuable as the fixed fields that show the part numbers and hours of labor used.

The one data mining technique that deals well with free text is memory-based reasoning. Recall that MBR is based on the ability to measure the *distance* from one record to all the other records in a database in order to form a neighborhood of similar records. Often, finding an appropriate distance metric is a stumbling block that makes it hard to apply MBR, but as it happens, researchers in the field of information retrieval have come up with good measures of the distance between two blocks of text. These measurements are based on the overlap in vocabulary between the documents, especially of uncommon words and proper nouns. You may have encountered this technology in the form of news retrieval services that give you the option to find articles "like this one."

Memory-based reasoning on free-form text has been used successfully to classify workers into industries and job categories based on written job descriptions they supplied on the United States census long form, and, as described in Chapter 9, to add keywords to new stories.

The Data Mining Report Card

In this section we rate each of the data mining techniques discussed in this book according to six criteria (see Table 17.2). The grades are necessarily subjective; they reflect our own experience and the general consensus of other data mining practitioners. We have assigned grades ranging from D (below average) to A (excellent) in the following categories:

- **Ease of understanding the model**—How easy is it to understand why the model makes the predictions it makes? Does the model add insight on the topic being studied or does it act as a black box, hiding the way it arrives at a solution.

Table 17.2   The Data Mining Report Card

	Ease of Understanding Model	Ease of Training Model	Ease of Applying Model	Generality	Utility	Availability
Standard Statistics	B	B	B	B	B	A+
Market Basket Analysis	A	A	A+	D	B	B
Memory-Based Reasoning	A–	B	B	A–	A–	C
Genetic Algorithms	B–	C–	A–	B+	C	C
Cluster Detection	B+	B+	A–	A–	B–	B
Link Analysis	A–	C	B	D	B	C+
Decision Trees	A+	B+	A+	A	A	B+
Neural Networks	C–	B–	A–	A	A	A

- **Ease of training the model**—How much effort is required to build a new model using this technique? What sorts of data transformations are involved? Does training the model require many iterations with manual intervention to adjust parameters between passes?
- **Ease with which the model can be applied**—Once a model has been generated, is it a straightforward matter to use it to score a database?
- **Generality**—Can this data mining technique be applied to a wide variety of problems and data types?
- **Utility**—How good are the results produced by this method? Are the models accurate enough to produce actionable results?
- **Availability**—Is there a choice of software packages that implement this technique? Are the tools available on a wide variety of computing platforms?

Consider Hybrid Approaches

Sometimes, a combination of techniques works better than any single approach. This may require breaking down a single data mining task into two or more subtasks. We saw an example of that in Chapter 3. Researchers found that the best way of selecting prospects for a particular car model was to first use a neural network to identify people likely to buy a car, then use a decision tree to predict the particular model each car buyer would select.

Earlier in this chapter we brought up the example of a bank that uses three variables as input to a credit solicitation decision. The three inputs are estimates for:

The likelihood of a response

The projected first year revenue from this customer

The risk of the new customer defaulting

These tasks vary considerably in the amount of relevant training data likely to be available, the input fields likely to be important, and the length of time required to verify the accuracy of a prediction. Soon after a mailing, the bank knows exactly who responded because the solicitation contains a deadline after which responses are considered invalid. A whole year must pass before the estimated first year revenue can be checked against the actual amount and it generally takes even longer for a customer to "go bad." Given all these differences, it would not be surprising if it turned out that a different data mining technique turned out to be best for each task.

WHAT TO LOOK FOR IN A DATA MINING SOFTWARE PACKAGE

Data mining software packages are proliferating, and marketing brochures and Web pages devoted to data mining are proliferating even faster. Any product even remotely related to decision support is now touted as a data mining tool. The brochures for these products make such similar claims that one might almost suspect plagiarism.

The following list of questions will help you to select the right data mining software for your company. We present the questions as an unordered list. The first thing you should do is order the list according to your own priorities. These priorities will necessarily be different from case to case, which is why we have not attempted to rank them for you. In some environments, for example, there is an established standard hardware supplier and platform-independence is a non-issue, while in other environments it is of paramount concern so different divisions can use the package or in anticipation of a future change in hardware.

Once you have determined which of these questions are most important to your organization, try to get honest answers to them from the software vendors or through an independent data mining consultant.

What is the range of data mining techniques offered by the vendor?

How scalable is the product in terms of the size of the data, the number of users, the number of fields in the data, and its use of the hardware?

For which hardware platforms and operating systems is the product available?

Does the product provide transparent access to databases and files?

Does the product efficiently make use of your network?

Does the product provide multiple levels of user interface?

Does the product generate comprehensible explanations of the models it generates?

Does the product support graphics, visualization, and reporting tools?

Can the product handle diverse data types?

Is the product well-documented and easy to use?

What is the availability of support and consulting?

How well will the product fit into the existing computing environment?

Does the vendor have credible references?

We will take up each of these issues in turn.

Range of Techniques

As must be clear by now, there is no single data mining technique that is applicable in all situations. Neural nets, decision trees, market basket analysis, genetic algorithms, memory-based reasoning, link analysis, and automatic cluster detection all have a place. As we have seen in the case studies, it is not uncommon for two or more of these techniques to be applied in combination to achieve results beyond the reach of any single method.

Assess the range of data mining tasks you need to address and use the report card provided earlier to figure out which data mining techniques will be most valuable. If you have a single application in mind, or a family of closely related applications, then it is likely that you will be able to select a single technique and stick with it. If you are setting up a data mining lab environment to handle a wide range of data mining applications, you will want to look for a coordinated suite of tools. You may discover that no single vendor addresses all of your requirements, in which case you will be faced with integrating tools from multiple vendors into your decision-support processing environment.

Scalability

Data mining provides the greatest benefit when the data to be mined is large and complex. But, data mining software is likely to be demonstrated on small, sample datasets. Be sure that the data mining software you are considering can handle the data volume you anticipate.

In the client/server architecture typical of decision-support computing environments, data mining is emphatically a server-side activity, with only control, presentation, and reporting activities performed on the desktop (see Figure 17.1). The databases needed to support intelligent marketing, sales, and customer support in a large corporation are huge. A data mining software tool must accommodate millions of records with hundreds of fields.

If the database management system runs on a scalable parallel machine, the data mining software should also run in that environment. Or, in a three-tiered architecture, the data mining software may run on the middle tier with much of the large-scale data manipulation still occurring on the database server.

Platform Independence

Ideally, you should be able to choose a data mining software package by taking an inventory of your data mining tasks, determining which data mining techniques best address them, and finding software that implements those techniques well. Unfortunately, unlike relational database management systems which, for the most part, are now platform-independent, many data mining software packages only run on one vendor's machines.

Since data mining is rarely the application that justifies a hardware purchase, you may have to rule out some software simply be-

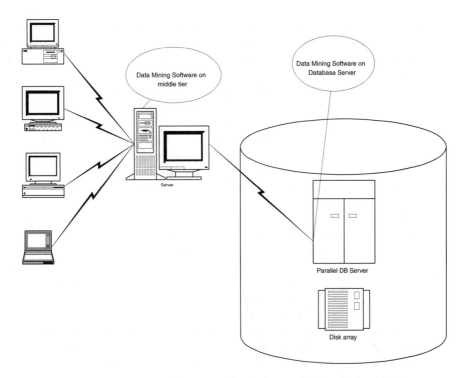

Figure 17.1   Where data mining software belongs in a client/server architecture.

cause it is not available for the hardware or operating system in use at your company. If there is any doubt about the stability of your current computing environment, it would be wise to look for a software package that has at least some degree of platform independence.

Where the data mining tools are to be made available to a diverse or widely scattered user community, support for multiple client-side environments is also important.

Transparent Access to Databases and Files

Increasingly, the data that makes up a corporation's memory is being stored in large relational data warehouses. These warehouses provide transparent access to the data through a wide variety of OLAP tools, statistical analysis packages, and query generators. Until recently, however, most data mining tools were islands unto themselves. In order to use them, it was necessary to construct data files in some format dictated by the tool. It is a relatively simple matter to extract data from a database into a flat file, but when there is a large quantity of data to be analyzed, the storage overhead of storing the same data twice can be prohibitive.

The task of translating data dictionary information into a form usable by the data mining tool can also be painful. Many tools require a descriptor file with an entry for each field to specify its offset in the file, its data type, whether it is continuous or categorical, and so on. Constructing this file may require special programming. It is preferable for the data mining software to be able to gather most of the information it needs from the metadata files of the warehouse.

Performance Issues

One reason that many data mining tools work from flat files rather than directly off of databases, is that data mining algorithms require access patterns not well-supported by relational database management systems. For instance, at every node in the decision tree, the CART algorithm reads each field or database *column* independently and sorts it in order to search for candidate splitters. Since database tables are generally stored with groups of *rows* contiguous on disk, this amounts to scanning the entire table as many times as there are fields under consideration at each node. Unless the entire table can be held in memory, this imposes a huge i/o penalty.

WARNING

Be very skeptical of data mining performance claims for a large database environment that are extrapolated from performance on a small demonstration system. For many data mining algorithms, the amount of computation and i/o required to solve a problem increases more than linearly with data size. Doubling the data size may quadruple the processing time.

Some data mining algorithms require random sampling or other access patterns not available through standard SQL. Some RDBMS vendors including Red Brick and Tandem have added proprietary features to their versions of SQL in order to better support data mining. Until these "Relational Data Mining" constructs become widely adopted, it will continue to be expedient to perform some data mining operations from flat-file extracts. This does not relieve data mining tools of the requirement to read from and, in some cases, to write to database tables.

Support for Scoring

The ability to write to as well as read from a database is desirable when data mining is used to develop models used for scoring. The models may be developed using samples extracted from the master database, but once developed, the models will score every record in the database.

The value of a response model decreases with time. Ideally, the results of one campaign should be analyzed in time to affect the next one. But, in many organizations there is a long lag between the time a model is developed and the time it can be used to append scores to a database; sometimes the time is measured in weeks. The delay is caused by the difficulty of moving the scoring model, which is often developed on a different computer from the database server, into a form which can be applied to the database. This can involve interpreting the output of a data mining tool and writing a computer program that embodies the rules that make up the model.

The problem is even worse when the database is actually stored at a third facility, such as with a list processor. The list processor is unlikely to accept a neural network model in the form of C source code as input to a list selection request! Building a unified model development and scoring framework requires significant integration effort, but if scoring large databases is an important application for your business, the effort will be repaid.

Multiple Levels of User Interface

In many organizations, several different communities of users use the data mining software. In order to accommodate their differing needs, the tool should provide several different user interfaces:

- A graphical user interface (GUI) for the casual user
- A command-line interface for when the GUI gets in the way, and to allow scripting
- An applications program interface (API) so that predictive modeling can be built into applications

Comprehensible Output

Tools vary greatly in the extent to which they explain themselves. Rule generators, tree visualizers, web diagrams, and association tables can all help.

Graphics and Visualization

Some vendors place great emphasis on visual representation of both data and rules. Tree visualizers, association rule visualizers, three-dimensional data terrain maps, geographic information systems (GIS), and cluster diagrams are among the techniques that can help make sense of complex relationships.

Ability to Handle Diverse Data Types

Many data mining software packages place restrictions on the kinds of data that can be analyzed. Before investing in a data mining software package, find out how it deals with the various data types you want to work with.

Some tools have difficulty using categorical variables (such as model, type, gender) as input variables and require the user to convert these into a series of yes/no variables, one for each possible class. Others can deal with categorical variables that take on a small number of values, but break down when faced with too many. Decision-tree tools that use an algorithm like ID3 that creates a branch for each value fall into this category. On the target field side, some tools can handle a binary classification task (good/bad), but have difficulty predicting the value of a categorical variable that can take on several values.

Some data mining packages on the market require that continuous variables (income, mileage, balance) be split into ranges by the user. This is especially likely to be true of tools that generate association rules, since these require a certain number of occurrences of the same combination of values in order to recognize a rule.

Most data mining tools cannot deal with text strings. If the text strings in your data are standardized codes (state, part number), this is not really a problem since character codes can easily be converted to numeric ones. If your application requires the ability to analyze free text, your choices will be more restricted.

Documentation and Ease of Use

A well-designed user interface should make it possible to start mining right away, even if mastery of the tool will require time and study. As with any complex software, good documentation can spell the difference between success and frustration. Before deciding on a tool, ask to look over the manual.

Availability of Training, Consulting, and Support

It is not easy to introduce unfamiliar data mining techniques into an organization. Before committing to a tool, find out the availability of user training and applications consulting from the tool vendor or third parties.

If the vendor is small and geographically remote from your data mining locations, customer support may be problematic. The Internet has shrunk the planet so that every supplier is just a few keystrokes away, but it has not altered the human tendency to sleep at night and work in the day; there is no overlap between the business day in San Francisco and the telephone support hours of a small company in Paris or Amsterdam.

Ease of Integration

Although we have already touched on a few integration issues, others to consider include:

- Where in the client/server hierarchy is the software to be installed?
- Will the data mining software require its own hardware platform? If so, will this introduce a new operating system into the mix?
- What software will have to be installed on the users' desktops in order to communicate with the package?
- What additional networking, SQL gateways, and middleware will be required?
- Does the package provide good interfaces to reporting and graphics packages?

Vendor Credibility

Data mining software vendors are popping up like mushrooms after a rain—and disappearing at a similar rate. Unless you are already familiar with the vendor, it is a good idea to learn something about its track record and future prospects. Ask to speak to references who have used the vendor's software and can substantiate the claims made in product brochures.

We are not saying that you should not buy software from a company just because it is new, small, or far away. Data mining is still at the leading edge of commercial decision-support technology. It is often small, start-up companies that first understand the importance of new techniques and successfully bring them to market.

18

Putting Data Mining to Work

You've read this book and you are ready to start putting data mining to work for your company. You are convinced that when you can properly weave data mining into its fabric, the whole enterprise will benefit from increased understanding of your customers and of the market, better focused marketing, more efficient utilization of sales resources, and more responsive customer support. How can you get started?

At MRJ Technology Solutions, where the authors gained much of their data mining experience, we have developed a four-stage process for integrating data mining into the marketing and management information systems functions of our clients. In this chapter, we concentrate on the front-end of that process because it is here, at the beginning of a project, that advice from a book is most likely to be helpful.

INTEGRATING DATA MINING INTO THE ENTERPRISE

Any large-scale systems integration project (and make no mistake, integrating data mining in a meaningful way *is* a large-scale project) should be approached incrementally, with achievable goals and measurable results along the way. The final goal is to have data mining fully integrated with a corporate data warehouse and incorporated, alongside other analytical and decision-support activities, into the day-to-day operating procedures of the enterprise. In order to achieve that goal, you must first demonstrate the real business value of data mining by producing measurable return on investment from a smaller, more manageable proof-of-concept project. The proof of concept should be chosen to be valuable in its own right and to provide a solid basis for the business case needed to justify the full-scale project.

At MRJ Technology Solutions, we divide a data mining systems integration project into four stages[1]:

1. Target
2. Prove
3. Build
4. Migrate

In the remainder of this chapter we discuss all four phases with special emphasis on the first two.

Target

In the target phase, you study the existing business process in order to identify areas where data mining can provide tangible benefits with results that can be measured in dollars and so used to create a solid business case for further integration of data mining into the company's marketing, sales, and customer-support operations.

During this phase, interview the potential users of new information and encourage them to imagine ways to develop a true learning relationship with customers. At the same time, inventory the available data sources and identify any additional data that may be required. Where data is already being warehoused, study the data dictionaries and database schema. Where these are not available, study the record layouts of the operational systems that will be supplying the data and interview people who are familiar with how it is used.

As part of the target phase, do some initial profiling of the available data to get a first-level understanding of relationships within it. This effort is likely to require some amount of data cleansing, filtering, and transformation. It may even be possible to build and evaluate some preliminary models.

By the end of the target phase, you will have produced all of the following:

---

1. We would like to thank Paul Becker of MRJ Technology Solutions. Our discussion of this four-stage methodology for data mining software integration projects draws heavily on a presentation he developed for MRJ's introductory data mining seminar.

- A statement of business objectives for the data mining pilot project
- The evaluation criteria and metrics by which the project will be judged
- A report on the results of the data profiling and preliminary analysis
- A project plan for the pilot or proof of concept
- The outline of a project plan for the eventual permanent data mining system

Prove

This stage has two primary goals. The first is to establish the expected return on investment for data mining in the context of your business. The second is to complete the definition of the full-scale data mining environment for which the proof-of-concept project serves as a pilot or demonstration project.

In the marketing arena, where most commercial data mining takes place, the best way to prove the value of data mining is with a demonstration project that goes beyond evaluating models to actually measuring the results of a campaign based on the models. Where that is not possible, careful thought must be given to how a dollar value will be attached to the results of the demonstration project. In some cases it is sufficient to test the new models derived from data modeling against historical data to show how much better you might have done.

If the proof of concept is being done in-house, the first step will be to implement the prototype model development system using software and hardware identified during the target phase. The model development environment must be rich enough to allow the testing of a variety of data mining techniques. One of the goals of the proof-of-concept project is to determine which techniques are most effective in addressing the particular business problem you have decided to tackle.

As you build and use the prototype data mining system, you will be refining the data extraction requirements and interfaces between the future data mining environment and the existing operational and MIS computing environment. By the end of the this phase, the requirements that were sketched in the target phase will have become actual specifications from which an integrated data mining system can be built.

When the prototype data mining environment has been built, use it to build predictive models to perform the initial high-payback task identified during the target phase. Carefully measure the performance of the models and use the results to construct a controlled experiment comparing the effects of the actions taken based on data mining with your current baseline.

Finally, use the results of this experiment to build a business case for integrating data mining into your business operations on a permanent basis. At the end of the Prove phase, you will have the following:

- A prototype model development system
- An evaluation of several data mining techniques and tools
- A plan for modifying your business processes and systems to incorporate data mining
- A development plan for the production data mining environment

It is entirely feasible, and often desirable, to accomplish the entire proof-of-concept project without actually building a prototype data mining environment in-house. There are a number of data mining consultancies that handle this kind of work on a service bureau basis.

There are advantages and disadvantages to outsourcing data mining effort for the proof of concept. On the positive side, the data mining consultancy will be able to bring insights gained through experience working with data from other companies to its work with your problem. Also, it is unlikely that anyone on your own staff has the knowledge and experience with the broad range of data mining tools and techniques that a specialist can bring to bear.

On the negative side, you and your staff will not learn as much about the data mining process if consultants do all the actual data mining work. Perhaps the best compromise is to put together a team which includes outside consultants along with people from your own company.

Build

Once the pilot project has been evaluated, if it is returning the expected value it is time to build the full system. This is a systems integration project much like any other, so we will not say too much about it here.

During the build phase, you will implement the full data extraction and cleaning procedures, and turn the prototype model development system into a production-quality system. You will develop interfaces to other operational and decision-support systems, and implement business process interfaces for the initial users.

At the end of the build phase, you will have produced:

- Data extraction and cleansing procedures and software
- A data mining model development system
- An initial version of the production data mining environment
- A solution implementation and migration plan

Migrate

Once the data mining system has been built, the remaining challenge is to successfully integrate data mining into the corporate culture. This means educating a wide range of users and departments to the capabilities of the new system and growing a community of data miners. It also means continually measuring the effectiveness of the data mining that you do and looking for ways to improve the process.

The Migrate phase includes rolling out the full productions system and providing mechanisms for ongoing feedback of results from business processes back to model development and operations.

At the end of the Migrate phase, you will have:

- A production data mining environment
- A community of data miners
- A tight feedback loop between operational business processes and data mining model development
- A system improvement plan

CHOOSING THE RIGHT PROOF OF CONCEPT

The purpose of a proof-of-concept project is to validate the utility of data mining for your company without risking a large sum of money. The project should be small enough to be manageable, but important enough to be interesting.

Tackle a Real Problem

The only way to attract attention and budget dollars to a project to develop your company's data mining infrastructure is to use data mining to meet a real business need. The most convincing proof-of-concept projects focus on areas that are already being measured and evaluated analytically, and where there is already an acknowledged need for improvement. Likely candidates include:

Response models

Default models

Attrition models

Usage models

Profitability models

These are areas where there is a well-defined link between improved accuracy of predictions and improved profitability. If you have chosen the right project, it should be easy to act on its results.

Act on Your Findings

Many data mining proof-of-concept projects fail to achieve the desired impact because they are designed to assess the technology rather than the results of its application. The link between better models and better business results must not be left hypothetical. Statisticians and analysts are likely to be impressed by theoretical results; senior management is not.

A graph showing the lift in response rates achieved by a new model on an evaluation dataset of preclassified historical data is impressive, but new customers gained because of the model are even more so.

Measure the Results of Your Actions

As described in Chapter 6, it is necessary to measure both the effectiveness of the data mining models themselves and the actual impact that the actions taken as a result of the models' predictions have on the business.

To measure the former, it is often appropriate to use lift, a measure of the change in concentration of records of some particular type (such as responders or defaulters) due to the model. To measure the latter, we need more information. If the pilot project builds a response model, we need to keep track of the following costs and benefits:

- What is the fixed cost of setting up the campaign and the model that supports it?
- What is the cost per recipient of making the offer?
- What is the cost per respondent of fulfilling the offer?
- What is the value of a positive response?

The last item seems obvious, but is often overlooked. We have seen more than one data mining initiative get bogged down because, although it was shown that data mining could reach more customers, there was no clear model of what a new customer was worth and therefore no clear understanding of the benefits to be derived.

Take Advantage of Outside Expertise

Once data mining has really taken hold within the corporation, it will probably grow and spread through internally generated excitement. One successful project leads to others, and with each one, you add to the breadth and depth of in-house data mining expertise. In the early stages, however, when you are still trying to establish the value of data mining, outside help can be very beneficial.

Use qualified and experienced outside consultants to help design or review the data mining pilot plan and to assist in the selection of hardware and software for the data mining laboratory. The field is moving so fast, that the only people who can keep up with it are people who do it for a living. Depending on the availability of internal systems development resources, you may also want to turn to outside help to integrate data mining software into your data warehousing environment.

HOW ONE COMPANY IS GETTING ITS FEET WET

At this writing, the authors are currently working with several very different companies who are in different stages in the process of putting data mining to work for their businesses. The companies include a catalog retailer, a cellular phone company, and the credit card division of a major bank.

These three companies are starting from very different positions. The cellular phone company gathers lots of data on customers and on calls, but does not have a data warehouse and currently does very little modeling or decision support based on this data. It is depending on outside consultants to find enough value in the data already collected to justify taking the next step.

The catalog company does have a data warehouse and is used to building analytical models using statistical packages, but recognizes the need to do more. Here too, outside consultants are being used to demonstrate the value of the less familiar techniques.

The bank already has a data warehouse and a very sophisticated group of analysts who are already applying many of the data mining techniques described in this book. They are looking for ways to speed up the cycle of analyzing the results of a marketing action, developing new models based on the analysis, and deploying the new models in production. For this client, we have designed a sophisticated data mining laboratory that will allow testing of the value of new techniques, new software, and new data.

The three companies have different needs and are taking different approaches to data mining, but in one respect they are all following the same path. They are all measuring the usefulness of data mining by looking at the results of the *actions* suggested by data mining. One of the companies, the wireless service provider, has agreed to let us describe the data mining pilot project we are doing for them.

A Controlled Experiment in Retention

Comcast Cellular offers wireless phone service in a market of 7.5 million people in a three-state area centered around Philadelphia. This rich market is attracting a lot of competition. In an industry where most companies are already losing customers at the rate of 7 to 8 percent a month, additional competition is cause for concern. This churn, as it is called in the industry, is very disturbing because even though the defectors are easily outnumbered by new subscribers, the acquisition cost for a new customer is often in the $500 to $600 range.

With a slew of new competitors, poised to enter the wireless communications market, Comcast Cellular knows that now is the time to reach out to subscribers with a proactive effort to ensure their continued happiness. As we write these words, Comcast is just beginning a pilot project whose aim is to assess the value of data mining as an aid to retention. The pilot is designed in such a way that when it is over, Comcast will know exactly how much investment in data mining is warranted. And, they will already be reaping the benefits of a better understanding of subscriber churn. Even when they are available, Comcast is unlikely to want to share the *results* of the pilot study, but they have given permission for us to describe its design.

Because Comcast Cellular is new to data mining, it decided to turn the design and implementation of the pilot project over to the data mining group at MRJ Technology Solutions, a systems integration and consulting company. The project is a three-way partnership.

- Comcast supplies data and expertise on its own business practices and procedures.
- MRJ uses the Comcast data to develop profiles of likely defectors.
- Sky Alland, a telemarketing service bureau, uses the profiles to develop scripts used to retain the potential defectors.

The Data

In the course of several interviews with the client, we identified two sources of data for use in the pilot. The first source is a customer profile database set up by a database marketing company. This database contains summary information for each subscriber including the billing plan, type of phone, local minutes of use by month, roaming minutes of use by month, number of calls to and from each identified cellular market in the United States, and dozens of other, similar fields.

The second source is call detail data collected from the cellular switching office. Each time a cellular phone is switched on, it begins a two-way conversation with the central switching office. The phone broadcasts a signal that is picked up by any nearby Comcast radio cell sites. The cell sites relay data from the telephone such as the serial number and phone type to a central switching office. Computers at the switching office figure out which cell site the phone should be talking to at the moment and send a message back to the phone telling it which cell it is using and what frequency to tune to.

When the subscriber enters a phone number and presses the send button, the number is relayed to the central switch which sets up the call over regular land lines or relays it to the cell closest to another wireless subscriber. Every cell generates a record that includes the subscriber id, the originating number, the number called, the originating cell, the call duration, and so on. For data mining purposes, this data is combined with the customer data so that each subscriber is described by a detailed calling pattern as well as by summary measures.

For the pilot program, we are using six months of data for around 50,000 subscribers. Over the course of those months, a number of subscribers have canceled their accounts. Thus, we have training data with examples of customers who have defected and customers who have remained loyal.

The Experiment

The experiment has four phases:

1. Data mining and model development
2. Selection of test and control groups based on the models
3. A telemarketing campaign designed to address concerns suggested by the models
4. Comparison of retention rates between the test and control groups

Data Mining and Model Development The data mining and model development phase will include both top-down hypothesis testing and bottom-up knowledge discovery as described in Chapter 5. The hypothesis testing will focus on issues such as mismatches between billing plans and usage patterns, and on the effects of factors, such as the number of different numbers calling the subscriber that have proved to be significant in other cases we have studied.

The knowledge discovery portion of the study will use automatic cluster detection and decision-tree models. The goal is to find clusters of subscribers that behave in similar ways and then, within each cluster, to come up with rules that predict who is likely to cancel the service. Our hope and expectation is that in addition to focusing attention on the customers who are most at risk, the rules generated by the decision-tree tool will also provide insight into *why* particular groups of subscribers are likely to defect.

Test and Control Groups   Once the attrition models have been built, they will be used to tag the entire subscriber population with a cluster membership and an attrition risk flag. Two groups of 24,000 subscribers will be selected at random from the scored population. Within the test group, the subscribers classified as high risk will be contacted proactively using telemarketing scripts tailored to the concerns suggested by the decision-tree rules that caused them to be labeled as potential defectors.

In the control group, the high-risk subscribers will continue to be treated no differently from the rest of the population. The difference in the attrition rate between high-risk and low-risk subscribers in the control group will provide a measure of the accuracy of the classification. The difference in the attrition rate between high-risk subscribers in the test group and high-risk subscribers in the control group will provide a measure of the effectiveness of data mining-based telemarketing as a way of stopping high-risk subscribers from defecting (see Figure 18.1).

The Telemarketing Campaign   The telemarketing campaign itself will have two parts serving two different purposes. The first goal is to probe the satisfaction level of the customers labeled as high risk and verify that the reported reasons for considering a cancellation agree with the reasons suggested by the data mining effort. The second goal is to offer the potential defectors something that will entice them to stay without costing much to Comcast.

The exact nature of the offers cannot be determined until after data mining has suggested the likely causes of dissatisfaction for different groups. As an example, we expect that the offer that appeals to a low-volume subscriber who has decided not to use any cellular service will differ from the offer that would appeal to a high-volume subscriber who is being lured away by a competing service.

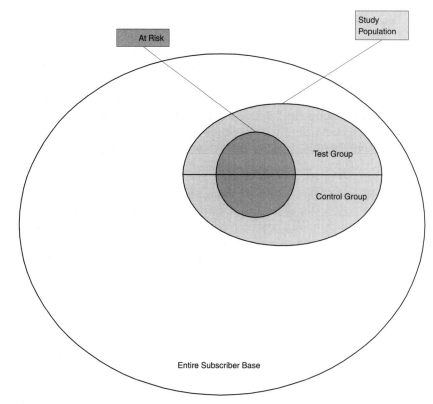

Figure 18.1 Overlapping areas of interest.

The Proof of the Pudding   At the end of six months, Comcast will be able to make a direct cost/benefit analysis of the combined data mining and telemarketing action plan. The costs of the project will be known exactly as will the difference in retention between the test and control groups and, more importantly, the difference in profitability between the two groups. Armed with this data, Comcast will be able to make an informed decision about how much to invest in future data mining efforts.

The company will also be faced with a whole new set of questions based on the data that comes back from the initial study. New hypotheses will be formed and tested. The response data from the telemarketing effort will be fodder for a new round of knowledge discovery. New product ideas and service plans will need to be tried out. The next round of data mining will start from a higher base because the company will know its customers better. That is the virtuous cycle of data mining.

Recommended Reading

ONE-TO-ONE MARKETING

Peppers, Don, & Martha Rogers. 1997. *Enterprise One to One: Tools for Competing in the Interactive Age*. New York: Doubleday.

Reichheld, Frederick F. 1996. *The Loyalty Effect: The Hidden Force Behind Growth, Profits, and Lasting Value*. Boston: Harvard Business School Press.

DATA WAREHOUSING

Inmon, William. 1996. *Building the Data Warehouse*, 2d ed. New York: John Wiley & Sons, Inc.

Kelly, Sean. 1996. *Data Warehousing: The Route to Mass Customization,* updated & expanded. New York: John Wiley & Sons, Inc.

Kimball, Ralph. 1996. *Data Warehouse Toolkit*. New York: John Wiley & Sons, Inc.

DATA MINING TECHNIQUES

Anderberg, David. 1973. *Cluster Analysis for Applications*. New York: Academic Press.

Bigus, Joseph P. 1996. *Data Mining with Neural Networks: Solving Business Problems—From Application Development to Decision Support*. New York: McGraw-Hill.

Goldberg, David E. 1989. *Genetic Algorithms in Search, Optimization, and Machine Learning*. New York: Addison Wesley.

Hartigan, J. A. 1975. *Clustering Algorithms*. New York: John Wiley & Sons, Inc.

Swingler, Kevin. 1996. *Applying Neural Networks: A Practical Guide*. London: Academic Press.

Quinlan, J. Ross. 1993. *C4.5 Programs for Machine Learning*. San Mateo: Morgan Kaufmann.

FOR FURTHER INFORMATION

The authors maintain a data mining web page at http://www.data-miners.com.

Index